Cybersecurity Measures for E-Government Frameworks

Noor Zaman
Taylor's University, Malaysia

Imdad Ali Shah
Shah Abdul Latif University, Pakistan

Samina Rajper
Shah Abdul Latif University, Pakistan

A volume in the Advances in
Electronic Government, Digital
Divide, and Regional Development
(AEGDDRD) Book Series

Published in the United States of America by
IGI Global
Information Science Reference (an imprint of IGI Global)
701 E. Chocolate Avenue
Hershey PA, USA 17033
Tel: 717-533-8845
Fax: 717-533-8661
E-mail: cust@igi-global.com
Web site: http://www.igi-global.com

Library of Congress Cataloging-in-Publication Data

Names: Zaman, Noor, 1972- editor. | Shah, Imdad Ali, 1975- editor. |
  Rajper, Samina, 1974- editor.
Title: Cybersecurity measures for E-government frameworks / Jhanjhi Noor
  Zaman, Imdad Ali Shah, and Samina Rajper, editors.
Description: Hershey, PA : Information Science Reference, 2022. | Includes
  bibliographical references and index. | Summary: "This book covers
  security issues that must be considered for E-governance applications,
  by helping and protecting them from possible cybersecurity attacks to
  alleviate the fraud potential as hackers use emerging technologies for
  cyber-attacks"-- Provided by publisher.
Identifiers: LCCN 2022001830 (print) | LCCN 2022001831 (ebook) | ISBN
  9781799896241 (hardcover) | ISBN 9781799896258 (paperback) | ISBN
  9781799896265 (ebook)
Subjects: LCSH: Internet in public administration--Security measures. |
  Computer security.
Classification: LCC JF1525.A8 C94 2022 (print) | LCC JF1525.A8 (ebook) |
  DDC 351.0285/4678--dc23/eng/20220215
LC record available at https://lccn.loc.gov/2022001830
LC ebook record available at https://lccn.loc.gov/2022001831

This book is published in the IGI Global book series Advances in Electronic Government, Digital
Divide, and Regional Development (AEGDDRD) (ISSN: 2326-9103; eISSN: 2326-9111)

British Cataloguing in Publication Data
A Cataloguing in Publication record for this book is available from the British Library.

All work contributed to this book is new, previously-unpublished material.
The views expressed in this book are those of the authors, but not necessarily of the publisher.

For electronic access to this publication, please contact: eresources@igi-global.com.

Advances in Electronic Government, Digital Divide, and Regional Development (AEGDDRD) Book Series

ISSN:2326-9103
EISSN:2326-9111

Editor-in-Chief: Zaigham Mahmood University of Derby, UK & North West University, South Africa

MISSION

The successful use of digital technologies (including social media and mobile technologies) to provide public services and foster economic development has become an objective for governments around the world. The development towards electronic government (or e-government) not only affects the efficiency and effectiveness of public services, but also has the potential to transform the nature of government interactions with its citizens. Current research and practice on the adoption of electronic/digital government and the implementation in organizations around the world aims to emphasize the extensiveness of this growing field.

The **Advances in Electronic Government, Digital Divide & Regional Development (AEGDDRD)** book series aims to publish authored, edited and case books encompassing the current and innovative research and practice discussing all aspects of electronic government development, implementation and adoption as well the effective use of the emerging technologies (including social media and mobile technologies) for a more effective electronic governance (or e-governance).

COVERAGE

- Public Information Management, Regional Planning, Rural Development
- Frameworks and Methodologies for E-Government Development
- Issues and Challenges in E-Government Adoption
- ICT Infrastructure and Adoption for E-Government Provision
- Knowledge Divide, Digital Divide
- Online Government, E-Government, M-Government
- E-Governance and Use of Technology for Effective Government
- Electronic Government, Digital Democracy, Digital Government
- Adoption of Innovation with Respect to E-Government
- E-Government in Developing Countries and Technology Adoption

IGI Global is currently accepting manuscripts for publication within this series. To submit a proposal for a volume in this series, please contact our Acquisition Editors at Acquisitions@igi-global.com or visit: http://www.igi-global.com/publish/.

Titles in this Series

For a list of additional titles in this series, please visit:
www.igi-global.com/book-series/advances-electronic-government-digital-divide/37153

Handbook of Research on Artificial Intelligence in Government Practices and Processes
Jose Ramon Saura (Rey Juan Carlos University, Spain) and Felipe Debasa (Rey Juan Carlos University, Spain)
Information Science Reference • © 2022 • 410pp • H/C (ISBN: 9781799896098) • US $285.00

Trends and Innovations in Urban E-Planning
Carlos Nunes Silva (University of Lisbon, Portugal)
Information Science Reference • © 2022 • 307pp • H/C (ISBN: 9781799890904) • US $195.00

Planning and Designing Smart Cities in Developing Nations
Saleem Gregory Zoughbi (Independent Researcher, Palestine)
Information Science Reference • © 2022 • 282pp • H/C (ISBN: 9781668435090) • US $215.00

Multidimensional Approach to Local Development and Poverty Causes, Consequences, and Challenges Post COVID-19
João Conrado de Amorim Carvalho (Centro de Ensino Superior Dom Bosco, Brazil) Francisco Espasandín Bustelo (Universidad de Sevilla, Spain) and Emmanuel M. C. B. Sabino (Centro de Ensino, Formação e Pesquisa. Brazil)
Information Science Reference • © 2022 • 353pp • H/C (ISBN: 9781799889250) • US $195.00

Blockchain Technologies and Applications for Digital Governance
Pradeep Nijalingappa (Bapuji Institute of Engineering and Technology, India) and Mangesh Manikrao Ghonge (Sandip Foundation's Institute of Technology and Research Centre, India)
Information Science Reference • © 2022 • 266pp • H/C (ISBN: 9781799884934) • US $225.00

For an entire list of titles in this series, please visit:
www.igi-global.com/book-series/advances-electronic-government-digital-divide/37153

701 East Chocolate Avenue, Hershey, PA 17033, USA
Tel: 717-533-8845 x100 • Fax: 717-533-8661
E-Mail: cust@igi-global.com • www.igi-global.com

Editorial Advisory Board

Table of Contents

Detailed Table of Contents

    Raja Majid Ali Ujjan, Independent Researcher, UK
    Imran Taj, Information System Branch, Ministry of Attorney General,
        BC Public Service, Canada
    Sarfraz Nawaz Brohi, University of the West of England (UWE), Bristol,
        UK

Currently, information and communication technologies are going in advance, allowing more information to be distributed globally via the internet superhighway. While being interconnected to the virtual world, people are becoming increasingly focused, large, and smart, needing the development of new solutions that will be implemented and robust network security systems. When the information is being handled in the applications, it is vulnerable to attack at every stage, and it is impossible to handle it in a separate manner, as traditional security systems have done. The introduction of software-defined networks (SDN) has provided a novel perspective on data security, since the network may assist in the construction of stable and safe continuity in the context of risks posed by the internet. The structure of SDN, particularly its gradual construction and centralization of network data and mechanisms, has pushed us to consider security from a strategy-practiced standpoint. The major goal of this chapter is to give detailed an overview of the current state-of-the-art in the area of SDN security and its significance in the context of e-government applications.

Chapter 2

Raja Majid Ali Ujjan, University of the West of Scotland, UK
Navid Ali Khan, Taylor's University, Malaysia
Loveleen Gaur, Amity University, Noida, India

The internet of things (IoT) is becoming more significant in everyday life as a mechanism for making major decisions in different fields as smart devices and data in real time are connected and updated. IoT is being used in a variety of ways to provide digital services to the public. Online payment, property purchase, and sailing are just a few examples. On the other hand, users' complaints about the safety and privacy of their personal information are growing. The internet of things (IoT) is becoming more popular and significantly enhances e-government. This chapter primarily focuses on how potential users can obtain information to use the internet of things and its related services within the e-government sectors. There are several technological, administrative, and political challenges to IoT adoption problems in e-government and legal problems that must be solved to develop effective and required applications. It's crucial to explore these problems and potential solutions.

Chapter 3

Saira Muzafar, King Faisal University, Saudi Arabia
Mamoona Humayun, Jouf University, Saudi Arabia
Syed Jawad Hussain, Abasyn University, Islamabad, Pakistan

The growing technologies in the world include machine learning (ML), the internet of things (IoT), and artificial intelligence (AI). Cybersecurity is the application of technologies that play a significant part in making secure data and reducing the risk among the users, such as computer programs, networks, data, and devices from the different cyber-attacks. In the current era of communication and information technologies, it is not possible to think of a good government without e-government. The main objective of this chapter is to look at the last 10 years of associated research articles, book chapters, and published reports on cybersecurity threats and attacks focused and founded on the e-government applications and emerging technologies for the measurement of cybersecurity. The results of this research have been used on machine learning techniques for taking authentic and scientific results. In the light of the studies, a new door will open for researchers and professionals.

    Imdad Ali Shah, Shah Abdul Latif University, Pakistan
    Sobia Wassan, Nanjing University, China
    Muhammad Hamza Usmani, The University of Lahore, Pakistan

In developing technology, hackers are actively collecting personal information. To achieve their goals and acquire simple access to information about any individual, they use a range of methods and techniques. A privacy breach occurs when hackers gain access to complete information without the user's permission. Threats and dangers to security can arise for a variety of reasons, including technological flaws and targeted attacks. The government provides digital public facilities to people and the business community. Consumers have the expectation that e-government provides security and protects their data and personal information. Users have expressed concerns about their personal data privacy and safety. The main object of this chapter is to give strategies for IT specialists and e-government services because they need continuous improvement in privacy and security issues. The findings of this chapter may be useful to new researchers and may aid in the avoidance of security breaches and privacy issues.

    Imdad Ali Shah, Shah Abdul Latif University, Pakistan
    Riyaz Ahamed Ariyaluran Habeeb, Taylor's University, Malaysia
    Samina Rajper, Department of Computer Science, Shah Abdul
        University, Pakistan
    Areeba Laraib, Mehran University of Engineering and Technology,
        Pakistan

The use of e-government is growing as the world is progressively becoming more interconnected. However, data security systems must be designed to address new and effective vulnerabilities that are increasing due to emerging technological innovations. In the dynamic and ever-changing world, the issues and challenges of protecting information infrastructure are growing. Due to various vulnerabilities in the system, these networks are vulnerable to cyber-attack. As a result, it is critical to speed security efforts that include application software and infrastructure to provide an efficient governance system without the risk of being rigged. It has been observed during review of associated articles that limited studies have been done on e-governance and cyber-attacks. The cyber-attacks influence e-governance and damage public trust. The main objective of this chapter is to review the last 15 years of associated research articles, and the result will be a comparison of every five years. The findings provide potential recommendations and solutions.

    Maurice Dawson, Illinois Institute of Technology, USA
    Damon Walker, University of Missouri, Saint Louis, USA

The Economic Community of West African States is an economic region located in West Africa. This region has a population of over 349 million and representation for approximately 15 countries. With the explosion of technological advances in agriculture, healthcare, and personal device use, cybersecurity has become an important issue. Coupled with dictatorships, corrupt regimes, religious extremists, and other illicit activities, it is imperative that cybersecurity become a cornerstone in local governments to ensure the safety of citizens. This chapter reviews recent literature that surrounds West African states to present an argument on why cybersecurity must be considered essential for local governments. Observations and interviews were conducted at a government facility concerning its security posture as it relates to physical and cybersecurity. This activity included interviews with senior government officials and employees to understand the state of affairs at the organization.

    Loveleen Gaur, Amity University, Noida, India
    Raja Majid Ali Ujjan, University of the West of Scotland, UK
    Manzoor Hussain, Indus University, Pakistan

The digitalization revolution plays a crucial role in every government administration. It manages a considerable volume of user information and is currently seeing an increase in internet access. The absence of unorganized information, on the other hand, adds to the difficulty of data analysis. Data mining approaches have recently become more popular for addressing a variety of e-governance concerns, particularly data management, data processing, and so on. This chapter identifies and compares several existing data mining and data warehouses in e-government. Deep learning is a subset of a larger class of machine learning techniques that combine artificial neural networks. The significance and difficulties of e-governance are highlighted for future enhancement. As a result, with the growth of e-governance, risk and cyber-attacks have increased these days. Furthermore, the few e-governance application performance evaluations are included in this chapter. The purpose of this chapter is to focus on deep learning applications of e-governance in detecting cyber-attacks.

N. Z. Jhanjhi, Taylor's University, Malaysia
Muneer Ahmad, National University of Science and Technology,
Pakistan
Muhammad Amir Khan, COMSATS University Islamabad, Abbottabad,
Pakistan
Manzoor Hussain, Indus University, Pakistan

A cyber-attack can damage data, computer programs, and network one or more computers through applying different methods and cybercriminal's activities to steal information. The increasing of new technologies among the users facilities them. The cyber-attacks are growing tremendously. E-governance is an application of IT and giving online services. These days the world is completely focused on creating social distance among the people, and billions of peoples around the world are working from home (online activities) and shops, and businesses are closed in the COVID-19 pandemic, which the WHO recommended. A remarkable cyber-crime has been recorded by the researcher's study in this environment, affecting society and businesses. This research's primary objective is to find cyber-attacks that steal information in the COVID-19 pandemic and assess the user loss. The results of five years have been compared on the machine learning techniques.

Manzoor Hussain, Indus University, Pakistan
Mir Sajjad Hussain Talpur, Sindh Agriculture University, Tandojam,
Pakistan
Mamoona Humayun, Jouf University, Saudi Arabia

With the development of new advanced technology, people's expectations and grievances of improving services and values in all aspects of life are growing. Changes in technology are offering better solutions to problems, hence improving existing systems. At the same time, new technologies are presenting new security and privacy violations. As information resources become more digitized, infrastructure and digital data are also facing increasing challenges. For advanced nations, the security parameters and optimization techniques have been thoroughly tested and are in good working order. However, these issues have yet to be adequately addressed in developing countries. An unauthorized person applies several different methods and techniques in the modern age for getting self-profit. The major goal of the research is to discover and assess the implications of integrity attacks and threats that have been used in e-governance research during the last 15 years. This research will be supported in assessing the security of various organizations that are working under e-governance.

Chapter 10

Raja Majid Ali Ujjan, University of the West of Scotland, UK
Khalid Hussain, Superior University, Pakistan
Sarfraz Nawaz Brohi, University of the West of England (UWE), Bristol,
    UK

Implementation of blockchain with e-government has raised several complexities. When an area has satisfied the requirements for e-government implementation, new challenges will appear. As a result of the information technology revolution, governments and industries are being forced to deliver more effective and secure internet services. Every government in the world attempts to provide the public with electronic services that are fast, quick, and beneficial for the users. Blockchain is considered to have significant potential benefits for the government since it is a combination of technologies such as distributed ledgers, privacy, authentication, and consensus mechanisms. However, this advanced technology is still in its development, and e-government faces a number of difficulties and challenges. The goal of this chapter is to evaluate this advanced technology in the context of high-level e-government security and privacy implementation measures and other technical issues during the adaption of blockchain technology.

Chapter 11

Gyankamal J. Chhajed, Bharati Vidyapeeth, India & Vidya
    Pratishthan's Kamalnayan Bajaj Institute of Engineering and
    Technology, India
Bindu R. Garg, Bharati Vidyapeeth, India

In today's digital world, it is noticeable that images are transferred in binary form which carries significant and confidential information. To secure and keep such information unnoticeable is the prime concern during transmission. Information hiding as watermarking or secret messaging are most acceptable ways to attain this. In this direction, a new information flow system using data hiding approach is proposed in this chapter. A decision tree is applied for locating the most suitable blocks for data hiding in the presented technique. Decision trees are one of the best techniques used as a classifier. In this approach, the decision tree classifies a particular block to be selected for hiding information, based on the LURD pattern of 3X3 pixel block of image and the blocks of information to be hidden. For security, information is encrypted and then scattered in the image. The receiver can retrieve the data without the original image. The results prove that the proposed scheme is capable of minimizing distortion caused due to data hiding.

Chapter 12
Imdad Ali Shah, Shah Abdul Latif University, Pakistan

Cyber-attacks can steal information by applying different methods and activities of cyber criminals, thereby destroying data, computer programs, and networking on one or more computers. There is an increase in new technology among users, and it provides them with more convenience. On the other hand, cyber-attacks are increasing dramatically today. The world is completely focused on creating social distancing between people. During the WHO-recommended COVID-19 pandemic, billions of people around the world are working from home, with shops and businesses closed. In their investigation of the environment, researchers have uncovered a notable type of cybercrime that has an impact on society and businesses. The pandemic has accelerated the transition of government employees and businesses to an actual workplace ecosystem. Dramatic changes in the workplace have created new and multi-layered challenges in dealing with cybersecurity risks and threats. Cyber-attacks can create problems that are detrimental to the economy, human privacy, and national security. These attacks have different perspectives on the problem and need to be understood first. In this chapter, the authors highlight several essential concerns and challenges facing e-government development as well as different departments that provide e-services. They also focus on and peer evaluate the major concerns and challenges facing e-government growth from a holistic perspective, offering methodologies and policy recommendations to address them in a complete and inclusive manner.

Preface

It gives us immense pleasure to publish the book titled *Cybersecurity Measures for E-Government Frameworks*. After the Covid-19 pandemic, the current world scenario even realizes more dependency on digitalization. E-Government got more attention, and the technology realizes its importance for the daily transaction as well. That is in several domains of our daily life. As an application of information technology (IT), e-government is used for delivery in government for services and information exchange between the government and the public. This electronic service delivery is an important innovation to society; however, it also attracts hackers and cyberattacks. It is essential to provide fast protection application software and structure.

Cybersecurity Measures for E-Government Frameworks provides security techniques and measures to e-governance applications. This book covers cyberattack detection, deep learning, and preventive approaches. It further discusses emerging technologies in the cybersecurity field as well as the specific uses they have for e-government technologies. It is an essential resource for government officials, security professionals, students and educators of higher education, IT professionals, researchers, and academicians.

This book will provide extensive knowledge and ways during this pandemic time, where most government businesses adopt the e-government approach to reach the public. Further, this will elaborate on the cybersecurity challenges for the e-government during this pandemic period.

Chapter 1: E-Government Cybersecurity Modeling in the Context of Software-Defined Networks

Currently, information and communication technologies are going in advance, allowing more information to be distributed globally via the internet superhighway. While being interconnected to the virtual world, people are becoming increasingly

focused, large, and smart, needing the development of new solutions that will be implemented and robust network security systems. When the information is being handled in the applications, it is vulnerable to attack at every stage, and it is impossible to handle it in a separate manner, as traditional security systems have done. The introduction of Software-Defined Networks (SDN) has provided a novel perspective on data security, since the network may assist in the construction of stable and safe continuity in the context of risks posed by the internet. The structure of SDN, particularly its gradual construction and centralization of network data and mechanisms, has pushed us to consider security from a strategy-practised standpoint.

Chapter 2: E-Government Privacy and Security Challenges in the Context of Internet of Things

The Internet of Things (IoT) is becoming more significant in everyday life as a mechanism for making major decisions in different fields. As smart devices and data in real-time are connected and updated. IoT is being used in a variety of ways to provide digital services to the public. Online payment, property purchase, and sailing are just a few examples. On the other hand, users' complaints about the safety and privacy of their personal information are growing. The Internet of Things (IoT) is becoming more popular and significantly enhances e-government. This chapter primarily focuses on how potential users can obtain information to use the Internet of Things and its related services within the e-government sectors. There are several technological, administrative, and political challenges to IoT adoption problems in e-government and legal problems that must be solved to develop effective and required applications. It's crucial to explore these problems and potential solutions.

Chapter 3: Emerging Cybersecurity Threats in the Eye of E-Governance in the Current Era

The growing technologies in the world, such as machine learning (ML), the Internet of Things (IoT), and Artificial Intelligence (AI). Cybersecurity is the application of technologies that play a significant part in making secure data and reducing the risk among the users, such as computer programs, networks, data, and devices from the different cyber-attacks. In the current era of communication and information technologies, it is not possible to think of a good government without e-government. The main object of this chapter is to peer-view on the last ten years' associated research articles, book chapters and published reports of cybersecurity threats and attacks have been focused and founded on the e-government applications and emerging technologies for the measurement of cybersecurity. The results of this research have been used on machine learning techniques for taking authentic and scientific results. In the light of our studies, the new door will open for the researchers and professionals.

Chapter 4: E-Government Security and Privacy Issues – Challenges and Preventive Approaches

In developing technology, hackers are actively collecting personal information. To achieve their goals and acquire simple access to information about any individual, they use a range of methods and techniques. A privacy breach occurs when hackers gain access to complete information without the user's permission. Threats and dangers to security can arise for a variety of reasons, including technological flaws and targeted attacks. The government provides digital public facilities to people and the business community. Consumers have the expectation that e-government provides security and protects their data and personal information. Users have expressed concerns about their personal data privacy and safety. The main object of this chapter is to give strategies for IT specialists and e-government services because they need continuous improvement in privacy and security issues. The findings of this chapter may be useful to new researchers and may aid in the avoidance of security breaches and privacy issues.

Chapter 5: The Influence of Cybersecurity Attacks on E-Governance

The use of e-government is growing as the world is progressively interconnected. However, need to use information and data. The data security system must design to address new and effective vulnerabilities increasing due to emerging technological innovations. In the dynamic and ever-changing world, the issues and challenges of protecting information infrastructure are growing. Due to various vulnerabilities in the system, these networks are vulnerable to cyber-attack. As a result, it is critical to speed security efforts that include application software and infrastructure to provide an efficient governance system without the risk of being rigged. It has been observed during review associated articles that limited studies have been done on e-governance and cyber-attacks. The cyber-attacks are influencing e-governance and damage public trust. The main object of this chapter is to review the last fifteen years of associate research articles, and the result will be a comparison every five years. Our findings provide potential recommendations and solutions.

Chapter 6: Argument for Improved Security in Local Governments Within the Economic Community of West African States

The Economic Community of West African States is an economic region located in West Africa. This region has a population of over 349 million and representation for approximately 15 countries. With the explosion of technological advances in agriculture, healthcare, and personal device use, cybersecurity has become an important issue. Coupled with dictatorships, corrupt regimes, religious extremists, and other illicit activities, it is imperative that cybersecurity is becoming a cornerstone in local governments to ensure the safety of citizens. This research paper reviews recent literature that surrounds West African states to present an argument on why cybersecurity must be considered essential for local governments. Observations and interviews were conducted at a government facility concerning its security posture as it relates to physical and cybersecurity. This activity included interviews with senior government officials and employees to understand the state of affairs at the organization.

Chapter 7: The Influence of Deep Learning in Detecting Cyber Attacks on E-Government Applications

Nowadays, the digitalization revolution plays a crucial role in every government administration. It manages a considerable volume of user information and is currently seeing an increase in internet access. The absence of unorganized information, on the other hand, adds to the difficulty of data analysis. Data mining approaches have recently become more popular for addressing a variety of e-governance concerns, particularly data management, data processing, and so on. This chapter identifies and compares several existing data mining and data warehouses in e-government. Deep Learning is a subset of a larger class of machine learning techniques that combine Artificial Neural Networks. The significance and difficulties of e-governance are highlighted for future enhancement. As a result, with the growth of e-governance, risk and cyber-attacks have increased these days. Furthermore, the few e-governance application performance evaluations are included in this chapter. The purpose of this chapter is to focus on deep learning applications of e-governance in detecting cyber-attacks.

Chapter 8: The impact of Cyber Attacks on E-Governance During the COVID-19 Pandemic

A cyber-attack can damage data, computer programs, and network one or more computers through applying different methods and cybercriminal's activities to steal information. The increasing of new technologies among the user and giving more facilities them. Another side the cyber-attacks are growing tremendously day today. E-governance is an application of IT and giving online services. These days the world is completely focused on creating social distance among the people and billions of peoples around the world are working from home (online activities) and shops and businesses are closed in the Covid-19 pandemic which the WHO recommended. A remarkable cyber-crime has been recorded by the researcher's study in this environment, affected society and businesses. This research's primary objective of this chapter is to find cyber-attacks and steal information in the Covid-19 Pandemic and assess the user's loss. The results of five years have been compared on the machine learning techniques.

Chapter 9: The Consequences of Integrity Attacks on E-Governance, Privacy, and Security Violation

With the development of new advanced technology, people's expectations and grievances improving services and values in all aspects of life are growing. Changes in technology are offering for better solutions to problems, hence improving existing systems. At the same time, new technologies are presenting new security and privacy violations. As information resources become more digitized, infrastructure and digital data are also facing increasing challenges. For advanced nations, the security parameters and optimization techniques have been thoroughly tested and are in good working order. However, these issues have yet to be adequately addressed in developing countries. An unauthorized person applies several different methods and techniques in the modern age for getting self-profit. The major goal of our research is to discover and assess the implications of integrity attacks and threats that are used in e-governance research during the last fifteen years. This research will be supported in assessing the security of various organizations which are working under e-governance.

Chapter 10: The Impact of Blockchain Technology on advanced Security Measures for E-Government

Currently implementation of blockchain with e-government has raised several complexities. When an area has satisfied the requirements for e-government implementation, new challenges will appear. As a result of the information technology revolution, governments and industries are being forced to deliver more effective and secure internet services. Every government in the world attempts to provide the public with electronic services that are fast, quick, and beneficial for the users. Blockchain is considered to have significant potential benefits for the government since it is a combination of technologies such as distributed ledgers, privacy, authentication, and consensus mechanisms. However, this advanced technology is still in its development, and e-government faces a number of difficulties and challenges. The goal of this chapter is to evaluate this advanced technology in the context of high-level e-government security and privacy implementation measures and other technical issues during the adaption of blockchain technology.

Chapter 11: Applying Decision Tree for Hiding Data in Binary Images for Secure and Secret Information Flow

In today's digital world, it is noticeable that images are transferred in binary form which carries significant and confidential information. To secure and keep such information unnoticeable is prime concern during transmission. Information hiding as watermarking or secret messaging are most acceptable way to attain this. In this direction, a new information flow system using data hiding approach is proposed in this paper. A decision tree is applied for locating the most suitable blocks for data hiding in the presented technique. Decision trees are one of the best techniques used as a classifier. In this approach, the decision tree classifies a particular block to be selected for hiding information, based on the LURD pattern of 3X3 pixel block of image and the blocks of information to be hidden. For security, information is encrypted and then scattered in the image. The receiver can retrieve the data without the original image. The results prove that the proposed scheme is capable of minimizing distortion caused due to data hiding.

Chapter 12: Cybersecurity Issues and Challenges for E-Government During COVID-19 – A Review

Cyber-attacks can steal information by applying different methods and activities of cyber criminals, thereby destroying data, computer programs, and networking on one or more computers. There is an increase in new technology among users and it provides them with more convenience. On the other hand, cyber-attacks are increasing dramatically today. The world is completely focused on creating social distancing between people. During the WHO-recommended COVID-19 pandemic, billions of people around the world are working from home, with shops and businesses closed. In this chapter, we will highlight several essential concerns and challenges facing e-government development as well as different departments that provide e-services. We'll also focus on and peer evaluate the major concerns and challenges facing e-government growth from a holistic perspective, offering methodologies and policy recommendations to address them in a complete and inclusive manner.

Acknowledgment

We would like to express our thanks to Almighty Allah SWT for his all blessings and then great appreciation to all of those we have had the pleasure to work with during this project. The completion of this project could not have been accomplished without their support. First, the editors would like to express deep and sincere gratitude to all the authors who shared their ideas, expertise, and experience by submitting chapters to this book and adhering to its timeline. Second, the editors wish to acknowledge the extraordinary contributions of the reviewers for their valuable and constructive suggestions and recommendations to improve the quality, coherence, and content presentation of chapters. Most of the authors also served as referees. Their willingness to give time so generously is highly appreciated. Finally, our heartfelt gratitude goes to our family members and friends for their love, prayers, caring, and sacrifices in completing this project well in time.

We dedicate this book to our best friend, Late Dr. G. Suseendran. We recently lost him during the Covid-19 Pandemic due to the Covid-19.

Noor Zaman
Taylor's University, Malaysia

Imdad Ali Shah
Shah Abdul Latif University, Pakistan

Samina Rajper
Shah Abdul Latif University, Pakistan

Introduction

Cybersecurity refers to defending critical systems and sensitive data against cyberattacks. Cybersecurity measures, also known as information technology (IT) security, are designed to keep networked systems and applications safe from attacks that come from both within and outside a firm. E-government can refer to anything from "Online government services" to "the electronic transfer of activities and resources among individuals, companies, and other government agencies."

During last half-century. Our modern, digital civilization has depended on information and communication technologies (ICT). Because the smart computer gadgets we use in our everyday lives are mainly powered by worldwide Internet access, the danger of data breaches or cyber-attacks is growing by the day. Therefore, preventing and defending ICT systems from various types of sophisticated cyber-attacks or threats, often known as ICT security, has recently become a top priority for security professionals and policymakers Arampatzis, A., & O'Hagan, L. (2022). Cybersecurity events have impacted significant governmental and private organizations in recent years—data breaches at IT businesses (Manancourt & Cerulus, 2021). Early detection of cybersecurity trends is critical for a thorough assessment of present and future capabilities. Armies and their research institutions were frequently the sources of significant technical advances in the 20th century. The Defense Advanced Research Projects Agency (DARPA), the Department of Defense's research and development arm, is credited with creating breakthrough technologies such as the Internet and drones (DARPA, 2021). Armies no longer lead the technical trends of the digital era in the twenty-first century. Defense organizations' conventional screening and development procedures are too sluggish to keep up with the rising innovation privatization. In this setting, there is an ever-widening gap in figure 1.

Software-defined networking (SDN) has emerged as a ground-breaking networking architecture capable of meeting future networking demands. Through OpenFlow technology, software-defined networking (SDN) decouples the control and data planes, allowing for more flexible network control. It has been widely used in several fields and has become a focal point in the future network. With the rise of SDN,

Figure 1. Overview Countries with the most high-quality cybersecurity patents are at the top of the list.

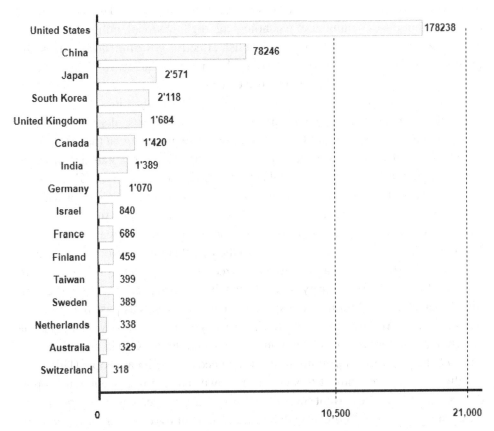

security has become a critical research problem that has to be addressed right now (Lee S, Kim J, Woo S). It vastly simplifies the network's control plane from the integrated nodes, replacing the traditional control plane based on system integration with an open and programmable soft control plane, in contrast to a normal network (Lv, Z., & Kumar, N. 2020). SDN has been used in various industries, including business networks and data centers, because of its openness and programmability. The separation of logical control and forwarding functions, on the other hand, widens the attack surface, posing security issues for the control plane, data plane, and application plane. Because the controller has a worldwide network vision, the whole network can be controlled once the network has been hijacked. As a result of extensive study and widespread deployment, security has steadily been a basic component restraining the SDN architecture's evolution (Wang, Y., Jiang, D., Huo, L 2021).

The use of IoT in e-government may be highly beneficial, allowing for the creation of new creative services and the transformation and augmentation of existing ones, all of which are informed by smart devices and real-time data. The use of IoT in e-government raises a number of technological, organizational, political, and legal issues that must be solved in order to establish effective government-to-citizen and government-to-society applications (Wang, Y., Jiang, D. 2021). IoT is an up-and-coming technology that is expected to thrive in the next years since 127 new devices connect to the Internet every second. (McKinsey, 2019). Machines and things are becoming dynamic, intelligent actors in networked contexts, delivering unique services due to the Internet of Things (IoT). The pervasive nature of the IoT delivers substantial changes to the way we work and live, with rising acceptance in different realms of personal and organizational activity (AlEnezi, A., AlMeraj, Z. 2018).

Cyber security is defined as the use of safety measures on PCs to provide an optimal level of assurance. The acronym CIA stands for Privacy, Authenticity, and Access, and it may be used to describe the problem of privacy (Humayun, M., Niazi, M. 2020).The term "accessibility" refers to the rule that information and computer assets should always be available to authorized clients. However, using the word "simple" to describe PC security is misleading, just as using "easy" to describe golf. Simply knock the ball through the space with as few strokes as possible given the circumstances (Almusaylim, Z 2020). Electronic governance (e-governance) is the integration of information and communication technology (ICT) in all activities to enhance the government's ability to meet the needs of the local people (Ullah, A., Pinglu 2021). E-government models have shown that e-government can support economic growth. The current study intends to fill in the research gaps mentioned in the existing literature. Addressing these flaws would allow e-government programs to run smoothly, especially in underdeveloped nations (Malodia, S., Dhir, A 2021). The current study combines computer systems and public administration perspectives by developing a multifunctional and multi-level paradigm on e-government that incorporates the perspectives of numerous e-government stakeholders.

E-Government results from governments' efforts to better their relationships with their citizens. If specific requirements are met, the valid estimate of digital transactions will be proportionate to the legal assessment of other forms of correspondence, such as the constructed structure. Data security best practices are required to ensure the success of e-government initiatives. Security rules, methods, and approaches and the use of security technology must be established to protect e-government frameworks from attack, recognize odd exercises administrations, and have a proven emergency plan in place (Sambana, B., Raju 2021). The Internet's core structure was built around better accessibility and trust, with security initiatives coming later. There are a number of widely used conventions that provide little to no security to their customers and instead rely on trust. When the Internet was originally developed, this concept seemed to work effectively because the data being transmitted was of little interest to anybody other than the owners. The Internet is now used to transfer data between individuals, banks, specialists, businesses, and government entities (El Khatib, M. 2020). As the present level of digital attacks, identity thefts, and phishing attacks demonstrates, this data may significantly induce others, even illegals.

Rural banditry is fast becoming one of the most dangerous types of domestic insurgency in the West African sub-region. The prevalence and intensity of rural banditry has intensified instability in the region, posing a threat to West Africa's regional cooperation (Abdullahi, A. 2019). This chapter investigates the nature and dynamics of rural banditry and increased security in local governments within the Economic Community of West African States. The Economic Community of West African States (ECOWAS) is a West African economic region. There are around 15 nations represented in this region, which has a population of over 349 million people (Ogunniyi, Olayemi Jacob, 2019). Cybersecurity has become a major concern with the rapid advancement of technology in agriculture, healthcare, and personal devices. With dictatorships, corrupt regimes, religious extremists, and other illegal activities on the rise, it's critical that local governments make cybersecurity a priority.

It's impossible to overestimate the importance of predicting cyber threats. Cyber-attack data has been shown to have unique properties, such as long-range dependence and high nonlinearity, which makes modeling and predicting cyber-attack rates extremely challenging (Lim, M., Abdullah, A., Jhanjhi, N. Z 2019). Deep learning software frameworks enable users to create, train, and evaluate deep neural networks using a variety of programming languages (Lim, M., Abdullah, A. 2019). Efforts by the government to develop and improve engagement with voters have produced e-government. A framework that is more than one framework is defined by the breadth of e-government control and its influence on a network. A network-based digital security methodology is needed to look at security concerns throughout the entire framework (El Khatib, M., Nakand, L. 2020). The results of current network-based activities have revealed possible development chances and indicated the estimation of these events. Their valuables endanger public safety, national security, and the universal network's general strength. It might be difficult to pinpoint the source of the disturbance.

The difficulty of combining safe operations with great confidentiality is the most concerning issue. To ensure that the government functions properly, it must have a high degree of openness, accountability, integrity, and secrecy. The risks and problems associated with establishing E-governance are primarily (Pal, S. K. (2019): In the field of information technology, cyber security plays a significant role. In today's world, protecting information has become a huge challenge. The major thing that comes to mind when thinking about cybersecurity is "cybercrimes," which occur on a massive scale on a regular basis

(Kalakuntla, R., Vanamala 2019). Various governments and groups are adopting a variety of steps to combat cybercrime. Aside from such steps, many people are still concerned about cybersecurity. The COVID-19 virus is a novel virus that belongs to the same viral family. This is a national emergency, and the world's forums and organizations work together to combat the sickness until an accurate vaccine for the virus is developed and life can resume normally (Ahmad, S. U., Kashyap 2020). The WHO advised creating social distance between people in this scenario. Hundreds of millions of individuals worldwide work from home and run companies from their homes, including financial activities, buying and selling, and shopping. The globe is still reeling from the COVID-19 assaults, which have had a broad impact on corporate activities and raised dangers in many parts of life, including the economy, politics, health, and security (Arampatzis, A 2020). E-government is rapidly being deployed around the world to provide comprehensive services to residents. They conduct online activities and provide teaching from their homes.

Exponential growth in service maturity levels from interactive, transactional, and transformational to connecting and integrating services and guaranteed service levels. The complexity of providing application security grows dramatically as e-government systems become more essential (Kumar, B. S., Sridhar 2022). The healthcare industry's data is sensitive and must be protected from theft or unauthorized changes. Security, privacy, data integrity, and non-repudiation are all important characteristics to have regarding healthcare data (Rao, P. M 2022). Security measures have become increasingly important as digital data in cyber settings has grown exponentially. National and international units are revealing cybersecurity dangers, and the number of these risks is growing every day (Savaş, S., & Karataş, S.2022). With a comprehensive cybersecurity plan, it is feasible to eliminate cybersecurity threats.

The current idea of centralization has been completely changed by blockchain technology. In blockchain technology, many methods are employed to connect and monitor transactions. This chapter provides an overview of blockchain technology, including its characteristics, classification, and applications (Gill, S. H., Razzaq 2022). Many advantages of blockchain technology have been recognized in this field. However, unique ways of safe and verified data transmission must be developed (Ronchi, A. M. 2019). Government entities manage and maintain many official records of individuals and businesses. Individuals must trust the government to protect the security and privacy of their personal information (Kassen, M.2022). Blockchain-based applications have the potential to transform the way these papers are managed through digital, secure, and immutable record-keeping figure 2.

Figure 2. Overview of e-government

REFERENCES

Abdullahi, A. (2019). Rural Banditry, Regional Security and Integration in West Africa. *Journal of Social and Political Sciences*, *2*(3). Advance online publication. doi:10.31014/aior.1991.02.03.107

Ahmad, S. U., Kashyap, S., Shetty, S. D., & Sood, N. (2022). Cybersecurity During COVID-19. In *Information and Communication Technology for Competitive Strategies (ICTCS 2020)* (pp. 1045–1056). Springer. doi:10.1007/978-981-16-0739-4_96

AlEnezi, A., AlMeraj, Z., & Manuel, P. (2018, April). Challenges of IoT based smart-government development. In *2018 21st Saudi Computer Society National Computer Conference (NCC)* (pp. 1-6). IEEE. https://ieeexplore.ieee.org/abstract/document/8593168

Almusaylim, Z. A., & Jhanjhi, N. Z. (2020). Comprehensive review: Privacy protection of user in location-aware services of mobile cloud computing. *Wireless Personal Communications*, *111*(1), 541–564. doi:10.100711277-019-06872-3

Arampatzis, A., & O'Hagan, L. (2022). Cybersecurity and Privacy in the Age of the Pandemic. In *Handbook of Research on Cyberchondria, Health Literacy, and the Role of Media in Society's Perception of Medical Information* (pp. 35-53). IGI Global. https://www.igi-global.com/chapter/cybersecurity-and-privacy-in-the-age-of-the-pandemic/293432

Arampatzis, A., & O'Hagan, L. (2022). Cybersecurity and Privacy in the Age of the Pandemic. In *Handbook of Research on Cyberchondria, Health Literacy, and the Role of Media in Society's Perception of Medical Information* (pp. 35-53). IGI Global. https://www.igi-global.com/chapter/cybersecurity-and-privacy-in-the-age-of-the-pandemic/293432

Cybersecurity Technologies: An Overview of Trends & Activities in Switzerland and Abroad. (2022). https://papers.ssrn.com/sol3/papers.cfm?abstract_id=4013762

Durst, M. (2019). Internet of things-enabled smart governance and the sustainable development of innovative data-driven urban ecosystems. *Geopolitics, History, and International Relations, 11*(2), 20-26. https://www.ceeol.com/search/article-detail?id=804059

El Khatib, M., Nakand, L., Almarzooqi, S., & Almarzooqi, A. (2020). E-Governance in Project Management: Impact and Risks of Implementation. *American Journal of Industrial and Business Management, 10*(12), 1785–1811. doi:10.4236/ajibm.2020.1012111

El Khatib, M., Nakand, L., Almarzooqi, S., & Almarzooqi, A. (2020). E-Governance in Project Management: Impact and Risks of Implementation. *American Journal of Industrial and Business Management, 10*(12), 1785–1811. doi:10.4236/ajibm.2020.1012111

Gill, S. H., Razzaq, M. A., Ahmad, M., Almansour, F. M., Haq, I. U., Jhanjhi, N. Z., ... Masud, M. (2022). Security and Privacy Aspects of Cloud Computing: A Smart Campus Case Study. *Intelligent Automation & Soft Computing, 31*(1), 117–128. doi:10.32604/iasc.2022.016597

Humayun, M., Niazi, M., Jhanjhi, N. Z., Alshayeb, M., & Mahmood, S. (2020). Cyber security threats and vulnerabilities: A systematic mapping study. *Arabian Journal for Science and Engineering, 45*(4), 3171–3189. doi:10.100713369-019-04319-2

Kalakuntla, R., Vanamala, A. B., & Kolipyaka, R. R. (2019). Cyber security. *HOLISTICA–Journal of Business and Public Administration, 10*(2), 115-128. https://sciendo.com/pdf/10.2478/hjbpa-2019-0020

Kassen, M. (2022). Blockchain and e-government innovation: Automation of public information processes. *Information Systems, 103*, 101862. doi:10.1016/j.is.2021.101862

Kumar, B. S., Sridhar, V., & Sudhindra, K. R. (2022). Generic Security Risk Profile of e-Governance Applications—a Case Study. In *Emerging Research in Computing, Information, Communication and Applications* (pp. 731–741). Springer. doi:10.1007/978-981-16-1342-5_57

Lee, S., Kim, J., Woo, S., Yoon, C., Scott-Hayward, S., Yegneswaran, V., Porras, P., & Shin, S. (2020). A comprehensive security assessment framework for software-defined networks. *Computers & Security*, *91*, 101720. doi:10.1016/j.cose.2020.101720

Lim, M., Abdullah, A., Jhanjhi, N. Z., Khan, M. K., & Supramaniam, M. (2019). Link prediction in time-evolving criminal network with deep reinforcement learning technique. *IEEE Access: Practical Innovations, Open Solutions*, *7*, 184797–184807. doi:10.1109/ACCESS.2019.2958873

Lim, M., Abdullah, A., Jhanjhi, N. Z., & Supramaniam, M. (2019). Hidden link prediction in criminal networks using the deep reinforcement learning technique. *Computers, 8*(1), 8. https://www.mdpi.com/2073-431X/8/1/8

Lv, Z., & Kumar, N. (2020). Software defined solutions for sensors in 6G/IoE. *Computer Communications*, *153*, 42–47. doi:10.1016/j.comcom.2020.01.060

Malodia, S., Dhir, A., Mishra, M., & Bhatti, Z. A. (2021). Future of e-Government: An integrated conceptual framework. *Technological Forecasting and Social Change*, *173*, 121102. doi:10.1016/j.techfore.2021.121102

Ogunniyi, O. J., & Akpu, J. O. (2019). The Challenge of Drug Trafficking to Democratic Governance and Human Security in West Africa. *Africa Development. Afrique et Developpement*, *44*(4), 29–50. https://www.jstor.org/stable/26873443

Pal, S. K. (2019). Changing technological trends for E-governance. In *E-governance in India* (pp. 79-105). Palgrave Macmillan. https://link.springer.com/chapter/10.1007/978-981-15-4451-4_52

Qi, M., & Wang, J. (2021). Using the Internet of Things e-government platform to optimize the administrative management mode. *Wireless Communications and Mobile Computing*, *2021*, 1–11. doi:10.1155/2021/2224957

Rao, P. M., & Deebak, B. D. (2022). Security and privacy issues in smart cities/industries: Technologies, applications, and challenges. *Journal of Ambient Intelligence and Humanized Computing*, 1–37. doi:10.100712652-022-03707-1

Ronchi, A. M. (2019). e-Government: Background, Today's Implementation and Future Trends. In e-Democracy (pp. 93-196). Springer.

Sambana, B., Raju, K. N., Satish, D., Raju, S. S., & Raja, P. V. K. (2021). *Impact of Cyber Security in e-Governance and e-Commerce* (No. 5533). EasyChair. file:///C:/Users/USER/Downloads/EasyChair-Preprint-5533%20(4).pdf

Savaş, S., & Karataş, S. (2022). Cyber governance studies in ensuring cybersecurity: an overview of cybersecurity governance. *International Cybersecurity Law Review*, 1-28. https://link.springer.com/article/10.1365/s43439-021-00045-4

Tsesmelis, M., Percia David, D., Maillart, T., Dolamic, L., Tresoldi, G., Lacube, W., . . . Mermoud, A. (2022). *Cybersecurity Technologies: An Overview of Trends & Activities in Switzerland and Abroad.* https://papers.ssrn.com/sol3/papers.cfm?abstract_id=4013762

Ullah, A., Pinglu, C., Ullah, S., Abbas, H. S. M., & Khan, S. (2021). The role of E-governance in combating COVID-19 and promoting sustainable development: a comparative study of China and Pakistan. *Chinese Political Science Review, 6*(1), 86-118. https://link.springer.com/article/10.1007/s41111-020-00167-w

Wang, Y., Jiang, D., Huo, L., & Zhao, Y. (2021). A new traffic prediction algorithm to software defined networking. *Mobile Networks and Applications, 26*(2), 716–725. doi:10.100711036-019-01423-3

Chapter 1
E-Government Cybersecurity Modeling in the Context of Software-Defined Networks

Raja Majid Ali Ujjan
Independent Researcher, UK

Imran Taj
Information System Branch, Ministry of Attorney General, BC Public Service, Canada

Sarfraz Nawaz Brohi
University of the West of England (UWE), Bristol, UK

ABSTRACT

Currently, information and communication technologies are going in advance, allowing more information to be distributed globally via the internet superhighway. While being interconnected to the virtual world, people are becoming increasingly focused, large, and smart, needing the development of new solutions that will be implemented and robust network security systems. When the information is being handled in the applications, it is vulnerable to attack at every stage, and it is impossible to handle it in a separate manner, as traditional security systems have done. The introduction of software-defined networks (SDN) has provided a novel perspective on data security, since the network may assist in the construction of stable and safe continuity in the context of risks posed by the internet. The structure of SDN, particularly its gradual construction and centralization of network data and mechanisms, has pushed us to consider security from a strategy-practiced standpoint. The major goal of this chapter is to give detailed an overview of the current state-of-the-art in the area of SDN security and its significance in the context of e-government applications.

DOI: 10.4018/978-1-7998-9624-1.ch001

1. INTRODUCTION

The new generation of healthcare incorporates innovative advancements to incorporate sustainable strategies improve patient care and a higher standard of living. As educing resource consumption and direct or indirect healthcare expenses. These unique clinical environments have a number of advantages, including the capability to support new possibilities, such as medical settings, monitoring vital signs of patients are collected and cognitively analyzed in order to diagnose disorders and ecosystems that aren't invaded anticipating unfavorable outcomes in the early stages, and digital support everywhere. This is made feasible by the combination of activities using actual hardware and virtual information flexible connectivity that fulfil not just the growing demand for speeds ranging and bandwidths (Stankovic, 2016), but also the agility and dynamic essential to control network activities in timely manner. Medical devices in medical contexts can be openly coordinated, controlled, and connected via ICE-based solutions (Mármol et al., 2016). Despite the advantages of existing solutions, SDN control plane's logical centralized approach and protocols introduce additional vulnerabilities that compromise the diagnostic products, communication network protection, and patient safety (Nespoli et al., 2017). Keeping in mind the prior problems, there are a number of open challenges that require additional attention. We emphasize the importance of designing and configurations that take into account the SDN paradigm's vulnerabilities; the Safety methods are being implemented in healthcare contexts (Díaz-López et al., 2016). To combat the overwhelming security threats, the fundamental features of a safe mechanism is required that its defenses become more powerful during its whole existence. It is particularly true when a harmful attempt is launched and unexpected information and investment loss, and both from within and external to the connection (Dunhill, 2020). A common network used to operate industrial applications and is accessible over the internet faces significantly. It faces more dangers than just its network counterpart. Traditionally, a hacker attack on the information assets of a company has entailed gaining access to the network through exploitation weaknesses in internet-facing systems. Used this devices of these victims, the stranger will have to put in a lot of effort to get access to the internal network and its various portions, which are all connected via a variety of intermediary boxes. These intermediate boxes could have their own set of vulnerabilities that would take a lot of time, skill, and effort to exploit (Huertas Celdran et al., 2018). Its central control and programmability, in particular, have changed the entire paradigm of enterprise security, eliciting mixed reactions. In one opinion, SDN's nature is considered a design flaw and the biggest threat in the cycle of networking safety precautions, has shifted our perspective on enterprise security in the face of current cyber threats (Fernandez Maimo et al., 2019). A novel definition of cyber antifragility is the ability to respond to a provocation, return to a

Figure 1. Overview of basic SDN architecture (Cheng et al., 2017)

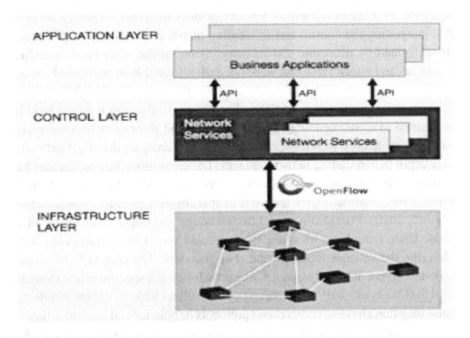

daily routine with minimal harm, and improve capabilities to thwart future threats of undiscovered or well-known forms. A simple SDN architecture that provides programmability and flexibility (Nguyen et al., 2016). It is necessary to incorporate a functional technique of recognizing issues related to the security of the application, control, and data planes, as well as their associated interfaces, to assure the system's security throughout its lifetime.

The following points will be highlighted in this chapter:

1. To provide a wide analysis, Networks that are defined by software (SDN)
2. To highlight the applications of e-government in the context of SDN
3. To focus on cybersecurity models in the context of SDN

2. LITERATURE REVIEW

SDN is a network design that physically divides network control from network-forwarding hardware (Cabaj et al., 2018). The software-based controllers in SDN give managers a better understanding of the system, permitting them to manage capabilities and regulate internet backbone flow of traffic. This permits the networks to be treated as a logical object while the underlying architecture is abstracted for applications and network services. Control plan protocols are used to make it easier for the control plane and network devices to communicate (Xiao et al., 2020). Integrating the control and forwarding planes provides lots of advantages, as demonstrated by academic and industry. SDN, on the other hand, introduces new dangers and attack risks that were not earlier available in traditional network topologies (Luo et al., 2020). To safeguard the network and data, it's critical to understand the security limits of SDN. The majority of research in this field has been devoted to recommending various solutions and techniques for constructing secure SDN structures. Researchers can explore and analyses the target network in greater depth by simulating network attacks. Different modelling techniques have been used in SDN studies to examine SDN structures and protocols. The STRIDE and attack tree methodologies are used to investigate OpenFlow protocol flaws (Lee et al., 2020). Provided a model for analyzing the safety mechanisms of the Separate Underlying Network of the Routing and Control plane (Lee et al., 2017). To describe the network topology and state transfers. The current SDN security risk models do not attempt to quantify the possibility of a specific attack (Smyth et al., 2016),(Cao et al., 2019). Support SDN controllers have a simpler architecture because they don't have to comprehend protocols or policies and can just follow the controllers' commands. As a result, the SDN architecture can be divided into three layers (Prabadevi et al., 2020),(Lv & Kumar, 2020). Rapid growth of mobile devices and the continual creation of large amounts of data necessitate high-bandwidth and a dynamic network environment. SDN has evolved into a networking paradigm that extends virtualization technology usage beyond servers to networks (Wang et al., 2021), (Al-Najjar et al., 2016),(Chen-xu & Jie-sheng, 2015). It has major scalability concerns due to the SDN controller's limited resources when dealing with a huge number of requests. A distributed SDN controller has been developed to address these difficulties. The general concept underlying the use of numerous controllers (Tan et al., 2017),(Li, Liu, & Yang, 2017). So far, we've examined logically centralized SDN controllers that presume the network is managed by a single. The network is managed by the same organization. Decentralize-SDN, often known as D-SDN, is an SDN architecture that allows the control plane to be distributed over administratively decentralized and heterogeneous networks. A hierarchy of main controllers and subordinate controllers is used to provide control distribution. Each controller has its own database, and update messages are used to communicate network state amongst the major controllers (Anwar et al., 2018), (Bannour et al., 2017), (Botelho et al., 2014), (El-Hassany et al., 2016). To satisfy the growing traffic demand in wireless networks. However, rising network density places a significant strain on backhaul networks and existing network protocols, necessitating a large-scale deployment of network devices. The authors developed a dynamic two-tier SDN controller hierarchy to overcome the difficulties created by densenets (Karki et al.,

2018), (Li, Jiang, Feng et al, 2017). Administration flight are the three components of the network architecture (Mace et al., 2018),(Ouyang et al., 2014). (Qian et al., 2017). (Schiff et al., 2016), (Wen et al., 2018), 35]. The SDN topic is a particularly active study area because of its rapid growth (Networking, n.d.). IDC can make a substantial contribution to energy efficiency by reducing energy consumption and power management in IT environments, owing to the large amount of energy used and the associated cost. It is for this reason that most research focuses on lowering the power consumption of IDCs. These initiatives involve developing creative DC architecture to reduce cool air loss, heat from IT equipment, and protection from outside heat, among other things. Additionally, computer scientists created energy-efficient workload reallocation techniques to spread peaks in server workloads and reduce energy usage and heat emission (Pena & Yu, 2014). E-government is described as the administration's use of digitalization (ICTs) to facilitate citizen availability and accessibility of administrative activities and services (Muzafar & Jhanjhi, 2020). E-government also relates to the use of technologies to boost government efficacy through better public services and collaboration (Hamid et al., 2020). It refers to a variety of government activities and operations that are impacted by the ongoing integration of ICTs with certain administration paradigms (Sharma et al., 2017). E-government can be viewed through the lenses of e-society, e-administration, and e-citizens. Its successful implementation can lead to increased internal efficiency, stakeholder satisfaction, and service improvement due to uniform operating methods, the shift of paper-based information into electronic form, and diverse databases figure 2.

3. THE EVOLUTION OF SOFTWARE DEFINED NETWORKS (SDN)

Several academics have increasingly become interested in the Software Defined Networks (SDN) concept. The SDN paradigm has the ability to produce a network system that is more secure, dynamic, and dependable. The primary innovation of SDN is still the independence of the centralized controller from the base network level. The message devices must be setup using a well-designed interface such as OpenFlow, which is managed by the controller. The controller can accommodate numerous tables of flow which is perused by the OpenFlow switch, permitting the SDN control layer to be programmable. The flow tables, depending on the controller policy, router that performs comparable functions. With everything, amazing advancements, SDN faces extra security vulnerabilities from numerous architectural components. When it comes to the various challenges and required to know them, the security of SDN is regarded as the most important. Among the many security risks,

Figure 2. Overview of SDN with main planes data, control, and application planes, and the communication channels (Sharma et al., 2017)

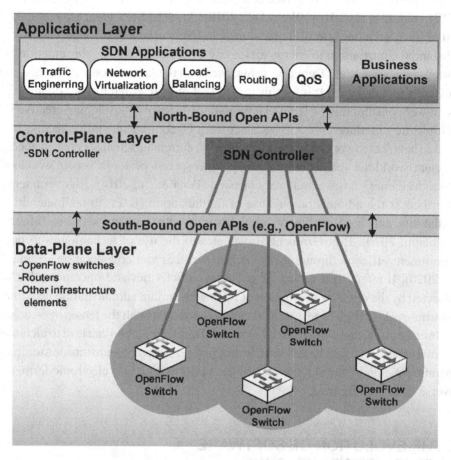

Distributed Denial of Service is one of the most serious (DDoS). The chief goal of this attack is to prevent legitimate users from accessing computing resources. This type of assault is frequently carried out by a group of bots that have been infiltrated by malicious software. The DDoS attack can swiftly grow and create huge network damage since the initial procedure is simple, but the defense phase is extremely difficult. Although a system of controller can detect a potential assault, it may not be practical to justification for simultaneous strikes instantaneously (Steichen et al., 2017). (Ryu, 2018). (Meng & Li, 2012). (Meng & Kwok, 2013), (Russo et al., n.d.). As a result, certain security restrictions must be imposed on the controller. As a result, for future network architectures such as SDN, an effective detection technique and mitigation procedures must be devised. Because the controller is the

SDN's brain, numerous approaches such as neural networks and ML can be utilized to improve information safety table 1

Table 1. Overview of existing DDoS attack detection techniques used in SDN

Citation	Applied method	Summary
(Ni et al., 2018)	Neural Network (Map of Self- Organization)	SOM techniques are used in categorization, APF, GDP, and GSF-like characteristics are utilized.
(Chin, Xiong, & Rahouti, 2018)	SVM	Traditional detection and prevention characteristics
(Rahouti et al., 2021)	Rate limiting and TRW-CB	Collect traffic and implement such techniques
(Chin, Rahouti, & Xiong, 2018)	BPNN	BPNN is used for packet trace-backing in the proposed SD-anti-DDoS.
(Palvia et al., 2018)	SPRT	The sequence chance ratio test was applied to a higher percentage of DDoS.
(Sharef et al., 2014)	Radial Basis Function	The RBF network is further enhanced by GA.
(Correia et al., 2017)	Gradient Boosting (XGBoost)	For higher accuracy, GA is utilized instead of XGBoost.
(He, Zhang, Zhu et al, 2016)	SVM	GA is a type of optimization tool.
(He, Zhang, & Liang, 2016)	Deep Learning-based sparse autoencoder (SAF)	The TCFI component is used to collect traffic.
(Abolhasan et al., 2015)	PSO-BP neural network	The techniques of sensitivity and machine learning are applied.
(Dong, 2017)	SVM	In image segmentation, GA is employed
(Huang et al., 2017)	SVM	PSO is a tool for adjusting settings.

4. SDN BACKGROUND

The concept of networks with programmability and separable control system has been around for a long time. a long time. SDN began in the 1980s (Dunhill, 2020). This section gives an overview of mentioned techniques that have aided in the evolution of SDN.

a. Central network control: Previously, circuits of telecommunications used signaling within the band, which carried both information (speech) and switch system over the same channel. The networks that resulted were invariably complicated and unsecure. The input and the command planes of AT & T's circuits of telecommunications were divided in the 1980s, and the idea of a NCP (Mukherjee et al., 2020) was established. The goal was to keep voice and command distinct, with command being handled by NCP. The NCP provided operators with a centralized, network-wide vantage point from which they could directly examine network behaviour. Eliminating in-band 9signaling allowed infrastructure, data, and services to evolve independently, making it easier to deliver new services to clients. As a result of NCP, the SDN concept was born: separation of control and data planes, as well as centralized network control.

b. Network gradually built: The DARPA research community proposed "Active Networks" in the mid-1990s, with the goal of creating a network architecture that could be programmable for bespoke services (Rahman et al., 2019), (Islam et al., 2019). Tempset was created in 1998 as a Cambridge project. Penn's Switchware project developed a controllable switch as well as a programming language to enable switchlets (Javaid et al., 2020). The BBN study Smart Packets focuses on extending the dynamic networks paradigm to the managed services operation (Ndiaye et al., 2020).

c. Virtualization of Network Resources: The depiction of one or more logical communication networks on top of the same architecture is known as network virtualization. It decouples the logical infrastructure from the physical infrastructure beneath it. Distinct configurations include Virtual LANs (VLANs), network simulation tools, and VMware (Cheng et al., 2018). The control framework has been removed from the switch in Switchlets, allowing the switch to be virtualized. The control and data planes were separated in VINI, and the control plane was a software routing protocol called XORP, which allowed routed methods to be run on network virtualization configurations.

d. Packet Switching Network Management: With the aforementioned progress of network technology, management separation was required for rapid network innovation. It was easier to adapt the current telephone network control logic since the control logic is related to hardware. It was able to have a different software controller and simply deploy new services to the telephone network because of the independent control channel. Software controllers also gave operators a centralized network-wide vantage point from which they could observe the telephone network's behaviour in real time. Packet switching networks attempt to divide the control plane from the data plane based on these motivations. Separate control channels, in-band protocols, modifying data plane hardware, and open hardware are the four basic methods packet switched networks use to achieve (Kumar et al., 2020). The FORCES architecture separated the control and data planes, they were kept on the same network device and portrayed as a single entity. The FORCES, on the other hand, required new hardware standardization, adoption, and deployment.

e. OpenFlow: Previously, the OpenFlow system was used on educational network systems (Karakus & Durresi, 2017a). Today, over nine colleges in the United States have adopted OpenFlow systems. OpenFlow has gotten attention from both academia and industry as a way to improve network functions while lowering costs and decreasing hardware complexity figure 3.

Figure 3. Overview of planes (Karakus & Durresi, 2017a)

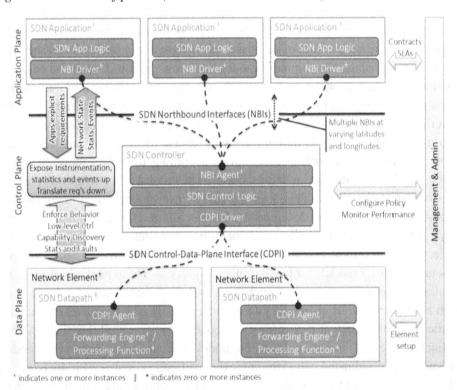

⁺ indicates one or more instances | * indicates zero or more instances

5. INFLUENCE OF SDN

The administration of IT infrastructure and network architecture has been greatly influenced by software-defined networking. As SDN technology advances, it alters not only network infrastructure architecture but also IT's job. SDN designs may make network control programmable, and they frequently use open protocols like

OpenFlow to do so. As a result, organizations can implement aware software control at the network's edges. Instead of using closed and proprietary firmware to setup, manage, secure, and optimize network resources, this allows access to network switches and routers. While SDN implementations can be found in any area, the technology's impact is greatest in technology-related fields and financial services. The way telecom firm's function is being influenced by SDN.

6. OVERVIEW E-GOVERNMENT AND SND

As a result of technological breakthroughs, various researchers have offered a variety of frameworks. Many of these ideas hold that the emergence of electronic government was continuous and ongoing, as the government matures through several stages. There are a maximum of six phases in the most commonly debated and cited models. A two-stage development model has been proposed, with the maturity phases defined as a catalogue, in which governments organize information in a catalogue that individuals and businesses may access, and a transaction, in which governments provide full-fledged e-government services. Governments first post information online, then communicate with stakeholders online, and ultimately allow consumers to do online transactions according to a three-stage paradigm called "publish, interaction, and transaction". They took a more balanced approach to government maturity models, stressing that e-governments might mature in four stages. The maturity model developed by Gartner differed from the others in several ways. According to the report, e-governments may complete transactions in the third stage, while others may do so in the second (Maharaj & Munyoka, 2019). Developed six-stage maturity models for the assimilation process. These methods allowed for a delayed absorption process in which the government began at a very basic level, such as with the use of an email system, and gradually advanced toward maturity. While evaluating current e-government models, we discovered that they had few distinct differences; in fact, most of the models were inherited from prior models and only slightly adjusted within the contexts of different countries. Produced nearly equivalent maturity models with a similar number of phases and metaphors for each step (Karakus & Durresi, 2017b). Current networks are becoming increasingly diverse, with a wide range of devices ranging from small sensors and appliances to network equipment like routers (Sahay et al., 2019), (Jacquenet & Boucadair, 2016). Despite the benefits of SDN in dealing with the complexities of today's networks, a significant concern in SDN at the moment is security; the current state of the art in SDN figure 4.

Figure 4. Overview e-government model and e-government services (Al Shuhaimi et al., 2016)

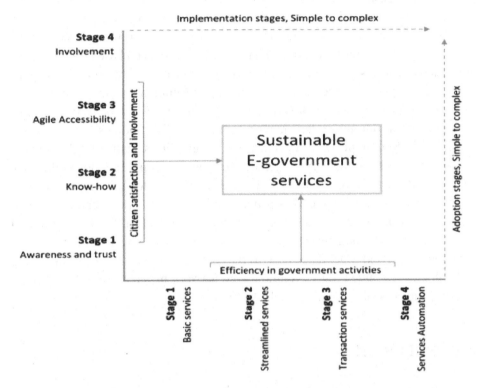

7. DISCUSSION

Thanks to the emergence of SDN, network designers now have the ability to remodel the network control plane. However, controllers must synchronize their states to keep a broad perspective. Synchronization may cause network overload since the status of the entire network changes frequently. Furthermore, Levin et al. discovered that the SDN's inconsistent control state lowers the performance of several applications significantly (Yassein et al., 2017). Furthermore, it can guarantee that at all times, at least one controller can respond to a request. The fact that each controller cannot identify the best answer for each flow is an unavoidable disadvantage of this technology. Each controller handles its own local domain in the distributed control plane (Chakraborty & Abougreen, 2021). Based on the observations, the data plane flow size appears to be different. The elephant flow is the flow that results in a massive volume of data transmission. Such fluxes have a significant impact on the load on underlying networks. On the other hand, elephants are in short supply.

When Kandoo identifies an elephant flow, the root controller uses the network-wide perspective to design an ideal path for the elephant flow.

Our contribution to this chapter is a number of determinants required to establish e-government operations that are long-term for a successful management system has been developed for e-government. We built a new model based on the factors and tested it in terms of e-government service sustainability. The proposed model's main characteristic was the merging of the implementation and adoption stages to make government services more efficient while also matching them with citizens' requirements. From an implementation standpoint. The findings of the last era regarding the SDN indicate that it is emerging as a growing scientific field, obtaining important focus from industry and academic. It was a deep discussion in different surveys of the state of the art in SDN, in the context of historical perspective, such as architecture, relating to the SDN pattern, and emerging in the deepest. We focus on giving definitions and concepts for a better a known of SDNs. The concept of networking devices and separable the concept of management has been known for a long time, and SDN dates back to the early 1980s. The four key supporting technologies that aided SDN evolution were network management from a central location and control of packet switched networks.

8. CONCLUSION

Currently information and communication technologies are going in advance, allowing more information to be distributed globally via the internet superhighway. While being interconnected to the virtual world, people are becoming increasingly focused, large, and smart, needing the development of new solutions that will be implemented and robust network security systems. When the information is being handled in the applications, it is vulnerable to attack at every stage, and it is impossible to handle it in a separate manner, as traditional security systems have done. The introduction of Software-Defined Networks (SDN) has provided a novel perspective on data security, since the network may assist in the construction of stable and safe continuity in the context of risks posed by the internet. The structure of SDN, particularly its gradual construction and centralization of network data and mechanisms, has pushed us to consider security from a strategy-practiced standpoint. The major goal of this chapter is to give detailed an overview of the current state-of-the-art in the area of SDN security and its significance in the context of e-government applications.

9. FUTURE WORK

SDN allows for a variety of network advances, but it lacks clear definitions and standard implementation in practice. Jarschel et al. examine the SDN definition in detail. On the other hand, many critical controller concerns must be solved in order to increase SDN development and usage.

a.   The controller, which is the fundamental component of a software-defined network, is used by operators to manage an underlying network. More abstractions, frameworks, and programming languages must be investigated in order to put more distinct control applications on the controller in order to effectively manage networks.

b.   There are an increasing number of programs available to manage the entire network. It's impractical to put all of your apps on each controller. As a result, more investigation into the application programming challenge is required.

c.   On the control plane, policies from various applications will be transformed into flow rules. There may be inconsistencies in the rules. Meanwhile, there is a requirement to combine the rules from several apps that will deal with the same flow. As a result, the rules multiply and the disputes avoided are worthwhile undertakings.

d.   The controller's security is always a significant issue. The software-defined network's functionality will be removed if the controller is successfully hacked. To secure the security of the controllers, new security-aware control applications must be developed. Meanwhile, further strategies are needed to provide safe controller-to-controller and controller-to-switch communications.

REFERENCES

Abolhasan, M., Lipman, J., Ni, W., & Hagelstein, B. (2015). Software-defined wireless networking: Centralized, distributed, or hybrid? *IEEE Network*, *29*(4), 32–38. doi:10.1109/MNET.2015.7166188

Al-Najjar, A., Layeghy, S., & Portmann, M. (2016). Pushing SDN to the end-host, network load balancing using OpenFlow. *Proc. PCCW'16*, 1–6. https://ieeexplore.ieee.org/abstract/document/7457129

Al Shuhaimi, F., Jose, M., & Singh, A. V. (2016, September). Software defined network as solution to overcome security challenges in IoT. In *2016 5th International Conference on Reliability, Infocom Technologies and Optimization (Trends and Future Directions)(ICRITO)* (pp. 491-496). IEEE. https://ieeexplore.ieee.org/abstract/document/7785005

Anwar, A., Cheng, Y., Huang, H., Han, J., Sim, H., Lee, D., . . . Butt, A. R. (2018, November). BESPOKV: Application tailored scale-out key-value stores. In *SC18: International Conference for High Performance Computing, Networking, Storage and Analysis* (pp. 14-29). IEEE. https://ieeexplore.ieee.org/abstract/document/8665756

Bannour, F., Souihi, S., & Mellouk, A. (2017). Distributed SDN control: Survey, taxonomy, and challenges. *IEEE Communications Surveys and Tutorials, 20*(1), 333–354. doi:10.1109/COMST.2017.2782482

Botelho, F., Bessani, A., Ramos, F. M., & Ferreira, P. (2014, September). *On the design of practical fault-tolerant SDN controllers. In 2014 third European workshop on software defined networks*. IEEE. https://ieeexplore.ieee.org/abstract/document/7780356

Cabaj, K., Gregorczyk, M., & Mazurczy, W. (2018). Softwaredefined networking-based crypto ransomware detection using http traffic characteristics. *Computers & Electrical Engineering, 66*, 353–368. doi:10.1016/j.compeleceng.2017.10.012

Cao, J., Li, Q., Xie, R., Sun, K., Gu, G., Xu, M., & Yang, Y. (2019). *The crosspath attack: disrupting the SDN control channel via shared links. In 28th USENIX Security symposium (USENIX Security* (Vol. 19). https://www.usenix.org/conference/usenixsecurity19/presentation/cao

Chakraborty, C., & Abougreen, A. N. (2021). Intelligent internet of things and advanced machine learning techniques for COVID-19. *EAI Endorsed Transactions on Pervasive Health and Technology, 7*(26), e1. http://eprints.eudl.eu/id/eprint/2578/1/eai.28-1-2021.168505.pdf

Chen-xu, N., & Jie-sheng, W. (2015, July). Auto regressive moving average (ARMA) prediction method of bank cash flow time series. In *2015 34th Chinese Control Conference (CCC)* (pp. 4928-4933). IEEE. https://ieeexplore.ieee.org/abstract/document/7260405

Cheng, J., Chen, W., Tao, F., & Lin, C. L. (2018). Industrial IoT in 5G environment towards smart manufacturing. *Journal of Industrial Information Integration, 10*, 10–19. doi:10.1016/j.jii.2018.04.001

Cheng, L., Li, Z., Zhang, Y., Zhang, Y., & Lee, I. (2017). Protecting interoperable clinical environment with authentication. *SIGBED Rev, 14*(2), 34–43. doi:10.1145/3076125.3076129

Chin, T., Rahouti, M., & Xiong, K. (2018). Applying software-defined networking to minimize the end-to-end delay of network services. *Applied Computing Review, 18*(1), 30–40. doi:10.1145/3212069.3212072

Chin, T., Xiong, K., & Rahouti, M. (2018). Kernel-Space Intrusion Detection Using Software-Deðned Networking. *EAI Endorsed Transactions on Security and Safety, 5*(15), e2. http://eprints.eudl.eu/id/eprint/2088/

Correia, S., Boukerche, A., & Meneguette, R. I. (2017). An architecture for hierarchical software-defined vehicular networks. *IEEE Communications Magazine, 55*(7), 80–86. doi:10.1109/MCOM.2017.1601105

Díaz-López, D., Dólera-Tormo, G., Gómez-Mármol, F., & Martínez-Pérez, G. (2016). Dynamic counter-measures for risk-based access control systems: An evolutive approach. *Future Generation Computer Systems, 55*, 321–335. doi:10.1016/j.future.2014.10.012

Dong, B. (2017). Software Defined Networking Based On-Demand Routing Protocol in Vehicle Ad-Hoc Networks. *ZTE Commun., 15*(2), 11-18. https://ieeexplore.ieee.org/abstract/document/7950235

Dunhill, J. (2020). *Critical patient dies after cyber attack disables hospital computers.* https://www.iflscience.com/technology/critical-patient-dies-after-cyber-attack-disables-hospital-computers

El-Hassany, A., Miserez, J., Bielik, P., Vanbever, L., & Vechev, M. (2016). SDNRacer: Concurrency Analysis for Software-defined Networks. In *37th ACM SIGPLAN Conference on Programming Language Design and Implementation (PLDI 16).* ACM. https://dl.acm.org/doi/abs/10.1145/2908080.2908124

Fernandez Maimo, L., Huertas Celdran, A., Perales Gomez, A.L., Garcıa Clemente, F.J., Weimer, J., & Lee, I. (2019). Intelligent and dynamic ransomware spread detection and mitigation in integrated clinical environments. *Sensors, 19*(5). doi:10.3390/s19051114

Hamid, B., Jhanjhi, N. Z., & Humayun, M. (2020). Digital Governance for Developing Countries Opportunities, Issues, and Challenges in Pakistan. In *Employing Recent Technologies for Improved Digital Governance* (pp. 36–58). IGI Global. doi:10.4018/978-1-7998-1851-9.ch003

He, Z., Zhang, D., & Liang, J. (2016). Cost-efficient sensory data transmission in heterogeneous software-defined vehicular networks. *IEEE Sensors Journal, 16*(20), 7342–7354. doi:10.1109/JSEN.2016.2562699

He, Z., Zhang, D., Zhu, S., Cao, J., & Liu, X. (2016, September). Sdn enabled high performance multicast in vehicular networks. In *2016 IEEE 84th Vehicular Technology Conference (VTC-Fall)* (pp. 1-5). IEEE. 10.1109/VTCFall.2016.7881215

Huang, X., Yu, R., Kang, J., He, Y., & Zhang, Y. (2017). Exploring mobile edge computing for 5G-enabled software defined vehicular networks. *IEEE Wireless Communications, 24*(6), 55–63. doi:10.1109/MWC.2017.1600387

Huertas Celdran, A., Garcıa Clemente, F.J., Weimer, J., & Lee, I. (2018). Ice++: Improving security, QoS, and high availability of medical cyber-physical systems through mobile edge computing. *IEEE 20th international conference one-health networking, applications and services (Healthcom), 1–8*. 10.1109/HealthCom.2018.8531185

Islam, M. J., Mahin, M., Roy, S., Debnath, B. C., & Khatun, A. (2019, February). Distblacknet: A distributed secure black sdn-iot architecture with nfv implementation for smart cities. In *2019 International Conference on Electrical, Computer and Communication Engineering (ECCE)* (pp. 1-6). IEEE. https://ieeexplore.ieee.org/abstract/document/8679167

Jacquenet, C., & Boucadair, M. (2016). A software-defined approach to IoT networking. *ZTE Commun., 1*, 1–12.

Javaid, M., Haleem, A., Vaishya, R., Bahl, S., Suman, R., & Vaish, A. (2020). Industry 4.0 technologies and their applications in fighting COVID-19 pandemic. *Diabetes & Metabolic Syndrome, 14*(4), 419–422. doi:10.1016/j.dsx.2020.04.032 PMID:32344370

Karakus, M., & Durresi, A. (2017a). A survey: Control plane scalability issues and approaches in software-defined networking (SDN). *Computer Networks, 112*, 279–293. doi:10.1016/j.comnet.2016.11.017

Karakus, M., & Durresi, A. (2017b). Quality of service (QoS) in software defined networking (SDN): A survey. *Journal of Network and Computer Applications, 80*, 200–218. doi:10.1016/j.jnca.2016.12.019

Karki, S., Nguyen, B., & Zhang, X. (2018). QoS Support for Scientific Workflows Using Software-Defined Storage Resource Enclaves. In *2018 IEEE International Parallel and Distributed Processing Symposium (IPDPS 18)*. IEEE. https://ieeexplore.ieee.org/abstract/document/8425164

Kumar, M. S., Raut, R. D., Narwane, V. S., & Narkhede, B. E. (2020). Applications of industry 4.0 to overcome the COVID-19 operational challenges. *Diabetes & Metabolic Syndrome, 14*(5), 1283–1289. doi:10.1016/j.dsx.2020.07.010 PMID:32755822

Lee, S., Kim, J., Shin, S., Porras, P., & Yegneswaran, V. (2017, June). Athena: A framework for scalable anomaly detection in software-defined networks. In *2017 47th Annual IEEE/IFIP International Conference on Dependable Systems and Networks (DSN)* (pp. 249-260). IEEE. https://ieeexplore.ieee.org/abstract/document/8023127

Lee, S., Kim, J., Woo, S., Yoon, C., Scott-Hayward, S., Yegneswaran, V., Porras, P., & Shin, S. (2020). A comprehensive security assessment framework for software-defined networks. *Computers & Security, 91*, 101720. doi:10.1016/j.cose.2020.101720

Li, N., Jiang, H., Feng, D., & Shi, Z. (2017). Customizable SLO and its near-precise enforcement for storage bandwidth. *ACM Transactions on Storage, 13*(1), 1–25. doi:10.1145/2998454

Li, Y., Liu, H., & Yang, W. (2017) Predicting inter-data-center network traffic using elephant flow and sublink information. *IEEE Trans Netw Serv Manag, 13*(4), 782–792. https://ieeexplore.ieee.org/abstract/document/8079318/

Luo, P., Zou, D., Du, Y., Jin, H., Liu, C., & Shen, J. (2020). Static detection of real-world buffer overflow induced by loop. *Computers & Security, 89*, 101,616. doi:10.1016/j.cose.2019.101616

Lv, Z., & Kumar, N. (2020). Software defined solutions for sensors in 6G/IoE. *Computer Communications, 153*, 42–47. doi:10.1016/j.comcom.2020.01.060

Mace, J., Roelke, R., & Fonseca, R. (2018). Pivot tracing: Dynamic causal monitoring for distributed systems. *ACM Transactions on Computer Systems, 35*(4), 1–28. doi:10.1145/3208104

Maharaj, M. S., & Munyoka, W. (2019). Privacy, security, trust, risk and optimism bias in e-government use: The case of two Southern African Development Community countries. *South African Journal of Information Management, 21*(1), 1–9. https://journals.co.za/doi/abs/10.4102/sajim.v21i1.983

Mármol, F. G., Pérez, M. G., & Pérez, G. M. (2016, July). I don't trust ICT: Research challenges in cyber security. In *IFIP International Conference on Trust Management* (pp. 129-136). Springer. 10.1007/978-3-319-41354-99

Meng, Y., & Kwok, L. F. (2013). Enhancing false alarm reduction using voted ensemble selection in intrusion detection. *International Journal of Computational Intelligence Systems, 6*(4), 626–638. doi:10.1080/18756891.2013.802114

Meng, Y., & Li, W. (2012, December). Intelligent alarm filter using knowledge-based alert verification in network intrusion detection. In *International Symposium on Methodologies for Intelligent Systems* (pp. 115–124). Springer. doi:10.1007/978-3-642-34624-8_14

Mukherjee, B. K., Pappu, S. I., Islam, M. J., & Acharjee, U. K. (2020, February). An SDN based distributed IoT network with NFV implementation for smart cities. In *International Conference on Cyber Security and Computer Science* (pp. 539–552). Springer. doi:10.1007/978-3-030-52856-0_43

Muzafar, S., & Jhanjhi, N. Z. (2020). Success Stories of ICT Implementation in Saudi Arabia. In *Employing Recent Technologies for Improved Digital Governance* (pp. 151–163). IGI Global. doi:10.4018/978-1-7998-1851-9.ch008

Ndiaye, M., Oyewobi, S. S., Abu-Mahfouz, A. M., Hancke, G. P., Kurien, A. M., & Djouani, K. (2020). IoT in the wake of COVID-19: A survey on contributions, challenges and evolution. *IEEE Access: Practical Innovations, Open Solutions*, 8, 186821–186839. doi:10.1109/ACCESS.2020.3030090 PMID:34786294

Nespoli, P., Papamartzivanos, D., Mármol, F. G., & Kambourakis, G. (2017). Optimal countermeasures selection against cyber attacks: A comprehensive survey on reaction frameworks. *IEEE Communications Surveys and Tutorials*, 20(2), 1361–1396. doi:10.1109/COMST.2017.2781126

Networking, S.-D. (n.d.). *The New Norm for Networks*. Available online: https://www.opennetworking. org/images/stories/downloads/sdn-resources/white-papers/wp-sdn-newnorm.pdf

Nguyen, H., Acharya, B., Ivanov, R., Haeberlen, A., Phan, L. T. X., Sokolsky, O., Walker, J., Weimer, J., Hanson, W., & Lee, I. (2016). Cloud-based secure logger for medical devices. *Proceedings of the IEEE first international conference on connected health: applications, systems and engineering technologies (CHASE)*, 89–94. 10.1109/CHASE.2016.48

Ni, H., Rahouti, M., Chakrabortty, A., Xiong, K., & Xin, Y. (2018, August). A distributed cloud-based wide-area controller with sdn-enabled delay optimization. In *2018 IEEE Power & Energy Society General Meeting (PESGM)* (pp. 1-5). IEEE. https://ieeexplore.ieee.org/abstract/document/8586040

Ouyang, J., Lin, S., Jiang, S., Hou, Z., Wang, Y., & Wang, Y. (2014, February). SDF: Software-defined flash for web-scale internet storage systems. In *Proceedings of the 19th international conference on Architectural support for programming languages and operating systems* (pp. 471-484). https://dl.acm.org/doi/abs/10.1145/2541940.2541959

Palvia, S., Aeron, P., Gupta, P., Mahapatra, D., Parida, R., Rosner, R., & Sindhi, S. (2018). *Online education: Worldwide status, challenges, trends, and implications.* https://www.tandfonline.com/doi/full/10.1080/1097198X.2018.1542262

Pena, J. G. V., & Yu, W. E. (2014, April). *Development of a distributed firewall using software defined networking technology. In 2014 4th IEEE International Conference on Information Science and Technology.* IEEE. https://ieeexplore.ieee.org/abstract/document/6920514

Prabadevi, B., Jeyanthi, N., & Abraham, A. (2020). An analysis of security solutions for ARP poisoning attacks and its effects on medical computing. *International Journal of System Assurance Engineering and Management, 11*(1), 1–14. 1. doi:10.100713198-019-00919-1

Qian, Y., Li, X., Ihara, S., Zeng, L., Kaiser, J., Süß, T., & Brinkmann, A. (2017, November). A configurable rule based classful token bucket filter network request scheduler for the lustre file system. In *Proceedings of the International Conference for High Performance Computing* (pp. 1–12). Networking, Storage and Analysis. doi:10.1145/3126908.3126932

Rahman, A., Islam, M. J., Sunny, F. A., & Nasir, M. K. (2019, December). DistBlockSDN: A distributed secure blockchain based SDN-IoT architecture with NFV implementation for smart cities. In *2019 2nd International Conference on Innovation in Engineering and Technology (ICIET)* (pp. 1-6). IEEE. https://ieeexplore.ieee.org/abstract/document/9290627

Rahouti, M., Xiong, K., Ghani, N., & Shaikh, F. (2021). SYNGuard: Dynamic threshold-based SYN flood attack detection and mitigation in software-defined networks. *IET Networks, 10*(2), 76–87. doi:10.1049/ntw2.12009

Russo, A. M., Rankothge, W., Ma, J., Le, F., & Lobo, J. (n.d.). *Towards making network function virtualization a cloud computing service.* https://ieeexplore.ieee.org/abstract/document/7140280

Ryu. (2018, May). Https://osrg.github.io/ryu/

Sahay, R., Meng, W., & Jensen, C. D. (2019). The application of Software Defined Networking on securing computer networks: A survey. *Journal of Network and Computer Applications, 131,* 89–108. doi:10.1016/j.jnca.2019.01.019

Schiff, L., Schmid, S., & Kuznetsov, P. (2016). In-Band Synchronization for Distributed SDN Control Planes. *Computer Communication Review, 46*(1), 37–43. doi:10.1145/2875951.2875957

Sharef, B. T., Alsaqour, R. A., & Ismail, M. (2014). Vehicular communication ad hoc routing protocols: A survey. *Journal of Network and Computer Applications, 40*, 363–396. doi:10.1016/j.jnca.2013.09.008

Sharma, P. K., Singh, S., Jeong, Y. S., & Park, J. H. (2017). Distblocknet: A distributed blockchains-based secure sdn architecture for iot networks. *IEEE Communications Magazine, 55*(9), 78–85. doi:10.1109/MCOM.2017.1700041

Smyth, D., Cionca, V., McSweeney, S., & O'Shea, D. (2016). *Exploiting pitfalls in software-defined networking implementation. In 2016 International conference on cyber security and protection of digital services (Cyber Security)*. IEEE. doi:10.1109/CyberSecPODS.2016.7502354

Stankovic, J. A. (2016). Research directions for cyber physical systems in wireless and mobile healthcare. *ACM Transactions on Cyber-Physical Systems, 1*(1), 1-12. https://dl.acm.org/doi/pdf/10.1145/2899006

Steichen, M., Hommes, S., & State, R. (2017, September). ChainGuard—A firewall for blockchain applications using SDN with OpenFlow. In *2017 Principles, Systems and Applications of IP Telecommunications (IPTComm)* (pp. 1-8). IEEE. https://ieeexplore.ieee.org/abstract/document/8169748

Tan, Y., Cheng, J., Zhu, H., Hu, Z., Li, B., & Liu, S. (2017, July). Real-time life prediction of equipment based on optimized ARMA model. In *2017 Prognostics and System Health Management Conference (PHM-Harbin)* (pp. 1-6). IEEE. https://ieeexplore.ieee.org/abstract/document/8079318

Wang, Y., Jiang, D., Huo, L., & Zhao, Y. (2021). A new traffic prediction algorithm to software defined networking. *Mobile Networks and Applications, 26*(2), 716–725. doi:10.100711036-019-01423-3

Wen, H., Cao, Z., Zhang, Y., Cao, X., Fan, Z., Voigt, D., & Du, D. (2018, September). Joins: Meeting latency slo with integrated control for networked storage. In *2018 IEEE 26th International Symposium on Modeling, Analysis, and Simulation of Computer and Telecommunication Systems (MASCOTS)* (pp. 194-200). IEEE.

Xiao, F., Zhang, J., Huang, J., Gu, G., Wu, D., & Liu, P. (2020). *Unexpected data dependency creation and chaining: a new attack to SDN. 2020 IEEE Symposium on Security and Privacy*.

Yassein, M. B., Aljawarneh, S., Al-Rousan, M., Mardini, W., & Al-Rashdan, W. (2017, November). Combined software-defined network (SDN) and Internet of Things (IoT). In *2017 international conference on electrical and computing technologies and applications (ICECTA)* (pp. 1-6). IEEE. https://ieeexplore.ieee.org/abstract/document/8252003

Zhu, T., Kozuch, M. A., & Harchol-Balter, M. (2017). WorkloadCompactor: Reducing Datacenter Cost While Providing Tail Latency SLO Guarantees. In *8th ACM Symposium on Cloud Computing (SoCC 17)*. ACM. https://dl.acm.org/doi/abs/10.1145/3127479.3132245

Chapter 2
E–Government Privacy and Security Challenges in the Context of Internet of Things

Raja Majid Ali Ujjan
University of the West of Scotland, UK

Navid Ali Khan
Taylor's University, Malaysia

Loveleen Gaur
 https://orcid.org/0000-0002-0885-1550
Amity University, Noida, India

ABSTRACT

The internet of things (IoT) is becoming more significant in everyday life as a mechanism for making major decisions in different fields as smart devices and data in real time are connected and updated. IoT is being used in a variety of ways to provide digital services to the public. Online payment, property purchase, and sailing are just a few examples. On the other hand, users' complaints about the safety and privacy of their personal information are growing. The internet of things (IoT) is becoming more popular and significantly enhances e-government. This chapter primarily focuses on how potential users can obtain information to use the internet of things and its related services within the e-government sectors. There are several technological, administrative, and political challenges to IoT adoption problems in e-government and legal problems that must be solved to develop effective and required applications. It's crucial to explore these problems and potential solutions.

DOI: 10.4018/978-1-7998-9624-1.ch002

INTRODUCTION

IoT works by utilizing gadgets to communicate data and take activity based on information. There can also be moments where a group of devices is cooperating for a shared goal and communicating through the internet. There are a variety of types of situations in which IoT can provide strategic, and operational benefits to management by designing apps to exploit the data collected by these devices. That is predicted by the literature review to increase in the coming years (McKinsey, 2018). Several Internet of Things devices is estimated to reach 65 billion by 2026 (Business Insider, 2019). With the introduction of the IoT, machines and things have become smart and dynamic agents in digital contexts, allowing for digital ideas, while the Internet of Things (IoT) is rapidly changing the nature of work, with a growing level of acceptance in a variety of personal and corporate settings. The better government market is anticipated to be worth USD 53.20 billion by 2027, according to industry estimates (Reports and Data, 2019). The smart government market is expecting IoT-enabled secret intelligence tools and apps to provide new services. Smart government can be defined as the technological intersection between e-government and smart cities (Qi et al., 2017). Hackers and cybercriminals are concentrating their attention on Internet of Things processor architectures and networks that hold (Balaji et al., 2021), (Maharaj & Munyoka, 2019) that is capable of making such intelligent selections while simultaneously saving a duplicate of the information, to ensure data is transmitted and processed swiftly to provide a vital choice that cannot wait till the data is transferred to the clouds. IoT mechanisms and apps allow the delivery of sophisticated solutions to individuals and societies as a whole, enhancing their protection against a range of challenges and in a variety of settings. The government provides these technical services to the public. Furthermore, theis electronic government-to-citizen and government-to-society services remove the risk of putting persons in danger who are responsible for dealing with such occurrences in danger, thanks to the deployment of IoT. They believe that IoT will add the most value to e-government in these key public functions (AlEnezi et al., 2018). Protection and shelter are vital to society, and they can take on even greater significance when they are linked to public health. IoT can enable the effective handling of public-sector security and safety concerns (Papadopoulou et al., 2020). Critical locations can substantially benefit from being monitored using IoT technology to permit appropriate and prompt action in aerial, maritime, and terrestrial contexts figure 1.

The chapter question organize as follows points:

1. In IoT E-government Applications, we identify both technological and non-technological challenges?
2. We will present our findings and recommendations?

3.   We will highlight the influence of the Internet of Things on E-government?

Figure 1. Overview IoT model with privacy and security policies

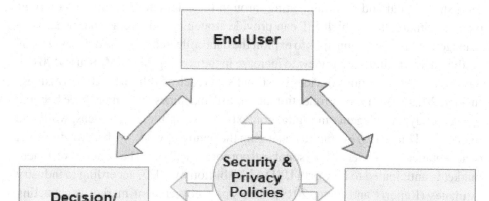

LITERATURE REVIEW

Internet of Things and e-government as a combined issue in several of research publications by AlEnezi et al. (2018) an attention towards IoT facilities. The author demonstrates the assistances of the IoT for economic growth and long-term development (Zaoui et al., 2014). With the advent of the Internet, e-government emerged, and e-government provided the ideal environment and technical assistance for the government to establish a provisional government. (Saxena, 2017) Propose connecting electronic government issues and service administration, and further propose that the connection of e-government and provider government is to force the government to adopt new changes and build high-quality, low-cost new service patterns, rather than to be based on current E-government. (Tingjun, 2015) The architecture and networking platform framework of the E-Government service explained the architecture and networking platform framework of the e-government service, which provided the government with the necessary institutional and technological assistance to build an e-government system (Tikkanen et al., 2018). Create the e-government application systems of various municipal management agencies and establish the "digital city" applications of diverse works (Alhawawsha & Panchenko, 2020). A novel way of integrating AJAX and the J2EE framework, which was successfully demonstrated in a real-world E-Government app. presented a network-based E-Government that meets certain standards and creates a typical hierarchical grid system conceptual structure. (Adjei-Bamfo et al., 2019). In the data age, the e-government authorization form paradigm based on cloud computing was developed. This framework includes the E-Government service mode, meets e-government security standards, adjusts to the background of a large data context, and supports cloud technology operational mechanisms (Al-Mushayt, 2019). The separation of the two network systems, the Intranet of Government Affairs and the Extranet of Government Affairs, the government internet, is a specially trained office preform. Because the Internet and other government affairs are physically separated, some flow of information and capacity transfer is possible behind a firewall (Lv et al., 2018). Urban environments are becoming increasingly rich in such instrumentation, which is being extensively investigated via the Internet of Things. These big data sets can be exploited and integrated into interconnected systems that bring together unstructured. They use the information to evaluate interconnected data, find trends, correlations, and results, as well as forecasting to find effective and quick solutions to improve production value, system organization, or process outcomes (Qi & Wang, 2021). The society area focuses on the topic from a global or intra-group perspective. Intergovernmental concerns are those that involve various public-sector organizations in e-government operations (Cheng et al., 2017). In an African context, similar challenges to incorporating ICT into local government were also identified. Low skill base to utilize current equipment, inability to repair, insufficient operating finance, uncoordinated ICT activities, and power fluctuations are among the most common hurdles to successful ICT integration in Uganda's ministry of local government, according to the findings. There have been certain e-Government programs that have fallen short of expectations, trying to make earlier claims of its transformative potential seem too hopeful. It's worth noting that the study has revealed considerable variation in its own approach to e-Government (Gershon et al., 2018). Competition in the industry has risen due to the fast development of information technology. As a result, customer behaviour has shifted, requiring firms to be more efficient and supply services at a lower cost. This helps to explain why there is such a constant need to accept new technology (AlEnezi et al., 2018). However, public sector organizations are slow to implement the same technologies. Meanwhile, research reveals that public organizations are still hesitant to use them, citing technical concerns like security and the fear of losing data control (Sava, 2018). Furthermore, educational institutions confront other common acceptance problems, such as the uncertainty of the value derived from cloud computing use (Nagowah et al., 2018). It also discusses some of the drawbacks of cloud computing, such as access control and resource ownership difficulties. While the benefits of cloud computing have accelerated its popularity among consumers, the obstacles connected with its use have drawn academics to improve its workability (Pradhan

& Shakya, 2018). The study indicates that if the quality of e-government services can be assured, global economies can profit considerably from financial development (Elezaj et al., 2018). Considering the significant early difficulties with e-government adoption, research has shown that this technology is useful, especially when geared towards economic growth. In light of the above framework, it is now time to identify the many e-government theories that are available (Henriksen, 2018). Concepts regarding e-government are essential because they have a big impact on how government websites are designed, implemented, benchmarked, and evaluated. It's probably accurate to say that no single theory dominates the current research and practice paradigm. As a result, study and practice in this field follow the lines of stakeholder theory, social exchange theory, and other theories. The fact that these theories have lasted this long and that they can be applied to e-government is ample evidence of their explanatory power (Chishiro et al., 2017). However, it is reasonable to conclude that governments around the world have adopted new technology at a considerably slower pace than business and industry, which is understandable. One reason for this cautious attitude is that, unlike industry, the government must be more cautious and risk-averse because the general public's interests are at stake (Máchová, 2017). E-government programs with a high failure rate incur significant direct and indirect financial expenses. Furthermore, it degrades employee morale, credibility, and confidence, limiting the delivery of e-government advantages. The absence of citizen access to these available online government services is one of the key reasons for failure (Mahmood, 2016). E-government refers to when the government uses the Internet and other communications technology capabilities to do activities in a more efficient, productive, and intelligent manner, resulting in high-quality services that meet the needs of the public (Le & Hoang, 2016),(Koo, 2019). When the phrase e-government was originally coined at the end of the 20th century, machines were being sold and popularized, and network infrastructures were being created. The United States was at the forefront of computer design and Internet expansion. Attempts were made by the government to apply digital resources to daily responsibilities to improve efficiency (Chinese Academy of Cyberspace Studies, 2019). Intelligent E-Government refers to next-generation E-government that employs cutting-edge intelligence information technology such as the Internet of Things, cloud, artificial intelligence, and big data. It refers to a government that blends intelligent information technology with human creativity to develop government management and create services that people value. It can also support intelligent government actions that communicate with the general population (Ma & Zheng, 2019). It can also be characterized as a government that locates and provides personalized services to individual citizens, as well as a government that transparently and securely opens and shares all government-run information. Because

Figure 2. Overview of IoT government application (Pathak et al., 2019)

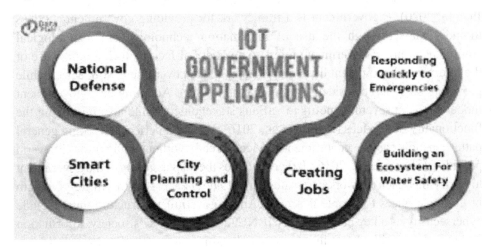

it incorporates innovative new technology, intelligent e-government is numerically and qualitatively superior to existing e-government.

It needs of an alternate solution to address existing e-government security challenges, such as the leakage of personal information, the propagation of misleading information, and the capture of national classified information. Intelligent e-government is presented as an option in this thesis. Intelligent information technologies, such as blockchains, secure clouds, and constantly changing cybersecurity programs, will be useful instruments for coping with these security concerns (Pathak et al., 2019), (Alexopoulos et al., 2019). Intelligent e-government keeps constant, continuous connection with the public, with the goal of not only resolving issues expressed by the public but also identifying issues ahead of time and suggesting solutions. Furthermore, citizens, not the government, are in charge of all policies and decisions when it comes to connecting with citizens via various channels such as the internet, mobile phones, and offline. This is not the same as providing set services; instead, it is the same as providing personalized services to specific citizen's figure 2.

ESTABLISH A FRAMEWORK FOR E-GOVERNMENT

The primary framework of the E-Government Internet of Things can also be separated into the government collecting layer, the government data link layer, and the government application layer, based on the features of the multiple Internet of Things' main architecture. The auxiliary architecture contains the service security architecture, service assurance architecture, and access terminal layer (Muzafar & Jhanjhi, 2020). E-government is a framework for providing government services to individuals through the use of information technology and technological communications. E-government refers to a variety of factors, including the use of the Internet and equipment like computers, to make government work easier while providing services to residents (Hamid et al., 2020). Adopting an e-government model can give several benefits to various stakeholders while also improving the functionality of services (Kumar et al., 2016). Within a perfectly working general pattern, people can use government services directly without going through several providers (Sharma et al., 2016). It then becomes the responsibility of the government to verify that such networks are safeguarded and, hence, that the entire paradigm of giving services to people is secure. Any e-government structure must include cybersecurity as a key component (CIRNU, 2016). In today's society, information systems play a critical role in interpersonal and inter-organizational relationships. They are large-scale sociotechnical, formal, and organizational systems for gathering, processing, storing, and disseminating information (Bhattacharya & Suri, 2017). Through the use of computer systems, information systems assist operations, management, and decision-making. Cybersecurity systems must be implemented into any information system to secure its overall integrity and functionality (Saqib & Al-Muqrashi, 2017). The core principle of e-government systems is to create a secure framework within which residents can access a variety of services. This framework must be protected to ensure social welfare (Baxter, 2017), (Nemèšanu & Pãžnzaru, 2017). Other aspects in the case of Saudi Arabia include the government's competitiveness in achieving efficiency and maintaining a positive view of the global arena in order to secure a variety of economic interests figure 3.

IN E-GOVERNMENT, IOT AND APPLICATIONS

The Internet of Things (IoT) can be used in e-government in a variety of ways. Data collected by IoT devices could be utilized to build several e-government applications. Every one of them might work to improve their analytics offerings to help people make better decisions faster (Elijah et al., 2018), (Yadav et al., 2018). IoT applications in e-government, with an emphasis on safety and protection of the public, Transport, healthcare, and smart cities are all issues that need to be addressed. The latter is divided into two categories, environmental pollution and natural occurrences such as fire, earthquakes, and weather. The healthcare sector offers a significant possibility for IoT adoption (Elijah et al., 2018) have mobility issues, such as the elderly or those with impairments, may benefit from the adoption of IoT systems. Citizens and society place a high value on security and safety. The

Figure 3. Overview of IoT e-government framework (Yadav et al., 2018)

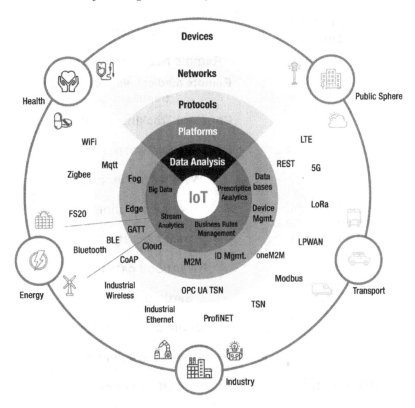

Internet of Things (IoT) can help with a variety of security and safety issues. Object detection and sensor information fusion are possible thanks to the autonomous nature of IoT nodes, as well as their sensing and powerful onboard processing capabilities (Khan & Salah, 2018). IoT nodes can be used to monitor country borders, whether they are on land, sea, or air, as well as other important places for the safety and protection of the public figure 4.

OVERVIEW OF CHALLENGES IN E-GOVERNMENT IN THE CONTEXT OF IOT

The use of IoT in e-government can be both exciting and problematic. We ponder on the technical and non-technical issues that arise from the usage of IoT in e-government figure 5.

Figure 4. Overview IoT domain and application in e-government

IoT Application Domain	IoT Applications
Health	Remote health monitoring
	Remote medical diagnosis and treatment
	Constant Tracking of patients
Environment (Incidents, Natural phenomena)	Pollution (air, water, sea, soil)
	Weather monitoring
	Noise pollution
	Forest fire detection
	River flood detection
	Earthquake alert
Transportation	Connected vehicles
	Driverless vehicles
	Traffic control
	Dynamic routing
	Emergency management
Security/Safety	Border Surveillance
	Critical security and safety areas control
	Surveillance of popular public areas
	Protection of critical infrastructure
Smart City	Structure conditions of buildings/bridges
	Lightning for buildings, roads, parks
	Road traffic and driving conditions
	Surveillance
	Emergency alert and response
	Parking

Figure 5. Overview of IoT e-government

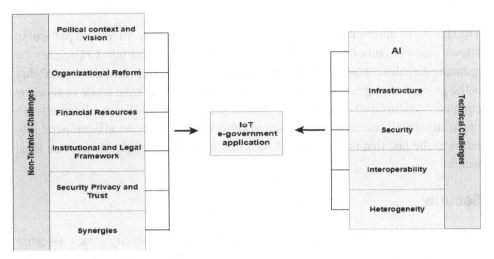

TECHNICAL CHALLENGES

The core idea of the Internet of Things interacts with one another in this era (Saleem et al., 2018). Data and information interchange between peers, as well as interaction with cloud-based back-end systems, are examples of such interactions. Because of the autonomous character of IoT devices, we can benefit as a result of numerous operations becoming automated, information and service interoperability, and the examination of automated entity behaviour and characteristics.

Heterogeneity

Furthermore, device heterogeneity is important in providing technologies that are supportable by the whole collection of nodes that are currently available. We will be able to establish Injecting smart government functions into devices through primary care. The variety of IoT gadgets makes connecting and communicating with them difficult (Papadopoulou et al., 2020). Connectivity is critical for resolving the aforementioned issue and making data collecting from homogenous or heterogeneous IoT devices easier. The most difficult part is gathering data from sensors and then transforming it into a coherent representation for further processing. On top of the integrated data, effective interfaces can be created to simplify access to the acquired data, allowing knowledge to be generated.

Interoperability

The sharing of information between communication entities, citizens, in particular, allows multiple authorities to communicate information and boost efficiency by reducing data discrepancies (Papadopoulou et al., 2020). Technical interoperability is the process of preparing for the technical challenges that arise while connecting computer systems and services. Whereas semantic interoperability is concerned with imparting specific meaning to transmitted information. Finally, legal interoperability refers to the law that is coordinated such that data shared is given adequate legal weight.

Security

The deployment of IoT in e-government is also beset by security issues. Because e-government services on the Cloud can be accessed by a variety of devices, it's critical to keep allowed info accessibility gathered, and inserted safely. This is one of the issues is severe when it comes to sensitive personal data. The self-contained nature of IoT networks creates issues. There has been a lot of talk regarding the dangers of hacking techniques and gadgets to get information and data. Which size the device, causing it to behave in a dangerous and insecure manner.

The architecture of IoT e-government services, adopting multi-layered security services could be a solution for application security (Birkel & Hartmann, 2019). To ensure the necessary level of safety, e-government IoT systems can use firewalls.

Infrastructure

The vast amount of data collected by IoT devices need a high-capacity (Ahmad et al., 2019) Network for storing and analysis to handle both in terms of the amount of information recorded and the rate at which it is produced. For optimal service provision, access to the Internet of Things Data from the e-government must be made public to make educated decisions in real-time and on a wide scale.

Artificial Intelligence

The use of artificial intelligence (AI) in e-government applications is another obstacle to the implementation of IoT in e-government. AI may be used to create intelligent apps based on data obtained from many sources. Once AI is implemented, the available e-government apps will be able to enable human-like thinking and behaviors once AI is implemented (Afzal et al., 2019). Machine learning could give systems and gadgets the ability to identify patterns, make judgments on their own, or learn from existing models and alter decisions based on the current state of the environment.

Non-Technical Challenges

The Internet of Things (IoT) in e-government includes non-technical difficulties that are just as important, if not more so, than technical ones. These issues include a variety of different institutional and legal concerns. They have a significant impact on the effectiveness of any effort to leverage IoT technology capabilities in electronic government platforms (Wang et al., 2019). They must be cautiously considered and handled, owing to their structural complications, as well as the multiple interrelations between them.

Political Context and Vision

Many factors may influence the strategic, tactical, and operational decisions that must be made and the actions that must be taken in the use of e-government in the context of IoT technology. Decisions and actions may relate to the expansion of existing e-government systems and services, as well as the development of new ones that take advantage of IoT (Tawalbeh et al., 2020). These kinds of considerations concerning strategies and activities for advancing smart government initiatives using IoT do not have to come from the top-down but might instead begin at the local level.

Organizational Reform

Introduce new ones based on IoT, the implementation of IoT in e-government necessitates organizational reform and process redesign. This may necessitate the establishment of new government authorities, institutions (Gupta & Quamara, 2020). Level of cooperation between organizations, involving the integration of many entities that must interact and rely on one another in an unbroken chain.

Financial Resources

As noted previously, the shift to e-government with IoT capabilities necessitates the reliability and accessibility of required funds and facilities, like 5G cellular systems (Nižetić et al., 2020). Additional funding for Internet of Things e-government applications is critical for their feasibility and long-term viability, including sufficient funding and proper billing structures.

Framework for Institutions and Law

IoT-based data sources and services must be formalized by institutional frameworks, meet legal requirements, and adhere to rules. As a result, effective IoT deployment in e-government necessitates substantial institutional backing. At the same time, institutions and legislation can encourage governments to use IoT by requiring technological evolution and implementation in government operations. For example, as part of its 2020 plan, Estonia intends to apply the "no legacy concept," which will be enacted into law and states that the public sector shall not use any ICT solution that is more than 13 years old (e-Estonia, 2018).

Security, Privacy and Trust

Data security and privacy are concerns that cut across practically every IoT e-government application. Safety and privacy are important challenges in IoT e-government, including components that require a non-technical approach in addition to their technological qualities (Sadeeq et al., 2021). Furthermore, personal data protection and administration are essential in nearly every area of e-government based on IoT, operating in highly sensitive sectors like healthcare.

Synergies

The successful use of IoT in e-government must be encouraged through collaboration with academic and research organizations, as well as public-private area synergies. This will allow for the creation of IoT applications and infrastructure, as well as the infrastructure required to support them effectively. As indicated in the World Bank Group (2017) study by lessons learned during the actual execution of IoT-oriented initiatives in numerous countries, public-private sector collaborations are a crucial aspect for the effective implementation of the Internet of Things in e-government (Makhshari & Mesbah, 2021). Such collaborations can also aid in the creation of IoT-based business models with long-term viability.

DISCUSSION

We take a comprehensive look at this chapter on IoT adoption in e-government. It gives an overview of the Internet of Things' potential in e-government across numerous application domains, stressing the difficulties that need to be addressed in each. We also look into the challenges that must be addressed and handled for IoT in e-government to achieve its full potential. With the use of IoT in e-government still in its initial stages. The publish-subscribe architecture allows for device interaction. The usage of final point via which gadgets used by end consumers can be connected and obtain information. The data required will be handled by the endpoint, which will be backed up by a data interchange mechanism.

The functions of the cybersecurity framework can provide a high-level and strategic focus of the lifecycle of e-government risk management connected to cybersecurity. The framework core can be considered essential in determining the important discrete outcomes for each e-government platform function. The implementation layers of the framework put the relationship between e-government systems and cybersecurity threats into context (Sadeeq et al., 2021). This contextualization takes place inside a complete framework that includes thorough risk mitigation considerations. The tiers are used to describe how far an organization and its cybersecurity risk reduction management system have progressed (Thakkar & Lohiya, 2021). A system of sensors could be used to monitor a forest to detect fires.

Our contribution to this chapter is regarding the government's public services and IoT implementation in terms of safety and privacy. Personal information security is discussed from a broad viewpoint. It evaluates how the government offers good public services that are acceptable to the public, as well as specific strategies and plans for achieving them in light of technological advancement and progress. In addition, the application domains and problems connected with IoT implementation in e-government were discussed in this chapter. The e-government platform can be adapted to particular user numbers and can allow various roles. The flexible, strategy based on roles may improve data delivery efficiencies, preparing the ground for a customized e-government platform. Additionally, people and IoT devices must be monitored, for the target application, as well as trackers and location-based information sharing, can only be authorized if citizen data security and privacy are maintained, and user consent is obtained. The application of mobile IoT systems can facilitate a broad range of safety and protection activities, including area monitoring and tracking, advanced threat detection, effective event management, quick response to emergency situations, security/safety risk alerts, and communication of current status to people. Such IoT-enabled activities can be used in a variety of settings, including unauthorized Management and controls, healthcare, transport, and climate analysis and forecasting are all areas that need to be monitored and forecasted.

CONCLUSION AND FUTURE WORK

The Internet of Things (IoT) is becoming more significant in everyday life as a mechanism for making major decisions in a variety of fields. As smart devices and data in real-time are connected and updated. IoT is being used in a variety of ways to provide digital services to the public, online payment, property purchase, and sailing are just a few examples. On the other hand, users' complaints about the safety and privacy of their personal information are growing. The Internet of Things (IoT) is becoming more popular and significantly enhances e-government. This chapter primarily focuses on how potential users can obtain information to use the Internet of Things and its related services within the e-government sectors. There are several technological, administrative, and political challenges to IoT adoption problems in e-government and legal problems that must be solved to develop effective and required applications. It's crucial to explore these problems and potential solutions. The adoption of mobile IoT systems can open up a world of possibilities of security and safety-related activities, including area surveillance and monitoring, threat detection, effective event management, quick response to emergency situations, security/safety risk alerts, and communication of current status to people. Such IoT-enabled activities can be used in a variety of settings, including Management and controls, healthcare, transport, and climate analysis and forecasting are all areas that need to be monitored and forecasted.

REFERENCES

Adjei-Bamfo, P., Maloreh-Nyamekye, T., & Ahenkan, A. (2019). The role of e-government in sustainable public procurement in developing countries: A systematic literature review. *Resources, Conservation and Recycling, 142*, 189–203. https://www.sciencedirect.com/science/article/abs/pii/S0921344918304579

Afzal, B., Umair, M., Shah, G. A., & Ahmed, E. (2019). Enabling IoT platforms for social IoT applications: Vision, feature mapping, and challenges. *Future Generation Computer Systems, 92*, 718–731. https://www.sciencedirect.com/science/article/abs/pii/S0167739X17312724

Ahmad, R., Asim, M. A., Khan, S. Z., & Singh, B. (2019, March). Green IOT—issues and challenges. In *Proceedings of 2nd International Conference on Advanced Computing and Software Engineering (ICACSE)*. https://papers.ssrn.com/sol3/papers.cfm?abstract_id=3350317

Al-Mushayt, O. S. (2019). Automating E-government services with artificial intelligence. *IEEE Access: Practical Innovations, Open Solutions, 7*, 146821–146829. https://ieeexplore.ieee.org/abstract/document/8862835

AlEnezi, A., AlMeraj, Z., & Manuel, P. (2018, April). Challenges of IoT based smart-government development. In *2018 21st Saudi Computer Society National Computer Conference (NCC)* (pp. 1-6). IEEE. https://ieeexplore.ieee.org/abstract/document/8593168

Alexopoulos, C., Lachana, Z., Androutsopoulou, A., Diamantopoulou, V., Charalabidis, Y., & Loutsaris, M. A. (2019, April). How machine learning is changing e-government. In *Proceedings of the 12th International Conference on Theory and Practice of Electronic Governance* (pp. 354-363). https://dl.acm.org/doi/abs/10.1145/3326365.3326412

Alhawawsha, M., & Panchenko, T. (2020, January). Open Data Platform Architecture and Its Advantages for an Open E-Government. In *International Conference on Computer Science, Engineering and Education Applications* (pp. 631–639). Springer. https://link.springer.com/chapter/10.1007/978-3-030-55506-1_56

Balaji, R. D., Jaboob, S., & Malathi, R. (2021). A Block Chain and IoT Based Hybrid Students Record System for E-Governance. *Current Journal of Applied Science and Technology*, 59-71. https://journalbank.org/index.php/CJAST/article/view/2453

Baxter, D. J. (2017). E-governance and e-participation via online citizen budgets and electronic lobbying: Promises and challenges. *World Affairs, 180*(4), 4-24. https://scholar.google.com/scholar?q=IoT+and+e-governance+challenges&hl=en&as_sdt=0%2C5&as_ylo=2017&as_yhi=2017

Bhattacharya, K., & Suri, T. (2017). The curious case of e-governance. *IEEE Internet Computing, 21*(1), 62–67. https://ieeexplore.ieee.org/abstract/document/7839849

Birkel, H. S., & Hartmann, E. (2019). Impact of IoT challenges and risks for SCM. *Supply Chain Management: An International Journal*. https://www.emerald.com/insight/content/doi/10.1108/SCM-03-2018-0142/full/html

Cheng, B., Solmaz, G., Cirillo, F., Kovacs, E., Terasawa, K., & Kitazawa, A. (2017). FogFlow: Easy programming of IoT services over cloud and edges for smart cities. *IEEE Internet of Things Journal, 5*(2), 696-707. https://ieeexplore.ieee.org/abstract/document/8022859/

Chinese Academy of Cyberspace Studies. (2019). The World e-Government Development. *World Internet Development Report 2017*, 159-197. https://link.springer.com/chapter/10.1007/978-3-662-57524-6_6

Chishiro, H., Tsuchiya, Y., Chubachi, Y., Abu Bakar, M. S., & De Silva, L. C. (2017, June). Global PBL for environmental IoT. In *Proceedings of the 2017 International Conference on E-commerce* (pp. 65–71). E-Business and E-Government. https://dl.acm.org/doi/abs/10.1145/3108421.3108437

CIRNU. (2016). *How EU and Japan Deal with the Challenges of Cybersecurity in the eGovernment Domain in the Emerging Age of IoT?* https://www.kgri.keio.ac.jp/en/docs/GWP_33.pdf

Elezaj, O., Tole, D., & Baci, N. (2018). Big Data in e-Government Environments: Albania as a Case Study. *Academic Journal of Interdisciplinary Studies, 7*(2), 117. https://www.mcser.org/journal/index.php/ajis/article/view/10285

Elijah, O., Rahman, T. A., Orikumhi, I., Leow, C. Y., & Hindia, M. N. (2018). An overview of Internet of Things (IoT) and data analytics in agriculture: Benefits and challenges. *IEEE Internet of Things Journal, 5*(5), 3758-3773. https://ieeexplore.ieee.org/abstract/document/8372905

Gershon, D., Prince, O., & Opoku, A. M. (2018). Promoting Inclusiveness and Participation in Governance: The Directions of Electronic Government in Ghana. *The International Journal of Social Sciences (Islamabad), 7*(3), 397–406. https://www.indianjournals.com/ijor.aspx?target=ijor:ijsw&volume=7&issue=3&article=007

Gupta, B. B., & Quamara, M. (2020). An overview of Internet of Things (IoT): Architectural aspects, challenges, and protocols. *Concurrency and Computation, 32*(21), e4946. https://onlinelibrary.wiley.com/doi/abs/10.1002/cpe.4946

Hamid, B., Jhanjhi, N. Z., & Humayun, M. (2020). Digital Governance for Developing Countries Opportunities, Issues, and Challenges in Pakistan. In *Employing Recent Technologies for Improved Digital Governance* (pp. 36–58). IGI Global. https://www.igi-global.com/chapter/digital-governance-for-developing-countries-opportunities-issues-and-challenges-in-pakistan/245975

Henriksen, H. Z. (2018). One step forward and two steps back: e-Government policies in practice. In *Policy Analytics, Modelling, and Informatics* (pp. 79–97). Springer. https://link.springer.com/chapter/10.1007/978-3-319-61762-6_4

Khan, M. A., & Salah, K. (2018). IoT security: Review, blockchain solutions, and open challenges. *Future Generation Computer Systems, 82*, 395–411. https://www.sciencedirect.com/science/article/abs/pii/S0167739X17315765

Koo, E. (2019). *Digital transformation of Government: from E-Government to intelligent E-Government* (Doctoral dissertation). Massachusetts Institute of Technology. https://dspace.mit.edu/handle/1721.1/121792

Kumar, P., Kunwar, R. S., & Sachan, A. (2016). A survey report on: Security & challenges in internet of things. In *Proc National Conference on ICT & IoT* (pp. 35-39). https://shop.iotone.ir/public/upload/article/5b8e38ead1f31.pdf

Le, N. T., & Hoang, D. B. (2016, December). Can maturity models support cyber security? In *2016 IEEE 35th international performance computing and communications conference (IPCCC)* (pp. 1-7). IEEE. https://ieeexplore.ieee.org/abstract/document/7820663

Lv, Z., Li, X., Wang, W., Zhang, B., Hu, J., & Feng, S. (2018). Government affairs service platform for smart city. *Future Generation Computer Systems, 81*, 443–451. https://www.sciencedirect.com/science/article/abs/pii/S0167739X17311391

Ma, L., & Zheng, Y. (2019). National e-government performance and citizen satisfaction: A multilevel analysis across European countries. *International Review of Administrative Sciences, 85*(3), 506–526. https://journals.sagepub.com/doi/abs/10.1177/0020852317703691

Máchová, R. (2017). Measuring the effects of open data on the level of corruption. In *Proceedings of the 21st International Conference Current Trends in Public Sector Research*. Masarykova univerzita. https://dk.upce.cz/handle/10195/66979

Maharaj, M. S., & Munyoka, W. (2019). Privacy, security, trust, risk and optimism bias in e-government use: The case of two Southern African Development Community countries. *South African Journal of Information Management, 21*(1), 1–9. https://journals.co.za/doi/abs/10.4102/sajim.v21i1.983

Mahmood, Z. (Ed.). (2016). *Connectivity frameworks for smart devices: the internet of things from a distributed computing perspective*. Springer. https://link.springer.com/book/10.1007%2F978-3-319-33124-9

Makhshari, A., & Mesbah, A. (2021, May). IoT bugs and development challenges. In *2021 IEEE/ACM 43rd International Conference on Software Engineering (ICSE)* (pp. 460-472). IEEE. https://ieeexplore.ieee.org/abstract/document/9402092

Muzafar, S., & Jhanjhi, N. Z. (2020). Success Stories of ICT Implementation in Saudi Arabia. In *Employing Recent Technologies for Improved Digital Governance* (pp. 151–163). IGI Global. https://www.igi-global.com/chapter/success-stories-of-ict-implementation-in-saudi-arabia/245980

Nagowah, S. D., Sta, H. B., & Gobin-Rahimbux, B. A. (2018, October). An overview of semantic interoperability ontologies and frameworks for IoT. In *2018 Sixth International Conference on Enterprise Systems (ES)* (pp. 82-89). IEEE.

Nemèšanu, F., & Pǎžnzaru, F. (2017). Smart city management based on IoT. *Smart Cities and Regional Development (SCRD) Journal, 1*(1), 91-97. https://www.ceeol.com/search/article-detail?id=624232

Nižetić, S., Šolić, P., González-de, D. L. D. I., & Patrono, L. (2020). Internet of Things (IoT): Opportunities, issues and challenges towards a smart and sustainable future. *Journal of Cleaner Production, 274*, 122877. https://www.sciencedirect.com/science/article/pii/S095965262032922X

Papadopoulou, P., Kolomvatsos, K., & Hadjiefthymiades, S. (2020). Internet of things in E-government: Applications and challenges. *International Journal of Artificial Intelligence and Machine Learning, 10*(2), 99–118. https://www.igi-global.com/article/internet-of-things-in-e-government/257274

Pathak, A., AmazUddin, M., Abedin, M. J., Andersson, K., Mustafa, R., & Hossain, M. S. (2019). IoT based smart system to support agricultural parameters: A case study. *Procedia Computer Science, 155*, 648-653. https://www.sciencedirect.com/science/article/pii/S1877050919310087

Pradhan, P., & Shakya, S. (2018). Big Data Challenges for e-Government Services in Nepal. *Journal of the Institute of Engineering, 14*(1), 216–222. https://www.nepjol.info/index.php/JIE/article/view/20087

Qi, M., & Wang, J. (2021). Using the Internet of Things e-government platform to optimize the administrative management mode. *Wireless Communications and Mobile Computing.* https://www.hindawi.com/journals/wcmc/2021/2224957/

Qi, R., Feng, C., Liu, Z., & Mrad, N. (2017). Blockchain-powered internet of things, e-governance and e-democracy. In *E-Democracy for Smart Cities* (pp. 509–520). Springer. https://link.springer.com/chapter/10.1007/978-981-10-4035-1_17

Sadeeq, M. M., Abdulkareem, N. M., Zeebaree, S. R., Ahmed, D. M., Sami, A. S., & Zebari, R. R. (2021). IoT and Cloud computing issues, challenges and opportunities: A review. *Qubahan Academic Journal, 1*(2), 1-7. https://journal.qubahan.com/index.php/qaj/article/view/36

Saleem, J., Hammoudeh, M., Raza, U., Adebisi, B., & Ande, R. (2018, June). IoT standardisation: Challenges, perspectives and solution. In *Proceedings of the 2nd international conference on future networks and distributed systems* (pp. 1-9). https://dl.acm.org/doi/abs/10.1145/3231053.3231103

Saqib, M., & Al-Muqrashi, N. (2017). Role and Importance of IoT in the smart city and E-Governance. *Journal of Student Research.* https://jsr.org/index.php/path/article/view/544

Sava, A. (2018). IoT Technologies: Realities of the Future. *Social-Economic Debates, 7*(1), 100-105. http://economic-debates.ro/art11-Sava-economic-debates-2018.pdf

Saxena, S. (2017). Factors influencing perceptions on corruption in public service delivery via e-government platform. *Foresight.* https://www.emerald.com/insight/content/doi/10.1108/FS-05-2017-0013/full/html

Sharma, P., Zawar, S., & Patil, S. B. (2016). Ransomware Analysis: Internet of Things (Iot) Security Issues, Challenges and Open Problems In the Context of Worldwide Scenario of Security of Systems and Malware Attacks. In *International conference on recent Innovation in Engineering and Management* (Vol. 2, No. 3, pp. 177-184). http://www.ijirse.com/wp-content/upload/2016/02/1089B.pdf

Tawalbeh, L. A., Muheidat, F., Tawalbeh, M., & Quwaider, M. (2020). IoT Privacy and security: Challenges and solutions. *Applied Sciences (Basel, Switzerland), 10*(12), 4102. https://www.mdpi.com/2076-3417/10/12/4102

Thakkar, A., & Lohiya, R. (2021). A review on machine learning and deep learning perspectives of IDS for IoT: Recent updates, security issues, and challenges. *Archives of Computational Methods in Engineering, 28*(4), 3211–3243. https://link.springer.com/article/10.1007/s11831-020-09496-0

Tikkanen, E., Gustafsson, S., & Ingelsson, E. (2018). Associations of fitness, physical activity, strength, and genetic risk with cardiovascular disease: Longitudinal analyses in the UK Biobank study. *Circulation, 137*(24), 2583–2591. https://www.ahajournals.org/doi/full/10.1161/CIRCULATIONAHA.117.032432

Tingjun, Z. (2015). The Analysis of Behavior and Effectiveness of Public Participating in E-government Platform of City Public Service—A Case Study of the Mayor's Hotline in Fuzhou. *Journal of Public Management,* 2. https://en.cnki.com.cn/Article_en/CJFDTotal-GGGL201502003.htm

Wang, N., Wang, P., Alipour-Fanid, A., Jiao, L., & Zeng, K. (2019). Physical-layer security of 5G wireless networks for IoT: Challenges and opportunities. *IEEE Internet of Things Journal, 6*(5), 8169-8181. https://ieeexplore.ieee.org/abstract/document/8758230

Yadav, E. P., Mittal, E. A., & Yadav, H. (2018, February). IoT: Challenges and issues in indian perspective. In *2018 3rd International Conference on Internet of Things: Smart Innovation and Usages (IoT-SIU)* (pp. 1-5). IEEE. https://ieeexplore.ieee.org/abstract/document/8519869

Zaoui, I., Elmaghraoui, H., Chiadmi, D., & Benhlima, L. (2014). Towards a personalized e-government platform. *International Journal of Computer Science: Theory and Application*, 2(2), 35–40. https://citeseerx.ist.psu.edu/viewdoc/download?doi=10.1.1.1018.918&rep=rep1&type=pdf

Chapter 3

Emerging Cybersecurity Threats in the Eye of E–Governance in the Current Era

Saira Muzafar
King Faisal University, Saudi Arabia

Mamoona Humayun
 https://orcid.org/0000-0001-6339-2257
Jouf University, Saudi Arabia

Syed Jawad Hussain
Abasyn University, Islamabad, Pakistan

ABSTRACT

The growing technologies in the world include machine learning (ML), the internet of things (IoT), and artificial intelligence (AI). Cybersecurity is the application of technologies that play a significant part in making secure data and reducing the risk among the users, such as computer programs, networks, data, and devices from the different cyber-attacks. In the current era of communication and information technologies, it is not possible to think of a good government without e-government. The main objective of this chapter is to look at the last 10 years of associated research articles, book chapters, and published reports on cybersecurity threats and attacks focused and founded on the e-government applications and emerging technologies for the measurement of cybersecurity. The results of this research have been used on machine learning techniques for taking authentic and scientific results. In the light of the studies, a new door will open for researchers and professionals.

DOI: 10.4018/978-1-7998-9624-1.ch003

INTRODUCTION

As digital changes and hyper-convergence give a chance to vulnerabilities, attacks, attacks, and failures, a cyber-flexibility approach is necessary for the smooth running of a business quickly. An effective approach helps businesses to decrease risk, reputational damages, and financial influence, and status losses. Cyber security has made significant progress in recent years to meet the changes that are taking place within cyberspace. Cyber security is to be said that any organization can utilize to shelter its data and products contained within cyberspace. A primary object of this research to identify challenges is to cyber security and governance issues, using machine learning techniques such as culture, risk management awareness, and developing threats. The researcher has reviewed 33 articles and other associated articles and chapters (Liu et al., 2020). The activities of criminal networks (CN), which are sneaky and secretive, can create difficulties by criminal network analysis due to lack of comprehensive data sets. Collected criminal data is insufficient and unreliable, which is echoed physically in the criminal network in the procedure of disappeared nodes and association. Criminal networks are generally studied by social network analysis models. MLTs mostly trust the metrics of SNA models in the emergence of secreted. Though supervised learning generally needs the obtainability of a large dataset, training link prediction models to get all-out routine levels. Hence, the author has conducted experiments to discover the application of deep reinforcement (DRL) in emerging CN secreted links production models from the rebuilding of corrupted CN datasets (Lim et al., 2019). The researchers have explored from their studies that great growth in research in the part of cyber security to sustenance cyber applications to evade crucial security threats handled by these applications. The main object of this research is to analyse and identify the usual cyber security weaknesses. After a comprehensive analysis of the chosen studies, the author has identified the key security weaknesses and their rate of incidence. There are synthesizes and studies have been done by available publication data, important targeted organisations and applications. The result of this research shows that the security measures mentioned so far usually only target security and find out the solutions provided in these studies essential for more experimental authentication and actual implementation Figure-1 (Humayun et al., 2020). One of the current tendencies of mobile and networking technology is mobile cloud computing (MCC) that is giving rich computational services in clouds and storing resources to mobile users. MCC applications give a variety of services to users and location-based services (LBS) applications are one of them. Using LBS and mobile applications, the mobile device is working as a thin client, wherever the abundant data locations are storing and collecting at the mobile cloud to give corresponding services. The user's location and privacy have opened new doors for the researchers and are widely studied in current years.

However, secrecy is one of the greatest challenges in MCC due to the location of users on mobile devices (MD) being offloaded from MD to cloud providers that may be exploited by third parties Figure-2 (Almusaylim & Jhanjhi, 2020).

The main objective of this study is to find out emerging cybersecurity threats in the eye of e-governance in the current era and using machine learning techniques for exact results.

Figure 1. Cyber security threats (Giles, 2019)

LITERATURE REVIEW

Number of cybersecurity attacks and threats continually increasing, organisations adopters have responded to security concerns that threaten their business in today's highly competitive environment. Several documented industrial cyber-attacks have effectively compressed technical solutions that are exploited by human-factor vulnerabilities linked to security skill and knowledge. This article focuses on human knowledge based on security knowledge and security skills to highlight the security capabilities and their quantity. The rise of information and communication technologies brought about new challenges that need to be dealt with if the citizens' security is considered. IoT ecosystem may be considered as a set of physical electronic devices joint with intelligence, linked through a network, allowing them to gather and exchange data, and agree these devices to be detected and worked remotely b/w

Figure 2. Emerging cybersecurity threats (Engineering,)

the physical and cyber domains. The devices are connected through the internet and affect every aspect of our lives, commercially, industrially, educationally, individually, socially, and are associated with governance as well. As we are related with a plethora of linked smart devices, and a great threat and risk of privacy and security in many points of view, such as device data theft, authentication, data falsification and device manipulation. The author focused on privacy and security connected implications (Khan et al., 2020). A major challenge for the smart factory is to ensure that its network security can withstand any cyber-attacks, such as botnet and distributed denial of service. They can cause a serious break to production and may cause financial losses to the company's producers. Among several security resolutions, there are some investigation studies that have explored botnet detection by honeypot. Further, the author has proposed a model of botnet detection and experimented (Lee et al., 2021). The interconnection happens through the exchange of data, info and helping our communication with the things around us. But now big questions about privacy and security continue. The hackers and attackers can have a favourable environment during the exchanging the massive amount of data. They proposed to work on current issues of security and privacy Figure-3 (Najmi et al., 2021). Breaking cybersecurity data is shared through a way of websites, including security blogs. The author proposed to work on investigate methods and analyze the severity of cybersecurity threats based on the language that is using to define them online (Zong et al., 2019). The authors have focused on changing technological tendencies for e-governance in India. Many trends are available that are need for development, such as digitally assisted services, enabling inclusive decision making, solution development for citizens, institutional initiatives, fulfilment of government to citizen services online and provide services with public-private partnership (Pal, 2019). The author is interested to study on implementing an information security self-assessment tool that can be applied by the government for giving security to e-governance systems from cyber security risk and threats. This tool applies a web-based model covering particular data security components and techniques for the different departments dealing with data security may evaluate their capability to protect e-governance systems. Further, this study has explored that government is investing heavily in technical information security measures but failed to evaluate and perform a repetitive review of its data security exercise (Korir et al., 2019). Different countries are interested in implementing e-governance on a complete scale. An important issue is to create a secure wall for data and transactions with complete secrecy in object to give surety that the government is running accordingly. The author apprised that this system needs complete transparency and accountability. Threats and risk are big challenges for accessing the e-services. The researcher proposed on the analysis of a few types of cyber-attacks by ML algorithms (Malhotra et al., 2019).

Coordination bright many opportunities in different features of life and controlled the blurring of the limitations between IT & Telecommunications. It has several measurements notably, such as technical, content, technological and carried a digital revolution. In view of speedy development in e-governance and other many e-service. Other hand, cybersecurity is also increasing the challenges where information and data are easily together and wrongly used. Threats and critical infrastructure are making products and Industrial systems extra vulnerable. It seems lack of security measurements and internationally affecting problems. Further, it is a challenging to make an effective cross-national policy of cybercrime about cloud computing (Ahmad, 2019). There are a good governance require a useful e-governance and look at e-governance and good governance in Nigeria. The primary aims are to look at the link between e-governance to show the relevance of the reality of good governance and to identify appropriate strategies for the effective application of e-governance to achieve good governance in Nigeria (Nosiri & Ndoh, 2018). IT has carried the new greatly progressive information society, such as information and industrial societies. The author proposed a new e-government model emerging model "E-Government Maturity Model based on Socio-political Development" this paper well-defined the 'smart society' as the great-advanced information society from the Korean case study Figure-4 (Sangki, 2018).

Figure 3. Cyber-security threats 2021(NSKT Global, 2020)

CYBERSECURITY THREATS AND RISK

With speedily emerging technology in the current era, the threats and risk also high-levels, shut the complete business down. Randomly occurring information breaches private and government, crypto-jacking, some newly appeared threats by the hackers to steal microchip apart from conventional information theft, unauthorized access, phishing, etc. There are no specific goals, each company that doesn't pay more or less attention to cybersecurity is a possible target of the present age (NSKT Global, 2020). Below are some present age threats:

1. IoT Hacking: IoT gets great popularity across the world, the risk and threats have also increased with the level of their complexity. The medical field is facing the largest exposure to this threat as there are several sophisticated IoMT devices. The greatest reason being, the nascence of such devices as they

Figure 4. Smart society & online services (Dreamstime,)

have not moved out completely, however emerging cybersecurity develops a challenge Figure-5. There is a set of broadly used network communication protocols that could affect millions of devices (Mello, 2021).

2.   Network Vulnerabilities: In many countries, with 5G exits and 5G-to-WiFi handovers, the hacker can easily exploit flows in cybersecurity skills and sophistication.In many countries, with 5G exits and 5G-to-WiFi handovers, hackers can easily exploit flaws in cybersecurity skills and sophistication. In order to save bandwidth, calls are converted to Wi-Fi, Hence, the vulnerabilities are present in the system between handover, the risk of breach increases (Kaur et al., 2018), (NSKT Global, 2020).

3.   API Breaches: Various firms that willingly use API for operations, have not a strong security for the API users. However, it is less importance than web security. A large portion of such firms provides external designers to modify the platform for enhanced and better. Risking the financial process can lead to misuse, peer-to-social media and messaging. This could be one of the major exploits point for cybersecurity threats and risk (Walden et al., 2020), (NSKT Global, 2020).

4.   Machine Learning Threat: The ML is being applied in every domain of the business to automate the process. Hackers may exploit their vulnerabilities to coordinate attacks. ML utilizes information from crowd-source that is related with ratings, financials, web traffic and reviews, etc. However, the hackers can misuse and threaten this data, also threatening the brand's image. AI fuzzing is used for tracing vulnerabilities and it can also co-operation to launch cyber-attacks Figure-6 (Liu et al., 2021), (NSKT Global, 2020).

5.   Deep fake: Moderately enhanced from cybersecurity, which involves disrupting the business activities such as fake audio or video for illegal purposes, financial ambiguity and spreading false information. This is a developing threat to cybersecurity that is causing great concern in the future Figure-7 (), (Research Gate, n.d.).

6.   Socially Engineered Attacks: Individuals and firms frequently disclose their sensitive information such as cards, engineer attacks and phishing attacks. The data is used to source financial fraud and information theft. It is one of the main cybersecurity threats and risks in the past era and millions of firms were affected by it, unknowingly or knowingly. In the present day, phishing is not limited to mails and has to extend to social media platforms, WhatApp and SMS too Figure-7 (Sharma, 2021), (Kaspersky,), (Le Blond et al., 2017), (Cowgill & Stevenson, 2020), (Dorr et al., 2020).

Figure 5. Concept of IoT (Mello, 2021)

E-GOVERNANCE IN CURRENT ERA

In the current era of communication and information technologies, it is not possible to think of a good government without e-government. In developing and smallest developed countries like Napal, e-government development has the potential to create good relations between citizens and government. Identifying the right things is important in order to overcome inborn difficulties and problems. The main objective of this research is to analyze the awareness of citizens in order to implement e-government, its related problems which are facing province 1 and local bodies Figure-9 (Bhagat et al., 2021).

Figure 6. Machine learning challenges for threat detection (Mello, 2021)

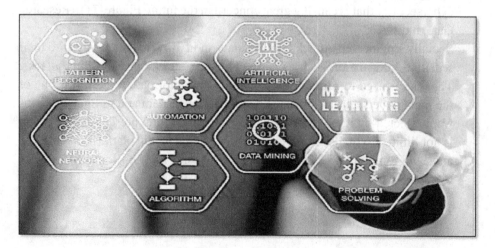

Figure 7. Number papers related to deepfake (Research Gate, n.d.)

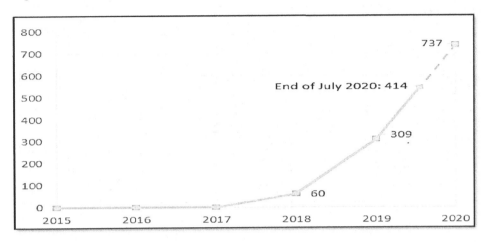

The author focused on the opportunities to present e-government in the institutional system of society based on digital, communication and information technologies. The concept of digitalization has developed from the point that information, communication and knowledge technologies form the social and legal infrastructure of a society. This shows that digital society forms the basis for the security of the modern globalized world, which is reflected in the standards of "e-government" (Arabadzhyiev et al., 2021). The aim of this study is to find out the effect of online services and telecommunication structure on the execution of e-government in military institutions in Yemen. The researcher has used an analytical approach

Figure 8. Concept of social engineering (Kaspersky,)

Figure 9. E-G awareness, E-G implement and Challenges E-G implementation (Bhagat et al., 2021)

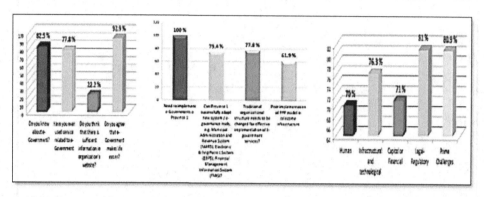

in this study. The result of this study found that there is no association between online service and the execution of e-government in military institutes in Yemen and there is a positive association between implementation of e-government and telecommunication infrastructure. Further, the author presented recommendations that consider carrying out programs and plans for the inclusion of novel technologies for the populations (Dahwan & Raju, 2021). The aim of this study was to analyze learning organization (LO) on the implementation of e-government in the city of Makassar and how application of LO in the government of this city. Research results show a positive trend but there are still several inadequacies and complaints against a service-based information technology. (Sadiq et al., 2021). The author focused on data privacy drawbacks in India, issues are related to the technical, precisely, political and legal and improvement in technology like data processing, cloud infrastructure, etc and portability. The main is threat and privacy of citizens. The increasing the modern technologies, globalization challenges are growing such ad threats, privacy and legalized structure systems like DPA act 1998 UK and communications privacy act1986 USA etc. further, research apprised that there is no such legalized structure that is related to the privacy problems (Mehrotra, 2021). In the current era, the information and communication technologies ICTs are playing a crucial part in our daily life. Many researchers have apprised in their study that there are many issues and challenges in the existing legacy of the governance system. Such as cost of service time-bound availability of service, delay in services, poor service collaboration and imperfect security of sensitive info. Researcher has designed a framework on cloud based e-governance. There are many researchers also focused on measuring the level of users' trust on online services provided by e-government and governance users Figure-10 & Figure-11(Muda et al., 2020).

Figure 10. Existing Ethiopia e-government challenges (Muda et al., 2020)

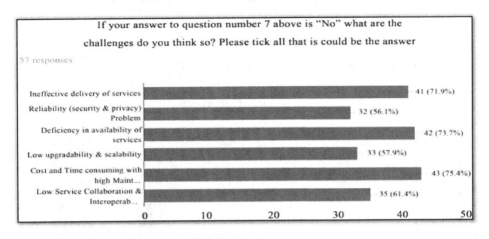

DISCUSSION AND DATA ANALYSIS

Several associated research articles, book chapters and published reports regarding the chosen for book chapter have comprehensively been focused and data also collected for analysis by machine learning techniques Figure-12, Figure-13 and Figure-14 (Razuleu, 2018), (Linkov et al., 2018), (Malhotra et al., 2017), (Soni, Anand, Dey et al, 2017), (Khatoun & Zeadally, 2017), (Soni, Dey, Anand et al, 2017), (Haran, 2016), (Ilves, 2016), (Norris et al., 2015), (Joshi, 2015), (Sithole, 2015), (Sony, 2015), (Dubey et al., 2015), (Mwangi, 2015). It has been observed during our study

Figure 11. Availability of service in existing e-government and end user satisfaction on the existing services (Muda et al., 2020)

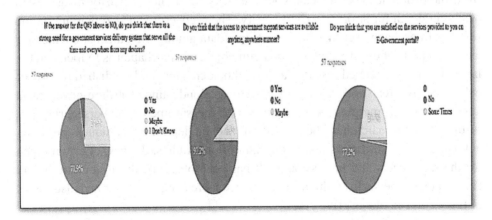

and find out that cybersecurity threats and risk are increasing year to year and also losses of the victims last five years.

Figure 12. Total complaints received and total losses

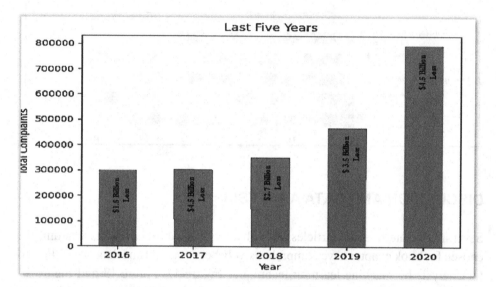

CONCLUSION

The growing technologies in the world, such as machine learning (ML), the Internet of Things (IoT), and Artificial Intelligence (AI). Cybersecurity is the application of technologies that play a significant part in making secure data and reducing the risk among the users, such as computer programs, networks, data, and devices from the different cyber-attacks. Cybersecurity needs new security measures to design in-depth for stronger cybersecurity. The e-government is providing online services to exchange services and electronic data among the citizens, businesses, and other parts of e-government. The main object of this chapter is to focus on the last ten years' associated research articles, book chapters and published reports of cybersecurity threats and attacks have been focused and founded on the e-government applications and emerging technologies for the measurement of cybersecurity. The results of this research have been used on machine learning techniques for taking authentic and scientific results. In the light of our studies, the new door will open for the researchers and professionals. It has been observed during our study and find out that cybersecurity threats and risk are increasing each year and also losses of the victims in the last five years.

Figure 13. Top 5 crime comparison last five years

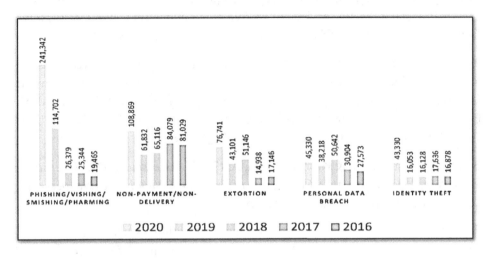

Figure 14. Victims comparison

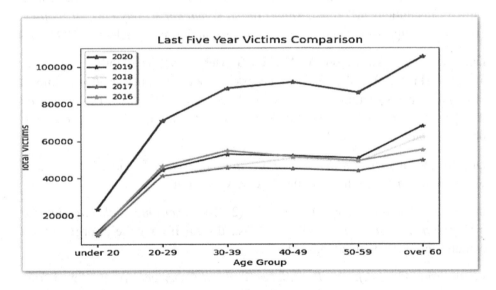

REFERENCES

Ahmad, T. (2019). Technology Convergence and Cybersecurity: A Critical Analysis of Cybercrime Trends in India. *27th Convergence India Pragati Maidan*, 29-31. https://papers.ssrn.com/sol3/papers.cfm?abstract_id=3326232

Almusaylim, Z. A., & Jhanjhi, N. Z. (2020). Comprehensive review: Privacy protection of user in location-aware services of mobile cloud computing. *Wireless Personal Communications, 111*(1), 541–564. doi:10.100711277-019-06872-3

Arabadzhyiev, D., Popovych, Y., Lytvynchuk, I., Bakbergen, K., & Kyrychenko, Y. (2021). Digital Society: Regulatory and Institutional Support of Electronic Governance in Modern Realities. In *SHS Web of Conferences* (Vol. 100, p. 03008). EDP Sciences. https://www.shsconferences.org/articles/shsconf/abs/2021/11/shsconf_iscsai2021_03008/shsconf_iscsai2021_03008.html

Bhagat, C., Sharma, B., & Kumar Mishra, A. (2021). *Assessment of E Governance for National Development–A Case Study of Province 1 Nepal*. https://papers.ssrn.com/sol3/papers.cfm?abstract_id=3857194

Cowgill, B., & Stevenson, M. T. (2020, May). Algorithmic social engineering. In *AEA Papers and Proceedings* (Vol. 110, pp. 96-100). https://www.aeaweb.org/articles?id=10.1257/pandp.20201037

Dahwan, A. A., & Raju, V. (2021). The Infleuence of Online Services and Telecommunication Infrastructure on the Implementation of E-government in Military Institutions in Yemen. *Annals of the Romanian Society for Cell Biology*, 1698–1710. https://www.annalsofrscb.ro/index.php/journal/article/view/2689

Dorr, B., Bhatia, A., Dalton, A., Mather, B., Hebenstreit, B., Santhanam, S., . . . Strzalkowski, T. (2020, April). Detecting asks in social engineering attacks: Impact of linguistic and structural knowledge. In *Proceedings of the AAAI Conference on Artificial Intelligence* (Vol. 34, No. 5, pp. 7675-7682). https://ojs.aaai.org/index.php/AAAI/article/view/6269

Dreamstime. (n.d.). *Online Services Illustrations & Vectors*. Retrieved from https://www.dreamstime.com/illustration/online-services.html

Dubey, A., Saquib, Z., & Dwivedi, S. (2015). *Electronic authentication for e-Government services-a survey*. https://digital-library.theiet.org/content/conferences/10.1049/cp.2015.0299

Engineering, C. (n.d.). *The Beginner's Guide to Cybersecurity*. Retrieved from https://bootcamp.cvn.columbia.edu/blog/the-beginners-guide-to-cybersecurity/

Giles, M. (2019). Five emerging cyber-threats to worry about in 2019. *MIT Technology Review*. Retrived from https://www.technologyreview.com/2019/01/04/66232/five-emerging-cyber-threats-2019/

Haran, M. H. (2016). Framework Based Approach for the Mitigation of Insider Threats in E-governance IT Infrastructure. *International Journal of Scientific Research, 3*(4), 5–10. http://citeseerx.ist.psu.edu/viewdoc/download?doi=10.1.1.5 66.4423&rep=rep1&type=pdf

Humayun, M., Niazi, M., Jhanjhi, N. Z., Alshayeb, M., & Mahmood, S. (2020). Cyber security threats and vulnerabilities: A systematic mapping study. *Arabian Journal for Science and Engineering, 45*(4), 3171–3189. doi:10.100713369-019-04319-2

Ilves, T. H. (2016). The consequences of cyber attacks. *Journal of International Affairs, 70*(1), 175–181.

Jazri, H., & Jat, D. S. (2016, November). A quick cybersecurity wellness evaluation framework for critical organizations. In *2016 International Conference on ICT in Business Industry & Government (ICTBIG)* (pp. 1-5). IEEE. https://ieeexplore.ieee. org/abstract/document/7892725

Joshi, S. (2015). E-Governance in Uttar Pradesh: Challenges and Prospects. *The Indian Journal of Public Administration, 61*(2), 229–240. doi:10.1177/0019556120150203

Kaspersky. (n.d.). *What is Social Engineering?* Retrieved from https://usa.kaspersky. com/resource-center/definitions/what-is-social-engineering

Kaur, K., Garg, S., Aujla, G. S., Kumar, N., Rodrigues, J. J., & Guizani, M. (2018). Edge computing in the industrial internet of things environment: Software-defined-networks-based edge-cloud interplay. *IEEE Communications Magazine, 56*(2), 44–51. doi:10.1109/MCOM.2018.1700622

Khan, A., Jhanjhi, N. Z., Humayun, M., & Ahmad, M. (2020). The Role of IoT in Digital Governance. In *Employing Recent Technologies for Improved Digital Governance* (pp. 128–150). IGI Global. doi:10.4018/978-1-7998-1851-9.ch007

Khatoun, R., & Zeadally, S. (2017). Cybersecurity and privacy solutions in smart cities. *IEEE Communications Magazine, 55*(3), 51–59. doi:10.1109/ MCOM.2017.1600297CM

Korir, G., Thiga, M., & Rono, L. (2019). *Implementing the Tool for Assessing Organisation Information Security Preparedness in E-Governance Implementation.* https://www.easpublisher.com/media/features_articles/EASJECS_210_284-299.pdf

Le Blond, S., Gilbert, C., Upadhyay, U., Gomez-Rodriguez, M., & Choffnes, D. R. (2017). A Broad View of the Ecosystem of Socially Engineered Exploit Documents. *NDSS.* https://www.ndss-symposium.org/wp-content/uploads/2017/09/ ndss2017_03B-4_LeBlond_paper.pdf

Lee, S., Abdullah, A., Jhanjhi, N., & Kok, S. (2021). Classification of botnet attacks in IoT smart factory using honeypot combined with machine learning. *PeerJ. Computer Science, 7*, e350. doi:10.7717/peerj-cs.350 PMID:33817000

Lim, M., Abdullah, A., Jhanjhi, N. Z., & Supramaniam, M. (2019). Hidden link prediction in criminal networks using the deep reinforcement learning technique. *Computers, 8*(1), 8. https://www.mdpi.com/2073-431X/8/1/8

Linkov, I., Trump, B. D., Poinsatte-Jones, K., & Florin, M. V. (2018). Governance strategies for a sustainable digital world. *Sustainability, 10*(2), 440. doi:10.3390u10020440

Liu, J., Wang, C., Li, C., Li, N., Deng, J., & Pan, J. Z. (2021). DTN: Deep triple network for topic specific fake news detection. *Journal of Web Semantics, 100646*. doi:10.1016/j.websem.2021.100646

Liu, Z., Wei, W., Wang, L., Ten, C. W., & Rho, Y. (2020). An Actuarial Framework for Power System Reliability Considering Cybersecurity Threats. *IEEE Transactions on Power Systems*. https://dl.acm.org/doi/abs/10.1145/3386723.3387847

Malhotra, H., Bhargava, R., & Dave, M. (2017). Implementation of E-Governance projects: Development, Threats & Targets. *International Journal of Information Communication and Computing Technology, 5*(2), 292-298. https://www.indianjournals.com/ijor.aspx?target=ijor:jims8i&volume=5&issue=2&article=001

Malhotra, H., Dave, M., & Lamba, T. (2019, November). Security Analysis of Cyber Attacks Using Machine Learning Algorithms in eGovernance Projects. In *International Conference on Futuristic Trends in Networks and Computing Technologies* (pp. 662-672). Springer.

MehrotraK. (2021). Data Privacy & Protection. *Available at* SSRN 3858581. https://papers.ssrn.com/sol3/papers.cfm?abstract_id=3858581

Mello, J. (2021). *DNS Flaws Expose Millions of IoT Devices to Hacker Threats.* Tech News World. Retrieved from https://www.technewsworld.com/story/87096.html

Muda, J., Tumsa, S., Tuni, A., & Sharma, D. P. (2020). Cloud-Enabled E-Governance Framework for Citizen Centric Services. *Journal of Computer and Communications, 8*(7), 63–78. doi:10.4236/jcc.2020.87006

Mwangi, N. M. (2015). *e-government adoption by Kenya ministries* (Doctoral dissertation). University of Nairobi. http://erepository.uonbi.ac.ke/handle/11295/94091

Najmi, K. Y., AlZain, M. A., Masud, M., Jhanjhi, N. Z., Al-Amri, J., & Baz, M. (2021). A survey on security threats and countermeasures in IoT to achieve users confidentiality and reliability. *Materials Today: Proceedings*. https://www.sciencedirect.com/science/article/pii/S221478532102469X

Norris, D., Joshi, A., & Finin, T. (2015, June). *Cybersecurity challenges to American state and local governments. In 15th European Conference on eGovernment*. Academic Conferences and Publishing Int. Ltd. https://ebiquity.umbc.edu/paper/abstract/id/774/Cybersecurity-Challenges-to-American-State-and-Local-Governments

Nosiri, U. D., & Ndoh, J. A. (2018). E-Governance. *South East Journal of Political Science, 4*(1). https://journals.aphriapub.com/index.php/SEJPS/article/view/833

NSKT Global. (2020). What are the biggest cybersecurity threats in 2021? *NSKT*. Retrieved from https://nsktglobal.com/what-are-the-biggest-cybersecurity-threats-in-2021-

Oxford Analytica. (2016). Estonia's e-governance model may be unique. *Emerald Expert Briefings*. https://www.emerald.com/insight/content/doi/10.1108/OXAN-DB214505/full/html

Pal, S. K. (2019). Changing technological trends for E-governance. In *E-governance in India* (pp. 79-105). Palgrave Macmillan. https://link.springer.com/chapter/10.1007/978-981-13-8852-1_5

Razuleu, L. (2018). *E-Governance and its associated cybersecurity: The challenges and best practices of authentication and authorization among a rapidly growing e-government*. https://scholarworks.calstate.edu/concern/theses/qj72pb20t

Research Gate. (n.d.). https://www.researchgate.net/figure/Number-of-papers-related-to-deepfakes-in-years-from-2015-to-2020-obtained-from_fig3_336058980

Sadiq, A. A. I., Haning, M. T., Nara, N., & Rusdi, M. (2021). Learning Organization on the Implementation of E-Government in the City of Makassar. *Journal Dimensie Management and Public Sector, 2*(3), 12–21. doi:10.48173/jdmps.v2i3.111

Sangki, J. (2018). Vision of future e-government via new e-government maturity model: Based on Korea's e-government practices. *Telecommunications Policy, 42*(10), 860–871. doi:10.1016/j.telpol.2017.12.002

Sharma, T. (2021). *Evolving Phishing Email Prevention Techniques: A Survey to Pin Down Effective Phishing Study Design Concepts*. https://www.ideals.illinois.edu/handle/2142/109179

Sithole, V. E. (2015). *An e-governance training model for public managers: The case of selected Free State Provincial departments* (Doctoral dissertation). http://repository.nwu.ac.za/handle/10394/16320

Soni, V., Anand, R., Dey, P. K., Dash, A. P., & Banwet, D. K. (2017). Quantifying e-governance efficacy towards Indian–EU strategic dialogue. *Transforming Government: People, Process and Policy.* https://www.emerald.com/insight/content/doi/10.1108/TG-06-2017-0031/full/html

Soni, V., Dey, P. K., Anand, R., Malhotra, C., & Banwet, D. K. (2017). Digitizing grey portions of e-governance. *Transforming Government: People, Process and Policy.* https://www.emerald.com/insight/content/doi/10.1108/TG-11-2016-0076/full/html

Sony, A. L. (2015). Solving e-Governance Challenges in India through the Incremental Adoption to Cloud Service. *Law: J. Higher Sch. Econ.*, 169. https://heinonline.org/HOL/LandingPage?handle=hein.journals/pravo2015&div=15&id=&page=

Walden, A., Cortelyou-Ward, K., Gabriel, M. H., & Noblin, A. (2020). To report or not to report health care data breaches. *The American Journal of Managed Care, 26*(12), e395–e402. doi:10.37765/ajmc.2020.88546 PMID:33315333

Zong, S., Ritter, A., Mueller, G., & Wright, E. (2019). *Analyzing the perceived severity of cybersecurity threats reported on social media.* doi:10.18653/v1/N19-1140

Chapter 4
E–Government Security and Privacy Issues:
Challenges and Preventive Approaches

Imdad Ali Shah
Shah Abdul Latif University, Pakistan

Sobia Wassan
Nanjing University, China

Muhammad Hamza Usmani
The University of Lahore, Pakistan

ABSTRACT

In developing technology, hackers are actively collecting personal information. To achieve their goals and acquire simple access to information about any individual, they use a range of methods and techniques. A privacy breach occurs when hackers gain access to complete information without the user's permission. Threats and dangers to security can arise for a variety of reasons, including technological flaws and targeted attacks. The government provides digital public facilities to people and the business community. Consumers have the expectation that e-government provides security and protects their data and personal information. Users have expressed concerns about their personal data privacy and safety. The main object of this chapter is to give strategies for IT specialists and e-government services because they need continuous improvement in privacy and security issues. The findings of this chapter may be useful to new researchers and may aid in the avoidance of security breaches and privacy issues.

DOI: 10.4018/978-1-7998-9624-1.ch004

INTRODUCTION

As the number of developed nations grows, the business and survival rates have each increased in recent years. Government has to make its internet service systems more robust. The idea of e-government, in general, might save time and resources by establishing communication between the public and government bodies. These are closely related concepts that are frequently used interchangeably. According to numerous reports, privacy violations in services for e-government have increased in the recent past. According to the UK administration's 2019 Cyber Security Breaches Survey, roughly 32% of businesses and 22% of charities reported cyber security breaches or assaults in 2019, including phishing, viruses, malware, ransomware attacks, and email impersonation (UK Cyber-Attacks, 2019). So far in 2019, malicious hackers in the U. S. have stolen more than 5.90 million records, credit card information, names, passwords, and addresses (US Cyber-Attacks, 2019). Suspected hackers recently leaked confidential information on 364 million Chinese citizens online, including user names, photographs, addresses, and identity card numbers (China Attacks, 2019). The measurement of area & collaborations focusing on e-government growth have increased dramatically, and the UN (RC) has played a key role in initiating or organising many of these activities. Many developing countries are dedicating a large portion of their money to e-government efforts around the world. Particularly in developing countries' places in the rural. Face as well as their hierarchical relationships. A thorough literature search and a survey of experts and CSC owners yielded a list of 15 problems (Sharma et al., 2021). AI is quickly gaining traction in a variety of disciplines, including e-government. AI, on the other hand, poses several problems and ethical considerations. This article traces the development of AI in business research over time, covering significant publications and leading publishing outlets. It discusses numerous major developmental patterns as well as the issues they provide. The field was created on the premise that can be precisely specified to the point that a machine may be simulated (Alqudah & Muradkhanli, 2021), (Herawati et al., n.d.). There is debate regarding what intelligence, and what forms of intelligence, human intelligence possesses, as well as how to imitate it. Artificial intelligence is a highly specialised field of study figure 1 concept of e-government.

The main purpose of this chapter is to focus more on security issues challenges and provide precautionary measures. The following are some points:

1. Evaluate e-government uncertainties in light of potential security threats
2. Evaluate the security and privacy challenges which affect e-government
3. Make an effort to provide potential preventative approaches
4. To provide strategies for IT specialists and e-governance

Figure 1. Concept of e-government (Meiyanti et al., 2018)

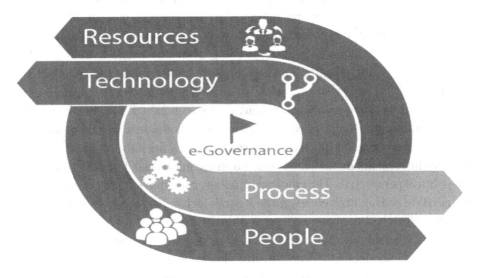

LITERATURE REVIEW

These OSI scores are focused on findings of ample review that looked at several areas of each of the 193 Member States' online presence. The poll evaluates national website technological aspects, while e-govt strategies and tactics are used generally. Improving e-government services by better utilising data is a prominent priority around the world. It necessitates that public administrations be honest, accountable, and provide dependable services to boost citizen confidence. Despite all of the technological advantages in developing such services and analysing security and privacy concerns, the literature lacks evidence of frameworks and platforms that enable privacy analysis from multiple perspectives and take citizens' needs into account in terms of transparency and use of citizens' data (Angelopoulos et al., 2017). The advent of e-government has had a significant impact on public administration, with information and communication technology (ICT) increasingly playing a role in redefining a government's goal. As a result, several governments around the world, including Malaysia, have adopted e-government as the slogan of service efficiency. Malaysian e-government has increased the quality of services and information supplied to citizens from its inception in 1996 under the banner of the multimedia super corridor (MSC). This research used a case study of Malaysian e-government projects (Ramli, 2017). The implementation of e-governance results in the creation of a new digital innovation platform for information distribution between citizens and the government. Although governments in developing economies are pouring money into making this initiative a major success, there are several risks to the system that must be addressed, but there hasn't been much research done on the subject. This article compares India to African countries in terms of numerous security risks linked to e-governance. It also contains several suggestions related to the problem (Malhotra et al., 2017). The goal of this article is to look at how e-government is implemented in a developing country in the Gulf Cooperation Countries (GCC) and what obstacles it faces. Within the State of Qatar, a case study (based on interview-based research) was conducted. Following a review of the literature, the study provides a conceptual model that was then utilised to investigate e-government-related transformation by taking into account the primary elements influencing implementation from an organisational, technological, social, and political perspective. The empirical findings corroborated previous findings in the literature and highlighted several new issues influencing e-government adoption in Qatar which had not been addressed directly in previous e-government studies (Ramzi & Weerakkody, n.d.). The use of e-government can help the government provide better services to its constituents. However, several obstacles stand in the way of its execution. The high failure rate of e-government promotes research on the difficulties of implementing e-government in poor countries. The goal of this research is to identify and propose a generic framework for addressing e-government implementation issues in poor nations (Meiyanti et al., 2018). Governments, residents, government agencies, and corporate sectors are increasingly using social networks as a platform for interaction. The widespread use of social media by users allows for the transformation of government administration into an open governance model and the alteration of government-citizen relationships. Social media has a variety of tools that allow users to communicate and exchange personal information (Alguliyev et al., 2018a). Potential dangers to each social network user's confidentiality and security are examined and classified. For the investigation of social network security threats, a multi-criteria evaluation method is provided (Dhonju & Shakya, 2019). E-government is a critical component of a Smart City. Information and communication technology transform people', enterprises', and government departments' relationships, allowing for the introduction of e-government and the speeding up of operational operations. This chapter explores current e-government deployment tactics and technology solutions in terms of security and privacy in a Smart City context, as well as the adoption problems (Yang et al., 2019). In government organisations, e-government improves the efficiency and efficacy of public service delivery. Efficiency and effectiveness are important, but so are cost savings and increased citizen participation. One of the government's public service providers in the Amhara national regional state land administration organisation (ANRS LA) (Abebe, 2019), (Alharmoodi & Lakulu, 2020). There is a growing demand for effective and efficient delivery of LA services as a result of urbanisation and the fact that land administration is an important public service delivery institution. However, service delivery in the LA

Figure 2. Overview e-government Service (Joshi & Islam, 2018)

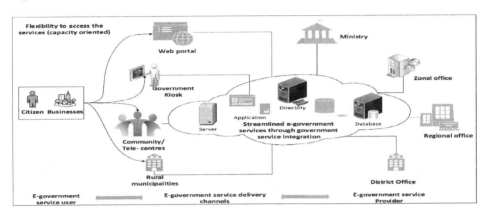

offices is time-consuming, costly, and convoluted, resulting in general inefficiency and ineffectiveness (Gouveia, 2020), (Malodia et al., 2021). These differences (gaps) existed between the expectations of service users and the actual service offered by the LA office. The current e-government status of the LA organisation is investigated in this study. To identify e-government status core e-government indicators were employed. Contexts and Challenges of e-Government and Smart Cities Adapting from Digital Exploration and Usage the current situation is both complicated and difficult. In addition, while considering the use and exploration of the digital, time and space possibilities add to the complexity (Sharma et al., 2021), (Alqudah & Muradkhanli, 2021), (Herawati et al., n.d.). Such issues exist for both nations and states, and they require digital change. Such challenges are necessary for their continued existence as we know them. As a result, we require additional information to discover novel solutions to both old and new challenges figure 2 overview e-government service.

EVALUATE E-GOVERNMENT UNCERTAINTIES

According to the literature, service organisations confront uncertainty from a variety of sources, including tasks, workflow, and the environment (Venkatesh et al., 2016). Task uncertainty refers to a limited knowledge about how to execute tasks; workflow uncertainty refers to a lack of knowledge about when inputs are arriving to be processed; and environmental uncertainty refers to the unpredictability of environmental variables that affect service performance. (Downey and Slocum 1975, Milliken 1987, Mills and Moberg 1982, Slocum and Sims 1980). Organisations will

Figure 3. Overview uncertainty e-government

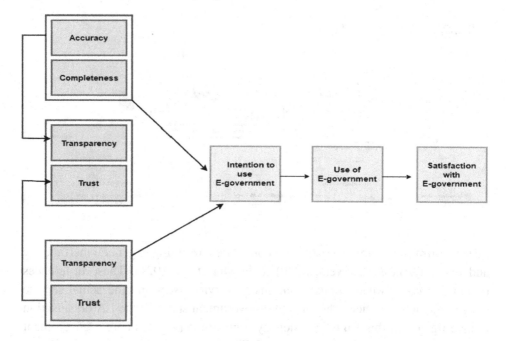

be able to effectively manage the volatility relating to service activities if they can differentiate the uncertainties figure 3 overview uncertainty e-government.

In the context of e-services, the principle of reliability. The concept of trust in the electronic marketer's reliability and honesty is referred to as adoption. (Bélanger and Carter 2008; Wibowo and Mubarak 2020; Yang et al. 2019). Citizens' perceptions about trustworthiness play a key part in public adoption of e-government operations, since their trust in service providers, as well as the applicable technologies, might impact their intentions to use them (Carter et al. 2016; Warkentin et al. 2018). Using objective criteria to assess risk for different users is difficult. As a result, studies in this sector tend to concentrate on people's risk perceptions (Ali et al. 2018; Palaco et al. 2019)

E-GOVERNMENT: SECURITY AND PRIVACY ISSUES

The limitations to E-government success were examined in this study, and therefore how various limitations potentially affect user dissatisfaction as a measure of E-government performance (Yang & Wibowo, 2020). In an unfavourable setting, the study explains more embedded relations of the Information System (IS) success model (Al-Rawahna et al., 2019). The research model was practically tested utilising

Table 1. Overview a summary of the limitation

citations	categorization	e-government limitations
(Yang et al., 2019) (Waller & Genius, 2015)	Vision	There is no implementation guidance available.
		Purpose and administrative approach are unknown.
		E-Government objectives that are too aggressive
(Al-Shboul et al., 2014) (Al-Soud et al., 2014) (Waller & Genius, 2015) (Gorla & Somers, 2014)	Scientific & IT Platform	Online crime includes are cases of privacy and security issues.
		Insufficient frequency as well as a deficiency of secure systems
		Insufficient government equipment/software privacy
		Global and local access to the information system that is not approved
(Rana et al., 2013) (Al-Soud et al., 2014) (Waller & Genius, 2015)	Policy and legal issues	There is a lack of legal grounds and a coherent strategy
		There are no security requirements, rules
		Conflict regarding data ownership

93 Jordanian government IT managers and IT specialists (Suleimany, 2021). Because of his higher statistical ability in dealing with complex causal models and limited sample sizes, PLS structural equation modelling (SEM) has been adopted (Grinin et al., 2022). The findings demonstrated that service offering falls short of stakeholder expectations. We discovered that a lack of IT infrastructure readiness is the most powerful element negatively impacting E-government performance and the most crucial cause causing user discontent. Users' discontent was found to be highly associated with the other parameters (AlMendah, 2021). Users' discontent was found to be highly associated with the other parameters. The relationship between system quality and service quality only differed between male and female groups, with males finding it inconsequential and females finding that low system quality directly related to low service quality, table 1 overview a summary of limitations.

CHALLENGES AND POTENTIAL IN E-GOVERNMENT

Africa has a 36 percent internet penetration rate. As the rate of technological innovation quickens, these gaps are responsible for inhibiting the development of e-government throughout Africa, posing severe obstacles to the continent's digital transformation. Throughout most parts of Africa, competing development goals

Figure 4 Overview of challenges and approaches

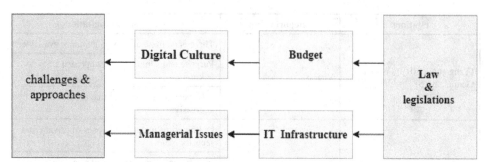

and a lack of domestic resource mobilization have resulted in severe monetary restrictions (Alguliyev et al., 2018a). Urgent requirement to enhance ownership in the digital world and minimise gaps have put greater strain on current technology and associated costs. Africa's digital transformation issues extend Facilities are only the beginning and financing to include management, financial and supervisory systems, structure of institutions, as well as capacity of people and institutions (Alguliyev et al., 2018a), (Meiyanti et al., 2018). That approach forward would be to develop national digitalization initiatives with improvement strategies that are detailed incorporate worldwide agendas figure 4 overview of challenges and approaches.

DISCUSSION

ECE member states have prioritised regional economic integration in their policymaking. ICT improves trade linkages and, as a result, regional integration. Digital services for the public and commercial sides are involved in this project. One area where there is a noticeable difference in advancement is trade facilitation. Countries that are not members of the union have greater problems on this front. Illegal network access, theft of employee or customer information, online financial fraud (Palanisamy & Mukerji, 2014). As things stand now, international organisations such as the United Nations and the World Bank must play a key role in fostering technology adoption in developing nations by providing the necessary financial resources (Susha & Grönlund, 2014). Governments can take advantage of new developing communication capabilities for utilizing cutting-edge technology and tools media applications (Alguliyev et al., 2018a), (Bouzas-Lorenzo et al., 2018b). While the issue of secrecy appears to be less of a concern for social media users, actual evidence reveals that when consumers engage directly with government authorities, these concerns are growing.

Table 2. Show the community facilities year 2018 and 2020

Electronic trading applications	2018	2020	Difference
Make an application of birth certificate	84	150	66
Obtaining construction permits	56	76	20
Obtain a trade licence	154	180	26
Submit an application for death certificates	75	149	74
Submit an application for a driver's licence	50	145	147
Submit an application for environmental permissions.	74	132	95
Submitting job applications on vacant positions	134	158	24
Submit an application for land registration	68	133	98
Submit an application for a marriage certificate.	78	148	65
Submit an application for a personal identification card	51	137	86
Submit an application for social assistance programes.	86	113	27
Submit a visa application	100	108	8
Appeal to the police	85	91	6
Submitted fine	112	116	4
Submit a utility payment	141	149	8
Obtain a vehicle registration	77	84	7
Submitted application for business reg:	126	164	38
Taxes payment	140	144	4

ELECTRONIC TRADING APPLICATION DEVELOPMENTS

The below applications are running and regional interfaces are available. The automation of fundamental executive operations, the improvement of community facilities, and the promotion of openness according to data for 2018 and 2020 table 2.

INFORMATION PROTECTION

There are a few in almost every country; this is a kind of official safety failure, but all of them make public. (Distel, 2018). the series of major cases is on the rise, resulting in financial or social consequences (Liu & Carter, 2018). Along with the growing need for information legislation to be adopted or amended, as well as the improvement of organization analytics capabilities, there is a growing requirement for data security and protection provisions to be enhanced and enforced (Agbozo et al., 2018), (Albrahim et al., 2018). Legitimate concerns about personal data loss are unaffected because the government is required by law to keep such information. Due to the rising use of official websites for online services, advanced security is essential.

ETHICS AND DATA PRIVACY

Authorities must use huge information sets to develop better algorithm models for regulation (Al-Nidawi et al., 2018), (Sagarik et al., 2018). However, concerns that governments' paternalistic tactics can lead them to compromise on human privacy should be measured against goals for more exposure in the use of data in government programmes in numerous areas (Véliz, 2021), (Alketbi, 2018). A number of high-profile occurrences have raised public awareness and flashed criticism about government surveillance, particularly the use of publicly available data.

EVALUATION OF SECURITY AND PRIVACY DATA

Every e-government system must ensure that the services are secret and available. When information is not exposed to unauthorised users and is safeguarded from any form of change, security is crucial not just for protecting data from external and internal dangers (College et al., 2020), (Ari et al., 2020), (Ferrag et al., 2020). Security is crucial not just for protecting data from external and internal dangers, but also for establishing.

CHAPTER'S CONTRIBUTION

In this chapter, we discovered that while extensive research has been conducted on the e-government and security and privacy issues challenges, and various preventive approaches to e-government have been implemented, security risk continues to grow in community networks despite the availability of security systems and networking devices. The staff members feel unsecure in the e-health environment. Which is cited below:

- Pin code
- Smart cards
- Patient data

Figure 5. Overview of challenges

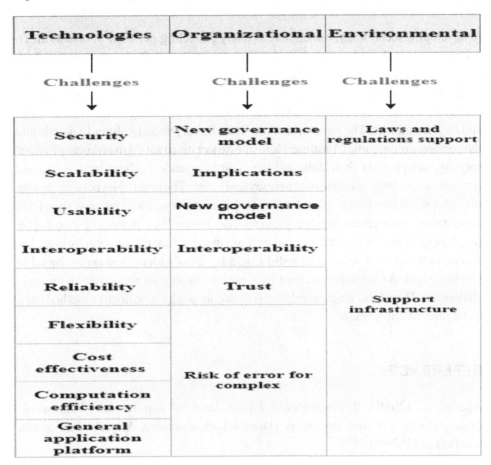

Technologies	Organizational	Environmental
Challenges	Challenges	Challenges
Security	New governance model	Laws and regulations support
Scalability	Implications	
Usability	New governance model	
Interoperability	Interoperability	
Reliability	Trust	
Flexibility		Support infrastructure
Cost effectiveness	Risk of error for complex	
Computation efficiency		
General application platform		

Usability is concerned with making apps and services simple to use. Usability is tied to security concerns since efforts to improve data security may reduce its usability. Access control in general has a broad meaning, encompassing everything from your automobile lock to the credit card security code. The primary function is to prevent unauthorized access. These access control methods will mostly be electronic and physically in the realm of e-government. As advanced technologies are increasing, so are privacy issues and challenges. Therefore, we currently need to deeply work on protective methods and techniques.

CONCLUSION AND FUTURE WORK

In developing technology, hackers are actively collecting personal information. To achieve their goals and acquire simple access to information about any individual, they use a range of methods and techniques. A privacy breach occurs when hackers gain access to complete information without the user's permission. Threats and dangers to security can arise for a variety of reasons, including technological flaws and targeted attacks. The government provides digital public facilities to people and the business community. Consumers have the expectation that e-government provides security and protects their data and personal information. Users have expressed concerns about their personal data privacy and safety. The main object of this chapter is to give strategies for IT specialists and e-government services because they need continuous improvement in privacy and security issues. The findings of this chapter may be useful to new researchers and may aid in the avoidance of security breaches and privacy issues. The issue of validating a business's identification is crucial in e-government. As advanced technologies are increasing, so are privacy issues and challenges. Therefore, we currently need to deeply work on protective methods and techniques of application.

REFERENCES

Abebe, B. (2019). *E-government based land administration framework; trends, challenges and prospects* (Doctoral dissertation). https://ir.bdu.edu.et/handle/123456789/10878

Agbozo, E., Alhassan, D., & Spassov, K. (2018, November). Personal data and privacy barriers to e-Government adoption, implementation and development in Sub-Saharan Africa. In *International Conference on Electronic Governance and Open Society: Challenges in Eurasia* (pp. 82–91). Springer. https://link.springer.com/chapter/10.1007/978-3-030-13283-5_7

Al-Nidawi, W. J. A., Al-Wassiti, S. K. J., Maan, M. A., & Othman, M. (2018). A review in E-government service quality measurement. *Indonesian Journal of Electrical Engineering and Computer Science, 10*(3), 1257–1265. https://www.mustaqbal-college.edu.iq/lecture/2018%20dr%20wael%20Paper.pdf

Al-Rawahna, A. S. M., Chen, S. C., & Hung, C. W. (2019). The barriers of e-government success: An empirical study from Jordan. *Available at SSRN 3498847*. https://papers.ssrn.com/sol3/papers.cfm?abstract_id=3498847

Al-Shboul, M., Rababah, O., Ghnemat, R., & Al-Saqqa, S. (2014). Challenges and factors affecting the implementation of e-government in Jordan. *Journal of Software Engineering and Applications, 7*(13), 1111. https://www.scirp.org/html/5-9302011_52812.htm?pagespeed=noscript

Al-Soud, A. R., Al-Yaseen, H., & Al-Jaghoub, S. H. (2014). Jordan's e-Government at the crossroads. *Transforming Government: People, Process and Policy.* https://www.emerald.com/insight/content/doi/10.1108/TG-10-2013-0043/full/html

Albrahim, R., Alsalamah, H., Alsalamah, S., & Aksoy, M. (2018). Access control model for modern virtual e-government services: Saudi Arabian case study. *International Journal of Advanced Computer Science and Applications, 9*(8), 357–364. https://pdfs.semanticscholar.org/ebb0/10ac868b6bb721a9db5d2bc33e24cf48895b.pdf

Alguliyev, R., Aliguliyev, R., & Yusifov, F. (2018a). Role of Social Networks in E-government: Risks and Security Threats. *Online Journal of Communication and Media Technologies, 8*(4), 363–376. https://www.ojcmt.net/article/role-of-social-networks-in-e-government-risks-and-security-threats-3957

Alguliyev, R., Aliguliyev, R., & Yusifov, F. (2018b, October). MCDM Model for Evaluation of Social Network Security Threats. In *the book.* In R. Bouzas-Lorenzo & A. Cernadas Ramos (Eds.), *ECDG 2018 18th European Conference on Digital Government* (pp. 1–7). University Santiago de Compostela. https://www.proquest.com/openview/bc2d4527ea3a433a65db63414c023e96/1?pq-origsite=gscholar&cbl=1796415

Alharmoodi, B. Y. R., & Lakulu, M. M. B. (2020). Transition from e-government to m-government: Challenges and opportunities-case study of UAE. *European Journal of Multidisciplinary Studies, 5*(1), 61–67. https://journals.euser.org/files/articles/ejms_v5_i1_20/Alharmoodi.pdf

Alketbi, H. (2018). *An evaluation of e-government effectiveness in Dubai smart government departments* (Doctoral dissertation). Southampton Solent University. https://ssudl.solent.ac.uk/id/eprint/3809/

AlMendah, O. M. (2021). A Survey of Blockchain and E-governance applications: Security and Privacy issues. *Turkish Journal of Computer and Mathematics Education, 12*(10), 3117–3125. https://turcomat.org/index.php/turkbilmat/article/view/4964

Alqudah, M. A., & Muradkhanli, L. (2021). Artificial Intelligence in Electric Government; Ethical Challenges and Governance in Jordan. *Electronic Research Journal of Social Sciences and Humanities, 3*, 65-74. https://papers.ssrn.com/sol3/papers.cfm?abstract_id=3806600

Angelopoulos, K., Diamantopoulou, V., Mouratidis, H., Pavlidis, M., Salnitri, M., Giorgini, P., & Ruiz, J. F. (2017, August). A holistic approach for privacy protection in E-government. In *Proceedings of the 12th International Conference on Availability* (pp. 1–10). Reliability and Security. https://dl.acm.org/doi/abs/10.1145/3098954.3098960

Ari, A. A. A., Ngangmo, O. K., Titouna, C., Thiare, O., Mohamadou, A., & Gueroui, A. M. (2020). Enabling privacy and security in Cloud of Things: Architecture, applications, security & privacy challenges. *Applied Computing and Informatics*. https://www.emerald.com/insight/content/doi/10.1016/j.aci.2019.11.005/full/pdf

College, C. C. C., Rajasingh, J. P., & Ramapuram, C. (2020). A Systematic Conceptual Review-Blockchain As A Next Generation E-Government Information Infrastructure. *European Journal of Molecular & Clinical Medicine*, 7(06). https://www.ejmcm.com/article_3906_fb90616fc37a6dd3497cdf923eff0558.pdf

Dhonju, G. R., & Shakya, S. (2019). Analyzing Challenges for the Implementation of E-Government in Municipalities within Kathmandu Valley. *Journal of Science and Engineering*, 7, 70–78. https://www.nepjol.info/index.php/jsce/article/view/26795

Distel, B. (2018). Bringing Light into the Shadows: A Qualitative Interview Study on Citizens' Non-Adoption of e-Government. *Electronic. Journal of E-Government*, 16(2), 98–105. https://academic-publishing.org/index.php/ejeg/article/view/654

Ferrag, M. A., Shu, L., Yang, X., Derhab, A., & Maglaras, L. (2020). Security and privacy for green IoT-based agriculture: Review, blockchain solutions, and challenges. *IEEE Access: Practical Innovations, Open Solutions*, 8, 32031–32053. https://ieeexplore.ieee.org/abstract/document/8993722

Gorla, N., & Somers, T. M. (2014). The impact of IT outsourcing on information systems success. *Information & Management*, 51(3), 320–335. https://www.sciencedirect.com/science/article/abs/pii/S0378720614000020

Gouveia, L. B. (2020). e-Government and Smart Cities: Contexts and Challenges Taking from Digital Usage and Exploration. *UNU-EGOV UM DSI PDSI talk*. https://bdigital.ufp.pt/handle/10284/8554

Grinin, L., Grinin, A., & Korotayev, A. (2022). COVID-19 pandemic as a trigger for the acceleration of the cybernetic revolution, transition from e-government to e-state, and change in social relations. *Technological Forecasting and Social Change*, 175, 121348. https://www.sciencedirect.com/science/article/pii/S0040162521007794

Herawati, A. R., Warsono, H., Afrizal, T., & Saputra, J. (n.d.). *The Challenges of Industrial Revolution 4.0: An Evidence from Public Administration Ecology in Indonesia.* http://www.ieomsociety.org/singapore2021/papers/846.pdf

Joshi, P. R., & Islam, S. (2018). E-government maturity model for sustainable e-government services from the perspective of developing countries. *Sustainability, 10*(6), 1882. https://www.mdpi.com/2071-1050/10/6/1882

Liu, D., & Carter, L. (2018, May). Impact of citizens' privacy concerns on e-government adoption. In *Proceedings of the 19th Annual International Conference on Digital Government Research* (pp. 1–6). Governance in the Data Age. https://dl.acm.org/doi/abs/10.1145/3209281.3209340

Malhotra, H., Bhargava, R., & Dave, M. (2017, November). Challenges related to information security and its implications for evolving e-government structures: A comparative study between India and African countries. In *2017 International Conference on Inventive Computing and Informatics (ICICI)* (pp. 30-35). IEEE.

Malodia, S., Dhir, A., Mishra, M., & Bhatti, Z. A. (2021). Future of e-Government: An integrated conceptual framework. *Technological Forecasting and Social Change, 173*, 121102. https://www.sciencedirect.com/science/article/pii/S0040162521005357

Meiyanti, R., Utomo, B., Sensuse, D. I., & Wahyuni, R. (2018, August). E-government challenges in developing countries: a literature review. In *2018 6th International Conference on Cyber and IT Service Management (CITSM)* (pp. 1-6). IEEE.

Palanisamy, R., & Mukerji, B. (2014). Security and Privacy issues in e-Government. In *Cyber Behavior: Concepts, Methodologies, Tools, and Applications* (pp. 880-892). IGI Global. https://www.igi-global.com/chapter/security-and-privacy-issues-in-e-government/107765

Ramli, R. M. (2017). Challenges and issues in Malaysian e-government. *Electronic Government, an International Journal, 13*(3), 242-273. https://www.inderscienceonline.com/doi/abs/10.1504/EG.2017.086685

Ramzi, E. H., & Weerakkody, V. (n.d.). *E-Government implementation Challenges: A Case study.* https://aisel.aisnet.org/cgi/viewcontent.cgi?article=1318&context=amcis2010

Rana, N. P., Dwivedi, Y. K., & Williams, M. D. (2013). Analysing challenges, barriers and CSF of egov adoption. *Transforming Government: People, Process and Policy.* https://www.emerald.com/insight/content/doi/10.1108/17506161311325350/full/html

Sagarik, D., Chansukree, P., Cho, W., & Berman, E. (2018). E-government 4.0 in Thailand: The role of central agencies. *Information Polity, 23*(3), 343-353. https://content.iospress.com/articles/information-polity/ip180006

Sharma, S. K., Metri, B., Dwivedi, Y. K., & Rana, N. P. (2021). Challenges common service centers (CSCs) face in delivering e-government services in rural India. *Government Information Quarterly, 38*(2), 101573.

Suleimany, M. (2021, May). Smart Urban Management and IoT; Paradigm of E-Governance and Technologies in Developing Communities. In *2021 5th International Conference on Internet of Things and Applications (IoT)* (pp. 1-6). IEEE. https://ieeexplore.ieee.org/abstract/document/9469713

Susha, I., & Grönlund, Å. (2014). Context clues for the stall of the Citizens' Initiative: Lessons for opening up e-participation development practice. *Government Information Quarterly, 31*(3), 454–465. https://www.sciencedirect.com/science/article/abs/pii/S0740624X14000860

Véliz, C. (2021). Privacy and digital ethics after the pandemic. *Nature Electronics, 4*(1), 10-11. https://www.nature.com/articles/s41928-020-00536-y

Venkatesh, V., Thong, J. Y., Chan, F. K., & Hu, P. J. (2016). Managing citizens' uncertainty in e-government services: The mediating and moderating roles of transparency and trust. *Information Systems Research, 27*(1), 87–111. https://pubsonline.informs.org/doi/abs/10.1287/isre.2015.0612

Waller, L., & Genius, A. (2015). Barriers to transforming government in Jamaica: Challenges to implementing initiatives to enhance the efficiency, effectiveness and service delivery of government through ICTs (e-Government). *Transforming Government: People, Process and Policy.* https://www.emerald.com/insight/content/doi/10.1108/TG-12-2014-0067/full/html?fullSc=1

Yang, L., Elisa, N., & Eliot, N. (2019). Privacy and security aspects of E-government in smart cities. In *Smart cities cybersecurity and privacy* (pp. 89–102). Elsevier. https://www.sciencedirect.com/science/article/pii/B978012815032000007X

Yang, R., & Wibowo, S. (2020). *Risks and Uncertainties in Citizens' Trust and Adoption of E-Government: A Proposed Framework.* https://aisel.aisnet.org/cgi/viewcontent.cgi?article=1073&context=acis2020

Chapter 5
The Influence of Cybersecurity Attacks on E-Governance

Imdad Ali Shah
Shah Abdul Latif University, Pakistan

Riyaz Ahamed Ariyaluran Habeeb
Taylor's University, Malaysia

Samina Rajper
ⓘD https://orcid.org/0000-0002-8635-8059
Department of Computer Science, Shah Abdul University, Pakistan

Areeba Laraib
Mehran University of Engineering and Technology, Pakistan

ABSTRACT

The use of e-government is growing as the world is progressively becoming more interconnected. However, data security systems must be designed to address new and effective vulnerabilities that are increasing due to emerging technological innovations. In the dynamic and ever-changing world, the issues and challenges of protecting information infrastructure are growing. Due to various vulnerabilities in the system, these networks are vulnerable to cyber-attack. As a result, it is critical to speed security efforts that include application software and infrastructure to provide an efficient governance system without the risk of being rigged. It has been observed during review of associated articles that limited studies have been done on e-governance and cyber-attacks. The cyber-attacks influence e-governance and damage public trust. The main objective of this chapter is to review the last 15 years of associated research articles, and the result will be a comparison of every five years. The findings provide potential recommendations and solutions.

DOI: 10.4018/978-1-7998-9624-1.ch005

1. INTRODUCTION

Improvement of the government's service and its efficiency have to increase. One of the most significant revolutions has been increased advancement of IT and improving the functioning of the government. Different applications e-government are functioning, putting a greater reliance on cyberspace, an area of "business" that few people are familiar with, particularly in the sphere of digital security (Razuleu, 2018). The practice of making the networks that make up cyberspace secure against invasions is known as cybersecurity. Through identifying interferences, the goal is to protect information confidentiality, availability, and integrity. The changing risk landscape, on the other hand, necessitates a more dynamic strategy. The government establishes a cyber-security plan and the government's flexible approach to solving cybersecurity concerns (Nzimakwe, 2018). Modern cities are viewed as a collection of main elements such as quality of life and socioeconomic development. Several important issues must be considered in the establishment and management of smart cities. These criteria were used to create a framework that conveys a more advanced understanding of efforts that have been made. Social, administration, economic, and legal dimensions are all significant pillars variables figure 1 (Nautiyal et al., 2018), (Pal, 2019) (Froehlich et al., 2020).

We hope that this chapter makes a complete overview last fifteen years associated on cyber-attacks. The primary object of this study is too focused following objectives:

i.   Based on current literature, our peer-review will depict the relationship and associate challenges and security issues.
ii. Overview on e-governance and influence of cybersecurity
iii. To provide discussion, actual findings, and recommendations.
iv. Overview cybersecurity attacks on e-government

2. LITERATURE REVIEW

Several nations implemented laws to control commerce and related e-governance applications after the UNICITRAL model on e-commerce was introduced in 1996. The Information Technology Act of 2000 was enacted by the Indian parliament to incorporate several sections of the UNICITRAL model law on e-commerce. This chapter review the existing regulations and proposed Data Protection Bill, which will ensure that e-governance runs smoothly. It also analyses possible gaps in the laws, such as a bill has to be addressed to prevent data privacy breaches. There are several terror and hackers collected illegally data to target the government, corporations, and individuals. The Indian government proposed more stringent laws to prohibit and punish criminal activities (Halder & Jaishankar, 2021). Today, the government has caught up with the technological revolution. The public administration's digitalization is inextricably linked to security concerns. Digitalization can be seen as one of the tools for effective governance, but it comes with its own set of issues. The current state and problems of cyber threats in e-administration services and practice in Hungarian municipalities will be examined in this article. The fragmented Hungarian municipal system, which limits the economic power of Hungarian. Experiments and opportunities are enormous. We look at the rule, we can see that it was created to develop a horizontally integrated e-administration. Legislation of governing this system has passed in recent years, and previous prohibitions on electronic administration have been lifted. The practice of Hungarian e-administration differs in some ways. New issues arose the expanded e-administration, which were partially addressed by the radical nationalization and centralization of formerly municipally handled activities. Municipal e-administration systems have primarily been established by the bigger municipalities. Their operation may be improved and so municipal cybersecurity is becoming an increasingly important component of Hungarian public administration chores. Applications of e-government and communication technology to govt functions and increasing transparency and accountability for government services. Growing efficiency within various institutional bodies and improving the government's interface with business and industry. This would typically entail the effective use of ICTs by various government entities for specific purposes. The author has examined the challenges that arise during the development and implementation of e-Government projects, as well as the risks that they face. The loss or compromise of confidential data and e-resources of government departments and other corporate entities can be caused by a variety of threat actors/agents. The many sorts of purposeful and inadvertent threats, as well as their consequences, have been further examined (Hoffman & Cseh, 2021).

3. EVOLUTION OF CYBERSECURITY AND E-GOVERNANCE

Government administrative machinery around the world was already transformed by implementation e-government techniques that have improved efficiency, openness, and accountability. Findings have been added in light of future studies and supporting administrators in selecting appropriate models and approaches. The manufacturers developing essential technical equipment for the next phase of symbiosis (Kiilu et al., n.d.), (Pal, 2019). E-government has become a critical component of govt operations around the world. Long-term applications, resources, and infrastructure are considered while developing e-governance initiatives. A lengthy procedure goes into the specifics of step-by-step roles and responsibilities in creating a digital/

Figure 1 Overview four phases of e-government model (Fang et al., 2019)

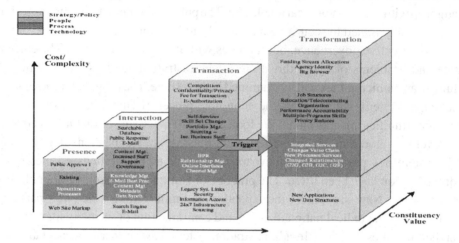

electronic equivalent of a physical service, which is frequently hampered by practical limits. This recent Covid-19/SARS-Cov2 corona epidemic has brought countries to a halt all over the world. The authors explore the importance of e-governance during pandemics and offer a framework and standard operating procedures for the successful operation of e-governance services even during disasters and pandemics with participation of government personnel and machines (Grinin et al., 2022). Outlines the various threats and vulnerabilities that may arise in the Insider's activities (Elbahnasawy, 2021). The authors have discussed the evolving technology trends in India's E-Government. Numerous new trends have been explored in his study. The evolving government strategy for E-Government was also mentioned. These writers have discussed changes such as digitally assisted services, citizen solution development, allowing inclusive decisions, delivering services, government service fulfilment online, and shared services in conjunction with public-private partnerships (Sibi Chakkaravarthy et al., 2018).

4. ISSUES OF CYBERSECURITY

Cyber-security has essentially defined the use of safety precautions to Computers to provide an optimal level of assurance. The acronym CIA stands for Confidentiality, Integrity, and Availability, and it is used to describe a security vulnerability. The term "classification" refers to the idea that information should only be visible to those who have been given permission to see it. The term "trustworthiness" refers to the rule that authorized customers are allowed to make changes to the data, and

Figure 2 Overview four e-government model (Krundyshev & Kalinin, 2019)

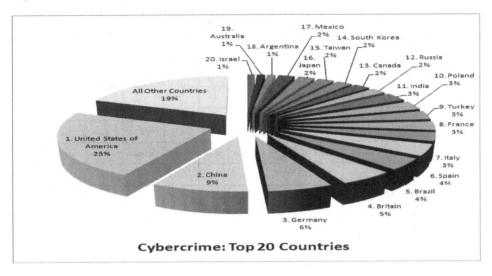

Cybercrime: Top 20 Countries

that these changes would be reflected consistently throughout all sections of the data. Term "accessibility" refers to the rule that information and computer assets shall always be available to authorized clients. The fundamental issue is that little details are missed. The history of PC security can be characterized as one of relapse. Early PC frameworks provided strong security, comparison to today's utility, they were almost non-accessible. Information accessibility grew significantly as programming vendors expanded their usefulness, shifting to PCs, then distributed registration, and finally online administrations. However, difficulties regarding classification and legitimacy arose as a result of such a development. Several driving principles behind the creation of a large portion of the product focused on the highlights first. The product business has cleared in the last few years due to an increase in security concerns. The Internet core structure was built around shared access and trust, with security initiatives coming later. Several widely used conventions provide little to no security to their clients and instead rely on trust (Krundyshev & Kalinin, 2019), (Sambana et al., 2021),(Manoharan et al., 2021),(Hackmageddon, 2021),(Lim et al., 2019),(Humayun et al., 2021),(Muzammal et al., 2020),(Humayun et al., 2020). Figure 2 and table 1 show a summary cybersecurity ranking.

5. TYPES OF CYBERATTACKS

Different research contexts were identified which will support the selection of features as below:

Table 1 show a summary of cybercrime ranking of different countries

Sno	Cybercrime	Country Ranking (Percentage/Number)									
		USA	China	Germany	Britain	Brazil	Spain	France	Turkey	Poland	India
1	Illegal activities on the computer	23%	9%	6%	5%	4%	3%	3%	3%	3%	3%
2	Malignant code's rank	1	2	12	4	16	11	8	15	23	3
3	Upload zombie' rank	1	4	2	10	1	6	14	5	9	11
4	Malware webpages are ranked by hosts	1	6	2	5	16	14	9	24	8	22
5	Bot with ranking	2	1	4	9	5	6	10	8	7	20
6	The origin of the ranking threat	1	2	4	3	9	8	5	12	17	19
		Russia	Canada	South Korea	Taiwan	Japan	Mexico	Argentina	Australia	Israel	All other countries
1	Illegal activities on the computer	2%	2%	2%	2%	2%	2%	1%	1%	1%	
2	Malignant code's rank	18	5	21	11	7	6	44	14	40	
3	Upload zombie' rank	7	40	19	21	29	18	12	37	16	19%
4	Malware webpages are ranked by hosts	7	3	4	12	11	31	20	17	15	
5	Bot with ranking	17	14	15	11	22	21	12	27	16	
6	The origin of the ranking threat	14	10	7	15	11	16	18	13	22	

- Attacks on the Network: A cross-site scripting (XSS) or node capture attack on CSC's networks can grant permission to make changes to the intelligent metering system, To modify its software inside the meters, change configuration utilising the distance security policy to circumvent controls, obstruct the system from accurately registering purchases or billings.

- Spyware Infection: When the antivirus is old and the software goes vulnerabilities, the hacker could install spyware and launch a cyber-attack remote to close the systems, and, as a result, the prepaid card settings an attacker can influence and prevent accurate readings for valid transactions by changing the parameters to use a protective relay method.

- Attack through Ransomware: The attacker might acquire information through reconnaissance and social engineering approaches, then launch a spear phishing-attack on targeted users to shut system down until a ransom is paid.

- An attempt at software tampering: When purchasing off-the-shelf software, most companies fail to reset the hard-coded password. The attacker could utilise advanced persistent threats and centralized control methods that attack these weaknesses and manage the system, resulting in cybercrime such as intellectual property theft, identity theft, and data theft.

- DDoS (Denial - of - service) or Data Leak: By injecting a rootkit into the OS server, the attackers can launch another Cyberattack which might result in voltages by causing echoing attacks on smart grid systems, causing the power system to vibrate.

- Attack mostly on Islands: Vendors are more vulnerable to attacks into CSC systems, but attackers include leveraging Malware or Island-hopping attacks to obtain access to big organisations Figure 3,4,5 the cyber-attacks and Figure 6 shows the most prevalent malware globally (Mitrokotsa & Douligeris, 2007), (Holt et al., 2021), (Kamiya et al., 2021), (Aliwa et al., 2021),(Rehman et al., 2021),(Roopak et al., 2020),(da Silva & Coury, 2020),(Dimolianis et al., 2020).

Figure 3 show Global Cyber-attacks

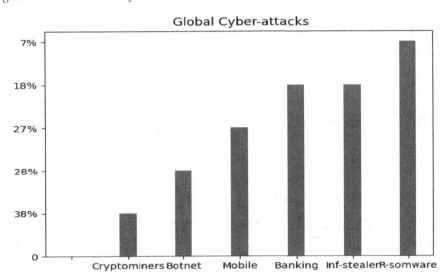

6. APPLICABILITY OF E-GOVERNMENT

The basic achievement factors in E-Government must be evaluated in light of the E-Government challenges and obstacles. High security, normalization, and information the board is unmistakable requirements of E-Governance, followed by the arrangement of explicit administrations and their quality, according to the method. The construction of all-around described frameworks and procedures, the use of appropriate innovation, and, most importantly, attracting the right kind of folks with reasonable mindfulness, morals, and conduct are all necessary for ensuring the internet's security. In light of the transformation of the internet and technology, the technical and legal challenges in ensuring the security of data, information technology, and networks, and also the impact on financial life throughout the state,

Figure 4 Show Cyber-attacks of America

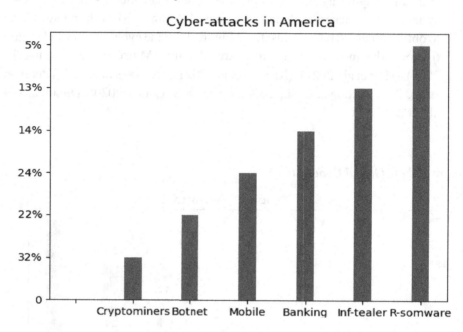

Figure 5 Show Cyber-attacks of Europe, Middle East, and Africa

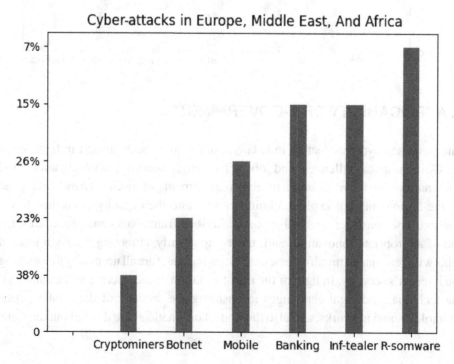

Figure 6 Most Prevalent Malware Globally Percentage of corporate networks impacted by each malware family year 2020

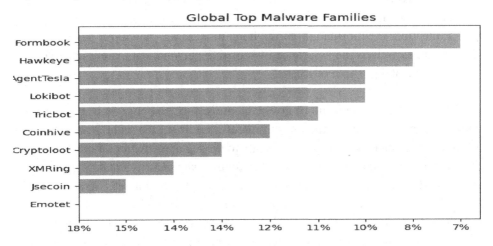

the requirements after an exercise to create a secure digital eco-framework include a variety of empowering forms, direct activities, and other measures.

a. Creation of a beneficial legal environment on the side of a safe and secure internet, adequate confidence and faith in electronic exchanges, and integration time capacities that can enable capable action of partners and viable arraignment.

b. IT systems and channels, as well as basic correspondence and data foundation, are all protected.

c. IT systems and channels, as well as basic correspondence and data foundation, are all protected.

d. Placing components for digital security crisis reaction and goals and emergency the board through feasible predictive, preventative, defensive, reaction, and recovery activities 24 hours a day, seven days a week.

e. Policy, advancement, and empowerment actions to ensure that International Security best practices and congruency evaluation (Product, Process, Technology, and People) are consistent, as well as impetuses for consistency.

f. Indigenous development of appropriate security techniques and innovation via outside innovation research, arrangement-based examination, concept verification, pilot development, and so on, as well as the organization of secure IT items/forms

g. The implementation of digital security had an impact on the culture of aware client behavior and activities.

h. Proactive and reactive alleviation activities to connect and kill the sources of difficulty, as well as support for the formation of a global security eco framework, including open private organization game plans, data sharing, and respective and multi-parallel agreements with appropriate foreign state offices, security offices, and security sellers, among other things.

i.   Protection of information throughout processing, handling, capacity, and travel, as well as the assurance of sensitive personal data, all contribute to a fundamental position of trust.

E-Government is the result of governments' efforts to better their relationships with their citizens. If certain requirements are met, the valid estimation of electronic exchanges will be proportionate to the legal estimation of other types of correspondence, such as the constructed structure. Data security standard procedures are needed to ensure the success of E-Government initiatives. Security rules, methods, and techniques, including the use of data information security, should be established to protect e-Government frameworks from attack, recognize odd exercises administrations, and have a demonstrated emergency plan in place. Essential elements include having a legitimate public key foundation that provides the required level of verification and integrity, and also maintaining constant awareness and planning a project to ensure individuals understand security dangers, know how to recognize potential issues, and act as needed to maintain a secure e-Government administration (Manoharan et al., 2021),(Sambana et al., 2021),(Hackmageddon, 2021),(Lim et al., 2019),(Humayun et al., 2021),(Muzammal et al., 2020). According to the report of timelines 2021 (Humayun et al., 2020),(Ullah, Azeem, Ashraf et al, 2021),(Malhotra et al., 2017), (Bindu et al., 2019), (Ullah, Pinglu, Ullah et al, 2021), (Abdulkareem, 2015).(Carstens et al., 2015),(Gajendra et al., 2012).

7. CHALLENGES TO INFRASTRUCTURAL DEVELOPMENT

In the 1990s, the fast growth of represents a feature and the development of a computer that is connected pushed the use of data innovation into a new era. As a consequence, digital e-commerce, e-government, and e-society are on the rise, which of the data age's achievements are noticeable, have really been blasting for the past ten years. The concept of e-government was initially proposed in the 1990s by Mr. Clinton, the former President of the United States, in 1992. Mr. Bill Clinton was elected President of the United States of America in 1992, he declared that his administration will be run entirely online (e-government).

The lack of infrastructure to support the 21st century style of instructing, studying, and communications are one of the problems that have come up often in the literature (Aduke, 2008). Electricity is one of the infrastructures required to encourage its use digitalization (ICT) for the sharing of ideas without the use of paper in University, which hasn't gotten nearly enough recent times' emphasis (Abdulkareem 2015). Energy is a substantial source of power as well as a critical infrastructure for supporting teaching and learning activities. Presently, the country's highest electrical output is 5000 megawatts, which it generates and distributes (Idowu 2020). That is less than the amount of power needed to run technology and facilities across the country's 170 universities (National Universities Commission, 2019) table 2 show summary of models (Gajendra et al., 2012),(Teiu, 2011),(Alshehri & Drew, 2010),(Ghiorghita et al., 2010).

8. CRITICAL EVALUATION

As a consequence, e-government is reduced to a means to an end (Yildiz, 2007). Believes that e-government use of ICT in public management, together with structural and skill improvements, to improve public services, generate democratic dividends, and raise support for public objectives (Denhardt 2009). View e-government as a tool for delivering services. Use of the internet to provide news and information to citizens, or the use of all information and communication technology platforms and applications in the public sector Adah (2015). The concept of e-government displays service delivery and information interchange both within and outside organizations (Intra-Governmental) that are monitored utilizing various digital instruments and is viewed as a mutual interaction between government and citizens, for government, non-profit groups, business people, employees, and the government itself are all benefited (Khalid & Lavilles, 2020) (Oke, 2009),(Chaturvedi et al., 2008).

We have deeply peer-viewed last fifteen years associated influence of cybersecurity attacks on e-governance that it is a two-edged sword, on the one hand, can be beneficial and, on the other hand, can be harmful, functions as a method for improving the government's internal working mechanism by reforming the back-end office, improving communication between and among various government agencies, and holding the government accountable. Another side, E-government aids in the improvement of government-citizen relations by developing public confidence and allowing communities to express themselves in decision-making. Increase the effectiveness and efficiency of service delivery, as well as equity and transparency. Consequently, the cyber-attacks are influenced e-governance and damage public trust figure 3 shows the new challenges.

Table 2 show summary models of the e-government year 2020

Models for e-government	Countries	Advantages	Disadvantages
Policy and funding coordination (Ministries with cross-cutting responsibilities, such as finances, treasury, trade, and budget)	Among the countries represented are, Brazil, China, Finland, France, Ireland, Israel, Japan, Rwanda, SL, the UK, Austria, Canada, and the US.	Has access authority completed monies establishing e-government by other ministries Assists with the integration of E-government and fiscal management in general	Can be inadequate in the focus and technical understanding needed to manage and implement e-government initiatives.
Administration activities coordination (administration reform, services, affairs, interiors, government)	Slovenia, Korea's, Bulgaria, Egypt, Germany, Korea, Mexico, and South Africa	Administrative changes and simplifying are incorporated into E-government is made easier.	Might be lacking in the technological capability needed to organise e-government, as well as financial and economic information needed to define significance.
System requirement coordination (industry science and technology)	Ghana, India, Jordan, Kenya, Pakistan, Romania, Singapore, Thailand, and Vietnam are among the countries represented.	Ensures the availability of technical personnel	It's possible that they're too focused on technology or industry and aren't paying attention to administrative reform.

9. E-GOVERNMENT IMPLEMENTATION CHALLENGES

One of the main barriers to e-government implementation in emerging countries is a lack of adequate ICT infrastructure. The developed country's government needs the resources to build a necessary Infrastructure facility for e-government (Glyptis et al., 2020). Information transformation is among the resources needed to implement e-government. Spread of the Internet network and tools and techniques for communications. Peoples of developing countries are still incapable access e-government due to a lack of internet connectivity (Samsor, 2020). The Internet connection is a requirement for using the services available on e-government web applications. Administrative processes are supported by e-government, in the perspective of advances and quality efficiency of service in the internal public sector increase (Arief et al., 2021).

10. DISCUSSION

Cybersecurity is seen as a national threat. Every nation's issue has the potential to affect residents' daily life (Mitrokotsa & Douligeris, 2007). The percentage for

Figure 7. Show new challenges framework of e-government implementation

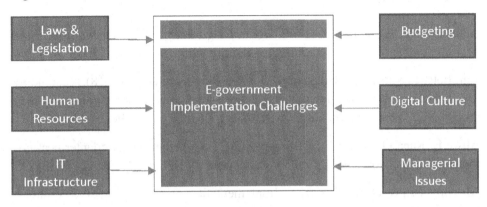

fulfilment will increase as powerful cybersecurity plans are implemented. In the interest of national security, cyber security policies to restrict self - expression is incompatible with human rights (Kamiya et al., 2021). Information security-based practices are needed for the protection of e-governance projects. Security requirements and plans help in the protection of e-government systems from attack and threats. The Internet core structure was built around shared access and trust, with security initiatives coming later (Dimolianis et al., 2020) regarding businesses, cyber-attacks, threats, and damage are a dangerous and growing problem. Almost every modern businesses require a computer network. Can handle workstations, printers, exchanges, wireless routers, and bridges. E-government has become a critical component of government operations around the world (Arief et al., 2021).

11. CONCLUSION AND FUTURE WORK

The use of e-government is growing as the world is progressively interconnected. However, need to use information and data. The data security system must design and address new and effective vulnerabilities increasing due to emerging technological innovations. In the dynamic and ever-changing world, the issues and challenges of protecting information infrastructure are growing. Due to various vulnerabilities in the system, these networks are vulnerable to cyber-attack. As a result, it is critical to speed security efforts that include application software and infrastructure to provide an efficient governance system without the risk of being rigged. It has been observed during review associated articles that limited studies have been done on e-governance and cyber-attacks. Consequently, the cyber-attacks are influencing e-governance and damage public trust. Further need to peer-review cybersecurity frameworks due to this is emerging technologies.

REFERENCES

Abdulkareem, A. K. (2015). *Challenges of e-government implementation in the Nigerian public service.* https://uilspace.unilorin.edu.ng/handle/20.500.12484/290

Agrafiotis, I., Nurse, J. R., Goldsmith, M., Creese, S., & Upton, D. (2018). A taxonomy of cyber-harms: Defining the impacts of cyber-attacks and understanding how they propagate. *Journal of Cybersecurity, 4*(1), tyy006. doi:10.1093/cybsec/tyy006

Aliwa, E., Rana, O., Perera, C., & Burnap, P. (2021). Cyberattacks and countermeasures for in-vehicle networks. *ACM Computing Surveys, 54*(1), 1–37. doi:10.1145/3431233

Alshehri, M., & Drew, S. (2010). Implementation of e-government: advantages and challenges. *International Association for Scientific Knowledge (IASK).* https://research-repository.griffith.edu.au/bitstream/handle/10072/40620/72631_1.pdf

Arief, A., Wahab, I. H. A., & Muhammad, M. (2021, May). Barriers and Challenges of e-Government Services: A Systematic Literature Review and Meta-Analyses. In *IOP Conference Series: Materials Science and Engineering* (Vol. 1125, No. 1, p. 012027). IOP Publishing. https://iopscience.iop.org/article/10.1088/1757-899X/1125/1/012027/meta

Baharin, A. M., & Zolkipli, M. F. (2021). Review on Current Target of Mobile Attacks. *Borneo International Journal, 4*(2), 17-24. http://majmuah.com/journal/index.php/bij/article/view/84

Bindu, N., Sankar, C. P., & Kumar, K. S. (2019). From conventional governance to e-democracy: Tracing the evolution of e-governance research trends using network analysis tools. *Government Information Quarterly, 36*(3), 385–399. doi:10.1016/j.giq.2019.02.005

Carlton, M., Levy, Y., & Ramim, M. (2019). Mitigating cyber attacks through the measurement of non-IT professionals' cybersecurity skills. *Information & Computer Security.* https://www.emerald.com/insight/content/doi/10.1108/ICS-11-2016-0088/full/html

Carstens, D. S., Kies, S., & Stockman, R. (2015). E-government transparency and citizen engagement increasing accountability. In *Digital Solutions for Contemporary Democracy and Government* (pp. 189–214). IGI Global. doi:10.4018/978-1-4666-8430-0.ch011

Chaturvedi, M. M., Gupta, M. P., & Bhattacharya, J. (2008). Cyber Security Infrastructure in India: A Study. In *Emerging Technologies in E-Government.* CSI Publication. http://citeseerx.ist.psu.edu/viewdoc/download?doi=10.1.1.542.8083 &rep=rep1&type=pdf

da Silva, L. E., & Coury, D. V. (2020). Network traffic prediction for detecting DDoS attacks in IEC 61850 communication networks. *Computers & Electrical Engineering, 87,* 106793. doi:10.1016/j.compeleceng.2020.106793

Dimolianis, M., Pavlidis, A., & Maglaris, V. (2020, February). A multi-feature DDoS detection schema on P4 network hardware. In *2020 23rd Conference on Innovation in Clouds, Internet and Networks and Workshops (ICIN)* (pp. 1-6). IEEE. https:// ieeexplore.ieee.org/abstract/document/9125016

Elbahnasawy, N. G. (2021). Can e-government limit the scope of the informal economy? *World Development, 139,* 105341. doi:10.1016/j.worlddev.2020.105341

Fang, X., Xu, M., Xu, S., & Zhao, P. (2019). A deep learning framework for predicting cyber attacks rates. *EURASIP Journal on Information Security, 2019*(1), 1-11. https://link.springer.com/article/10.1186/s13635-019-0090-6

Froehlich, A., Ringas, N., & Wilson, J. (2020). E-Governance in Africa and the World. In *Space Supporting Africa* (pp. 53–124). Springer. doi:10.1007/978-3-030-52260-5_2

Gajendra, S., Xi, B., & Wang, Q. (2012). E-government: Public participation and ethical issues. *Journal of e-Governance, 35*(4), 195-204. https://content.iospress. com/articles/journal-of-e-governance/gov00320

GhiorghitaE.GherasimZ.AndronieM. (2010). E-Government Implications on Project Management in the Metallurgical Fields. *Available at* SSRN 1741882. doi:10.2139/ ssrn.1741882

Glyptis, L., Christofi, M., Vrontis, D., Del Giudice, M., Dimitriou, S., & Michael, P. (2020). E-Government implementation challenges in small countries: The project manager's perspective. *Technological Forecasting and Social Change, 152,* 119880. doi:10.1016/j.techfore.2019.119880

Grinin, L., Grinin, A., & Korotayev, A. (2022). COVID-19 pandemic as a trigger for the acceleration of the cybernetic revolution, transition from e-government to e-state, and change in social relations. *Technological Forecasting and Social Change, 175,* 121348. doi:10.1016/j.techfore.2021.121348 PMID:34789950

Hackmageddon. (2021). https://www.hackmageddon.com/2021/04/13/q1-2021-cyber-attack-statistics/

Halder, D., & Jaishankar, K. (2021). Cyber governance and data protection in India: A critical legal analysis. In *Routledge Companion to Global Cyber-Security Strategy* (pp. 337–348). Routledge. doi:10.4324/9780429399718-28

Hoffman, I., & Cseh, K. B. (2021). E-administration, cybersecurity and municipalities–the challenges of cybersecurity issues for the municipalities in Hungary. *Cybersecurity and Law, 4*(2), 199-211. https://www.cybersecurityandlaw.pl/E-administration-cybersecurity-and-municipalities-the-challenges-of-cybersecurity,133999,0,1.html

Holt, T. J., Stonhouse, M., Freilich, J., & Chermak, S. M. (2021). Examining ideologically motivated cyberattacks performed by far-left groups. *Terrorism and Political Violence, 33*(3), 527–548. doi:10.1080/09546553.2018.1551213

Humayun, M., Jhanjhi, N., Alruwaili, M., Amalathas, S. S., Balasubramanian, V., & Selvaraj, B. (2020). Privacy protection and energy optimization for 5G-aided industrial Internet of Things. *IEEE Access: Practical Innovations, Open Solutions, 8*, 183665–183677. doi:10.1109/ACCESS.2020.3028764

Humayun, M., Jhanjhi, N. Z., Alsayat, A., & Ponnusamy, V. (2021). Internet of things and ransomware: Evolution, mitigation and prevention. *Egyptian Informatics Journal, 22*(1), 105-117. https://www.sciencedirect.com/science/article/pii/S1110866520301304

Kamiya, S., Kang, J. K., Kim, J., Milidonis, A., & Stulz, R. M. (2021). Risk management, firm reputation, and the impact of successful cyberattacks on target firms. *Journal of Financial Economics, 139*(3), 719–749. doi:10.1016/j.jfineco.2019.05.019

Kiilu, P., Shingala, H., & Bondavalli, A. (n.d.). *Framework Based Approach for the Mitigation of Insider Threats in E-governance IT Infrastructure.* file:///C:/Users/imdad/Downloads/Framework_Based_Approach_for_the_Mitigat%20(1).pdf

Kotenko, I., Saenko, I., & Lauta, O. (2019). Modeling the impact of cyber attacks. In *Cyber Resilience of Systems and Networks* (pp. 135–169). Springer. doi:10.1007/978-3-319-77492-3_7

Krundyshev, V., & Kalinin, M. (2019, September). Hybrid neural network framework for detection of cyber attacks at smart infrastructures. In *Proceedings of the 12th International Conference on Security of Information and Networks* (pp. 1-7). https://dl.acm.org/doi/abs/10.1145/3357613.3357623

Lim, M., Abdullah, A., Jhanjhi, N. Z., & Supramaniam, M. (2019). Hidden link prediction in criminal networks using the deep reinforcement learning technique. *Computers*, *8*(1), 8. https://www.mdpi.com/2073-431X/8/1/8

Malhotra, H., Bhargava, R., & Dave, M. (2017). Implementation of E-Governance projects: Development, Threats & Targets. *JIMS8I-International Journal of Information Communication and Computing Technology*, *5*(2), 292-298. https://www.indianjournals.com/ijor.aspx?target=ijor:jims8i&volume=5&issue=2&article=001

Manoharan, A. P., Ingrams, A., Kang, D., & Zhao, H. (2021). Globalization and worldwide best practices in E-Government. *International Journal of Public Administration*, *44*(6), 465–476. doi:10.1080/01900692.2020.1729182

Mitrokotsa, A., & Douligeris, C. (2007). E-Government and Denial of Service Attacks. In *Secure E-Government Web Services* (pp. 124–142). IGI Global. doi:10.4018/978-1-59904-138-4.ch008

Muzammal, S. M., Murugesan, R. K., & Jhanjhi, N. Z. (2020). A comprehensive review on secure routing in internet of things: Mitigation methods and trust-based approaches. *IEEE Internet of Things Journal*. https://ieeexplore.ieee.org/abstract/document/9223748

Nautiyal, L., Malik, P., & Agarwal, A. (2018). Cybersecurity system: an essential pillar of smart cities. In *Smart Cities* (pp. 25–50). Springer. doi:10.1007/978-3-319-76669-0_2

Nzimakwe, T. I. (2018). Government's Dynamic Approach to Addressing Challenges of Cybersecurity in South Africa. In *Handbook of Research on Information and Cyber Security in the Fourth Industrial Revolution* (pp. 364–381). IGI Global. doi:10.4018/978-1-5225-4763-1.ch013

Oke, O. (2009). *Evaluating the Security of E-government in West Africa*. http://cs.lewisu.edu/mathcs/msis/projects/msis595_SolaOke.pdf

Pal, S. K. (2019). Changing technological trends for E-governance. In *E-governance in India* (pp. 79-105). Palgrave Macmillan. https://link.springer.com/chapter/10.1007/978-981-13-8852-1_5

Peng, C., Sun, H., Yang, M., & Wang, Y. L. (2019). A survey on security communication and control for smart grids under malicious cyber attacks. *IEEE Transactions on Systems, Man, and Cybernetics. Systems*, *49*(8), 1554–1569. doi:10.1109/TSMC.2018.2884952

Razuleu, L. A. (2018). *E-Governance and Its Associated Cybersecurity: The Challenges and Best Practices of Authentication and Authorization Among a Rapidly Growing E-government* (Doctoral dissertation). California State University, Northridge. https://scholarworks.calstate.edu/downloads/mc87pt75n

Rehman, S., Khaliq, M., Imtiaz, S. I., Rasool, A., Shafiq, M., Javed, A. R., ... Bashir, A. K. (2021). DIDDOS: An approach for detection and identification of Distributed Denial of Service (DDoS) cyberattacks using Gated Recurrent Units (GRU). *Future Generation Computer Systems, 118*, 453-466. https://www.sciencedirect.com/science/article/abs/pii/S0167739X21000327

Roopak, M., Tian, G. Y., & Chambers, J. (2020, January). *An intrusion detection system against ddos attacks in iot networks. In 2020 10th Annual Computing and Communication Workshop and Conference (CCWC) (pp. 0562-0567).* IEEE. https://ieeexplore.ieee.org/abstract/document/9031206/

Sambana, B., Raju, K. N., Satish, D., Raju, S. S., & Raja, P. V. K. (2021). *Impact of Cyber Security in e-Governance and e-Commerce* (No. 5533). EasyChair. file:///C:/Users/imdad/Downloads/EasyChair-Preprint-5533.pdf

Samsor, A. M. (2020). Challenges and Prospects of e-Government implementation in Afghanistan. *International Trade, Politics and Development*. https://www.proquest.com/openview/8aabcd1bad4fe2b6ff590619c704defd/1?pq-origsite=gscholar&cbl=4931636

Sibi Chakkaravarthy, S., Sangeetha, D., Venkata Rathnam, M., Srinithi, K., & Vaidehi, V. (2018). Futuristic cyber-attacks. *International Journal of Knowledge-based and Intelligent Engineering Systems, 22*(3), 195–204. doi:10.3233/KES-180384

Teiu, C. (2011). The Impact Of The Financial Crisis On European E-Government Development. *CES Working Papers, 3*(3), 429-439. https://www.ceeol.com/search/article-detail?id=137053

Ullah, A., Azeem, M., Ashraf, H., Alaboudi, A. A., Humayun, M., & Jhanjhi, N. Z. (2021). Secure healthcare data aggregation and transmission in IoT—A survey. *IEEE Access: Practical Innovations, Open Solutions, 9*, 16849–16865. doi:10.1109/ACCESS.2021.3052850

Ullah, A., Pinglu, C., Ullah, S., Abbas, H. S. M., & Khan, S. (2021). The role of e-governance in combating COVID-19 and promoting sustainable development: A comparative study of China and Pakistan. *Chinese Political Science Review, 6*(1), 86–118. doi:10.100741111-020-00167-w

Yarovoy, T. S., Kozyrieva, O. V., Bielska, T. V., Zhuk, I. I., & Mokhova, I. L. (2020). The E-government development in ensuring the country financial and information security. *Financial and credit activity: Problems of theory and practice, 2*(33), 268-275. http://fkd1.ubs.edu.ua/article/view/206853

Chapter 6
Argument for Improved Security in Local Governments Within the Economic Community of West African States

Maurice Dawson
https://orcid.org/0000-0003-4609-3444
Illinois Institute of Technology, USA

Damon Walker
University of Missouri, Saint Louis, USA

ABSTRACT

The Economic Community of West African States is an economic region located in West Africa. This region has a population of over 349 million and representation for approximately 15 countries. With the explosion of technological advances in agriculture, healthcare, and personal device use, cybersecurity has become an important issue. Coupled with dictatorships, corrupt regimes, religious extremists, and other illicit activities, it is imperative that cybersecurity become a cornerstone in local governments to ensure the safety of citizens. This chapter reviews recent literature that surrounds West African states to present an argument on why cybersecurity must be considered essential for local governments. Observations and interviews were conducted at a government facility concerning its security posture as it relates to physical and cybersecurity. This activity included interviews with senior government officials and employees to understand the state of affairs at the organization.

DOI: 10.4018/978-1-7998-9624-1.ch006

INTRODUCTION

Economic Community of West African States (ECOWAS) is a regional group of fifteen countries that was created in 1975. These countries are Benin, Burkina Faso, Cape Verde, Côte d' Ivoire, The Gambia, Ghana, Guinea, Guinea Bissau, Liberia, Mali, Niger, Nigeria, Sierra Leone, Senegal, and Togo (See Figure 1.). ECOWAS' fundamental Principles are a vital component of its survival. Principles such as equality and interdependence of its Member States, solidarity and collective self-reliance, non-aggression between the Member States, maintenance of regional peace, and accountability, economic and social justice are the driving force behind ECOWAS' success.

The main purpose of creating ECOWAS was to create a region where West African citizens could have access to the resources from the member countries without difficulties for all Member States to grow individually and collectively. It is important to note that both the countries and their population would benefit from this vision. However, there is a major setback associated with such freedom as the knowledge of cyber fraud gets easily spread among these fifteen countries.

AFRICA'S GIANT

Nigeria is Africa's most populous nation and largest economy. Nigeria is a country in the western part of Africa, bordering the Gulf of Guinea, between Benin and Cameroon (See Figure 1.). It has an estimated population of over 190 million people, with the largest black population in the world. It is one of the major oil-producing counties in the world and has a lot of natural resources. The land area of Nigeria is approximately 900,000 square kilometers and has had Abuja as its capital since 1991. Nigeria has more than 250 ethnic groups, with Hausa and the Fulani tribes making up 29% of the population. The Yoruba tribes have about 21%, Igbo or Ibo has 18%, Ijaw has a little over 10%, Kanuri has over 4%, Ibibio has about 3.5%, and the Tiv with about 2.5%. The major religions in Nigeria are Christianity and Islam. The Northern part of Nigeria is majority Muslim while the southern part of Nigeria is made of mostly Christians and Muslims. In the north of Nigeria, where the population is mostly Muslims, there is a lot of unrest today due to the presence of a group called Boko Haram.

Nigeria is a significant maker of oil and is an individual from the Organization of Petroleum Producing Countries (OPEC). Nigeria is one of the main oil and gas makers in Africa and is the seventh most elevated maker of oil and gas on the planet (Taiwo, 2010). The oil areas represent over 70% of government income and over 90% of fares. Nigeria has a tremendous store of oil and gas inside the nation. The

Figure 1. ECOWAS Region
Reprinted from the Member States, by ECOWAS, n.d., retrieved from https://www.ecowas.int/member-states/.

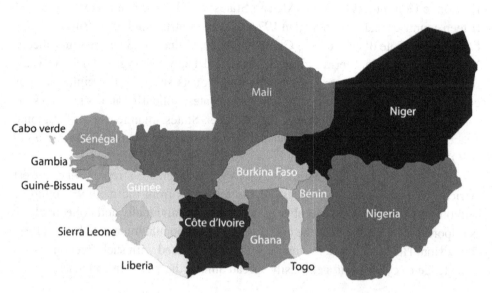

abuse of the stores of oil and gas has improved the monetary status of the nation anyway Nigeria's economy is reliant on oil and gas, which is the essential wellspring of subsidizing for the economy. A large portion of Nigeria's oil is in the Niger Delta district of the nation. The investigation of the oil in Nigeria is completed on a joint endeavor among Nigeria and some unfamiliar worldwide associations, for example, Shell, Exxon-Mobil, Agip, Chevron, Total, Texaco, among others. There are major rustic metropolitan and provincial pressures because of normal asset enrichments, inconsistent admittance to political forces, helpless government administrations to different gatherings, and lopsided portions of public riches (AfDB, OECD, UNDP, and ECA, 2013).

The Nigerian Military Forces are the armed security forces of the country called Nigeria and currently have over 200,000 military personnel in three-armed service groups. The three-armed service groups are the Army, Navy, and Air Forces. The military group in Nigeria has the major responsibility for protecting the citizens and borders of the Federal Republic of Nigeria. The Nigerian military forces have been involved in various combat efforts in the past in protecting the sovereignty of the country, including the Nigerian civil war (1967-1970), conflicts in the Niger Delta, and recently the Boko Haram insurgency in the northern part of the country.

Boko Haram is a religious terrorist group in Nigeria that started in 2002. It is a conservative Islamic group that attempts to impose its religious ideology in the country (Adesoji, 2010). The name Boko Haram means "non-Islamic education is a sin," and it is the belief of this group that Muslims should avoid Western education but embrace Islamic education. Boko Haram is derived from the Hausa word "Boko' meaning book, and the Arabic word "haram," meaning sinful or ungodly. The first internationally published Boko Haram crisis started on the 25th of July 2009, and went on till the 30th of July 2009, with the crisis spreading through four states, including Bauchi, Kano, Yobe, and Borno (Adesoji, 2010). Borno State has received several casualties, serving as the base of the leadership. Boko Haram has grown to other states in Nigeria over time and has been involved in a few terrorist acts since 2009. Boko Haram has attacked cities like Abuja, the capital of Nigeria, and Chibok (Borno State), where 276 female students were abducted by the Islamist militants. The kidnapping of the Chibok female students has attracted a lot of international attention, with many human rights organizations calling on the Boko Haram sects to release the kidnapped children. Although Boko Haram has its main base in Nigeria, it has also carried out attacks in Nigeria's neighboring countries like Chad, Benin, Niger, and Cameroon. It is reported that the terror group has killed about 17,000 people and is responsible for the displacement of more than two million inhabitants (most of the northern hemisphere of Nigeria). Today, Boko Haram is causing a lot of unrest in Nigeria (mostly in the north part of Nigeria), and the government of Nigeria has dispatched a lot of military personnel to combat rising cases of Boko Haram attacks. The United States of America (USA) has also launched a surveillance and intelligence mission in Nigeria against the militant group as part of its support for Nigeria in its combat against Boko Haram. Nigeria and its neighboring countries have also formed a joint task force to combat the efforts of the militant group in the region. This has resulted in the reduction of Boko Haram attacks in Nigeria. However, the Islamic State of Iraq (ISIS) is overtaken by Boko Haram as the world's deadliest terror organization (Buchanan, 2015). In 2015, Boko Haram changed its name to Islamic State West Africa Province (ISWAP).

Nigeria is not only home to the terrorist group Boko Haram but also to the Fulani Militants, which is another Islamic militant group. This is not to be confused with the Fula people or Fulana, who are a nomadic tribe dispersed all over western Africa. The Fula are also found in Egypt and Sudan. As of November 2015, the Global Terrorism Index (GTI) lists the Fulani Militants as the fourth deadliest terror group in the world (Buchanan, 2015).

NIGERIA 419 SCAM

The data discussed has shown the multitude of national security issues in the country. However, the largest technological problem is information warfare in the form of the 419 advance fee fraud scam (Edelson, 2003). This 410 scam is derived from the penal code in Nigeria, and the rise of this criminal activity continues to grow. The problem encompasses illicit activities such as fake lotteries, money scams, and similar activities. Due to the rapid growth of social media and online communities, this scam has flourished (Isacenkova, Thonnard, Costin, Francillon, and Balzarotti, 2014).

ESPIONAGE

At the highest government levels, such as the African Union (AU), they have claimed that the Chinese are performing cyber espionage on a building funded by Beijing for $200 million (Aglionby, 2018). A Chinese state-owned company constructed the entire building, which allowed them uncontrolled access to the building. A security researcher discovered that systems within the AU were compromised (Tilouine & Kadiri, 2018). This is a significant issue as China has developed many telecom backbones and served as a supplier for the majority of computing equipment. Coincidentally, technical staff within the AU has employed encryption and changed the supply chain for acquiring equipment. However, this measure is too late as across the continent to include ECOWAS, the Chinese have enormous investments in infrastructure and continue to provide computing devices that serve over 100 million people. Due to these events and similar ones at varying levels, some African governments have been securing their systems.

OBSERVATIONS

As there have been alarming security breaches at the AU level, it is not surprising that these events are also found at the local government. Through multiple visits with the Ministry of Agriculture in Senegal, numerous issues have been discovered. In this West African nation, the systems for this ministry have shown the following deficiencies as they relate to the National Institute for Standards and Technology (NIST) Special Publication (SP) 800-53 (Rev. 4). Security Controls and Assessment Procedures for Federal Information Systems and Organizations. Since there is no governing policy in the AU or ECOWAS regarding controls, a survey was done using NIST SP 800-50 (Rev. 4). This document provides control families and associated minimum security controls that can serve as a baseline. There are 18 control families with three levels of minimum-security controls (Ross, 2013). This document can serve as the baseline for implementing security. For this paper, only Low-Impact Baseline security controls shall be evaluated.

ATTACKS ON WEST AFRICAN COUNTRIES

Several attacks had cut off Liberia's internet connection from the rest of the world. These attacks showed the hackers' well-coordinated effort in using a massive network of hijacked servers to reach their targets. In 2016, the website of Ghana's electoral commission was targeted by hackers after its citizens cast their votes to elect a new president. Hackers went a step further by announcing results on several social media. However, the commission urged people to ignore "the fake results" circulating on social media.

A man who describes himself as a nationalist Turkish hacker group claimed to have hacked most of the Ghanaian government websites and its main site (BBC, 2015). This was not the first incident with the Ghanaian government and will not be the last, unfortunately. For instance, the ministry of justice's website was hijacked. The hijack is widely believed to have been caused by hackers who felt terrible about the Argentine vessel, detained by Ghanaian authorities after it was determined that Argentina owed money to Ghana. Moreover, two banks were simultaneously hacked as well.

INITIATIVES

The need for cybersecurity keeps growing bigger every year in West Africa and worldwide, for that matter. There has been an increase of senior members and stakeholders to learn the new developments in the cybersecurity industry during the West African Cyber Security Summit. The 2017 event was held from March 10 to March 11 and featured speakers from KPMG, Ernst & Young, and G3, among others.

Cyber Security Expert Association of Nigeria, CSEAN has urged the Nigerian President to sign the Electronic Transaction bill. With the sophistication of cyber fraud in Nigeria, this bill will "enable the validity of contracts expressed in electronic forms, matters relating to evidence, the security of online transactions, electronic signatures, the disclosure of information, protection of personal data, and protecting the rights of consumers" (Maseko, 2018). Also, this bill will help financial institutions file criminal claims against the "bad guys."

Senegal has decided to join forces with the Netherlands to combat cybersecurity activities in Senegal and West Africa (GFCE, 2018). This initiative has placed its focus on the following actions. First, a cybersecurity capacity review of Senegal was conducted by the Global Cyber Security Capacity Center to enable the government of Senegal to prioritize areas of capacity investments. Secondly, there were two expert meetings on cybersecurity to address issues and challenges relevant to the West African region.

ECOWAS and International Telecommunication Development Sector (ITU-D) will collaborate to work on questions of shared interest in the field of cybersecurity that includes the elaboration of regional Cybersecurity initiatives through ECOWAS and the enhancing the Cybersecurity posture of ECOWAS member countries through country-specific initiatives as well as regional initiatives (ECOWAS, 2018). The regional initiatives include:

- The National CIRT/CERT program.
- Enhancing Cybersecurity in ECOWAS countries.
- The Global Cybersecurity Index.
- The harmonization and enhancement of legislation address the prosecution of cybercriminals effectively.
- The elaboration of national cybersecurity strategies.

The challenge with these initiatives is still the number of organizations that fall significantly short of the expected outcomes that have been conveyed through government heads. These unaddressed items pose a local risk, and a national security issue as these are unaddressed security controls at government facilities. After conducting onsite interviews and surveys, there were huge discrepancies between what is being proposed to what is occurring at the sites.

INTERVIEWS AND SITE SURVEYS

Interviews and site surveys were conducted in several areas regarding the organization's security posture related to technology and physical security. The location of the site surveys was in Senegal and Guinea. Through the interviews, a few themes were discovered. Regarding physical security between all sites, there were inconsistencies in how the buildings were secured. No guard was remaining on or near the premises in the event there was a breach for locations outside capital cities. A six-foot gate secured the building with barbed wire. There were no alarms on the actual building with the physical equipment or servers present. Only during the organizations' operating hours were there some form of guard in place. The guards at the locations seemed uninterested in the post and went through daily tasks to include not routinely checking all checkpoint areas around the site. The received training was minimal to nonexistent, while fewer than 10% had any formal military training. There were no alarms present, fire extinguishers, or Closed-Circuit Televisions (CCTVs) present in more than one location. The lack of these security controls is alarming as several ECOWAS nations have terrorism, high poverty, and criminal activities such as theft.

An investigation of the computing equipment used for conducting work found numerous vulnerabilities and issues. There was no Change Management (CM) system within the organization or handling changes to the system. The specifics of the hardware and software list were incomplete and usually out of date. Computers had unverified licenses for Microsoft Windows Operating System (OS) and office products. This meant that the computers were not receiving patches and updates critical for the system, which left them vulnerable to actions such as zero-day exploits. Upon further review, there was no Anti-Virus (AV) or firewall present. The password policy was relatively simple and not enforced to become more complex, requiring standards found through low-security requirements in the National Institute of Standards (NIST) Risk Management Framework (RMF). A few systems ran older versions of Microsoft, such as Windows XP, which was unsupported as of 8 April 2014. This meant that there were devices with different configurations within the network, which made patch management difficult, if not completely nonexistent.

CONCLUSION

According to the NIST guidelines, after reviewing sites that supported agriculture in Guinea and Senegal, it was determined that the computer-based systems be placed on a secure network, all OS updated and patched appropriately. Password policies need to be created, managed, and maintained by each organization. Lastly, physical sites need to be secured by moderate to highly skilled professionals 24 hours a day. Breaches at the local level can prove to be a great vantage point for those seeking to disrupt and pillage data at the national level.

To effectively address the deficiencies, it is essential to address fundamental security controls and create a plan to address these to mitigate associated risks. First, organizations must address issues with power outages. This is because power outages frequently happen in many parts of the country, even in rural areas. Many businesses rely on fuel-burning generators for backup power. These power outages also contribute to the loss of internet connectivity and may result in data loss (McDonnell, 2019). The power comes from government-run entities. It is detrimental that these countries' governments raise funds to build the power grid to provide adequate power for all of its residents and businesses. Organizations should review and adhere to NIST SP PE-3 documentation on physical security, handling information sites, and logging access authorizations. Immediately stop the nonuse of government-regulated emails. Organizations ought to review and adhere to NIST SP 800-177 for Trust Worthy Emails (Rose et al., 2016). Address the lack of standardization documentation. Organizations should review and adhere to NIST

SP 800-16 for standardization in the training of all personnel and documentation of organizational processes (Wilson et al., 1998).

There was no plan for business continuity or disaster recovery. The guidance that needs to be used to baseline controls and requirements needs to be NIST 800-34. This document is an effective resiliency program that includes risk management, contingency and continuity planning, and other security and emergency management activities (Swanson, Bowen, Phillips, Gallup, & Lynes, 2010). Lastly, the implementation of annual security checks. Organizations ought to review and adhere to NIST SP 800-115 for annual information security testing and assessments (Scarfone et al., 2008).

REFERENCES

Aglionby, J. (2018, January 29). *African Union accuses China of hacking headquarters.* Retrieved October 27, 2018, from https://www.ft.com/content/c26a9214-04f2-11e8-9650-9c0ad2d7c5b5

BBC. (2015, January 21). *Ghana government websites targeted by hackers.* Retrieved October 27, 2018, from https://www.bbc.com/news/world-africa-30914000

ECOWAS. (n.d.). *Economic Community of West African States (ECOWAS).* Retrieved October 27, 2018, from https://www.ecowas.int/member-states/

Edelson, E. (2003). The 419 scam: Information warfare on the spam front and a proposal for local filtering. *Computers & Security, 22*(5), 392–401. doi:10.1016/S0167-4048(03)00505-4

Harris, S., & Meyers, M. (2002). *CISSP.* McGraw-Hill/Osborne.

Isacenkova, J., Thonnard, O., Costin, A., Francillon, A., & Balzarotti, D. (2014). Inside the scam jungle: A closer look at 419 scam email operations. *EURASIP Journal on Information Security, 2014*(1), 4. doi:10.1186/1687-417X-2014-4

Maseko, F. (2018, September 17). *Nigeria: Cyber security advocacy group calls president to sign electronic transaction bill.* Retrieved October 27, 2018, from http://www.itnewsafrica.com/2018/09/nigeria-cyber-security-advocacy-group-calls-president-to-sign-electronic-transaction-bill/

McDonnell, T. (2019, November 24). *The Powerlessness Of Nigeria's Tech Startups.* Retrieved October 12, 2020, from https://www.npr.org/sections/goatsandsoda/2019/11/24/781132932/the-powerlessness-of-nigerias-tech-startups

Rose, S. W., Nightingale, S. J., Garfinkel, S. L., & Chandramouli, R. (2016). *Trustworthy Email*. doi:10.6028/NIST.SP.800-177

Ross, R. S. (2013). *Security and Privacy Controls for Federal Information Systems and Organizations (includes updates as of 5/7/13)*. No. Special Publication (NIST SP)-800-53 Rev 4.

Scarfone, K. A., Souppaya, M. P., Cody, A., & Orebaugh, A. D. (2008). *Technical guide to information security testing and assessment*. doi:10.6028/NIST.SP.800-115

Swanson, M., Bowen, P., Phillips, A. W., Gallup, D., & Lynes, D. (2010). *Contingency planning guide for federal information systems*. doi:10.6028/NIST.SP.800-34r1

Tilouine, J., & Kadiri, G. (2018, January 27). *A Addis-Abeba, le siège de l'Union africaine espionné par Pékin*. Retrieved October 27, 2018, from https://www.lemonde.fr/afrique/article/2018/01/26/a-addis-abeba-le-siege-de-l-union-africaine-espionne-par-les-chinois_5247521_3212.html

Wilson, M., Zafra, D. E. D., Pitcher, S. I., Tressler, J. D., & Ippolito, J. B. (1998). *Information technology security training requirements*. doi:10.6028/NIST.SP.800-16

ADDITIONAL READING

Aker, J. C., & Fafchamps, M. (2015). Mobile phone coverage and producer markets: Evidence from West Africa. *The World Bank Economic Review*, 29(2), 262–292. doi:10.1093/wber/lhu006

Asongu, S. A., Orim, S. M. I., & Nting, R. T. (2019). Inequality, information technology and inclusive education in sub-Saharan Africa. *Technological Forecasting and Social Change*, 146, 380–389. doi:10.1016/j.techfore.2019.06.006

Dalton, W., van Vuuren, J. J., & Westcott, J. (2017). Building cybersecurity resilience in Africa. In *12th International Conference on Cyber Warfare and Security* (pp. 112-120). Academic Press.

Gcaza, N., & Von Solms, R. (2017). A strategy for a cybersecurity culture: A South African perspective. *The Electronic Journal on Information Systems in Developing Countries*, 80(1), 1–17. doi:10.1002/j.1681-4835.2017.tb00590.x

Orji, U. J. (2018). The African Union Convention on Cybersecurity: A Regional Response Towards Cyber Stability? *Masaryk University Journal of Law and Technology*, 12(2), 91-129.

Oshikoya, T. W., & Hussain, M. N. (1998). Information technology and the challenge of economic development in Africa. *African Development Review*, *10*(1), 100–133. doi:10.1111/j.1467-8268.1998.tb00099.x

KEY TERMS AND DEFINITIONS

Authentication: Security measure designed to establish the validity of a transmission, message, or originator, or a means of verifying an individual's authorization to receive specific categories of information (Harris, 2002).

Availability: Timely, reliable access to data and information services for authorized users (Harris, 2002).

Confidentiality: Assurance that information is not disclosed to unauthorized individuals, processes, or devices (Harris, 2002).

Cyber Terrorism: Attacks with the use of the Internet for terrorist activities, including acts of deliberate, large-scale disruption of computer networks, especially of personal computers attached to the Internet, by the means of tools such as computer viruses, worms, Trojans, and zombies (Janczewski & Colarik, 2008).

Integrity: Quality of an IS reflecting the logical correctness and reliability of the OS; the logical completeness of the hardware and software implementing the protection mechanisms; and the consistency of the data structures and occurrence of the stored data. Note that, in a formal security mode, integrity is interpreted more narrowly to mean protection against unauthorized modification or destruction of information (Harris, 2002).

Non-Repudiation: Assurance the sender of data is provided with proof of delivery and the recipient is provided with proof of the sender's identity, so neither can later deny having processed the data (Harris, 2002).

Chapter 7
The Influence of Deep Learning in Detecting Cyber Attacks on E-Government Applications

Loveleen Gaur
ⓘ D https://orcid.org/0000-0002-0885-1550
Amity University, Noida, India

Raja Majid Ali Ujjan
University of the West of Scotland, UK

Manzoor Hussain
Indus University, Pakistan

ABSTRACT

The digitalization revolution plays a crucial role in every government administration. It manages a considerable volume of user information and is currently seeing an increase in internet access. The absence of unorganized information, on the other hand, adds to the difficulty of data analysis. Data mining approaches have recently become more popular for addressing a variety of e-governance concerns, particularly data management, data processing, and so on. This chapter identifies and compares several existing data mining and data warehouses in e-government. Deep learning is a subset of a larger class of machine learning techniques that combine artificial neural networks. The significance and difficulties of e-governance are highlighted for future enhancement. As a result, with the growth of e-governance, risk and cyber-attacks have increased these days. Furthermore, the few e-governance application performance evaluations are included in this chapter. The purpose of this chapter is to focus on deep learning applications of e-governance in detecting cyber-attacks.

DOI: 10.4018/978-1-7998-9624-1.ch007

1. INTRODUCTION

E-Government is the result of governments' efforts to enhance and improve their relationships with their citizens. If certain requirements are met, the legitimate estimation of electronic exchanges will be comparable to the legitimate estimation of other types of correspondence, such as written structure. Very effective and feasible data security practices and prevention measures are required to ensure the success of e-government ventures. Security rules, methods, and techniques must be established, as well as the use of security innovation, which helps to secure e-government frameworks against attack (Shorten et al., 2021) Distinguish odd exercises from administrations, and have a documented emergency course of action built up. Essential parts include having a legal public key foundation that provides the appropriate level of verification and integrity, as well as having ongoing awareness and planning a project to ensure individuals comprehend security risks, understand how to spot any concerns, and act as needed to keep up a safe e-government administration. Residents' desire for efficient and cost-effective governments is boosting the growth of e-government projects (Sit et al., 2020). The scope of e-government control and its impact on a network characterize a framework that is more than just a single framework. A network-based digital security approach is required to investigate security issues across the entire framework. The outcomes of recent network-based activities have provided insight into potential opportunities for advancement and have demonstrated the estimation of these events. Their valuables pose a serious threat to public safety, national security, and the overall strength of the globally connected universal network. It can be difficult to identify the source, attacker's origin, and behavior, or the motivation for the disruption (Kuutti et al., 2020). Criminals must frequently be deduced from the objective, the impact, or other unintentional evidence. On-screen actors who are dangerous can work from almost anywhere. Displaying specialized talent to stealing information. Hackers and programmers are responsible for a wide range of harmful gadgets and systems. The growing complexity and scale of crime raise the risk of destructive behavior. E-government is the result of legislators' efforts to strengthen relations with their constituents. Given the Internet's norms, e-governance brings governments even closer to their citizens (Zhang et al., 2019). As a result, e-government has a greater societal advantage because it ensures a more extensive and agent-majority rules system. The ability to respond to changing conditions due to the constant ageing and exploitation of new information is crucial in an information economy. Many businesses are unable to function without the use of ICT in their daily operations. Deep Learning has had a sign of success with "Natural Language Processing" (NLP). Literature mining, misinformation detection, and public sentiment analysis are some of the applications for COVID-19 (Lee et al., 2019). Deep learning (DL)

Figure 1. Overview of Deep Learning for security intrusion detection (Gupta, Pal, & Muttoo, 2020)

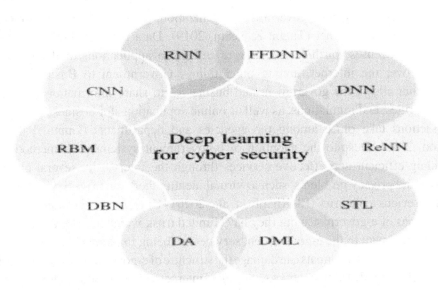

is a subset of machine learning (ML) and artificial intelligence (AI) and is based on an artificial neural network (ANN). It is one of the primary technologies of the Fourth Industrial Revolution (Thabit & Jasim, 2019). "Cyber security" and "Deep learning" are becoming increasingly popular around the world. Deep neural network learning techniques, as well as their ensembles and hybrid approaches, can be used to intelligently handle various cybersecurity concerns, such as intrusion detection, malware or botnet identification, phishing, forecasting cyber-attacks, such as denial of service (DoS), fraud detection, or cyber-anomalies figure 1 Overview of Deep Learning for security intrusion detection . Deep learning has advantages in terms of building security models because it is more accurate, especially when learning from massive amounts of security datasets.

The following points are discussed in this chapter:

1. We focus on e-governance, deep learning applications, cyber-attacks detection in-depth
2. We compare deep learning applications for identifying cyber-attacks.
3. We discuss the impact of deep learning on e-governance.
4. We provide potential solutions and recommendations for deep learning application
5. This chapter also discusses the challenges that existing research and outstanding issues face.

2. LITERATURE REVIEW

Citizens, businesses, and government organizations can access e-government services over the internet (Thabit & Jasim, 2019). Data is accessible to people for driving licenses, birth/death/marriage certificate applications, and payment of taxes over the internet, among other things. Government to Business is a system that allows the government and businesses to share information such as policies, rules, and regulations, as well as online applications for business permits. Transactions take place among the agencies and departments (Gupta, Pal, & Muttoo, 2020). Despite the adoption of e-government systems as a method of providing efficient and effective services through the internet by several cities, security and privacy problems, such as virtual identity theft and privacy violations, remain serious concerns (El Khatib et al., 2020). Citizens are hesitant to use applications of e-governance but they have limited trust, which has been cited as a major impediment to the e-government services are being implemented (Jha, n.d.). Computer hackers and threats can damage the structure of e-government. (Hammouri et al., 2021). Denial of service attacks, unwanted internet access, personal information, internet financial crime and entry attacks are the most prevalent cyberattacks. In any of these three operations (Setiya et al., 2021). Because of the pervasiveness of these devices, security and privacy are issues that standard cyber security solutions may not be able to address (Froehlich et al., 2020). Cyber thieves develop more sophisticated attack strategies sdaily, making it difficult to foresee the kind of attacks that e-government systems will face in the next years, given the capacity of automated equipment to initiate interactions without human intervention (Gupta, Muttoo, & Pal, 2020). As mentioned in the following section, cyber-attacks can take many forms, causing system damage, disrupting communication, and stealing critical information (Shivpuri, 2021) hackers are experts at tracking down information on the internet (Shivpuri, 2021). With the tremendous number of information, cybersecurity keeps personal data secure, and any attacks are automatically reported to the entire corporation. Furthermore, anomalous detection features, event correlation, and pattern identification are characterized using data science ideas applied to cybersecurity. Because of the restricted battery capacity, mobility, and energy consumption characteristics of mobile devices, the Intrusion Detection System (IDS) cannot defend them. With the use of machine learning algorithms, a protective shield can be developed to safeguard apps employing cybersecurity (Shah et al., 2021), (Kumar et al., 2018), (Romaniuk & Omona, 2021), (Sahoo et al., 2018), (Anand et al., 2018). Deep learning is a more effective way to detect cybersecurity risks. Deep learning is one of the most powerful AI-powered machine learning approaches, and this study focuses on it. Deep learning approaches can efficiently process a large volume of data in cybersecurity datasets while also surviving attacks (Witti & Konstantas,

2018), (Sharma & Singh, 2018). These scholars are doing research (Wang et al., 2018), (Komar et al., 2018), (Taormina & Galelli, 2018), (Taormina & Galelli, 2018), (Xin et al., 2018), (Sujatha et al., 2021),(Tayyab et al., 2021), (Lee et al., 2021), (Jhanjhi et al., 2019) recommended a comprehensive analysis and discussion of existing deep learning-based cybersecurity solutions. These studies were primarily undertaken to encourage various scholars working in the same sector to improve the security of various businesses that are exposed to various types of attacks. These papers, however, did not explore the wide range of cybersecurity datasets used or the flaws in deep learning approaches. As a result, the primary goal of this paper is to present a bibliometric analysis of the deep learning approach for detecting potential cybersecurity vulnerabilities. We identified research papers from 2011 to 2020 that are based on cybersecurity challenges using deep learning techniques table 1 shows cyber-attacks of different countries.

Table 1. Overview cyber-attacks of different countries

S.NO	Name of countries	Percentage of cyber-attacks
1	United State	39%
2	India	18%
3	Japan	12%
4	Taiwan	8%
5	Ukraine	7%
6	South Korea	12%
7	Brunei	5%
8	Russia	5%
9	Vietnam	6%
10	Pakistan	5%

3. THE EVOLUTION OF DEEP LEARNING AND E-GOVERNMENT APPLICATIONS

Deep learning (DL) is a difficult but easy-to-understand process. Deep learning is a subset of machine learning, which is itself a subset of artificial intelligence. It is a method of doing automated data analysis using artificial neural networks algorithms that effectively replicate the structure and function of the human brain. While it's still a work in progress, it has limitless potential (Khan et al., 2020) figure 2 overview of the deep learning application. We discussed on following several DL applications:

Figure 2. Overview of DL applications

Prevention of fraud	System for managing customer relationship	Vision software
Natural languages processing (NLP)	Clean up the data	Vehicle Autonomous
Vocal AL	E-commerce	Manufacturing

1. Prevention of fraud: In the digital age, fraud is on the rise. According to an FTC report, customers reported losing more than $3.3 billion in fraud to the FTC in 2020, nearly doubling the amount consumers lost the previous year (Gao et al., 2020). The most common types of fraud were identity theft and imposter fraud.

2. System for managing customer relationships: customer relationship management solutions are commonly referred to as the "single source of truth." They include emails, phone call records, and notes on all of the company's present and former clients, as well as potential consumers (Panwar et al., 2020). While aggregating that data has aided revenue teams in providing a better customer experience, deep learning in CRM systems has unlocked yet another layer of customer insights.

3. Vision software: Deep learning tries to replicate how the human mind processes information and recognizes patterns, making it an ideal method for training vision-based AI applications (Panwar et al., 2020). Those platforms can take in a succession of tagged photo sets and learn to detect objects like airplanes, faces, and weaponry using deep learning models.

4. Natural language processing (NLP): Robots can now comprehend communications and deduce meaning thanks to the emergence of natural language processing technology (Hong et al., 2019). Even so, the procedure might be oversimplified, failing to account for the various ways in which words join to alter the meaning or intent of a sentence.

5. Cleaning up the data: It's difficult for data scientists to spot trends, draw conclusions, or accomplish anything with enormous amounts of raw data. It should be processed (Purwins et al., 2019). Deep learning models can take that raw data and turn it into usable information. Descartes Labs refines data using a cloud-based supercomputer.

6. Vehicles Autonomous: Driving is all about observing and reacting to external circumstances such as other automobiles, street signs, and pedestrians to safely

navigate from point A to point B. While completely autonomous vehicles are still a long way off, deep learning has played a critical part in bringing the technology to reality (Pathirage et al., 2019). It enables autonomous vehicles to consider where you want to go, forecast what obstacles will happen in your environment, and construct a safe path to bring you there.

7. Vocal AI: Deep learning is becoming increasingly important in the process of replicating human speech or translating voice to text. Deep learning models allow systems like Google Voice Search and Siri to listen to audio, recognize speech patterns, and convert them to text (Tang et al., 2019). Then there's DeepMind's WaveNet model, which uses neural networks to identify syllable patterns, inflection points, and other features in the text.

8. E-commerce: Although online shopping has become the de facto method of purchasing things, scrolling through dozens of pages to locate the right pair of shoes to match your style can be stressful. To make the hunt easier, several e-commerce companies are turning to deep learning. Users can upload a photo of their favorite furniture piece to the website Cora, which then uses computer vision wizardry to identify comparable goods (Koirala et al., 2019). A service that helps brands with picture labelling to enhance SEO traffic and reveal alternative goods for consumers when an item is out of stock is one of Clarifai's many deep learning capabilities.

9. Manufacturing: Machines, humans, and robots working together as effectively as possible to generate a reproducible product are often critical to a factory's success (Singh & Arat, 2019). When one aspect of the manufacturing process goes awry, it can be extremely costly to the organization. Deep learning is being utilized to improve the efficiency of the process and reduce faults.

4. OVERVIEW OF E-GOVERNANCE AND CYBER-ATTACKS

Technical, administrative, scientific, legal, economic, and informational challenges all play a role in e-government security (Ozdemir & Koc, 2019). Security techniques, careful system design, and policy measures are frequently used to solve these issues (Kumar et al., 2019). Security, firewalls, and operating system security, among other things, are used to construct security mechanisms to detect, prevent, and recover from security attacks. Management and authorities implement policy measures by establishing new rules and procedures for e-government system development, testing, certification, monitoring, auditing, and certification. Numerous studies and academic institutions have created e-government maturity models to guide and benchmark e-government development from a management perspective. For example, the Information Security Maturity Model for E-Government (ISMM) was suggested by

(Anand & Khemchandani, 2019). Security measures in an e-government system can be implemented at the physical, technological, or management levels, depending on the circumstances (Dhaoui, 2019). Cyber security is essentially defined as the use of safety measures to PCs to provide an optimal level of assurance. The acronym CIA stands for Confidentiality, Integrity, and Availability, and it can be used to describe a security vulnerability (Loukas et al., 2020). The term "classification" refers to the fact that information should only be visible to those who have been given permission to see it. Trustworthiness refers to the rule that only authorized customers are permitted to update information and that these changes are consistently represented throughout all portions of the information (El-Gendy & Azer, 2020). The term "accessibility" refers to the rule that information and computer assets shall always be available to authorized clients (Calderaro & Craig, 2020). However, using the word "simple" to describe PC security is misleading, just as using the word "easy" to describe golf is. Simply knock the ball into the space with as few strokes as possible under the circumstances. The fundamental issue is that little details are missed (Mehta et al., 2021). Early PC frameworks provided strong security, but in comparison to today's utility, they were almost non-accessible. As programming vendors expanded their usefulness, shifting to PCs, then to distributed registers, their banks, specialists, businesses, and government entities (Nadrah et al., 2021). As the present level of digital attacks, character robberies, and phishing assaults demonstrate, this data can be a significant inducement to others, even lawbreakers Figure 3 overview type attacks in cyber-attacks.

5. ARTIFICIAL INTELLIGENCE AND MACHINE LEARNING

In the development of aberrant network traffic, such as intrusion detection, machine learning methods have been widely deployed (Sambana et al., 2021). This could be used in smart cities these systems are typically created by training ML algorithms with sets of data containing typically comes at the expense of privacy. In recent decades, the increased digitalized contacts among the e-government, and consumers has raised privacy and confidentiality problems (Tkatchenko, 2020). Privacy concerns have been cited as a major problem to policy, regulation, and legislation in the twenty-first century. Furthermore, electronic computers are used by e-government systems to acquire a great deal of personal information about people, employees, consumers, products, research, and financial condition. Consumers' confidence has been weakened, as well as growth and economic prospects, financial advantages figure 4 show AI, ML and DL.

Figure 3. Overview type attacks in cyber-attacks (Sambana et al., 2021)

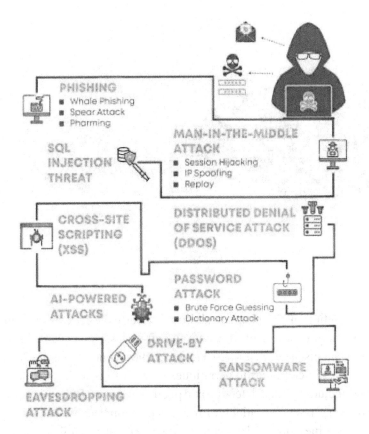

6. DISCUSSION

The basic achievement factors in e-governance must be studied in light of the e-government obstacles and blockages. High security, normalization, and information the board is undeniable requirements of e-government, followed by the arrangement of explicit administrations and their quality, according to the procedure. The construction of all-around described frameworks and procedures and most significantly, attracting the correct type of expert with reasonable mindfulness, morals, and conduct are all necessary for ensuring the internet's security. Given the global nature of IT and the internet, the technical and legal challenges in safeguarding data and networks, an activity to create a secure digital eco-framework is required. Government divisions or offices should focus on developing realistic Information Security strategies and rules, as well as energizing the use of appropriate technology and applications in the organization.

Figure 4. Overview of AI, ML, DL and definition

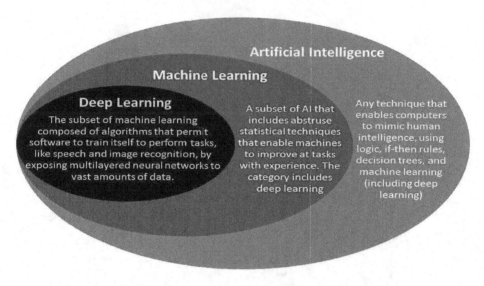

Our contribution of this chapter, we could never have envisaged deep learning applications bringing us self-driving cars and virtual assistants like Alexa, Siri, and Google Assistant just a few years ago. However, these innovations are already a part of our daily lives. Deep Learning continues to inspire us with its almost limitless applications, including fraud detection and pixel restoration. Effective e-government builds up the very assets essential for further expansion because capital is produced by profitable business tasks. This capital improvement capability is not available to government organizations. This might severely limit the government's ability to respond to new opportunities and requests from its citizens. The purpose of government elements is to serve society. While businesses exist to assist their investors, governments exist to serve the networks to which they speak. This connection to the network is critical in government functions. People consider commercial enterprises to be a hotspot for specific services or products. Networks consider the legislature as a provider of numerous administrations in a broader sense. To assure the use of security best practices in basic division associations and frequent tests of consistency, a "Data Security Assurance Framework" must be created, arranged, and managed.

7. CONCLUSION AND FUTURE WORK

Nowadays, the digitalization revolution plays a crucial role in every government administration. It manages a considerable volume of user information and is currently seeing an increase in internet access. The absence of unorganized information, on the other hand, adds to the difficulty of data analysis. Data mining approaches have recently become more popular for addressing a variety of e-governance concerns, particularly data management, data processing, and so on. This chapter identifies and compares several existing data mining and data warehouses in e-government. Deep Learning is a subset of a larger class of machine learning techniques that combine Artificial Neural Networks. The significance and difficulties of e-governance are highlighted for future enhancement. As a result, with the growth of e-governance, risk and cyber-attacks have increased these days. We also highlight frequent issues and challenges related to applying deep learning, such as what steps are necessary to establish a deep learning network, which tools are accessible to assist, and what data and computing power are required. Furthermore, the few e-governance application performance evaluations are included in this chapter. According to global research on the vulnerabilities of e-government sites, more than 80% of e-government sites are vulnerable to standard web server assaults such as cross-site scripting and SQL injection.

REFERENCES

Anand, D., & Khemchandani, V. (2019). Unified and integrated authentication and key agreement scheme for e-governance system without verification table. *Sadhana*, *44*(9), 1–14. doi:10.100712046-019-1163-4

Anand, R., Medhavi, S., Soni, V., Malhotra, C., & Banwet, D. K. (2018). Transforming information security governance in India (A SAP-LAP based case study of security, IT policy and e-governance). *Information & Computer Security*. https://www.emerald. com/insight/content/doi/10.1108/ICS-12-2016-0090/full/html

Calderaro, A., & Craig, A. J. (2020). Transnational governance of cybersecurity: Policy challenges and global inequalities in cyber capacity building. *Third World Quarterly*, *41*(6), 917–938. doi:10.1080/01436597.2020.1729729

Dhaoui, I. (2019). *Electronic governance: An overview of opportunities and challenges*. https://mpra.ub.uni-muenchen.de/92545/

El Khatib, M., Nakand, L., Almarzooqi, S., & Almarzooqi, A. (2020). E-Governance in Project Management: Impact and Risks of Implementation. *American Journal of Industrial and Business Management*, *10*(12), 1785–1811. doi:10.4236/ ajibm.2020.1012111

El-Gendy, S., & Azer, M. A. (2020, December). Security Framework for Internet of Things (IoT). In *2020 15th International Conference on Computer Engineering and Systems (ICCES)* (pp. 1-6). IEEE. https://ieeexplore.ieee.org/abstract/document/9334589

Froehlich, A., Ringas, N., & Wilson, J. (2020). E-Governance in Africa and the World. In *Space Supporting Africa* (pp. 53–124). Springer. doi:10.1007/978-3-030-52260-5_2

Gao, Z., Luo, Z., Zhang, W., Lv, Z., & Xu, Y. (2020). Deep learning application in plant stress imaging: a review. *AgriEngineering, 2*(3), 430-446. https://www.mdpi.com/2624-7402/2/3/29

Gupta, R., Muttoo, S. K., & Pal, S. K. (2020). Regional e-governance development index for developing nations. *Digital Government: Research and Practice, 1*(3), 1-26. https://dl.acm.org/doi/abs/10.1145/3386163

Gupta, R., Pal, S. K., & Muttoo, S. K. (2020). Cyber Security Assessment Education for E-Governance Systems. In *Innovations in Cybersecurity Education* (pp. 181–212). Springer. doi:10.1007/978-3-030-50244-7_10

Halder, D., & Jaishankar, K. (2021). Cyber governance and data protection in India: A critical legal analysis. In *Routledge Companion to Global Cyber-Security Strategy* (pp. 337–348). Routledge. doi:10.4324/9780429399718-28

Hammouri, Q. M., Abu-Shanab, E. A., & Nusairat, N. M. (2021). Attitudes Toward Implementing E-Government in Health Insurance Administration. *International Journal of Electronic Government Research, 17*(2), 1–18. doi:10.4018/IJEGR.2021040101

Hong, S. J., Han, Y., Kim, S. Y., Lee, A. Y., & Kim, G. (2019). Application of deep-learning methods to bird detection using unmanned aerial vehicle imagery. *Sensors (Basel), 19*(7), 1651. doi:10.339019071651 PMID:30959913

Jha, R. (n.d.). *Review of Data Mining and Data Warehousing Implementation in E-Governance.* https://ijisrt.com/assets/upload/files/IJISRT20OCT033.pdf

Jhanjhi, N. Z., Brohi, S. N., & Malik, N. A. (2019, December). Proposing a rank and wormhole attack detection framework using machine learning. In *2019 13th International Conference on Mathematics, Actuarial Science, Computer Science and Statistics (MACS)* (pp. 1-9). IEEE. https://ieeexplore.ieee.org/abstract/document/9024821

Khan, M. A., Ashraf, I., Alhaisoni, M., Damaševičius, R., Scherer, R., Rehman, A., & Bukhari, S. A. C. (2020). Multimodal brain tumor classification using deep learning and robust feature selection: A machine learning application for radiologists. *Diagnostics (Basel), 10*(8), 565. doi:10.3390/diagnostics10080565 PMID:32781795

Koirala, A., Walsh, K. B., Wang, Z., & McCarthy, C. (2019). Deep learning–Method overview and review of use for fruit detection and yield estimation. *Computers and Electronics in Agriculture, 162*, 219–234. doi:10.1016/j.compag.2019.04.017

Komar, M., Sachenko, A., Golovko, V., & Dorosh, V. (2018, May). Compression of network traffic parameters for detecting cyber attacks based on deep learning. In *2018 IEEE 9th International Conference on Dependable Systems, Services and Technologies (DESSERT)* (pp. 43-47). IEEE. https://ieeexplore.ieee.org/abstract/document/8409096

Kumar, B. S., Sridhar, V., & Sudhindra, K. R. (2019). A Case Study: Risk Rating Methodology for E-Governance Application Security Risks. *i-Manager's Journal on Software Engineering, 13*(3), 39. www.proquest.com/openview/ee2f52533cd40f06b66288ca835e4501/1?pq-origsite=gscholar&cbl=2030612

Kumar, C., Singh, A. K., & Kumar, P. (2018). A recent survey on image watermarking techniques and its application in e-governance. *Multimedia Tools and Applications, 77*(3), 3597–3622. doi:10.100711042-017-5222-8

Kuutti, S., Bowden, R., Jin, Y., Barber, P., & Fallah, S. (2020). A survey of deep learning applications to autonomous vehicle control. *IEEE Transactions on Intelligent Transportation Systems, 22*(2), 712–733. doi:10.1109/TITS.2019.2962338

Lee, S., Abdullah, A., Jhanjhi, N., & Kok, S. (2021). Classification of botnet attacks in IoT smart factory using honeypot combined with machine learning. *PeerJ. Computer Science, 7*, e350. doi:10.7717/peerj-cs.350 PMID:33817000

Lee, S. M., Seo, J. B., Yun, J., Cho, Y.-H., Vogel-Claussen, J., Schiebler, M. L., Gefter, W. B., van Beek, E. J. R., Goo, J. M., Lee, K. S., Hatabu, H., Gee, J., & Kim, N. (2019). Deep learning applications in chest radiography and computed tomography. *Journal of Thoracic Imaging, 34*(2), 75–85. doi:10.1097/RTI.0000000000000387 PMID:30802231

Loukas, G., Patrikakis, C. Z., & Wilbanks, L. R. (2020). Digital deception: Cyber fraud and online misinformation. *IT Professional, 22*(2), 19–20. doi:10.1109/MITP.2020.2980090

Mehta, S., Sharma, A., Chawla, P., & Soni, K. (2021, May). The Urgency of Cyber Security in Secure Networks. In *2021 5th International Conference on Intelligent Computing and Control Systems (ICICCS)* (pp. 315-322). IEEE. https://ieeexplore. ieee.org/abstract/document/9432092

Nadrah, R., Gambour, Y., Kurdi, R., & Almansouri, R. (2021). E-government service in Saudi Arabia. *PalArch's Journal of Archaeology of Egypt/Egyptology, 18*(16), 21-29. https://archives.palarch.nl/index.php/jae/article/view/8156

Ozdemir, R., & Koc, M. (2019, September). A quality control application on a smart factory prototype using deep learning methods. In *2019 IEEE 14th International Conference on Computer Sciences and Information Technologies (CSIT)* (Vol. 1, pp. 46-49). IEEE. https://ieeexplore.ieee.org/abstract/document/8929734

Panwar, H., Gupta, P. K., Siddiqui, M. K., Morales-Menendez, R., & Singh, V. (2020). Application of deep learning for fast detection of COVID-19 in X-Rays using nCOVnet. *Chaos, Solitons, and Fractals, 138*, 109944. doi:10.1016/j. chaos.2020.109944 PMID:32536759

Pathirage, C. S. N., Li, J., Li, L., Hao, H., Liu, W., & Wang, R. (2019). Development and application of a deep learning–based sparse autoencoder framework for structural damage identification. *Structural Health Monitoring, 18*(1), 103–122. doi:10.1177/1475921718800363

Purwins, H., Li, B., Virtanen, T., Schlüter, J., Chang, S. Y., & Sainath, T. (2019). Deep learning for audio signal processing. *IEEE Journal of Selected Topics in Signal Processing, 13*(2), 206–219. doi:10.1109/JSTSP.2019.2908700

Romaniuk, S. N., & Omona, D. A. (2021). Building a Cyber Fortress in Africa: Uganda's cyber security capacities and challenges. In *Routledge Companion to Global Cyber-Security Strategy* (pp. 573–590). Routledge. doi:10.4324/9780429399718-49

Sahoo, B., Behera, R. N., & Mohanty, S. (2018, July). International Cyber Attackers Eyeing Eastern India: Odisha-A Case Study. In *Science and Information Conference* (pp. 1328–1339). Springer. https://link.springer.com/ chapter/10.1007/978-3-030-01177-2_97

Sambana, B., Raju, K. N., Satish, D., Raju, S. S., & Raja, P. V. K. (2021). *Impact of Cyber Security in e-Governance and e-Commerce* (No. 5533). EasyChair. file:///C:/ Users/USER/Downloads/EasyChair-Preprint-5533%20(1).pdf

Setiya, R., Pandey, S., Singh, A. K., & Sharma, D. K. (2021). Citizen e-governance using blockchain. In *Blockchain for Smart Cities* (pp. 119–152). Elsevier. doi:10.1016/ B978-0-12-824446-3.00010-7

Shah, Rajper, & ZamanJhanjhi. (2021). Using ML and Data-Mining Techniques in Automatic Vulnerability Software Discovery. *International Journal (Toronto, Ont.)*, *10*, 3.

Sharma, L., & Singh, V. (2018, October). India Towards Digital Revolution (Security and Sustainability). In *2018 Second World Conference on Smart Trends in Systems, Security and Sustainability (WorldS4)* (pp. 297-302). IEEE. https://ieeexplore.ieee.org/abstract/document/8611564

Shivpuri, D. (2021). Cyber Crime: Are the Law Outdated for this Type of Crime. *International Journal of Research in Engineering, Science and Management, 4*(7), 44-49. https://www.journals.resaim.com/ijresm/article/view/958

Shorten, C., Khoshgoftaar, T. M., & Furht, B. (2021). Deep Learning applications for COVID-19. *Journal of Big Data, 8*(1), 1–54. doi:10.118640537-020-00392-9 PMID:33457181

Singh, K. B., & Arat, M. A. (2019). *Deep learning in the automotive industry: Recent advances and application examples.* https://arxiv.org/abs/1906.08834

Sit, M., Demiray, B. Z., Xiang, Z., Ewing, G. J., Sermet, Y., & Demir, I. (2020). A comprehensive review of deep learning applications in hydrology and water resources. *Water Science and Technology, 82*(12), 2635–2670. doi:10.2166/wst.2020.369 PMID:33341760

Sujatha, R., Chatterjee, J. M., Jhanjhi, N. Z., & Brohi, S. N. (2021). Performance of deep learning vs machine learning in plant leaf disease detection. *Microprocessors and Microsystems, 80*, 103615. doi:10.1016/j.micpro.2020.103615

Tang, B., Pan, Z., Yin, K., & Khateeb, A. (2019). Recent advances of deep learning in bioinformatics and computational biology. *Frontiers in Genetics, 10*, 214. doi:10.3389/fgene.2019.00214 PMID:30972100

Taormina, R., & Galelli, S. (2018). Deep-learning approach to the detection and localization of cyber-physical attacks on water distribution systems. *Journal of Water Resources Planning and Management, 144*(10), 04018065. doi:10.1061/(ASCE)WR.1943-5452.0000983

Tayyab, M., Marjani, M., Jhanjhi, N. Z., & Hashem, I. A. T. (2021, March). A Light-weight Watermarking-Based Framework on Dataset Using Deep Learning Algorithms. In *2021 National Computing Colleges Conference (NCCC)* (pp. 1-6). IEEE. https://ieeexplore.ieee.org/abstract/document/9428845

Thabit, T. H., & Jasim, Y. A. (2019). The challenges of adopting E-governance in Iraq. *Current Res. J. Soc. Sci. & Human., 2*, 31. https://heinonline.org/HOL/LandingPage?handle=hein.journals/crjssh2&div=6&id=&page=

Tkatchenko, A. (2020). Machine learning for chemical discovery. *Nature Communications, 11*(1), 1–4. doi:10.103841467-020-17844-8 PMID:32807794

Veeramani, K., & Jaganathan, S. (2020). Land registration: Use-case of e-Governance using blockchain technology. *Transactions on Internet and Information Systems (Seoul), 14*(9), 3693–3711. https://www.koreascience.or.kr/article/JAKO202030161655507.page

Wang, H., Ruan, J., Wang, G., Zhou, B., Liu, Y., Fu, X., & Peng, J. (2018). Deep learning-based interval state estimation of AC smart grids against sparse cyber attacks. *IEEE Transactions on Industrial Informatics, 14*(11), 4766–4778. doi:10.1109/TII.2018.2804669

Witti, M., & Konstantas, D. (2018, December). A secure and privacy-preserving internet of things framework for smart city. In *Proceedings of the 6th International Conference on Information Technology* (pp. 145–150). IoT and Smart City. doi:10.1145/3301551.3301607

Xin, Y., Kong, L., Liu, Z., Chen, Y., Li, Y., Zhu, H., Gao, M., Hou, H., & Wang, C. (2018). Machine learning and deep learning methods for cybersecurity. *IEEE Access: Practical Innovations, Open Solutions, 6*, 35365–35381. doi:10.1109/ACCESS.2018.2836950

Zhang, T., Gao, C., Ma, L., Lyu, M., & Kim, M. (2019, October). An empirical study of common challenges in developing deep learning applications. In *2019 IEEE 30th International Symposium on Software Reliability Engineering (ISSRE)* (pp. 104-115). IEEE. https://ieeexplore.ieee.org/abstract/document/8987482

Chapter 8
The Impact of Cyber Attacks on E-Governance During the COVID-19 Pandemic

N. Z. Jhanjhi
https://orcid.org/0000-0001-8116-4733
Taylor's University, Malaysia

Muhammad Amir Khan
https://orcid.org/0000-0003-3669-2080
COMSATS University Islamabad, Abbottabad, Pakistan

Muneer Ahmad
https://orcid.org/0000-0001-5047-1108
National University of Science and Technology, Pakistan

Manzoor Hussain
Indus University, Pakistan

ABSTRACT

A cyber-attack can damage data, computer programs, and network one or more computers through applying different methods and cybercriminal's activities to steal information. The increasing of new technologies among the users facilities them. The cyber-attacks are growing tremendously. E-governance is an application of IT and giving online services. These days the world is completely focused on creating social distance among the people, and billions of peoples around the world are working from home (online activities) and shops, and businesses are closed in the COVID-19 pandemic, which the WHO recommended. A remarkable cyber-crime has been recorded by the researcher's study in this environment, affecting society and businesses. This research's primary objective is to find cyber-attacks that steal information in the COVID-19 pandemic and assess the user loss. The results of five years have been compared on the machine learning techniques.

DOI: 10.4018/978-1-7998-9624-1.ch008

1. INTRODUCTION

The covid-19 is a new virus that is related to the same family of viruses. This is a national emergency and collectively steps are made by the world's forums and organizations to face this disease till getting an accurate vaccine of this virus and smoothly running life. In this situation, the WHO recommended creating social distance among the people. Billions of people around the world are working from home and operating businesses from home, such as financial transactions, buy and selling, shopping, etc. Presently, the world remains in shock of covid-19 attacks and broadly impacts on business activities and rising threats to many aspects, such as economy, politics, health, and security. World Health Organization WHO has apprised that during the covid-19 pandemic that may happen all over the world in the economic aspect and it can cause huge losses due to the situation this pandemic also changed the way of organization and Government's departments' activities. They are operating online activities and instruction from home. E-governance is being speedily implemented all over the world for giving seamless facilities to the citizens. While the threats and attacks are also increasing to the organization and digital data. Indonesia has predicted future threats and risks, it needs huge investment to deal with this virus, especially in health (McKibbin & Fernando, 2020). It is very important to estimate the current gap, strengthen health structure, funding, and management, and increase the research measurements and evidence-based strategy making (Rodela et al., 2020). Government and Private Organizations are essential to securing information and data. The detailed report of GESTR 2019 apprised that 42% of endpoints are insecure (Ahmad, 2020). Cyber-crime and cyberattacks have been analyzed during the covid-19 pandemic picture-1 and 2 show detail (Lallie et al., 2021). The experts of cybersecurity have appraised that $450 billion annually is the total universal cost of malicious hacking activities. CTI experts have suggested that investigation and examination are necessary for the international online hacker community. The aim of this research is to identify developing threats in terms of admiration and tool functionality (Samtani et al., 2020). The health industries faced great losses due to the growing number of cyber-attacks recently in the medical field. Medical information plays a significant part in human health, a primary object of this research to conduct a comprehensive survey in connection with possible cyber-attacks and finding proper solutions to these types of threats and attacks.(Razaque et al., 2019) The world has estimated the cost of cybersecurity attacks and threats is US $6 trillion a year in 2021, while the number of threats and attacks has bigger increased after COVID-19. The large literature is available in the prospect of health care industries on threats technological vulnerabilities. The author focused on the reason for increasing the number of cybersecurity threats and attacks during the COVID-19 pandemic (Williams et al., 2020). The main object of this chapter is to

Figure 1. Detail of cyberattacks in the different region during the covid-19 pandemic (Williams et al., 2020)

Date	Country	Type of attack	Details of attack
March 2020	Czech Republic	Ransomware	The Brno University Hospital as one of COVID-19 testing laboratories in the country has been hit by a cyber-attack and was forced to shutdown its entire IT network.[16]
March 2020	UK	Ransomware	The Maze ransomware group has published personal and medical details of thousands of former patients of a London-based medical research company which provide COVID-19 testing.[17]
March 2020	France	DDoS	The systems of a group of hospitals in Paris which plays an important role in fighting COVID-19 crisis in the capital were the target of a DDoS attacks disrupted access to server and email.[18]
March 2020	US	DDoS	The US Department of Health and Human Services Department which heavily dealing with COVID-19 issue in the country were the target of a DDoS attacks.[24]
May 2020	Taiwan	Phishing	Emails contained a remote access hacking tool impersonating Taiwan's top infection-disease official urging recipients to get coronavirus tests.[19]
June 2020	Germany	Phishing	Phishing emails to senior executives at the company which supply personal protective equipment (PPE). The phishing links were designed to direct executives to fake Microsoft login pages to steal their credentials.[20]
June 2020	US	Ransomware	The University of California San Francisco (UCSF) which working on COVID-19 vaccine was the target of a ransomware attacks and forced to pay $1.14 m to cybercriminals called Netwalker.[21]
June 2020	Canada	Ransomware	CryCryptor ransomware masquerades as COVID-19 contact-tracing apps on Android device.[22]

focus on the last ten years' research articles of cybersecurity threats and attacks that were founded on the e-government applications and emerging technologies for the measurement of cybersecurity. The result of this research will be analyzed on the machine learning techniques.

This research's main objective is to find cyber-attacks and steal information in the Covid-19 Pandemic and assess the user's loss on machine learning techniques.

2. LITERATURE REVIEW

The covid-19 pandemic has moved online implementation of digital technologies, such as shopping, industry, finance transactions, and business activities. Unfortunately, the ratio of cybercrimes is rising in frequency and severity, latest reports published (Samtani et al., 2020). Has identified the top ten cybersecurity threats which were

Figure 2. Cyber-attacks different region during the covid-19 pandemic (Hiscox, 2019)

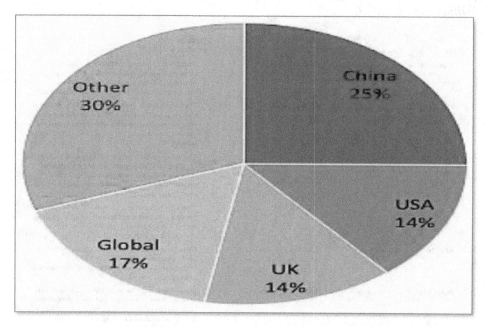

recorded by the researcher during the covid-19 picture-3 shows the detail (Razaque et al., 2019). Has investigated for endorsing future research and emerging to produce solutions using AI, HPC, 3DPT, TT, and BDA (Williams et al., 2020). The ratio of cybersecurity issues has increased due to staff working from homes, such as ransomware and phishing. The author has given several practical approaches to decrease the risks of cyber-attacks (Hiscox, 2019). Has identified significant cybersecurity challenges in a review article on grooving the cyberattacks during the covid-19 pandemic (ransomware and phishing campaigns attacks) (Khan et al., 2020). The IT industry and professionals have taken huge benefits to provide services and applications. While a few undesirable influences as well, growing new cybersecurity risk and threats due to highway workload and continuously increasing, picture-4 shows the detail (Brohi et al., 2020). WHO has apprised that a dramatically growing number of cyber-attacks are directed at its staff, and email scams targeting the public at large (He et al., 2021). Highlighted several cybersecurity challenges linked during the pandemic and cybersecurity involve lack of budgets. Security and Privacy are yet big queries in human-computer interactions HCI (Weil & Murugesan, 2020). Pandemic has wedged the route of EU cybersecurity policy. From the crisis of the Pandemic, the significant growing cybersecurity risk and businesses, citizens, and states are facing (World Health Organization, 2020). The growing level of IT and computer use in a pandemic will disturb the scale of cybercrime vulnerability behavior (Ferreira & Cruz-Correia, 2021). The pandemic led to broader use of digital applications prompting government and business activities to change whole work processes that have been done online. The passable actions have been implemented and are increasing the dependence of government and private sector proper running of their IT systems. It has been said that millions of people work from their homes during the pandemic. Further, it has highlighted security risks and threats (Carrapico & Farrand, 2020). The pandemic has accelerated the move to practical workplace ecosystems for the government's employees and businesses. The Dramatic move of the workplace has created novel multi-layered challenges around handling cybersecurity risk and threats (Wijayanto & Prabowo, 2020). Research articles have been reviewed on the cybersecurity influence of the coronavirus fear on digital systems and cyberspace. Additionally, recommendations have been made to privacy protection online applications (Wiggen, 2020). Top priority has been given to the citizens, the problem of cybersecurity in the medical domain instead of the given priority to a real threat to national security during a pandemic and measuring the implementation of cybersecurity and spreading fake news (Burrell, 2020). It has highlighted the influence of government and e-government performance on the implementation of e-government facilities by integrating it into the Technology Acceptance Model (TAM). It was exposed in the TAM that positively to be seen in the prediction of e-government performance. Figure-3 shows the cyber-attacks (Okereafor & Adebola, 2020). There is an inevitable development of e-government clouds throughout the world, and a growing need to explore the determinants and their mechanism of e-Government cloud implementation among the government agencies in China. Picture-4 shows the detail of data and Figure-5 shows the concept of e-Government (Karpenko et al., 2021). With the number of cybersecurity attacks and threats continually increasing, organization adopters have responded to security concerns that threaten their business in today's highly competitive environment. Several documented industrial cyber-attacks have effectively compressed technical solutions that are exploited by human-factor vulnerabilities linked to security skills and knowledge. This article focuses on human knowledge based on security knowledge and security skills to highlight the security capabilities and their quantity. Demonstrates authenticity by providing a framework and computational method (Mensah, 2019). Today, IoT, cloud computing, social networks mobile, and mobile are making changes in the social procedure. This technology transformation stands for new security attacks and threats in complex cybersecurity situations with huge capacities of data and different attack vectors. Which may exceed the academic capabilities of security analysts. This paper presents a reasoning security model that combines security solutions (Gupta & Agarwal, 2017; Williams et al., 2020). The rise of information and communication technology has met new challenges that are essential to be addressed, including the security of citizens.

Figure 3. Cyber-attacks (Okereafor & Adebola, 2020)

Figure 4. IC3 core function (Karpenko et al., 2021)

COLLECTION	ANALYSIS	PUBLIC AWARENESS	REFERRALS
The IC3 is the central point for Internet crime victims to report and alert the appropriate agencies to suspected criminal Internet activity. Victims are encouraged and often directed by law enforcement to file a complaint online at www.ic3.gov. Complainants are asked to document accurate and complete information related to Internet crime, as well as any other relevant information necessary to support the complaint.	The IC3 reviews and analyzes data submitted through its website to identify emerging threats and new trends.	Public service announcements, industry alerts, and other publications outlining specific scams are posted to the www.ic3.gov website. As more people become aware of Internet crimes and the methods used to carry them out, potential victims are equipped with a broader understanding of the dangers associated with Internet activity and are in a better position to avoid falling prey to schemes online.	The IC3 aggregates related complaints to build referrals, which are forwarded to local, state, federal, and international law enforcement agencies for potential investigation. If law enforcement conducts an investigation and determines a crime has been committed, legal action may be brought against the perpetrator.

3. CYBERSECURITY ATTACKS AND MEASUREMENTS (SA&M)

Attempts from any person to obtain illegal access to a computer or computer network in the interest of damaging data or information from the computer systems. The object of cyber-attacks to destroy, disable, block, delete, disrupt and steal information

Figure 5. Detail of international Victim Counter(Mensah, 2019)

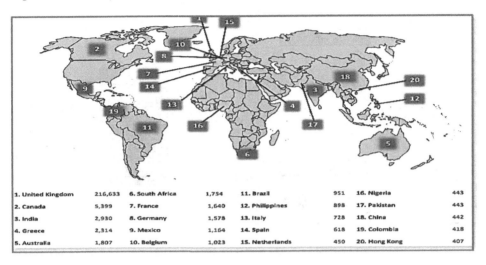

1. United Kingdom	216,633	6. South Africa	1,754	11. Brazil	951	16. Nigeria	443
2. Canada	5,399	7. France	1,640	12. Philippines	898	17. Pakistan	443
3. India	2,930	8. Germany	1,578	13. Italy	728	18. China	442
4. Greece	2,314	9. Mexico	1,164	14. Spain	618	19. Colombia	418
5. Australia	1,807	10. Belgium	1,023	15. Netherlands	450	20. Hong Kong	407

from the computer system Picture-7 shows the detail. The growing population in the world, another side the cyber-attacks and threats are also increasing in variation and frequency, such as cyber terrorism, cybercrime, cyber ware, cyber espionage, etc. This article has focused on identifying the vulnerable target and its assessment impact on the economy (Liang et al., 2017; Mensah, 2019). Cyber-attacks create problems that are harmful to the economy, human privacy, and national security. These attacks have various perspectives of problems and need to be understood first. Further, the author proposed to find out the rate of cyber-attacks through modeling and predicting (Liang et al., 2017; Williams et al., 2020). There is widespread implementation of the IoT, the threats and risks are significantly growing and various issues arise on the digital technology of many areas (Gupta & Agarwal, 2017; Williams et al., 2020). The world is interconnected digitally and there are serious issues of targeted attacks and threats to conventional computer systems and serious infrastructure. The 123 articles were reviewed and 60 were identified as related in the context of the study. Chosen the associated articles were broadly reviewed and evaluated (Gupta & Agarwal, 2017; Peng et al., 2017). Has been approached to detect a broad range of cyber-attacks (DDoS) attacks account hijacking, attacks, and data breaches (Peng et al., 2017). A new line of security is required for cyber-attacks in the modern age. Organizations need to collect and share on due time connecting the cyber threat information and give it to threat intelligence (TI) in the interest to stop attacks (Saleem et al., 2017). The result of literature review and publicly presented reports that cyber-attacks are increasing and threatening for the business. The object of this survey is to understand cyber-attack in a systemic process (Luh et al., 2017).

Figure 6. Cybersecurity attacks classification (Tounsi & Rais, 2018)

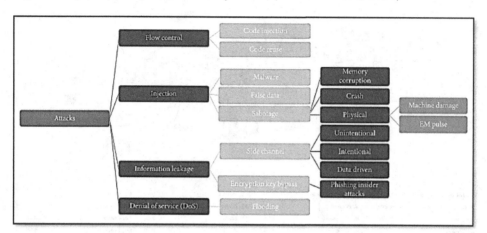

It has been observed by the review article associate IoT and public know that the use of IoT is increasing. Further, various news cyber-attacks are IoT-enabled. This is a survey article linked to IoT-enabled cyber-attacks that were founded altogether in application domains since 2010 (Khandpur et al., 2017). This article is giving an overview of current developments in security control and industrial CPSs and attack detection from a control theory perspective Figure-6 shows the detailed cybersecurity and Figure-7 shows the detailed literature review. (Huang et al., 2018; Tounsi & Rais, 2018).

4. FRAUD COMPLAINTS AND THEFT REPORTS

Fraud complaints have been tracked by the Federal Trade Commission (FTC) that were filed by the state, federal, private organizations and local law agencies. 4.8 million fraud complaints and theft reports have been received by FTC in the year 2020 and 3.3 million in the year 2019, its 113 percent fraud complaints and theft reports, further, the figure-8 shows detail of complaints (Stellios et al., 2018).

5. CYBERCRIME COMPLAINTS

IC3 is to be known as Internet Crime Complaint Center, it plays a significant role to provide reliable and suitable reporting mechanisms to the Federal Bureau of Investigation (FBI) associate suspected internet-facilitated criminal activities and to emerging alliances with industries and law enforcement partners. In 2020 the IC3 came and treated 791, 790 complaints. While 69 percent increased from 467,361 in 2019. Total $4.2 billion losses in 2019. Further, Figure-9 shows the details of losses (Stellios et al., 2018).

Figure 7. Thematic flow diagram of literature review

Figure 8. Identify theft and fraud report from 2016 to 2020 (Stellios et al., 2018)

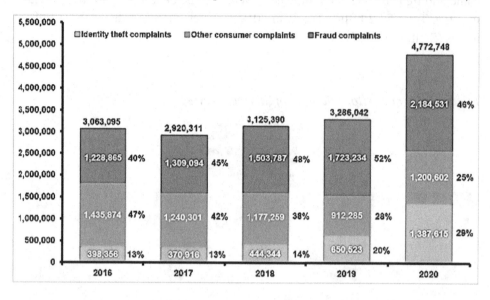

Figure 9. Cybercrime complaints report from 2016 to 2020 (Stellios et al., 2018)

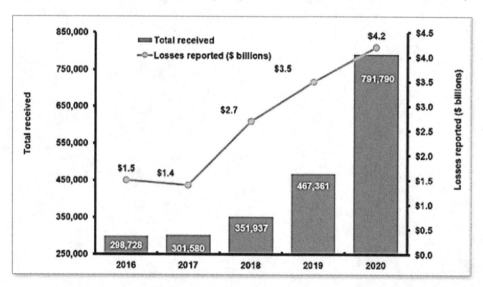

6. COVID-19 PANDEMIC AND CYBER ATTACKS

Recently, interest has increased in cybersecurity in COVID-19 pandemic started. Cybersecurity attacks and threats have been classified based on publicly documented and reported cases and associated review articles during the COVID-19 pandemic, further figure-10 shows the cybersecurity attack types and related references (Ramadan et al., 2021).

Figure 10. Covid-19 cyberattacks and threats (Ramadan et al., 2021)

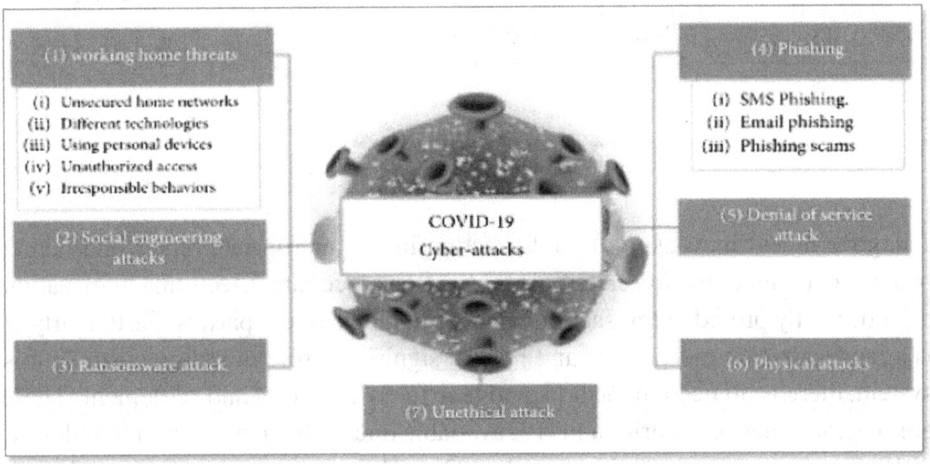

7. WORKING FROM HOME MALICIOUS CYBER THREATS

The COVID-19 pandemic caused many citizens to work for the first time from home. Working from home has other cybersecurity threats, such as intentional cybercrime. When any personal computer or mobile phone is compromised, unauthorized access to the stored information can have a devastating effect on personal, emotional, financial, and working life. Figure-11 classifies the different types of working from home threats. In the following sections, major working from home threats is discussed (Ding et al., 2018; Ramadan et al., 2021).

8. E-GOVERNANCE FRAMEWORK

E-Governance plays a significant role to provide facilities and decrease difficulties for the business, giving fast data, and allowing digital communication to the e-business.

Figure 11. Threats of working from home (Ding et al., 2018)

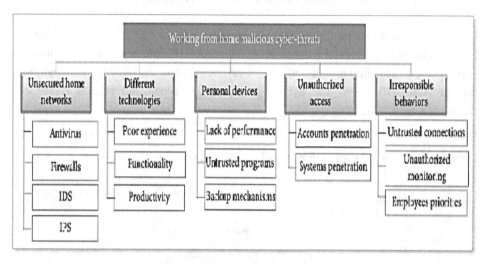

The government is re-using the information in the appropriate report and taking benefits of communication electronic transaction procedure. Electronic information has efficiently provided transaction services to the different parties. Particularly, it is a modernization mechanism and plays a significant role in saving costs. In this system, there is no need to meet face to face for information and settlement. There are several issues of security and risk available due to this new system (Cradduck, 2019; Scarfone et al., 2009; Uyar et al., 2021). The primary aim of this article is to examine the role of e-governance during the fighting covid-19 through participating in the applications of the CPEC. Further, the author focused on analyzing the e-government emerging index, reports, and ranking issues that have been raised by the UN and big data implications in the covid-19 pandemic (Ullah et al., n.d.; Uyar et al., 2021). 65% of the population belongs to rural villages according to the report of the world bank. Further, this has explored that the majority of the population belongs to rural areas in India. Therefore, the Government has a desire to give facilities to the rural people effectively on a top priority basis, to meet their multiple challenges, and provide basic requirements and needs. E-governance plays a significant role to provide due facilities through E-government and it is one of the most successful platforms to communicate rural citizens to rural citizens especially in the covid-19 pandemic situation. The researcher explored in the association different articles that several people are accessing the government websites and getting e-governance health care facilities to take safety measures covid-19 situation Figure-12 shows the concept of the E-government (Bhuvana & Vasantha, 2021; Gaur et al., 2021; Hussain et al., 2021; Lim et al., 2019).

Figure 12. Definition of E-Government (Scarfone et al., 2009)

9. CONCLUSION

A cyber-attack can damage data, computer programs, and network one or more computers through applying different methods and cybercriminal's activities to steal information. The increase of new technologies among the users and giving them more facilities. Cyber-attacks are growing tremendously today. E-governance is an application of IT and giving online services. These days the world is completely focused on creating social distance among the people and billions of peoples around the world are working from home (online activities) and shops and businesses are closed in the Covid-19 pandemic which the WHO recommended. A remarkable cyber-crime has been recorded by the researcher's study in this environment, affecting society and businesses, the comparison of years of losses has been conducted by machine learning, table-1 shows the detail of cyber-attacks and Figure-13 show the research results and comparison last five years. Business email compromise typically involves a criminal mimicking a legitimate email address received from Internet Complaint Center year 2016 losses $298,728, 2017 losses $301,580, 2018 losses $351,937,2019 losses $467,361, 2020 losses $791,790. Further, the result apprised that the year 2020 will remain on top in cyber-attacks during the covid-19 pandemic.

Table-1 shows the results of the research

Year	Identify theft complaints	Percentage	Other Consumer complaints	Percentage	Fraud complaints	Percentage	Total
2016	1,228,865	40%	1,435,874	47%	398,356	13%	3,063,095
2017	1,309,094	45%	1,240,301	42%	370,916	14%	2,920,311
2018	1,503,787	48%	1,177,259	38%	444,344	14%	3,125,390
2019	1,723,234	52%	912,285	28%	650,523	20%	3,286,042
2020	2,184,531	46%	1,200,602	25%	1,387,615	29%	4,772,748

Figure 13. Comparison of Five

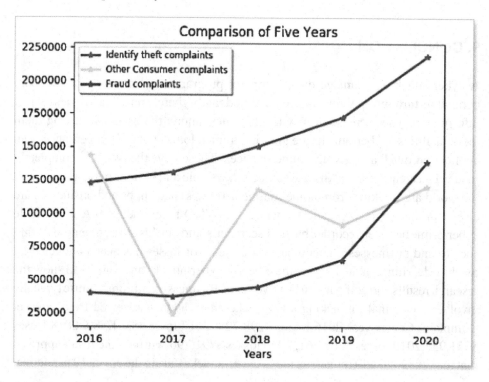

REFERENCES

AhmadT. (2020). *Corona virus (covid-19) pandemic and work from home: Challenges of cybercrimes and cybersecurity.* https://papers.ssrn.com/sol3/papers.cfm?abstract_id=3568830 doi:10.2139/ssrn.3568830

Bhuvana, M., & Vasantha, S. (2021). The Impact of COVID-19 on Rural Citizens for Accessing E-Governance Services: A Conceptual Model Using the Dimensions of Trust and Technology Acceptance Model. *Recent Advances in Technology Acceptance Models and Theories, 335*, 471. https://www.ncbi.nlm.nih.gov/pmc/articles/PMC7979245/

Brohi, S. N., Jhanjhi, N. Z., Brohi, N. N., & Brohi, M. N. (2020). *Key Applications of State-of-the-Art technologies to mitigate and eliminate COVID-19.* file:///C:/Users/imdad/Downloads/Key%20Applications%20of%20State-of-the-Art%20Technologies%20to%20Mitigate%20and%20Eliminate%20COVID-19%20(1).pdf

Burrell, D. N. (2020). Understanding the talent management intricacies of remote cybersecurity teams in covid-19 induced telework organizational ecosystems. *Land Forces Academy Review, 25*(3), 232-244. https://www.armyacademy.ro/reviste/rev3_2020/Burrell.pdf

Carrapico, H., & Farrand, B. (2020). Discursive continuity and change in the time of Covid-19: The case of EU cybersecurity policy. *journal of European Integration, 42*(8), 1111–1126. doi:10.1080/07036337.2020.1853122

Cradduck, L. (2019). E-conveyancing: a consideration of its risks and rewards. *Property Management.* https://www.emerald.com/insight/content/doi/10.1108/PM-04-2019-0021/full/html

Ding, D., Han, Q.-L., Xiang, Y., Ge, X., & Zhang, X.-M. (2018). A survey on security control and attack detection for industrial cyber-physical systems. *Neurocomputing, 275*, 1674–1683. doi:10.1016/j.neucom.2017.10.009

Ferreira, A., & Cruz-Correia, R. (2021). COVID-19 and cybersecurity: finally, an opportunity to disrupt? *JMIRx Med, 2*(2), e21069. https://xmed.jmir.org/2021/2/e21069/

Gaur, L., Bhatia, U., Jhanjhi, N. Z., Muhammad, G., & Masud, M. (2021). Medical image-based detection of COVID-19 using Deep Convolution Neural Networks. *Multimedia Systems*, 1–10. doi:10.100700530-021-00794-6 PMID:33935377

Gupta, R., & Agarwal, S. P. (2017). A Comparative Study of Cyber Threats in Emerging Economies. *Globus: An International Journal of Management & IT, 8*(2), 24-28. https://globusjournal.com/wp-content/uploads/2018/07/826Ruchika.pdf

He, Y., Aliyu, A., Evans, M., & Luo, C. (2021). Health Care Cybersecurity Challenges and Solutions Under the Climate of COVID-19: Scoping Review. *Journal of Medical Internet Research, 23*(4), e21747. doi:10.2196/21747 PMID:33764885

Hiscox. (2019). *The hiscox cyber readiness report 2019.* https://www.sciencedirect. com/science/article/pii/S0167404821000729

Huang, K., Siegel, M., & Madnick, S. (2018). Systematically understanding the cyber attack business: A survey. *ACM Computing Surveys, 51*(4), 1–36. doi:10.1145/3199674

Hussain, S. J., Irfan, M., Jhanjhi, N. Z., Hussain, K., & Humayun, M. (2021). Performance enhancement in wireless body area networks with secure communication. *Wireless Personal Communications, 116*(1), 1–22. doi:10.100711277-020-07702-7 PMID:33558792

III. (n.d.). https://www.iii.org/fact-statistic/facts-statistics-identity-theft-and-cybercrime

Karpenko, O., Kuczabski, A., & Havryliak, V. (2021). Mechanisms for providing cybersecurity during the COVID-19 pandemic: Perspectives for Ukraine. *Security and Defence Quarterly.* http://yadda.icm.edu.pl/yadda/element/bwmeta1.element. doi-10_35467_sdq_133158

Khan, N. A., Brohi, S. N., & Zaman, N. (2020). *Ten deadly cyber security threats amid COVID-19 pandemic.* https://www.techrxiv.org/articles/preprint/Ten_Deadly_ Cyber_Security_Threats_Amid_COVID-19_Pandemic/12278792/1

Khandpur, R. P., Ji, T., Jan, S., Wang, G., Lu, C. T., & Ramakrishnan, N. (2017, November). Crowdsourcing cybersecurity: Cyber attack detection using social media. In *Proceedings of the 2017 ACM on Conference on Information and Knowledge Management* (pp. 1049-1057). https://dl.acm.org/doi/abs/10.1145/3132847.3132866

Lallie, H. S., Shepherd, L. A., Nurse, J. R., Erola, A., Epiphaniou, G., Maple, C., & Bellekens, X. (2021). Cyber security in the age of covid-19: A timeline and analysis of cyber-crime and cyber-attacks during the pandemic. *Computers & Security, 105*, 102248. doi:10.1016/j.cose.2021.102248

Liang, Y., Qi, G., Wei, K., & Chen, J. (2017). Exploring the determinant and influence mechanism of e-Government cloud adoption in government agencies in China. *Government Information Quarterly, 34*(3), 481–495. doi:10.1016/j.giq.2017.06.002

Lim, M., Abdullah, A., & Jhanjhi, N. Z. (2019). Performance optimization of criminal network hidden link prediction model with deep reinforcement learning. *Journal of King Saud University-Computer and Information Sciences.* https://onlinelibrary. wiley.com/doi/abs/10.1002/ett.4171

Luh, R., Marschalek, S., Kaiser, M., Janicke, H., & Schrittwieser, S. (2017). Semantics-aware detection of targeted attacks: A survey. *Journal of Computer Virology and Hacking Techniques, 13*(1), 47–85. doi:10.100711416-016-0273-3

McKibbin, W., & Fernando, R. (2020). The economic impact of COVID-19. *Economics in the Time of COVID-19, 45*. https://www.incae.edu/sites/default/files/covid-19.pdf#page=52

Mensah, I. K. (2019). Impact of government capacity and E-government performance on the adoption of E-Government services. *International Journal of Public Administration*. https://www.tandfonline.com/doi/10.1080/01900692.2019.1628059

Okereafor, K., & Adebola, O. (2020). Tackling the cybersecurity impacts of the coronavirus outbreak as a challenge to internet safety. *Int J IT Eng, 8*(2). https://papers.ssrn.com/sol3/papers.cfm?abstract_id=3568830

Peng, C., Xu, M., Xu, S., & Hu, T. (2017). Modeling and predicting extreme cyber attack rates via marked point processes. *Journal of Applied Statistics, 44*(14), 2534–2563. doi:10.1080/02664763.2016.1257590

Ramadan, R. A., Aboshosha, B. W., Alshudukhi, J. S., Alzahrani, A. J., El-Sayed, A., & Dessouky, M. M. (2021). Cybersecurity and Countermeasures at the Time of Pandemic. *Journal of Advanced Transportation, 2021*, 1–19. doi:10.1155/2021/6627264

Razaque, A., Amsaad, F., Khan, M. J., Hariri, S., Chen, S., Siting, C., & Ji, X. (2019). Survey: Cybersecurity vulnerabilities, attacks and solutions in the medical domain. *IEEE Access: Practical Innovations, Open Solutions, 7*, 168774–168797. doi:10.1109/ACCESS.2019.2950849

Rodela, T. T., Tasnim, S., Mazumder, H., Faizah, F., Sultana, A., & Hossain, M. M. (2020). Economic Impacts of Coronavirus Disease (COVID-19) in Developing Countries. doi:10.31235/osf.io/wygpk

Saleem, J., Adebisi, B., Ande, R., & Hammoudeh, M. (2017, July). A state of the art survey-Impact of cyber attacks on SME's. *Proceedings of the International Conference on Future Networks and Distributed Systems*. https://dl.acm.org/doi/abs/10.1145/3102304.3109812

Samtani, S., Zhu, H., & Chen, H. (2020). Proactively Identifying Emerging Hacker Threats from the Dark Web: A Diachronic Graph Embedding Framework (D-GEF). *ACM Transactions on Privacy and Security, 23*(4), 1-33. https://dl.acm.org/doi/abs/10.1145/3409289

Scarfone, K., Hoffman, P., & Souppaya, M. (2009). Guide to enterprise telework and remote access security. *NIST Special Publication, 800*, 46. https://csrc.nist.rip/library/alt-SP800-46r1.pdf

Stellios, I., Kotzanikolaou, P., Psarakis, M., Alcaraz, C., & Lopez, J. (2018). A survey of iot-enabled cyberattacks: Assessing attack paths to critical infrastructures and services. *IEEE Communications Surveys and Tutorials, 20*(4), 3453–3495. doi:10.1109/COMST.2018.2855563

Tounsi, W., & Rais, H. (2018). A survey on technical threat intelligence in the age of sophisticated cyber attacks. *Computers & Security, 72*, 212–233. doi:10.1016/j.cose.2017.09.001

Ullah, A., Pinglu, C., Ullah, S., Abbas, H. S. M., & Khan, S. (n.d.). *The Role of E-Governance in Combating COVID-19 and Promoting Sustainable Development: A Comparative Study of China and Pakistan*. https://link.springer.com/article/10.1007/s41111-020-00167-w

Uyar, A., Nimer, K., Kuzey, C., Shahbaz, M., & Schneider, F. (2021). Can e-government initiatives alleviate tax evasion? The moderation effect of ICT. *Technological Forecasting and Social Change, 166*, 120597. doi:10.1016/j.techfore.2021.120597

Weil, T., & Murugesan, S. (2020). IT Risk and Resilience-Cybersecurity Response to COVID-19. *IT Professional, 22*(3), 4–10. doi:10.1109/MITP.2020.2988330

Wiggen, J. (2020). *Impact of COVID-19 on cyber crime and state-sponsored cyber activities*. Konrad Adenauer Stiftung. https://www.jstor.org/stable/pdf/resrep25300.pdf?acceptTC=true&coverpage=false

Wijayanto, H., & Prabowo, I. A. (2020). Cybersecurity Vulnerability Behavior Scale in College During the Covid-19 Pandemic. *Jurnal Sisfokom (Sistem Informasi dan Komputer), 9*(3), 395-399. https://www.aimspress.com/article/id/6087e948ba35de2200eea776

Williams, C. M., Chaturvedi, R., & Chakravarthy, K. (2020). Cybersecurity Risks in a Pandemic. *Journal of Medical Internet Research, 22*(9), e23692. doi:10.2196/23692 PMID:32897869

World Health Organization. (2020). *WHO reports fivefold increase in cyber-attacks, urges vigilance. WHO reports fivefold increase in cyber attacks, urges vigilance*. WHO.

Chapter 9

The Consequences of Integrity Attacks on E-Governance:
Privacy and Security Violation

Manzoor Hussain
Indus University, Pakistan

Mir Sajjad Hussain Talpur
Sindh Agriculture University, Tandojam, Pakistan

Mamoona Humayun
ⓘ https://orcid.org/0000-0001-6339-2257
Jouf University, Saudi Arabia

ABSTRACT

With the development of new advanced technology, people's expectations and grievances of improving services and values in all aspects of life are growing. Changes in technology are offering better solutions to problems, hence improving existing systems. At the same time, new technologies are presenting new security and privacy violations. As information resources become more digitized, infrastructure and digital data are also facing increasing challenges. For advanced nations, the security parameters and optimization techniques have been thoroughly tested and are in good working order. However, these issues have yet to be adequately addressed in developing countries. An unauthorized person applies several different methods and techniques in the modern age for getting self-profit. The major goal of the research is to discover and assess the implications of integrity attacks and threats that have been used in e-governance research during the last 15 years. This research will be supported in assessing the security of various organizations that are working under e-governance.

DOI: 10.4018/978-1-7998-9624-1.ch009

Figure 1. Health Data Breaches (HIPAA Journal, 2021)

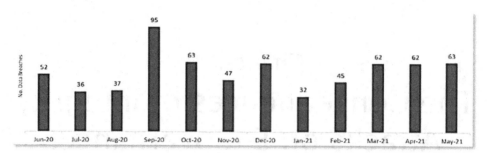

INTRODUCTION

Cyber-attacks damage your businesses and can reduce your customers' faith in you. As a result, there's a chance you'll lose customers. Sales are down. It's no secret that as new technologies emerge, so do new opportunities for illicit activity. They pose a threat not only to the narrow-minded but also to the world's active progress. The sum of money. The accumulation of data follows a geometrical pattern that leads to a compromise of some sort. Confidentiality, integrity, and availability are the three pillars of information security (Reda et al., 2021), (Najmi et al., 2021). A growing number of cyber security holes have harmed corporate competence in the modern technological era, particularly in the context of Industry 4.0, by exploiting the vulnerabilities of networked business gear. In some circumstances, cyber-attacks on critical industrial equipment can undermine a company's business model (Humayun, 2021), (Saleh et al., n.d.). There has been a substantial increase in cyber security research to aid cyber applications and prevent major security flaws that these apps face. (Humayun, 2021). The rapid rise of IoT and broad acceptance of wireless technology has opened up new development opportunities in a range of real-world sectors, like e-health & smart cities applications (Almusaylim et al., 2020). We observe that the clicks we make on our computer machine bring us to a wealth of fresh knowledge while we are taking a break, eating lunch, resting, or unplugging from the information network for a few moments. However, we now have access to hundreds of new software programs and apps in the field of information technology Figure-1 (Jashari & Avdyli, 2020), (Matteson, 2021).

We expect that this paper makes a comprehensive overview of the consequences of Integrity Attacks on E-Governance, Privacy, and security violation and focused to discover and assess the implications of integrity attacks and threats. Our study provides deep discussion, suggests effective findings and critical evaluation.

Health Data Breaches have increased and their severity is 6,535,130 according to the healthcare records. The breaches have crossed 63 incidents and the record of healthcare exposes for each month is 3,323,116. Additionally, the past 12 months have 40 million recorded (HIPAA Journal, 2021)

LITERATURE REVIEW

The author focused to identify how possible is to implement efficiently e-government perform securely like a developing country. This study focuses on Estonia and the way this country has been analyzed which were taken regarding e-government (Adeodato & Pournouri, 2020). To maintain the security of large data in e-government, determining the data's dependability has become a crucial first step. This study focuses on e-government large data dependability evaluation, evaluates the limitations of classic iterative filtering algorithms as a starting point for research, and concludes that traditional algorithms cannot withstand joint attacks. A novel iterative filtering algorithm is proposed by redesigning the old approach. This strategy has the benefits of data aggregation, resistance to simple and combined attacks, and is an excellent way to assess data trustworthiness Figure-4 (Hoque et al., 2018). Since the internet became a part of life, data security has always been a contentious issue. The internet, Web 2.0, and Web 3.0 have made it possible for citizens to use a wide range of applications. One of them is e-government. Data security in E-government apps and services has always been a source of concern. This article examines the effectiveness of security policies in the face of threats and vulnerabilities. These issues will be examined from the viewpoint of the Saudi Arabian e-government of Saudi Arabian. When it comes to security, e-government, anywhere in the globe, is a very delicate issue (Fu, 2020). People can communicate and obtain information more easily with the help of (ICT). Strategic information must be protected, and stakeholders must be aware of any potential vulnerabilities in information and communication system transactions. To develop information security in e-government, various requirements must be accomplished. Confidentiality and privacy are the fundamental requirements. The Republic of Indonesia's Ministry of Law and Human Rights is currently integrating e-government in internal business operations and public services. The utilization of the Correctional Database System is one of them (SDP). Because one of them includes data, the data and information in SDP are confidential. The research method employed was a qualitative method with a case study approach, and the defense in depth model was used to assess information security incorporating multiple levels of security to keep information safe. The results of the descriptive study show that the essential concepts of information security, such as confidentiality, integrity, and availability of data, are taken into account in the design and development of SDPs. Information security flaws, on the other hand, are very likely to arise at the layers of host defense, network defense, and physical protection Figure-2 (Shafiq et al.,

2021). The e-governance system allows countries all over the world to access online government services. To make services more accessible to their residents, many governments have built e-governance platforms. However, the system confronts significant difficulties, including security and privacy concerns. The public's trust in the system has been badly weakened as a result of these difficulties. This article examines current research towards protecting the e-governance framework. We found 16 relevant e-governance studies on a variety of platforms. Our research reveals that securing e-government platforms and services with blockchain technology is a viable alternative. As a result, a new paradigm for integrating blockchain into e-governance is offered, with Saudi Arabia as a case study (Assiri et al., 2020), (Zoppelt & Kolagari, 2019), (Dagba, 2020).

E-governance is gaining popularity in several parts of the world. Threats to infrastructure and digital data are also developing within government agencies as resources become more digitized. Security criteria and reform processes are well-regulated in industrialized countries, while security parameters are not yet strictly addressed in emerging countries like India. Based on information system principles, the paper presents a framework for security evaluation between e-governance departments (Khan et al., 2020), (Gupta et al., 2017), (Lim, Abdullah, Jhanjhi, & Supramaniam, 2019), (HIPAA Journal, 2021).

INTEGRITY ATTACKS

In the context of information security, integrity refers to the accuracy and completeness of data. Integrity-focused security processes are designed to keep data from being tampered with or misused by unauthorized individuals. One of the security measures used to maintain the integrity of data is encryption. There are three sorts of attacks: access, denial of service, and reconnaissance (Javed et al., 2020), (Yau, 2021). We investigate how to attack detection techniques that prevent integrity attacks are affected by differential privacy. We look at how an attacker might use differential privacy's extra noise to create covert attacks with the most physical impact on the system (Humayun et al., 2020). We put these attacks to the test on 20 different capacitive MEMS accelerometer models from five different vendors. According to our research, 75% of people are prone to output distorting, and 65% are vulnerable to output control. We demonstrate how to inject bogus steps into a Fitbit using a $5 speaker to demonstrate end-to-end ramifications. We use a malicious music file played from a smartphone's speaker to control the onboard MEMS accelerometer trusted by a local app to fly a toy RC car in our self-stimulating attack (Lim, Abdullah, & Jhanjhi, 2019). We discuss a general approach in which an adversary compromises automobiles via wireless communication networks, manipulates real-time traffic data

Figure 2. Estimate 5-year skill demand growth (HIPAA Journal, 2021)

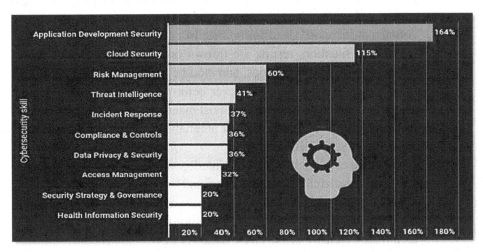

generated or forwarded by these vehicles, and then broadcasts the forged real-time traffic data onto vehicular networks. We provide a formal model of the attack and examine its impact on the effectiveness of route guidance schemes quantitatively (Lim, Abdullah, Jhanjhi, Khan et al, 2019). We investigate the enlarged e-government area on a worldwide scale and in the Russian Federation using a scientometrics technique to address these two challenges. The findings imply that global e-government is a well-defined field, due to limited globalisation and little impulses for knowledge development, Russian e-government research is trailing behind (Saeed et al., 2019).

Data Integrity (DI)

There are DI is constructed on the following four important points that support DI.

1. Enterprise-wide E-W
2. Accuracy & Consistency (A & C)
3. Location Intelligence LI
4. Data enrichment (DE)
   a. E-W: presents a substantial issue in keeping data integrity. When departments run separate systems of software to satisfy its own demands, those organizations have due necessities to bring into line. In several situations, the corporations became celluloid themselves. We share information in supply partners to each other and it reduces resistances in the process of business, but it also increases number of data models, business processes, and software systems, posing data integrity concerns.

b. A & C: Another issue arises as a result of this. Data integrity issues get increasingly difficult as the network's storage capacity and number of computers increase. Even in the best of circumstances, invalid. In the worst-case situation, results are thrown out. With the introduction of IoT devices, smartphone apps, and cloud connectivity, enterprises now have access to more data than ever before. To eliminate these errors, effective data integrity strategies must manage and evaluate data across different systems, identify gaps or anomalies, and mobilize procedures and processes. Qualified.

c. LI: The use of geographic data in intelligence location to decrease risk, better understand customer behaviour, and boost efficiency. Almost every data point on the planet can be linked to somewhere else. Companies, in particular, engaging in digital transformation projects should be considered an intrinsic element of the entire data strategy.

d. DE On a different level, intelligence location can provide context to data that already exists. When we have a greater understanding of the borders, movement, and environment that surrounds a customer, a seller, a business location, or any other company. To make much better business judgments, we can gather as much information as feasible (Hussain et al., 2019), (HIPAA Journal, 2021), (Javed et al., 2020), (Fu, 2020), (Yang et al., 2017).

APPRAISAL OF E-GOVERNMENT

The 2020 survey shows continued progress in global e-government development patterns. Many countries are lowering their EGDI levels. There are 57 countries represented in this season. EGDI ratings of 0.75 to 1.00 are much higher than those of 40 nations in 2018. The number of people in this group has increased by 43%. For a total of 69 countries, EGDI values vary from 0.50 to 0.75. The EGDI group contains 59 countries with values ranging from 0.25 to 0.50. Only eight countries have lower EGDI values (range from 0.00 to 0.25), implying a 50% decrease. The number of countries in this category reached an all-time high in 2018 (Giraldo et al., 2017). With the spread of technologies, the world is undergoing a transformation. It can assist governments in simplifying, speeding up, and securing processes. It may be used to automatically and quickly transfer data across multiple departments. (Trippel et al., 2017). The study focuses mostly on the transaction stage of e-government implementation. Poor ICT infrastructure, insufficient human resources, a lack of citizen readiness to use e-government services, and an unsupportive atmosphere are all challenges to the development of e-government in Indonesia. Due to these difficulties, the Indonesian government should design comprehensive plans and progress assessments that integrate technological, organisation, citizen, and environmental elements to aid in the growth of e-government Figure-3 (Lin et al., 2017), (Khan et al., 2019).

Figure 3. Types of e-government (Javed et al., 2020)

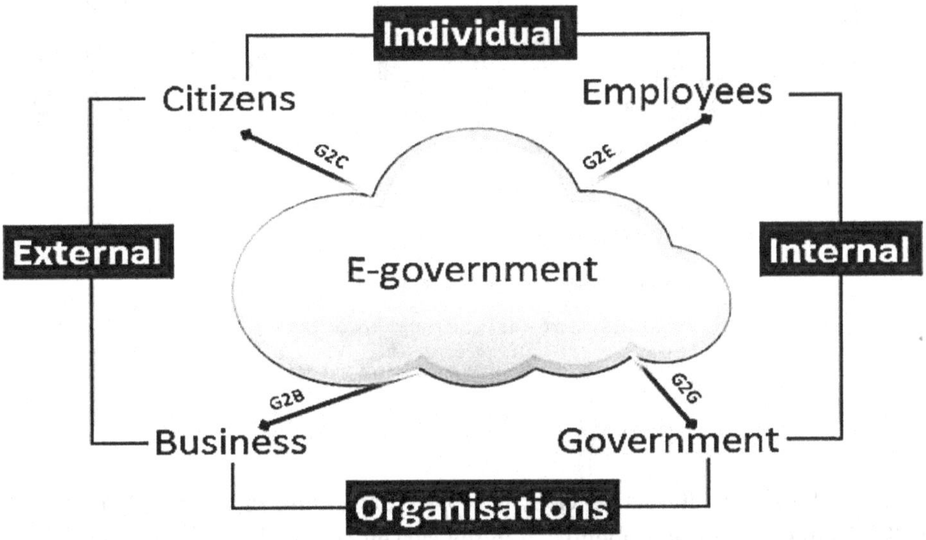

PUBLIC INFORMATION ONLINE SHARED

Helps throughout the general sharing of information and official data effective, accountable, and comprehensive institutions (according to SGD16). As a result, conduct surveys regularly. Examine whether governments share information about certain industries and policies. Official data in machine-readable and non-machine-readable formats are available online. This is to show that there is a positive trend. Sector-specific information is becoming more widespread on dedicated government websites. 80-90% percent of people in member states will have provided information on sector-specific policies and programs by 2020. Many countries also publish their public spending and budgets openly. In comparison to 2018, this number has climbed by around 50%. Sector-related information in machine-readable formats is provided by OGD portals. The very best. There has been an increase in the number of countries with OGD portals in the environment sector. Since 2018, the number of companies offering machine-readable information has risen from 58 to 101 (74 percent) Figure 4 (Sabani et al., 2019).

Figure 4. Trends in sharing public information online, 2020 (Sabani et al., 2019)

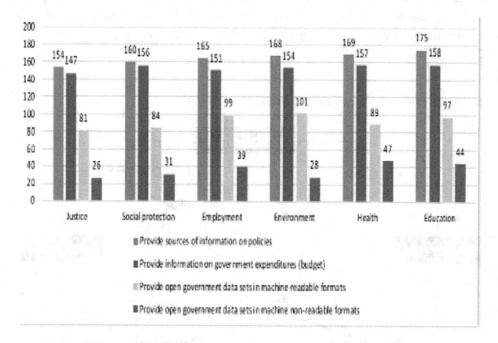

The offering of internet services is rapidly expanding in various domains. 16 of the 20 internet services identified in the survey are available in more than 60% of nations in the United States and Asia. Half of the nations in Africa and Oceania offer 12 to 14 distinct types of online services. Internet services for registering a business and applying for a business license are available in 65-70 percent of African countries. Obtaining birth, death, and marriage certificates, as well as applying for government jobs. Certificates are another popular online service in Africa, with over 55% of countries offering them (Kabanov et al., 2019), (Vardell et al., 2021), (Sambana et al., 2021), (Martins, 2018), (Basyal et al., 2018).

Filing a change of address is the cheapest current online service in Africa, however, it is only offered in 9% of nations. According to 94 percent of countries, the most common internet services in the United States include registering a business, paying for services, and requesting a marriage, birth, or death certificate. Applying for a visa online and reporting a change of address online are two of the most popular services in the region. Around 90% of Asian countries offer online services for business registration and licensing applications. Applying for government positions and paying utilities online are the next two most popular services, with 85 percent and 81 percent of countries in the area offering them, respectively. Automobile registration and address updates are the least current online services (offered by less than half of

Asian countries). Applying for government jobs is the most popular online service in Oceania (86 percent), while motor vehicle registration is the least popular (14 percent). In truth, online automotive registration is one of the few choices available in each location (20 percent of countries in Africa, 46 percent in the United States, 47 percent in Asia, and 72 percent in Europe). During the last two years, the most significant growth in online service delivery has occurred in business enrolment, registering for a birth/marriage certificate, applying for a driver's license, and applying for a personal ID card in all regions. This study looked into cosplayers' information habits, as well as the social norms, social types, and information architecture of the Rey Cosplay Community, an online cosplay Facebook community (RCC). The findings imply that the RCC can be seen as an information community where fans can learn about cosplay costume making and share it. Ample and well-organized information, as well as a healthy community culture, substantially assist community members in creating their costumes Figure 5 (Sharma, 2018), (Lee-Geiller & Lee, 2019), (Vaddiraju & Manasi, 2019).

DISCUSSION

Tech support fraud is becoming more prevalent. To mislead unwary individuals, a criminal pretends to give customers, security, or technical assistance or service. Criminals may act as support or service agents, offering to resolve difficulties such as a hacked email account or bank account, a computer virus, or a software license renewal. Criminals acting as customer service representatives for banking institutions, utility companies, or virtual currency exchanges have been the subject of recent complaints. Many victims say they were told to send money to overseas accounts or buy big volumes of prepaid cards. Although pandemic lockdowns temporarily slowed fraud activities, victims reported a rise in the number of incidents due to tech support fraud table-1 and figure 6 (Vaddiraju & Manasi, 2019), (Pandey & Risal, 2019), (De & Shukla, 2020), (Romansky & Noninska, 2020).

CRITICAL EVALUATION

E-government suffers the same challenges as e-business faced (Sambana, B. 2021). Increase integrity attacks and threats insider the e-governance (Kiilu, P. 2021). The services of e-governance make it easier to access services in a timely and effective manner. While the other side the potential risk increase of breaching security and privacy (Salam, S. 2021).

Figure 5. Different countries giving online facilities (Vardell et al., 2021)

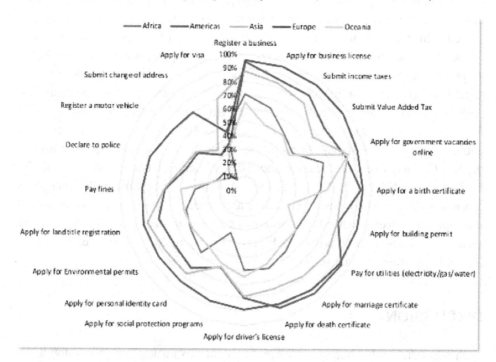

From the peer-review of previous research articles on implementation of e-government and its integrity attacks, privacy and security violation. The applications of e-government are increasing dramatically and it needs to take great steps for security violation and privacy. The integrity attacks increase during the Covid-19 pandemic and users face great losses.

CONCLUSION AND FUTURE WORK

With the development of new advanced technology, people's expectations and grievances for improving services and values in all aspects of life are growing. Changes in technology are offering far better solutions to problems, hence improving existing systems. At the same time, new technologies are presenting new security and privacy violations. Electronic government is fast gaining traction around the world to provide citizens with consistent services. As information resources become more digitised, Infrastructure and digital data are also facing increasing challenges. For advanced nations, the security parameters and optimization techniques have been thoroughly tested and are in good working order. However, these issues have yet to

Table 1. Shows the 20 top victim countries year 2020

Name of Victim Country	Complaints Received
'United Kingdom'	217,640
Canada	5,480
India	3,177
Greece	2,518
Australia	2,112
South Africa	1,865
France	1,751
Germany	1,615
Mexico	1,270
Belgium	1,100
Brazil	982
Philippines	910
Italy	802
Spain	627
Netherlands	512
Nigeria	488
Pakistan	456
China	477
Colombia	420
Hong Kong	410

be adequately addressed in developing countries. There is also a requirement for individuals involved in the advance and operation of e-government systems to be educated and informed. An unauthorized person applies several different methods and techniques in the modern age for getting self-profit. Mostly the understandable consequence of several attacks is particularly targeted financial institutes and money stealing. Such as unauthorized transfer amounts fraudulently from their personal accounts. E-governance is an application of IT and it gives online services to the users to operate online financial transactions from home. Electronic government is quickly adopting info and communication technology to deliver public facilities to numerous entities and institutions efficiently and transparently. Future work, in the perspective of providing e-governance applications in different regions and dramatically increasing potential risk and privacy violation, needs to work on e-government applications.

Figure 6. 20 top victim countries

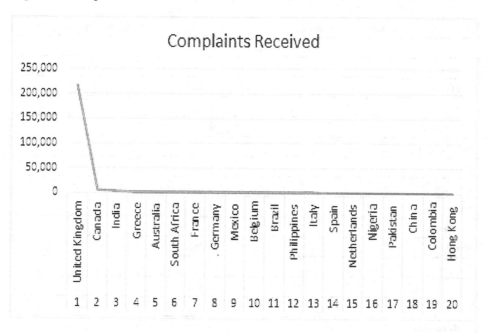

REFERENCES

Adeodato, R., & Pournouri, S. (2020). Secure Implementation of E-Governance: A Case Study About Estonia. In *Cyber Defence in the Age of AI, Smart Societies and Augmented Humanity* (pp. 397–429). Springer. doi:10.1007/978-3-030-35746-7_18

Almusaylim, Z., Jhanjhi, N. Z., & Alhumam, A. (2020). Detection and Mitigation of RPL Rank and Version Number Attacks in the Internet of Things: SRPL-RP. *Sensors (Basel)*, 20(21), 5997. doi:10.339020215997 PMID:33105891

Assiri, H., Nanda, P., & Mohanty, M. (2020). *Secure e-Governance Using Blockchain.* https://ieeexplore.ieee.org/abstract/document/9428825

Basyal, D. K., Poudyal, N., & Seo, J. W. (2018). Does E-government reduce corruption? Evidence from a heterogeneous panel data model. *Transforming Government: People, Process and Policy.* https://www.emerald.com/insight/content/doi/10.1108/TG-12-2017-0073/full/html

Dagba G. (2020). *Exploring Citizens' Perceptions of Social Media Use in E-governance in Punjab.* https://papers.ssrn.com/sol3/papers.cfm?abstract_id=3763121 doi:10.2139/ssrn.3763121

De, S. J., & Shukla, R. (2020). Privacy policies of e-governance initiatives: Evidence from India. *Journal of Public Affairs, 20*(4), e2160. https://onlinelibrary.wiley.com/doi/abs/10.1002/pa.2160

Fu, Y. (2020, April). Evaluation Method of Big Data Reliability in Electronic Government. In *2020 International Conference on E-Commerce and Internet Technology (ECIT)* (pp. 142-144). IEEE. https://ieeexplore.ieee.org/abstract/document/9134119

Giraldo, J., Cardenas, A. A., & Kantarcioglu, M. (2017, May). Security vs. privacy: How integrity attacks can be masked by the noise of differential privacy. In *2017 American Control Conference (ACC)* (pp. 1679-1684). IEEE. https://ieeexplore.ieee.org/abstract/document/7963194

Gupta, R., Muttoo, S. K., & Pal, S. K. (2017, March). Proposed framework for information systems security for e-governance in developing nations. In *Proceedings of the 10th International Conference on Theory and Practice of Electronic Governance* (pp. 546-547). https://dl.acm.org/doi/abs/10.1145/3047273.3047285

HIPAA Journal. (2021). *Healthcare Data Breach Report.* https://www.hipaajournal.com/may-2021-healthcare-data-breach-report/

Hoque, T., Wang, X., Basak, A., Karam, R., & Bhunia, S. (2018, April). Hardware trojan attacks in embedded memory. In *2018 IEEE 36th VLSI Test Symposium (VTS)* (pp. 1-6). IEEE. https://ieeexplore.ieee.org/abstract/document/8368630

Humayun, M. (2021). Industry 4.0 and Cyber Security Issues and Challenges. *Turkish Journal of Computer and Mathematics Education, 12*(10), 2957–2971. https://turcomat.org/index.php/turkbilmat/article/view/4946

Humayun, M., Niazi, M., Jhanjhi, N. Z., Alshayeb, M., & Mahmood, S. (2020). Cyber security threats and vulnerabilities: A systematic mapping study. *Arabian Journal for Science and Engineering, 45*(4), 3171–3189. doi:10.100713369-019-04319-2

Hussain, S. J., Ahmed, U., Liaquat, H., Mir, S., Jhanjhi, N. Z., & Humayun, M. (2019, April). IMIAD: intelligent malware identification for android platform. In *2019 International Conference on Computer and Information Sciences (ICCIS)* (pp. 1-6). IEEE. https://ieeexplore.ieee.org/abstract/document/8716471

Jashari, R., & Avdyli, M. (2020). *Security of information systems-legal and ethical rules, chalenges of appying in Kosova.* https://knowledgecenter.ubt-uni.net/conference/2020/all_events/61/

Javed, M. A., Khan, M. Z., Zafar, U., Siddiqui, M. F., Badar, R., Lee, B. M., & Ahmad, F. (2020). ODPV: An efficient protocol to mitigate data integrity attacks in intelligent transport systems. *IEEE Access: Practical Innovations, Open Solutions*, *8*, 114733–114740. doi:10.1109/ACCESS.2020.3004444

Kabanov, Y., Chugunov, A. V., & Nizomutdinov, B. (2019, September). E-Government Research Domain: Comparing the International and Russian Research Agenda. In *International Conference on Electronic Government* (pp. 18–30). Springer. doi:10.1007/978-3-030-27325-5_2

Khan, N. A., Brohi, S. N., & Jhanjhi, N. Z. (2020). UAV's applications, architecture, security issues and attack scenarios: a survey. In *Intelligent Computing and Innovation on Data Science* (pp. 753–760). Springer. doi:10.1007/978-981-15-3284-9_81

Khan, S. N., Shael, M., & Majdalawieh, M. (2019, July). Blockchain technology as a support infrastructure in E-Government evolution at Dubai economic department. In *Proceedings of the 2019 International Electronics Communication Conference* (pp. 124-130). https://dl.acm.org/doi/abs/10.1145/3343147.3343164

Lee-Geiller, S., & Lee, T. D. (2019). Using government websites to enhance democratic E-governance: A conceptual model for evaluation. *Government Information Quarterly*, *36*(2), 208–225. doi:10.1016/j.giq.2019.01.003

Lim, M., Abdullah, A., & Jhanjhi, N. Z. (2019). Performance optimization of criminal network hidden link prediction model with deep reinforcement learning. *Journal of King Saud University-Computer and Information Sciences*. https://www.sciencedirect.com/science/article/pii/S1319157819308584

Lim, M., Abdullah, A., Jhanjhi, N. Z., Khan, M. K., & Supramaniam, M. (2019). Link prediction in time-evolving criminal network with deep reinforcement learning technique. *IEEE Access: Practical Innovations, Open Solutions*, *7*, 184797–184807. doi:10.1109/ACCESS.2019.2958873

Lim, M., Abdullah, A., Jhanjhi, N. Z., & Supramaniam, M. (2019). Hidden link prediction in criminal networks using the deep reinforcement learning technique. *Computers, 8*(1), 8. https://www.mdpi.com/2073-431X/8/1/8

Lin, J., Yu, W., Zhang, N., Yang, X., & Ge, L. (2017, January). On data integrity attacks against route guidance in transportation-based cyber-physical systems. In *2017 14th IEEE Annual Consumer Communications & Networking Conference (CCNC)* (pp. 313-318). IEEE. https://ieeexplore.ieee.org/abstract/document/7983125

Martins, I. (2018). The role of e-government in nigeria: Legal issues and barriers against complete implementation. In *The Stances of e-GovernmentPolicies* (pp. 23-30). Chapman and Hall/CRC. https://www.taylorfrancis.com/chapters/edit/10.1201/9780203731451-3/role-government-nigeria-legal-issues-barriers-complete-implementation-ishaya-martins

Matteson. (2021). *Cybersecurity: There's no such thing as a false positive.* TechRepublic. https://www.techrepublic.com/article/cybersecurity-theres-no-such-thing-as-a-false-positive/

Najmi, K. Y., AlZain, M. A., Masud, M., Jhanjhi, N. Z., Al-Amri, J., & Baz, M. (2021). A survey on security threats and countermeasures in IoT to achieve users confidentiality and reliability. *Materials Today: Proceedings.* https://www.sciencedirect.com/science/article/pii/S221478532102469X

Pandey, D. L., & Risal, N. (2019). Impact of social governance on e-governance in Nepal. *ITIHAS The Journal of Indian Management, 9*(4), 40-48. https://www.indianjournals.com/ijor.aspx?target=ijor:ijim&volume=9&issue=4&article=006

Reda, H. T., Anwar, A., Mahmood, A. N., & Tari, Z. (2021). *A Taxonomy of Cyber Defence Strategies Against False Data Attacks in Smart Grid.* https://arxiv.org/abs/2103.16085

Romansky, R., & Noninska, I. (2020). Business virtual system in the context of e-governance: Investigation of secure access to information resources. *Journal of Public Affairs, 20*(3), e2072. doi:10.1002/pa.2072

Sabani, A., Deng, H., & Thai, V. (2019, January). Evaluating the development of E-government in Indonesia. In *Proceedings of the 2nd International Conference on Software Engineering and Information Management* (pp. 254-258). https://dl.acm.org/doi/abs/10.1145/3305160.3305191

Saeed, S., Jhanjhi, N. Z., Naqvi, M., & Humayun, M. (2019). Analysis of Software Development Methodologies. *International Journal of Computing and Digital Systems, 8*(5), 446–460. http://journal.uob.edu.bh/handle/123456789/3583

Saleh, M., Jhanjhi, N. Z., Abdullah, A., & Saher, R. (n.d.). *Design Challenges of Securing IoT Devices: A survey.* http://www.ripublication.com/irph/ijert20/ijertv13n12_149.pdf

Sambana, B., Raju, K. N., Satish, D., Raju, S. S., & Raja, P. V. K. (2021). *Impact of Cyber Security in e-Governance and e-Commerce* (No. 5533). EasyChair. file:///C:/Users/imdad/Downloads/EasyChair-Preprint-5533%20(1).pdf

Shafiq, D. A., Jhanjhi, N. Z., & Abdullah, A. (2021, March). Machine Learning Approaches for Load Balancing in Cloud Computing Services. In *2021 National Computing Colleges Conference (NCCC)* (pp. 1-8). IEEE.

Sharma, S. (2018). *Good Governance and its Challenges in India.* https://www.indianjournals.com/ijor.aspx?target=ijor:ijmss&volume=6&issue=11&article=009

Trippel, T., Weisse, O., Xu, W., Honeyman, P., & Fu, K. (2017, April). WALNUT: Waging doubt on the integrity of MEMS accelerometers with acoustic injection attacks. In *2017 IEEE European symposium on security and privacy (EuroS&P)* (pp. 3-18). IEEE. https://ieeexplore.ieee.org/abstract/document/7961948

Vaddiraju, A. K., & Manasi, S. (2019). E-governance: Learning from Karnataka. *The Indian Journal of Public Administration, 65*(2), 416–429. doi:10.1177/0019556119844582

Vardell, E., Wang, T., & Thomas, P. A. (2021). "I found what I needed, which was a supportive community": An ethnographic study of shared information practices in an online cosplay community. *Journal of Documentation.* https://www.emerald.com/insight/content/doi/10.1108/JD-02-2021-0034/full/html

Yang, Q., An, D., Min, R., Yu, W., Yang, X., & Zhao, W. (2017). On optimal PMU placement-based defense against data integrity attacks in smart grid. *IEEE Transactions on Information Forensics and Security, 12*(7), 1735–1750. doi:10.1109/TIFS.2017.2686367

Yau. (2021) *What is Data Integrity? Precisely.* https://www.precisely.com/blog/data-integrity/what-is-data-integrity

Zoppelt, M., & Kolagari, R. T. (2019, October). What today's serious cyber attacks on cars tell us: consequences for automotive security and dependability. In *International Symposium on Model-Based Safety and Assessment* (pp. 270–285). Springer. doi:10.1007/978-3-030-32872-6_18

Chapter 10

The Impact of Blockchain Technology on Advanced Security Measures for E-Government

Raja Majid Ali Ujjan
University of the West of Scotland, UK

Khalid Hussain
Superior University, Pakistan

Sarfraz Nawaz Brohi
University of the West of England (UWE), Bristol, UK

ABSTRACT

Implementation of blockchain with e-government has raised several complexities. When an area has satisfied the requirements for e-government implementation, new challenges will appear. As a result of the information technology revolution, governments and industries are being forced to deliver more effective and secure internet services. Every government in the world attempts to provide the public with electronic services that are fast, quick, and beneficial for the users. Blockchain is considered to have significant potential benefits for the government since it is a combination of technologies such as distributed ledgers, privacy, authentication, and consensus mechanisms. However, this advanced technology is still in its development, and e-government faces a number of difficulties and challenges. The goal of this chapter is to evaluate this advanced technology in the context of high-level e-government security and privacy implementation measures and other technical issues during the adaption of blockchain technology.

DOI: 10.4018/978-1-7998-9624-1.ch010

INTRODUCTION

New tactics are being developed to provide a better living for humanity. In a variety of ways, new initiatives and new technology are driving a new wave of innovation in city services. Nonetheless, despite the continual advancement of cities and digital technologies, certain problems relating to including citizens in social decisions remain unsolved and must be addressed (Alqahtani & Braun, 2021). E-governance appears as a critical tool and the first stage in this transition in this setting (Avina et al., 2017). The rise of e-governments and associated services has presented governments with new instruments to improve public life, service delivery, citizen engagement, and work procedures (Barrane et al., 2018). As a result of this development, there is now a risk of data leakage and illegal access to secret and private data associated with e-government apps. This could stymie the development and implementation of e-governments as a whole. As a result of these concerns, cyber security is crucial for the development and adoption of e-government (Chen et al., 2018). Most researchers emphasized security, privacy, and trust as essential elements that have a substantial impact on e-government adoption, acceptance, and implementation. Thus, in order to trust and encourage the public to embrace and utilize e-government systems and services, governments must appropriately handle security concerns (Choi et al., 2018). Understanding how organizational, psychological, and technical elements interact to affect the network security outcome of enterprises is one of the primary cyber security concerns in organizations. Although cybercriminals are frequently mentioned in the news for data breaches and attacks, evidence suggests that the majority of security breaches are caused by personnel within the organization, whether purposefully or accidentally, due to non-compliance with cyber security standards (Alqahtani & Braun, 2021). Compliance with cyber security measures has been given a lot of thought in order to achieve successful cyber security (Donalds & Osei-Bryson, 2020). In its simplest form, a blockchain is a decentralized ledger that keeps track of all transactions made by the system's users. This refers to a technology that stores data on the outcomes of all interactions between citizens and government entities in the context of electronic government. Importantly, all members of the system interlink, code, and store the data, which is then automatically updated to reflect the changes made (Harris & Martin, 2019).The egoistic impulses that drive some people to engage in corrupt actions to the harm of society and state sovereignty are controlled by blockchain technology. It also generates a compelling motivation to follow the rules that apply equally to all participants, promoting a sense of shared responsibility (Hofbauer et al., 2019). Blockchain is a technology that allows users to agree on nearly any topic without the need for an intermediary, laying the groundwork for decentralized governance, and a fair balance of interests that benefits society (Huang & Madnick, 2021). The security provided by traditional

Figure 1. Overview of propriety distributed ledger technology (Krishnaraju et al., 2016)

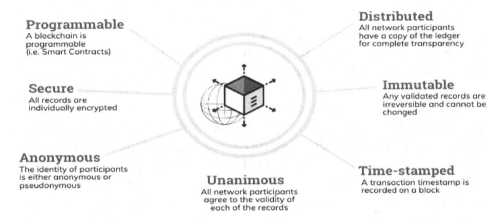

registers can be improved by a registration system based on blockchain technology. By eliminating the payment of governmental duties and middleman fees, transaction costs can be drastically lowered while transactions themselves can become faster, more transparent, and more secure figure 1 overview of propriety Distributed ledger Technology.

The chapter questions organize as follows:

1. What are the concerns and limitations of blockchain technology in terms of security?
2. What impact does blockchain technology have on e-governance?
3. How effective is blockchain technology in detecting cyber-threats?

LITERATURE REVIEW

The use of information and communication technology to combine government and public services for citizens is known as e-governance. The goals and objectives of e-governance are to provide citizens with more properly recognized services to attain overall social and economic leverage with high performance and capabilities in the major inspiring points. Since its birth in early 2009, Bitcoin's underlying technology, blockchain, has demonstrated strong application potential and captured the imagination of both academic and industrial. Blockchain approaches have inspired a slew of new applications and have been effectively embraced in a variety of areas, even if the financial industry is viewed as the blockchain's primary beneficiary.

Security, decentralization, transparency, traceability, immutability, distributed ledgers, transparent logs, and irreversible data storage are all characteristics of blockchain (Galvez et al., 2018). The Blockchain is based on an ordered list of nodes that store data and are connected by chains. Investigate the role of Blockchain in the long-term viability and power of electronic services, particularly e-governance systems, without the need for centralized data storage (Li et al., 2019). One of the primary motives for doing this research is the governments and industries recent attention to SC associated concepts and initiatives. In order to illustrate how widely these notions have been adopted (Kim & Kim, 2021). The past government and former countries of our modern globe have always changed; now, with the current globalization of communication, we can consider citizens' opinions (Liu et al., 2020). Due to its extensive application for simple or more complicated transactions, the blockchain (BC) as a fresh and revolutionary technology concept is gaining traction in a variety of industries (Galvez et al., 2018). As a result, it has a wide range of applications, ranging from the corporate and financial sectors to the social sector, which includes healthcare, education, and government administration (Liu & Carter, 2018). One subject that is particularly confronted with complicated obstacles is public administration, where old processes, as well as trust, autonomy, and facilitators, are just a few examples of key issues (Ronchi, 2019). The BC, with its underlying complicated structure, is frequently mentioned as a possible e-Government development solution. The BC has the property of storing information that is dispersed across multiple nodes, with each node's consensus required (Muller & Lind, 2020). All transactions will be saved in a protocol, so they can't be changed, moved, or deleted. The required rules are originally described in so-called payment systems to create the legislative regime. (Simonova, 2020). This approach eliminates reliance on a single central party, the possibility of manipulation, and It allows for the collection of data and the execution of operations, exchanged, and regulated between the users in a decentralized network (Twizeyimana & Andersson, 2019). The attributes outlined above provide a convincing explanation for the BC's emergence as a possible technology to transform government procedures and transactions with enterprises or individuals by supporting key concepts like trust, privacy, inclusion, and participation (Yazdanmehr et al., 2020). Various BC systems and applications have already been implemented in a number of nations. While the BC implementation already provides for land and property registrations in Sweden and Brazil, it also helps to track real estate transactions in Dubai and India (Yoo et al., 2018). While blockchain technology (BCT) shows promise in terms of how it may be used to not just digitalize but also revolutionize the public sector, there are various obstacles to overcome when it comes to applying and adopting BCT in this industry (Agbo et al., 2019). Guidelines and best practices must be defined and offered to ensure adequate and reliable implementation of BC solutions, as well as general acceptability within the government sector and society. The majority of current research focuses on the qualities of BCT, and the several potential domains of request, but it continues to overlook the concerns in between, such as political and legal issues. Furthermore, there is little study on participation models and platforms in the current literature, with an emphasis on important driver values and procedures involving all relevant stakeholders. There are no implementation techniques or frameworks that support proactive engagement to modernize procedures between the government and citizens to understand and solve welfare concerns and generate additional public benefit (Salam & Kumar, 2021), (Bao et al., 2020), (De Filippi et al., 2020), (El Haddouti & El Kettani, 2019),(Fan et al., 2018), (Kim & Laskowski, 2018),(Han et al., 2018). The organization and division of government have a considerable impact on how new services and policies for citizens are implemented. The interconnectedness between central and local government is challenged by their various spheres of competence, as well as their divergent interests and political discretion. The normal connection between central and local government can be stated Local governments perform the role of the centralized administration, with the federal government deciding how much money, how quickly, and how prioritized local services should be produced and implemented (Han et al., 2018), (Mengelkamp et al., 2018), (Naik & Jenkins, 2020). Several journal publications and conference papers discuss the immaturity of this technical notion, citing its extremely sophisticated yet opaque underlying processes as well as the lack of well-proven best practices. Furthermore, society's general mistrust of new technologies is counterproductive. As a result, both the public sector and society bear responsibilities for establishing trust.

THE MOST SIGNIFICANT CHARACTERISTICS OF BLOCKCHAIN TECHNOLOGY

- There is no centralized organization or agency in charge of administering the blockchain and managing the keys to data rectification.
- It is always in action. Because the system's data is duplicated simultaneously to networks of nodes, 99% of them will be available even if 99% of them fall offline, and it will be updated automatically as soon as they reconnect to the internet. There is only one way to bring the system to a halt: shut off power and Internet access to all computers on the globe.
- Blockchain technology is based on open-source code that has never been hacked. The algorithm allows for cryptographic auditing, which is a mathematical test that determines whether or not evidence has been changed.

Figure 2. Overview of structure of blockchain (Su et al., 2018)

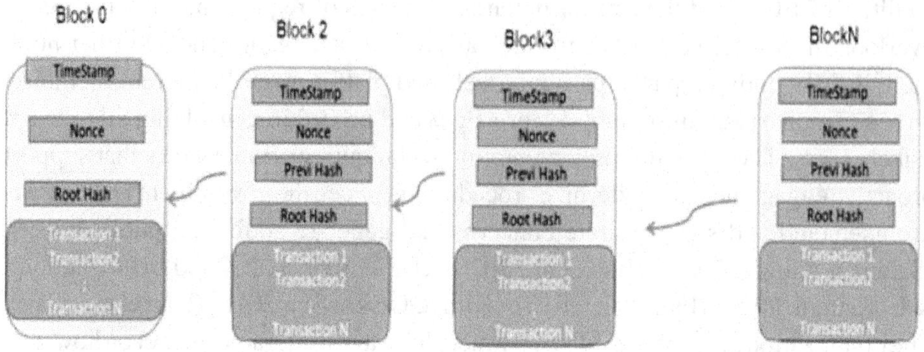

- The code facilitates the development of new services, software, and other goods, is not the property of any one agency or organization, and is not copyright protected.

OVERVIEW OF BLOCKCHAIN TECHNOLOGY AND APPLICATIONS

The blockchain is made up of a series of linked blocks, each of these has a shared public ledger that records all confirmed transactions across the whole network automatically. A linked list of blocks organizes the ledger, each of which maintains a transaction log. (Nawari & Ravindran, 2019). Digital data transfer assets is represented by the transaction. Block chain nodes are run on computers donated by volunteers all around the world. Blockchain is impervious to network attacks due to its decentralized architecture.

Asymmetric cryptography methods encrypt the transactions in a block chain, ensuring anonymity and confidentiality. The blockchain is made up of a series of blocks that are connected together as shown in figure 2.

Consensus procedures are another critical component for preserving blockchain integrity. A distributed ledger maintained by all nodes in a decentralized network is known as a block chain. The insertion of additional blocks and transaction verification require agreement among nodes, which is accomplished through distributed consensus methods. The majority of nodes in the network vote on whether or not to add a fresh block. After a consensus, a new block is added to the BC, and all nodes are brought up to date with the most recent version of the ledger. The consensus protocol ensures that the integrity of the block chain is not affected by the compromise or failure of individual systems, further figure 3 describe. Smart contracts allow participants to

Figure 3. Overview transaction execution of bloackchain

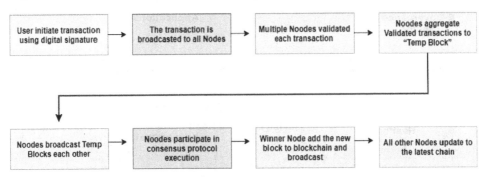

express the rules and penalties that govern a contract as a set of executable instructions that execute transactions automatically when certain criteria are met.

THE USE OF BLOCKCHAIN IN E-GOVERNMENT

Many official records of persons and businesses are managed and maintained by government entities. Individuals must put their trust in the government to safeguard the security and privacy of their personal information. Through digitalization, secure and immutable record keeping, blockchain-based apps have the potential to transform how these papers are managed. (United Nations, 2018). Through automation and accountability, blockchain can make government services more efficient and democratically accountable (Zheng et al., 2018). The goal of blockchain-based governance is to provide decentralized and efficient public services while retaining their integrity. This section examines how blockchain can be used in a variety of public settings.

Public Administration Applications

Existing e-voting systems, on the other hand, rely on centralized authorities, which may risk the voting system's confidence and confidentiality. From this perspective, blockchain-based e-voting solutions appear to be promising. South Africa, a West African country, was the first to use BCT to run a general election (Singh et al., 2020), (Kumar et al., 2021), (Ravi et al., 2021). It makes use of "message boards," a permissioned blockchain. The bulletin board is made up of code-associated write-permissioned nodes for tracking individual votes, third-party witness nodes for witnessing votes, and read-only nodes for vote verification open to all users.

Figure 4. Overview sectors of e-governance and use cases

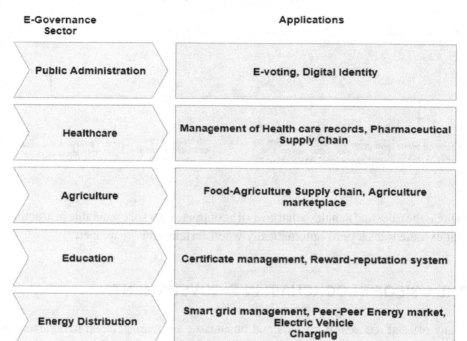

Health-Care Applications

In healthcare, blockchain can be used for a variety of things, including safe storing (Alamri et al., 2019).

Advances in digital technologies have had an impact on how health-care services are delivered and how data is stored. Hospital automation and the growing popularity of online patient consultations, among other things, have changed how electronic health records are stored and accessed (EHR) (Choi et al., 2019). Sharing an individual's health records between hospitals and verifying their accuracy is a complex task.

Agricultural Applications

The application cases of blockchain in agriculture are primarily divided into three categories: food and agricultural supply chain, business, and finance (Tosh et al., 2017). The blockchain-based supply chain apps provide provenance monitoring across multiple phases of agricultural products, preventing food fraud and contamination (Yang et al., 2017). The technology automates the entire commodity transfer process, including buyer and seller verification, quality assurance, and shipping.

Educational Applications

The education sector has a lot of potential use cases for Blockchain technology (Tasca & Tessone, 2017). Design a blockchain-based mechanism for verifying educational records. Universities use a blockchain platform to create digitally signed certificates. The certificate can be shared with companies or other institutions, and verification can be done by following the transaction that records the certificate's issuance (Xia et al., 2017). The technology delivers self-verifiability and transparency, in addition to increased security. Blockchain-based educational incentive and reputation system

Energy-Related Applications

The growth of small-scale renewable energy generation puts existing centralized energy management systems to the test (Cachin & Vukolić, 2017). The widespread adoption of blockchain technology in the energy sector is due to dispersed energy resources and the integration of IoT technology for a distributed platform for energy management and exchange is required for metering energy output and consumption.

LIMITATIONS AND CHALLENGES

While being studied by practitioners and academia, concerns and challenges arise, just as they do with any other novel technology with the potential to disrupt particular industries. The resulting challenges limit blockchain (BC) enormous potential and widespread application across industries. As a result, this section examines the numerous technical and business limitations. Despite the fact that the characteristics show that the BC technological idea is very promising in terms of establishing exceptional data security, several technical issues must be investigated. The BC's security is enhanced by both hash algorithms and smart contracts, but the cryptographic technique is still vulnerable to attack (McKinney et al., 2017), (Millard, 2017). Time jacking is a third well-known cyber-attack in which a hacker attempts to change the timestamps of BC before they are recorded to the protocol in order to introduce inauthentic records and phoney BCs. One of the other issues that must be investigated is the loss of privacy. On the one hand, keeping the whole information and history of transaction data on each node seems to be useful from a security standpoint, but also raises doubts about the technology concept's general viability for use cases requiring greater anonymity. Furthermore, the immutability of all transaction data highlights another shortcoming of this system, as some business use cases necessitate changes to specific transactions (Risius & Spohrer, 2017). There are significant concerns about the BC protocol's long-term viability, particularly for blockchains that are utilized for public-facing applications. The mining grid's security measures and corresponding consensus methods squander a large amount of energy (Casino, Dasaklis & Patsakis, 2019; Yli-Huumo, 2016). Taking a closer look at China's energy use, the country that leads BC mining, exemplifies this. China consumes more electricity than 159 countries combined, according to the bitcoin energy consumption index (Index, 2017).This overall complexity is the source of a lack of acceptance, not only from the viewpoint of proper technological operation and handling by users, but also from the perspective of legal and regulatory compliance by authorities. The key drivers of BCTs' increasing acceptability are a lack of knowledge and faith in technology, the legality of the transaction, and general data protection (Hughes et al., 2019). Aspects to examine include, among other things, the horrific costs of implementation and energy usage, as well as the hazards of opening up the business model and infrastructure to third parties. Using this technology to bring additional economic value while still ensuring the integrity of the data will put the entire concept and implementation to the test (Seebacher & Schüritz, 2017; Hughes et al., 2019).

Concerns regarding the Block chain technology has limits in a variety of uses areas were raised in the literature linked to block chain application as explain in figure 5 the obstacles that limit blockchain adoption are primarily divided into three categories: Technical, economic, and human factors issues.

DISCUSSION

From the perspective of current technology, the entire potential has yet to be realized. The combination of the internet and BC allows government institutions to fully exploit the revolutionary technology's full potential to align novel capacities to achieve individual citizen goals while simultaneously creating societal value (Paintner, 2021). Some of these ideas have already been implemented, but with a more basic premise. As a result, the maturity of the distribution channel must be considered while evaluating the type of service delivery. Services with a higher level of maturity address not just basic office concerns, but also more complex challenges involving multiple departments and organizational bodies (Ahmad & Shah, 2021). BCT and public administration, two distinct disciplines, have been thoroughly explored. Beyond the hurdles and constraints that practically any innovative innovation faces, there is a strong chance that BCT and BC-based systems can be used to enable multidimensional practices for a wide range of public administration applications. There has never been any interference between these two domains in the past. By combining them, new multidisciplinary solutions for individuals, corporations, and other governments can be developed. Similarly, to propose and construct a new

Figure 5. Overview of Limitation of Blockchain

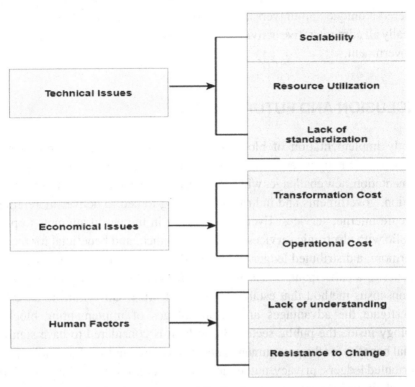

sector, namely "e-gov," which consists of a collection of artefacts developed and built in accordance with essential normative structures and executive principles.

Our contribution to this chapter is that, in today's information world, citizens have grown to demand an easy and effective government-to-citizen connection. Electronic government solutions, these systems, which are aimed at automating choice systems on a large basis, are assisting with meeting these goals while also improving government and social communications efficiency for all members of society. E-government significantly transforms the distributed governance system and has an impact on all document management and processing duties. Among the numerous technological alternatives available, which vary in speed, dependability, and data security, a few recent technology advancements stand out as being founded on radically new compatible principles and showing substantial promise for electronic administration. The logical outcome of blockchain-based solutions and their integration into electronic governance systems will be increased government efficacy, lower transaction costs, and a simpler, faster, more effective, and thus more convenient way of engaging the government with citizens. An administrative procedure entails recording civil status, property rights, health information, and other information in an official registry. As a result, blockchain technology may be considered a unique and universal technology that helps streamline and automate practically all administrative activities while boosting the transparency and efficacy of e-government.

CONCLUSION AND FUTURE WORK

Currently implementation of blockchain with e-government has raised several complexities. When an area has satisfied the requirements for e-government implementation, new challenges will appear. As a result of the information technology revolution, governments and industries are being forced to deliver more effective and secure internet services. Every government in the world attempts to provide the public with electronic services that are fast, quick, and beneficial for the users. Furthermore, a distributed ledger is described as a "blockchain" that is accessible among network participants and is used to record transactions that are authenticated by a consensus method that establishes network trust. Governments have begun to investigate the advantages and disadvantages of implementing blockchain technology inside the public sector. Blockchain is considered to have significant potential benefits for the government since it is a combination of technologies such as distributed ledgers, privacy, authentication, and consensus mechanisms. The use of blockchain technology in the public sector appears to benefit citizens and also organizations. However, this advanced technology is still in its development, and e-government faces a number of difficulties and challenges. Furthermore, more study can be conducted to determine the extent to which a single platform or ecosystem might aid in the intensification of collaboration between the government, society, and enterprises, as well as contribute to an increase in government confidence and capacities. Not least, further research is needed to determine the extent to which the government's digital services generate value through the usage of BCT while also increasing trust in the public sector.

REFERENCES

Agbo, C. C., Mahmoud, Q. H., & Eklund, J. M. (2019, June). Blockchain technology in healthcare: a systematic review. In *Healthcare* (Vol. 7, No. 2, p. 56). Multidisciplinary Digital Publishing Institute. https://www.mdpi.com/2227-9032/7/2/56

Ahmad, M. S., & Shah, S. M. (2021). Moving Beyond the Crypto-Currency Success of Blockchain: A Systematic Survey. *Scalable Computing: Practice and Experience, 22*(3), 321-346. https://link.springer.com/chapter/10.1007/978-3-030-77637-4_6

Alamri, M., Jhanjhi, N. Z., & Humayun, M. (2019). Blockchain for Internet of Things (IoT) research issues challenges & future directions: A review. *Int. J. Comput. Sci. Netw. Secur, 19*, 244–258.

Alqahtani, M., & Braun, R. (2021). *Examining the Impact of Technical Controls, Accountability and Monitoring towards Cyber Security Compliance in E-government Organizations.* https://web.archive.org/web/20210428072623id_/https://www.researchsquare.com/article/rs-196216/v1.pdf

Avina, G. E., Bogner, K., Carter, J., Friedman, A., Gordon, S. P., Haney, J., . . . Wolf, D. (2017). *Tailoring of cyber security technology adoption practices for operational adoption in complex organizations.* https://citeseerx.ist.psu.edu/viewdoc/download?doi=10.1.1.549.7147&rep=rep1&type=pdf

Bao, J., He, D., Luo, M., & Choo, K. K. R. (2020). A survey of blockchain applications in the energy sector. *IEEE Systems Journal.* https://www.revistageintec.net/index.php/revista/article/view/2409

Barrane, F. Z., Karuranga, G. E., & Poulin, D. (2018). Technology adoption and diffusion: A new application of the UTAUT model. *International Journal of Innovation and Technology Management, 15*(06), 1950004. https://www.worldscientific.com/doi/abs/10.1142/S0219877019500044

Cachin, C., & Vukolić, M. (2017). *Blockchain consensus protocols in the wild.* https://arxiv.org/abs/1707.01873

Chen, X., Chen, L., & Wu, D. (2018). Factors that influence employees' security policy compliance: An awareness-motivation-capability perspective. *Journal of Computer Information Systems, 58*(4), 312–324. https://www.tandfonline.com/doi/abs/10.1080/08874417.2016.1258679

Choi, B. G., Jeong, E., & Kim, S. W. (2019). Multiple security certification system between blockchain based terminal and internet of things device: Implication for open innovation. *Journal of Open Innovation, 5*(4), 87.

Choi, M., Lee, J., & Hwang, K. (2018). Information Systems Security (ISS) of EGovernment for Sustainability: A Dual Path Model of ISS Influenced by Institutional Isomorphism. *Sustainability.* https://www.mdpi.com/2071-1050/10/5/1555

De Filippi, P., Mannan, M., & Reijers, W. (2020). Blockchain as a confidence machine: The problem of trust & challenges of governance. *Technology in Society*, *62*, 101284. doi:10.1016/j.techsoc.2020

Donalds, C., & Osei-Bryson, K. M. (2020). Cybersecurity compliance behavior: Exploring the influences of individual decision style and other antecedents. *International Journal of Information Management*, *51*, 102056. https://www.sciencedirect.com/science/article/abs/pii/S0268401218312544

El Haddouti, S., & El Kettani, M. D. E. C. (2019, April). Analysis of identity management systems using blockchain technology. In *2019 International Conference on Advanced Communication Technologies and Networking (CommNet)* (pp. 1-7). IEEE. https://ieeexplore.ieee.org/abstract/document/8742375/

Fan, K., Wang, S., Ren, Y., Li, H., & Yang, Y. (2018). Medblock: Efficient and secure medical data sharing via blockchain. *Journal of Medical Systems*, *42*(8), 1–11. https://link.springer.com/article/10.1007/s10916-018-0993-7

Galvez, J. F., Mejuto, J., & Simal-Gandara, J. (2018). Future challenges on the use of blockchain for food traceability analysis. *Trends in Analytical Chemistry*, *107*, 222–232.

Han, M., Li, Z., He, J., Wu, D., Xie, Y., & Baba, A. (2018, September). A novel blockchain-based education records verification solution. In *Proceedings of the 19th Annual SIG Conference on Information Technology Education* (pp. 178-183). https://dl.acm.org/doi/abs/10.1145/3241815.3241870

Harris, M. A., & Martin, R. (2019). Promoting cybersecurity compliance. In *Cybersecurity education for awareness and compliance* (pp. 54–71). IGI Global. https://www.igi-global.com/chapter/promoting-cybersecurity-compliance/225917

Hofbauer, D., Ivkic, I., & Tauber, M. (2019). On the Cost of Security Compliance in Information Systems. *10th International Multi-Conference on Complexity, Informatics and Cybernetics 2019 (IMCIC)*. https://www.igi-global.com/chapter/promoting-cybersecurity-compliance/225917

Huang, K., & Madnick, S. (2021, January). Does High Cybersecurity Capability Lead to Openness in Digital Trade? The Mediation Effect of E-Government Maturity. In *Proceedings of the 54th Hawaii International Conference on System Sciences* (p. 4352). https://papers.ssrn.com/sol3/papers.cfm?abstract_id=3542552

Kim, C., & Kim, K. A. (2021). The institutional change from E-Government toward Smarter City; comparative analysis between royal borough of Greenwich, UK, and Seongdong-gu, South Korea. *Journal of Open Innovation*, 7(1), 42. https://www.mdpi.com/2199-8531/7/1/42

Kim, H. M., & Laskowski, M. (2018). Agriculture on the blockchain: Sustainable solutions for food, farmers, and financing. *Supply Chain Revolution*. https://papers.ssrn.com/sol3/papers.cfm?abstract_id=3028164

Krishnaraju, V., Mathew, S. K., & Sugumaran, V. (2016). Web personalization for user acceptance of technology: An empirical investigation of E-government services. *Information Systems Frontiers*, 18(3), 579–595.

Kumar, M. S., Vimal, S., Jhanjhi, N. Z., Dhanabalan, S. S., & Alhumyani, H. A. (2021). Blockchain based peer to peer communication in autonomous drone operation. *Energy Reports*. https://www.sciencedirect.com/science/article/pii/S2352484721006752

Li, L., He, W., Xu, L., Ash, I., Anwar, M., & Yuan, X. (2019). Investigating the impact of cybersecurity policy awareness on employees' cybersecurity behavior. *International Journal of Information Management*, 45, 13–24. https://www.sciencedirect.com/science/article/abs/pii/S0268401218302093

Liu, C., Wang, N., & Liang, H. (2020). Motivating information security policy compliance: The critical role of supervisor-subordinate guanxi and organizational commitment. *International Journal of Information Management*, 54, 102152. https://www.sciencedirect.com/science/article/abs/pii/S0268401219302877

Liu, D., & Carter, L. (2018, May). Impact of citizens' privacy concerns on e-government adoption. In *Proceedings of the 19th Annual International Conference on Digital Government Research* (pp. 1–6). Governance in the Data Age. https://dl.acm.org/doi/abs/10.1145/3209281.3209340

McKinney, S. A., Landy, R., & Wilka, R. (2017). Smart contracts, blockchain, and the next frontier of transactional law. *Wash. JL Tech. & Arts, 13*, 313. https://heinonline.org/HOL/LandingPage?handle=hein.journals/washjolta13&div=18&id=&page=

Mengelkamp, E., Gärttner, J., Rock, K., Kessler, S., Orsini, L., & Weinhardt, C. (2018). Designing microgrid energy markets: A case study: The Brooklyn Microgrid. *Applied Energy, 210*, 870–880. https://dl.acm.org/doi/abs/10.1145/3241815.3241870

Millard, J. (2017). European Strategies for e-Governance to 2020 and Beyond. In *Government 3.0–Next Generation Government Technology Infrastructure and Services* (pp. 1–25). Springer. https://link.springer.com/chapter/10.1007/978-3-319-63743-3_1

Muller, S. R., & Lind, M. L. (2020). Factors in Information Assurance Professionals' Intentions to Adhere to Information Security Policies. *International Journal of Systems and Software Security and Protection, 11*(1), 17–32. https://www.igi-global.com/article/factors-in-information-assurance-professionals-intentions-to-adhere-to-information-security-policies/249763

Naik, N., & Jenkins, P. (2020, April). Self-Sovereign Identity Specifications: Govern your identity through your digital wallet using blockchain technology. In *2020 8th IEEE International Conference on Mobile Cloud Computing, Services, and Engineering (MobileCloud)* (pp. 90-95). IEEE. https://ieeexplore.ieee.org/abstract/document/9126742

Nawari, N. O., & Ravindran, S. (2019). Blockchain and the built environment: Potentials and limitations. *Journal of Building Engineering, 25*, 100832. https://www.sciencedirect.com/science/article/abs/pii/S2352710218312294

Paintner, P. (2021). *Blockchain technology in the area of e-Governance–Guidelines for implementation* (Doctoral dissertation). https://run.unl.pt/handle/10362/123244

Ravi, N., Verma, S., Jhanjhi, N. Z., & Talib, M. N. (2021, August). Securing VANET Using Blockchain Technology. In *Journal of Physics: Conference Series* (Vol. 1979, No. 1, p. 012035). IOP Publishing. https://iopscience.iop.org/article/10.1088/1742-6596/1979/1/012035/meta

Risius, M., & Spohrer, K. (2017). A blockchain research framework. *Business & Information Systems Engineering, 59*(6), 385–409. https://link.springer.com/article/10.1007/s12599-017-0506-0

Ronchi, A. M. (2019). e-Government: Background, Today's Implementation and Future Trends. In e-Democracy (pp. 93-196). Springer.

Salam, S., & Kumar, K. P. (2021). Survey on Applications of Blockchain in E-Governance. *Revista Geintec-Gestao Inovacao E Tecnologias, 11*(4), 3807-3822. https://www.revistageintec.net/index.php/revista/article/view/2409

Simonova, A. (2020). *An Analysis of Factors Influencing National Institute of Standards and Technology Cybersecurity Framework Adoption in Financial Services: A Correlational Study* (Doctoral dissertation). Capella University. https://www.proquest.com/openview/8482434364a539361dbd14f5dd872752/1?pq-origsite=gscholar&cbl=18750&diss=y

Singh, A. P., Pradhan, N. R., Luhach, A. K., Agnihotri, S., Jhanjhi, N. Z., Verma, S., ... Roy, D. S. (2020). A novel patient-centric architectural framework for blockchain-enabled healthcare applications. *IEEE Transactions on Industrial Informatics, 17*(8), 5779–5789. https://ieeexplore.ieee.org/abstract/document/9259231

Su, Z., Wang, Y., Xu, Q., Fei, M., Tian, Y. C., & Zhang, N. (2018). A secure charging scheme for electric vehicles with smart communities in energy blockchain. *IEEE Internet of Things Journal, 6*(3), 4601-4613. https://ieeexplore.ieee.org/abstract/document/8457186

Tasca, P., & Tessone, C. J. (2017). *Taxonomy of blockchain technologies. Principles of identification and classification.* arXiv preprint arXiv:1708.04872.

Tosh, D. K., Shetty, S., Liang, X., Kamhoua, C., & Njilla, L. (2017, October). Consensus protocols for blockchain-based data provenance: Challenges and opportunities. In *2017 IEEE 8th Annual Ubiquitous Computing, Electronics and Mobile Communication Conference (UEMCON)* (pp. 469-474). IEEE.

Twizeyimana, J. D., & Andersson, A. (2019). The public value of E-Government–A literature review. *Government Information Quarterly, 36*(2), 167–178. https://www.sciencedirect.com/science/article/pii/S0740624X1730196X

United Nations. (2018). https://publicadministration.un.org/egovkb/en-us/data/compare-countries

Xia, Q., Sifah, E. B., Smahi, A., Amofa, S., & Zhang, X. (2017). BBDS: Blockchain-based data sharing for electronic medical records in cloud environments. *Information, 8*(2), 44. https://www.mdpi.com/2078-2489/8/2/44

Yang, T., Guo, Q., Tai, X., Sun, H., Zhang, B., Zhao, W., & Lin, C. (2017, November). *Applying blockchain technology to decentralized operation in future energy internet. In 2017 IEEE Conference on Energy Internet and Energy System Integration (EI2).* IEEE. https://ieeexplore.ieee.org/abstract/document/8244418

Yazdanmehr, A., Wang, J., & Yang, Z. (2020). Peers matter: The moderating role of social influence on information security policy compliance. *Information Systems Journal, 30*(5), 791–844. https://onlinelibrary.wiley.com/doi/abs/10.1111/isj.12271

Yoo, C. W., Sanders, G. L., & Cerveny, R. P. (2018). Exploring the influence of flow and psychological ownership on security education, training and awareness effectiveness and security compliance. *Decision Support Systems, 108*, 107–118. https://www.sciencedirect.com/science/article/abs/pii/S0167923618300381

Zambrano, R., Seward, R. K., & Sayo, P. (2017). *Unpacking the disruptive potential of blockchain technology for human development.* https://idl-bnc-idrc.dspacedirect. org/handle/10625/56662

Zheng, Z., Xie, S., Dai, H. N., Chen, X., & Wang, H. (2018). Blockchain challenges and opportunities: A survey. *International Journal of Web and Grid Services, 14*(4), 352-375. https://www.inderscienceonline.com/doi/abs/10.1504/IJWGS.2018.095647

Chapter 11
Applying Decision Tree for Hiding Data in Binary Images for Secure and Secret Information Flow

Gyankamal J. Chhajed

ⓘ https://orcid.org/0000-0002-9478-5579

Bharati Vidyapeeth, India & Vidya Pratishthan's Kamalnayan Bajaj Institute of Engineering and Technology, India

Bindu R. Garg

Bharati Vidyapeeth, India

ABSTRACT

In today's digital world, it is noticeable that images are transferred in binary form which carries significant and confidential information. To secure and keep such information unnoticeable is the prime concern during transmission. Information hiding as watermarking or secret messaging are most acceptable ways to attain this. In this direction, a new information flow system using data hiding approach is proposed in this chapter. A decision tree is applied for locating the most suitable blocks for data hiding in the presented technique. Decision trees are one of the best techniques used as a classifier. In this approach, the decision tree classifies a particular block to be selected for hiding information, based on the LURD pattern of 3X3 pixel block of image and the blocks of information to be hidden. For security, information is encrypted and then scattered in the image. The receiver can retrieve the data without the original image. The results prove that the proposed scheme is capable of minimizing distortion caused due to data hiding.

DOI: 10.4018/978-1-7998-9624-1.ch011

INTRODUCTION

Nowadays, people prefer images of information that is in any form to avoid time-consuming writing, preserving or transferring as it is possible to have it with just a few clicks. In such an open world of information, exchanging messages safely and securely is an important topic of research. Media files are best suitable for covered communication because of their large size. Steganography on images is one of the most popular forms of steganography, since images occur frequently on websites, as an attachment, etc. There are many ways or methods used before for hiding data in images which usually distorts images. So a popular decision tree, a machine learning approach is adopted for which will support to minimize the distortion. This algorithm is used to find suitable blocks where the data can be hidden taking care of the least distortion. In this technique, a specific pattern of four bits of 3X3 pixel block called as LURD pattern is matched with a block of 4-bit encrypted data to be hidden and accordingly decided whether the 3X3 pixel block is suitable for data hiding or not. The encryption with the key is applied for security purpose. Scattering data over the partitions of the image makes this technique more difficult for unauthorized access.

Background

Many Information hiding techniques were proposed where common approaches are using LSB bits, block based processing, edge pixel utilization, frequency domain transformations, applying some machine learning algorithms etc. Image encryption and support vector machine (SVM) used for data hiding, extraction, and image recovery in (Manikandan & Masilamani, 2018). It uses image blocks and in each block, the one-bit message can be embedded. In this scheme, encryption keys have been used at 3 levels and only authorized receiver is able to get the hidden message. A support vector machine (SVM) model is also trained for extraction. A small-block-based technique is proposed in (Ding & Wang, 2018) in which information is hidden adapting image block pattern. The technique claims highest data hiding rate. It applied the principle of Webb's law and used blind data extraction. Data hiding and extraction algorithm have very low computational complexity. In (Feng & Weng, 2017), a binary image steganalysis scheme proposed which checks the effect of embedding and identifies that the data is hidden. The l-shape pattern is considered and distortion is calculated for 4 classes of patterns. It used images to constitute a 32-dimensional Steganography feature set. Further, a 2-dimensional feature set that only involves the distribution of 2 patterns is computed. They are then combined with the soft-margin Support Vector Machine (SVM) to construct steganalysis. The proposed scheme presents a significant performance in detecting state-of-the-art data hiding schemes. In (Wu, 2017), the combination theory applied to reduce visual distortion. A special matrix is used which increases hiding capacity reducing the visual artifacts. In this technique one pixel is changed at most for each block and [log2(m x n +1)] bits are hidden into a block of size m x n. The scheme yields capability of a higher payload embedding maintaining noise. Block classification and local complexity calculation is used in (Wu, 2016). In this scheme, at most only two pixels are modified to embed three bits data into each selected block. The complex region of the image is used to hide the secret data so that it is difficult to detect with whether data is hidden or not. This also avoids grabbing attention from attackers. The texture property of binary images is considered in (Honey Mol & Reji, 2016) and proposed an efficient binary image data hiding with similarity matching method based on texture. A new information security method is proposed in (Nguyen, 2015). The proposed technique targets more unnoticeable and secure transmission of data that is secretly hidden compare to the generally used LSB algorithm. A novel scheme for authentication of binary image is proposed in (Udhayavene & Aathira, 2015) that has a small distortion in the cover image. Hamming codes-based scheme is used in the data-embedding algorithm is proposed in (Lee et al., 2009) where the ELSSM (Edge Line Segment Similarity Measure) algorithm is used for selecting and flipping pixels. A new multi-class steganalysis method was proposed in (Chiew & Pieprzyk, 2010). The proposed method is capable of identifying the technique used for hiding data. The data hiding in binary text documents is proposed in (Mei et al., 2001) where the 8-connected boundary of character is used for embedding. Five-pixel boundary with a fixed set of pairs of patterns utilized to embed data by adding or deleting the center foreground pixel in a pair. An image quality maintaining scheme is proposed in (Tseng & Pan, 2002) after data hiding .The imperceptibility after embedding is identified by comparing modified bit and its adjacent bits . In (Lu et al., 2002) discrete cosine transform (DCT) domain is used by checking for watermark embedding possibility in the binary images. The method in (Chhajed et al., 2008; Chhajed & Shinde, 2010; Wu & Liu, 2004) uses relationships within the block to identify "flippable" pixels which causes minimum visual distortion. Visual alteration detection and accordingly deciding hiding data in such a way that visual quality is maintained for all types of binary images is proposed in(Kim & de Queiroz, 2004) . Variety of proposed scheme also presented which locates updated region. The connectivity of pixels in a neighborhood preserving method is proposed in (Yang & Kot, 2007). In a 3X3 moving window, the "flippability" is identified centered at pixel. In (Yang & Kot, 2006), a blind binary image authentication scheme which uses two-layer where the first layer is used for the authentication and the second layer locates the tampering locations. A scheme which uses morphological transform domain is proposed in (Yang et al., 2008). (Xuan & Yun, 2008) Proposed, reversible data hiding scheme where run-length (RL) histogram is monitored and modified to embed data. The sequence of RL couples was used to hide data which are formed by black RL and white RL. Review and analysis of exiting watermarking and steganography techniques presented in (Chhajed et al., 2011) considering image processing in spatial and transform domain. Regression analysis model used in (Garg, 2016) to accomplish the efficient de-fuzzification operation. An ordered weighted aggregation (OWA) proposes in (Garg et al., 2018) for fuzzy time series and further designed forecasting model signifying efficacy of the proposed concept.

PROPOSED APPROACH

The proposed model uses a novel approach to hide information in binary image. The novelty of this approach is in first utilization of 3X3 image block in such a way that it carries 4 bits of information. Second the selection of block is matching the Information bits to minimize distortion. Third, the information is distributed in image partition so that imperceptibility will be increased and fourth, the information is encrypted before hiding. Fifth, decision tree is utilized for selection of suitable blocks in images for again minimizing distortion and distribution of information. Figure 1 represents the information hiding process. As shown very first, the image is divided into blocks of size 3X3 pixels. For distribution of distortion, the image is partitioned into image partitions horizontally distributing 3X3 pixels blocks equally. Data to be hidden is considered a message which is in textual form. This is represented in binary form concatenating ASCII codes of characters. Encryption is applied to secure this stream of message bits. The message blocks of sizes 4 bits are prepared from the encrypted message stream. Each image block represents the LURD pattern as shown in Figure 2. For message block embedding, matching image partition number, its predecessor and successor partitions are considered. Unique LURD patterns are identified and block which matches with message block patterns are prepared as indicator blocks by utilizing remaining pixels of the block so that correct message can be extracted. As shown in Figure 3, the decision tree is used to select suitable blocks from partitions that are considered for respective message blocks. The message block is embedded in the image block which is decided by the decision tree. In the same way, all message blocks are embedded.

The extraction process is shown in Figure 4. Very first, the image is divided into blocks of size 3X3 pixels. Image is partitioned into image partitions horizontally distributing 3X3 pixels blocks equally. Indicator blocks are located and LURD patterns in those blocks are considered as message block patterns. The extracted message blocks are combined and decrypted with the shared key among sender and receiver and original the message is obtained.

Figure 1. Information hiding process

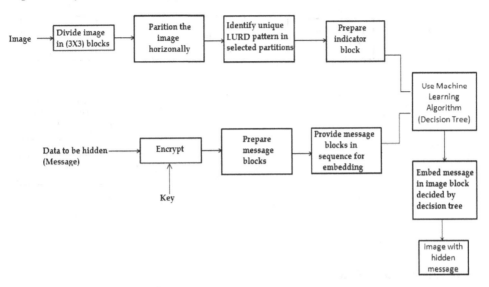

Figure 2. (a)LURD pattern representation (b) e.g. LURD: 1100

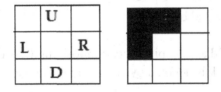

Figure 3. Decision tree

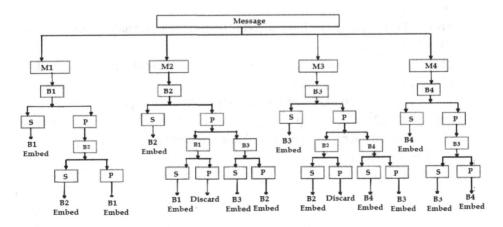

Figure 4. Data extraction process

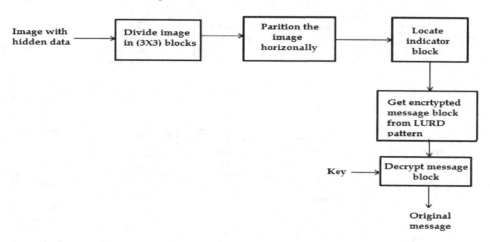

Mathematical Model

1. Let I be the image of size mxn, partitioned into blocks of 3x3 pixels
   I = (B|1 <= i <= m/3; 1 < j <=n/3)
2. Each B is represented by 9 bits
   B = b0, b1... b8
3. Let Bl, Bu, Br, Bd are the pixel location forming LURD pattern central pixel in 3X3 pixel block is denoted by Bij and they are denoted as follows
   Bl = Bi-1, j
   Bu= Bi, j+1
   Br = Bi+1, j
   Bd= Bi, j-1
4. D = d1, d2............,dp
   where, D is the data to be hidden and is represented in binary p bits
5. Db = (d0,d1,d2,d3)
   where, Db is the block of data to be hidden and is represented in binary four bits
6. K = k1, k2,.............,kq
   where, K is the secret keys and is represented in binary q bits.
7. Let E = e1, e2,............ep
   where, E is the encrypted data to be hidden represented in p bits.
8. E = Encrypt(D,K)
9. D = Decrypt(E,K)

Algorithm

Decision tree is an algorithm to get decision based on existing different situations. In proposed work it is build considering all possible situations and is capable of providing decision for supplied situation. In proposed system, it is used to get suitable blocks for data hiding in respective set of image partitions for respective message block to avoid unnecessary distortion due to flipping of pixels. As shown in Figure 3, "S" is indicating message blocks matching fully with LURD pattern and indicator bits and hence such blocks are selected blocks. "P" indicates partial matching and in this situation, same LURD patterns are checked in respective image partition and accordingly decision is made.

Input: Message
Output: Decision of selection of blocks where message blocks to be embedded

Step 1. Take the image and divide it in four parts (consider A B C D).
Step 2. Take the message and divide it in four parts (consider M1, M2, M3, M4).
Step 3. Now try to store the four parts of message in four different blocks (i.e. M1 in A, M2 in B, M3 in C and M4 in D).
Step 4. Store the first part of message in first part of block.
Step 5. If any part of message cannot be stored in its own block then try to store in its adjacent block.
Step 6. If any part of message can be stored in its own block but needs to change one bit in indicator and its adjacent block of image can store that part of message without any charge one bits than that message bits are stored in that adjacent part but the sequence of message should not get disturbed.
Step 7. In this way store all the message bits in scattered format.

Experimental Setup and Performance Evaluation

Experiments on standard images and other sample images are conducted using NetBeans IDE 8.2, JAVA 8. The Mean Squared error (MSE) and peak signal-to-noise ratio (PSNR) are standard measurement generally used as metrics for performance evaluation of data hiding techniques. The high value of PSNR indicates less distortion after hiding data in image. If the cover image is C of size M × N and the image

Figure 5. Sample images for testing (a) before data hiding (b)after data hiding

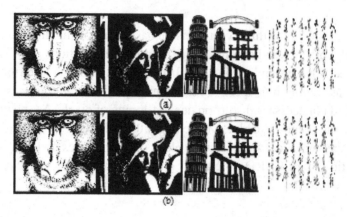

after data hiding is S of size M × N, then C and S image will have pixel value (x,y) from 0 to M-1and 0 to N-1 respectively. The PSNR is then calculated as follows:

$$MSE = \frac{1}{MN} \sum_{x=0}^{M-1} \sum_{y=0}^{N-1} \left(C(x,y) - S(x,y) \right)^2 \tag{1}$$

$$PSNR = 10.\log_{10} \left[\frac{MAX^2}{MSE} \right] \tag{2}$$

RESULT ANALYSIS

The technique is tested with set of standard images. The sample figures are as shown in Figure 5 before and after hiding information. The result analysis is presented in Table 1. The flipped pixel to number of bits of information hidden is the basis for evaluating the technique performance. The performance metrics PSNR and MSE are used to check the performance of the technique. A textual message "success" represented in 56 bits encrypted message is embedded in the images.

Table 1. Result analysis table with sample images

SN	Image	Image size	Total Pixels	Image DPI	Message size (no of bits)	Flipped pixel count (no. in bits)	MSE 10-3	PSNR
1	Baboon	200X200	40000	96	56	15	5.63	32.04
2	Lena	299X295	88205	96	56	22	5.49	32.15
3	Image 1	256X256	65536	96	56	17	4.41	33.10
4	Image2	300X298	83400	96	56	24	6.91	31.14
5	Image3	297X172	51084	96	56	16	5.01	32.54

Figure 6. Comparison of size of message embedded versus flipped pixels

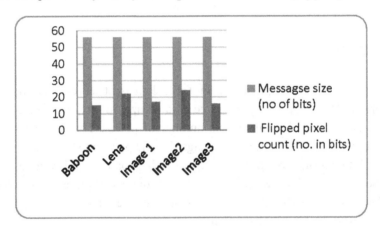

Figure 7. Performance analysis using MSE

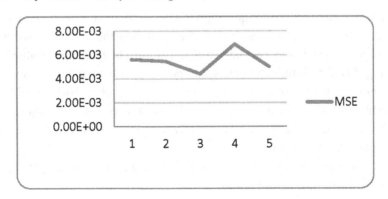

Figure 8. Performance analysis using PSNR

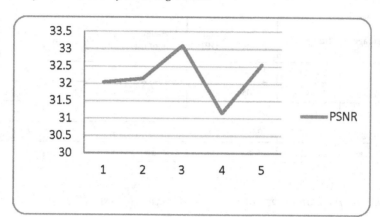

DISCUSSION

From the obtained results presented in Table 1, it is observed that flipped pixel count range is 15-24 for hiding the same data of size 56 bits. Figure 6 graphically represents flipped pixel count versus number of pixels. The number of Flipped pixels is dependent on the size of the image, LURD pattern in the image block, and data block bit pattern. More the matching of LURD pattern and data bit block less will be the distortion. Figure 7 shows the Mean square error due to embedding and Figure 8 shows the PSNR value. The decision tree takes care of selecting a suitable block that causes minimum distortion.

CONCLUSION

The proposed data hiding technique applies a decision tree for hiding data in binary images. It collectively provides the benefits of hiding the data with security and minimized distortion. It uses a decision tree algorithm which selects suitable block for data hiding. The data is hidden in the scattered form so that locating data is difficult for unauthorized users. Since the message block is matched with LURD patterns of image blocks and indicator bits, it minimizes distortion. The experimental result shows that the proposed scheme significantly uses existing image patterns flipping very few pixels to hide data.

This research received no specific grant from any funding agency in the public, commercial, or not-for-profit sectors.

REFERENCES

Chhajed, Deshmukh, & Kulkarni. (2011). Review on Binary image Stegnography and Watermarking. *International Journal in Computer Science and Engineering, 3*(11), 3545-3651.

Chhajed, Inamdar, & Attar. (2008). Steganography in Black and White Picture Images. In *Congress on Image and Signal Processing, CISP 2008.* IEEE Computer Society. DOI: doi:10.1109/CISP.2008.626

Chhajed, G. J., & Shinde, S. A. (2010). Efficient Embedding in B&W picture Images. *2nd IEEE International conference ICIME 2010*, 525-528. 10.1109/ICIME.2010.5478204

Chiew & Pieprzyk. (2010). Binary Image Steganographic Techniques Classification Based on Multi-class Steganalysis. LNCS, 6047, 341–358.

Ding, W., & Wang, Y. (2018). Data Hiding in Binary Image with High Payload. *Arabian Journal for Science and Engineering, 2018*(43), 7737–7745. doi:10.100713369-018-3130-5

Feng, B., & Weng, J. (2017). *Stegnalysis of content adaptive binary image data hiding.* Elsevier ScienceDirect., doi:10.1016/j.jvcir.2017.01.008

Garg, B. (2016). *Enhanced accuracy of fuzzy time series model using ordered weighted aggregation. Elsevier Applied Soft Computing, 48.*

Garg, B., Aggarwal, S., & Sokhal, J. (2018). Crop yield forecasting using fuzzy logic and regression model. *Computers & Electrical Engineering, 67*, 383–403. doi:10.1016/j.compeleceng.2017.11.015

Honey Mol, M., & Reji, P. I. (2016). A secure binary data hiding and comparison technique. *International Journal of Scientific & Engineering Research, 7*(7).

Kim, H. Y., & de Queiroz, R. L. (2004). Alteration-locating authentication watermarking for binary images. *Proc. Int. Workshop Digital Watermarking*, 125–136.

Lee, Y., Kim, H., & Park, Y. (2009). A new data hiding scheme for binary image authentication with small image distortion. *Information Sciences, 179*(22), 3866–3884. doi:10.1016/j.ins.2009.07.014

Lu, H., Shi, X., Shi, Y. Q., Kot, A. C., & Chen, L. (2002). Watermark embedding in DC components of DCT for binary images. *Proc., IEEE Workshop on Multimedia Signal Processing*, 300–303.

Manikandan, V. M., & Masilamani, V. (2018). Reversible data hiding scheme during encryption using machine learning. *Procedia Computer Science, 133*, 348–356. doi:10.1016/j.procs.2018.07.043

Mei, Q., Wong, E. K., & Memon, N. (2001). Data hiding in binary text document. *Proceedings of the Society for Photo-Instrumentation Engineers, 4314*, 369–375. doi:10.1117/12.435420

Nguyen. (2015). *High capacity data hiding for binary image based on block classification.* Springer. doi:10.100711042-015-2768-1

Tseng, Y. C., & Pan, H.-K. (2002). Data hiding in 2-color images. *IEEE Transactions on Computers, 51*(7), 873–878. doi:10.1109/TC.2002.1017706

Udhayavene, S., & Aathira, T. (2015). New data hiding technique in encrypted image:DKL algorithm. *Procedia Computer Science, 54*, 790–798. doi:10.1016/j.procs.2015.06.093

Wu. (2016). *Separable Reversible data hiding for encrypted palette images with color partitioning and flipping verification.* IEEE. doi:10.1109/TCSVT.2016.2556585

Wu. (2017). *Development of data hiding schema based on combination theory for lowering the visual noise in binary image.* Elsevier ScienceDirect. doi:10.1016/j.displa.2017.07.009

Wu, M., & Liu, B. (2004). Data hiding in binary images for authentication and annotation. *IEEE Transactions on Multimedia, 6*(4), 528–538. doi:10.1109/TMM.2004.830814

Xuan, G., & Yun, Q. (2008). Reversible Binary Image Data Hiding By Run-Length Histogram Modification. *International Conference on Pattern Recognition*, 1651-1653.

Yang, H., & Kot, A. C. (2006). Binary Image Authentication With Tampering Localization by Embedding Cryptographic Signature and Block Identifier. *IEEE Signal Processing Letters, 13*(12), 741–744. doi:10.1109/LSP.2006.879829

Yang, H., & Kot, A. C. (2007). Pattern-based date hiding for binary images authentication by connectivity-preserving. *IEEE Transactions on Multimedia, 9*(3), 475–486. doi:10.1109/TMM.2006.887990

Yang, H., Kot, A. C., & Rahardja, S. (2008). Orthogonal data embedding for binary images in Morphological Transform domain-A high capacity approach. *IEEE Transactions on Multimedia, 10*(3), 339–351. doi:10.1109/TMM.2008.917404

Chapter 12
Cybersecurity Issues and Challenges for E-Government During COVID-19:
A Review

Imdad Ali Shah
Shah Abdul Latif University, Pakistan

ABSTRACT

Cyber-attacks can steal information by applying different methods and activities of cyber criminals, thereby destroying data, computer programs, and networking on one or more computers. There is an increase in new technology among users, and it provides them with more convenience. On the other hand, cyber-attacks are increasing dramatically today. The world is completely focused on creating social distancing between people. During the WHO-recommended COVID-19 pandemic, billions of people around the world are working from home, with shops and businesses closed. In their investigation of the environment, researchers have uncovered a notable type of cybercrime that has an impact on society and businesses. The pandemic has accelerated the transition of government employees and businesses to an actual workplace ecosystem. Dramatic changes in the workplace have created new and multi-layered challenges in dealing with cybersecurity risks and threats. Cyber-attacks can create problems that are detrimental to the economy, human privacy, and national security. These attacks have different perspectives on the problem and need to be understood first. In this chapter, the authors highlight several essential concerns and challenges facing e-government development as well as different departments that provide e-services. They also focus on and peer evaluate the major concerns and challenges facing e-government growth from a holistic perspective, offering methodologies and policy recommendations to address them in a complete and inclusive manner.

DOI: 10.4018/978-1-7998-9624-1.ch012

1. INTRODUCTION

The COVID-19 pandemic has brought together public health and cybersecurity in unprecedented ways, revealing underlying problems and ignoring warnings that have plagued both sectors of the United States for decades. By providing fast data and allowing digital communication to the e-business (McKibbin & Fernando, 2020),(Rodela et al., 2020),(Ahmad, 2020). The government is re-using the information in the appropriate report and is taking advantage of the benefits of communication electronic transaction procedures. Electronic information has efficiently provided transaction services to the different parties (Lallie et al., 2021),(Samtani et al., 2020),(Razaque et al., 2019),(Williams et al., 2020). In particular, it is a modernization mechanism and plays a significant role in saving costs. In this system, there is no need to meet face-to-face for information and settlement. This is a national emergency and collectively steps are being taken by the world's forums and organizations to face this disease until they get an accurate vaccine for it and can smoothly run life. In this situation, the WHO recommended creating social distance between the people. Billions of people around the world are working from home and operating businesses from home, such as financial transactions, buying and selling, shopping, etc. At the moment, the world is still reeling from the COVID-19 attacks and their widespread effects on business operations, as well as rising threats to many aspects such as the economy, politics, health, and security (Brohi et al., 2020; He et al., 2021; Hiscox, 2019; Khan, Brohi, & Zaman, 2020; Weil & Murugesan, 2020). Which could occur anywhere in the world, could result in massive economic losses, and that the pandemic has changed the way organizations and government departments operate. They are operating online activities and instruction from home. E-governance is being speedily implemented all over the world to give seamless facilities to the citizens. While threats and attacks on organizations and digital data are on the rise, Indonesia has predicted future threats and risks. It needs a huge investment to deal with this virus, especially in health (Carrapico & Farrand, 2020; Ferreira & Cruz-Correia, 2021; Wiggen, 2020; Wijayanto & Prabowo, 2020; World Health Organization, 2020). It is very important to estimate the current gap, strengthen health structure, funding, and management, and increase research measurements and evidence-based strategy making. Securing information and data is essential to government and private organizations. The detailed report of GESTR 2019 stated that 42% of endpoints are insecure (Burrell, 2020; Karpenko et al., 2021; Liang et al., 2017; Mensah, 2019; Okereafor & Adebola, 2020). Cybersecurity experts have estimated that $450 billion annually is the total universal cost of malicious hacking activities. CTI experts have suggested that investigation and examination are necessary for the international online hacker community (Gupta & Agarwal, 2017; Luh et al., 2017; Peng et al., 2017; Saleem et al., 2017; Williams et al., 2020). Medical information plays a significant part in human health. The primary object of this research is to conduct a comprehensive survey in connection with possible cyber-attacks and find proper solutions to these types of threats and attacks the world has estimated the cost of cybersecurity attacks and threats, while the number of threats and attacks has bigger increased after COVID-19 (Huang et al., 2018; Khandpur et al., 2017; Stellios et al., 2018; Tounsi & Rais, 2018). The large literature is available in the prospect of health care industries on threats technological vulnerabilities. The major revolutions are the advancement of information technology and the improvement of government functions. Different applications of e-government are working, more reliant on cyberspace, a lesser-known area of "business" especially in digital security (Ding et al., 2018), (Ramadan et al., 2021), (Scarfone et al., 2009). The practice of keeping the networks that make-up cyberspace safe from intrusion is called cybersecurity. Integrity of information. On the other hand, the changing risk landscape requires a more dynamic strategy. Governments develop cybersecurity plans and flexible approaches for governments to address cybersecurity issues (Bhuvana & Vasantha, 2021; Cradduck, 2019; Hussain et al., 2021; Lim, Abdullah, Jhanjhi et al, 2019; Ullah et al., n.d.). A modern city is seen as a collection of major elements such as quality of life and socio-economic development. The construction and management of smart cities must consider several important issues. These standards are used to create a framework to gain a deeper understanding of the efforts that have been made. Social, administrative, economic, and legal dimensions are all important pillar variables. The government has caught up with the technological revolution. The digitalization of public administration is inextricably linked to security issues. Digitization can be seen as one of the tools of effective governance, but it also has its own set of problems (Gaur et al., 2021; Lim, Abdullah, & Jhanjhi, 2019; Lim, Abdullah, Jhanjhi et al, 2019). This article will explore the current status and issues of cyber threats to Hungarian urban e-administrative services and practices. Hungary's fragmented municipal system limits the country's economic strength (Humayun, Niazi, Jhanjhi et al, 2020). The experiments and opportunities are huge. We take a look at the rules and we can see that they were created to develop horizontally integrated electronic management. Legislation governing the system has been passed in recent years, and the previous ban on electronic administration has been lifted. Hungarian e-governance practices differ in some respects (Almusaylim & Jhanjhi, 2020; Amir Latif et al., 2020; Khan, Jhanjhi, Humayun et al, 2020; Kumar et al., 2021; Lee et al., 2021). A new problem arises from the expanded e-administration, which partly addresses the radical nationalization and centralization of activities previously managed by municipalities. Municipal e-government systems are mainly established by large cities. Their functioning is likely to improve, so municipal cybersecurity is becoming an increasingly important part of Hungarian public administration. Apply e-government and communication technologies to government functions to improve

Figure 1. Overview of strategies for the chapter

transparency and accountability of government services. Increase the efficiency of various agencies and improve government interaction with business and industry. This often requires the effective use of ICTs for specific purposes by individual government entities. Loss or disclosure of confidential data and electronic resources of government departments and other corporate entities can be caused by various threat actors or agents (Najmi et al., 2021),(NSKT Global, n.d.),(Zong et al., 2019). Further research has been conducted on a variety of intentional and unintentional threats and their consequences Figure 1 shows the strategies for the chapter.

The main object of this chapter is to focus on the following points, which will be discussed in depth:

1. We will present an overview of cybersecurity and issues for e-government
2. We will discuss the e-government experience COVID-19
3. We will discuss and explore cybersecurity issues and challenges facing during COVID-19
4. We will present recommendations and solutions

2. LITERATURE REVIEW

The covid-19 pandemic has moved online implementation of digital technologies, such as shopping, industry, finance transactions, and business activities. Unfortunately, the ratio of cybercrimes is rising in frequency and severity, latest reports published (Singh et al., 2020), (Korir et al., 2019). Has investigated for endorsing future research and emerging to produce solutions using AI, HPC, 3DPT, TT, and BDA. The ratio of cybersecurity issues has increased due to staff working from homes. The IT industry and professionals have taken huge benefits to provide services and applications. While a few undesirable influences as well, growing new cybersecurity risk and threats due to highway workload and continuously increasing (Ahmad, 2019; Humayun, Jhanjhi, Hamid et al, 2020; Nosiri & Ndoh, 2018; Ravi et al., 2021; Sangki, 2018). Highlighted several cybersecurity challenges linked during the pandemic and cybersecurity involving lack of budgets. Security and Privacy are yet big queries in human-computer interactions HCI. Pandemic has wedged the route of EU cybersecurity policy. From the crisis of the Pandemic, the significant growing cybersecurity risk businesses, citizens, and states are facing (Alamri et al., 2019; Kaur et al., 2018; NSKT Global, n.d.; Rajmohan et al., 2020). The growing level of IT and computer use in a pandemic will disturb the scale of cybercrime vulnerability behavior. The pandemic led to broader use of digital applications prompting government and business activities to change whole work processes that have been done online. The passable actions have been implemented and are increasing the dependence of government and private sector proper running of their IT systems. It has been said that millions of people work from their homes during the pandemic. Further, it has highlighted security risks and threats. The pandemic has accelerated the move to practical workplace ecosystems for the government's employees and businesses. The Dramatic move of the workplace has created novel multi-layered challenges around handling cybersecurity risk and threats. Research articles have been reviewed on the cybersecurity influence of the coronavirus fear on digital systems and cyberspace (Liu et al., 2021; NSKT Global, n.d.; Research Gate, n.d.; Walden et al., 2020). Additionally, recommendations have been made to privacy protection online applications. Top priority has been given to the citizens, the problem of cybersecurity in the medical domain instead of the given priority to a real threat to national security during a pandemic and measuring the implementation of cybersecurity and spreading fake news. It was exposed in the TAM that positively to be seen in the prediction of e-government performance (Cowgill & Stevenson, 2020; Dorr et al., 2020; Kapersky, n.d.; Le Blond et al., 2017; Sharma, 2021). There is an inevitable development of e-government clouds throughout the world, and a growing need to explore the determinants and their mechanism of e-Government cloud implementation among the government agencies in China. With the number of cybersecurity attacks and threats continually increasing, organization adopters have responded to security concerns that threaten their business in today's highly competitive environment. Several documented industrial cyber-attacks have effectively compressed technical solutions that are exploited by human-factor vulnerabilities linked to security skills and knowledge. This article focuses on human knowledge based on security knowledge and security skills to highlight the security capabilities and their quantity. Demonstrates authenticity by providing a framework and computational method (Bhagat et al., 2021), (Arabadzhyiev et al., 2021). Today, IoT, cloud computing, social networks mobile, and mobile are making changes in the social procedure. This technology transformation stands for new security attacks and threats in complex cybersecurity situations with huge capacities of data and different attack vectors. Which may exceed the academic capabilities of security analysts (Dahwan & Raju, 2021), (Sadiq et al., 2021). The rise of information and communication technology has met new challenges that are essential to be addressed, including the security of citizen's (Mehrotra, 2021). Government administrative mechanisms around the world have been transformed through the implementation of e-government technologies that increase efficiency, openness, and accountability. Findings were added based on future research and to support administrators in selecting appropriate models and methods. A manufacturer develops the necessary technical equipment for the next phase of symbiosis (Muda et al., 2020). The authors discuss evolving technology trends in e-government in India. Many new trends are explored in his research. Reference was also made to the evolving e-government government strategy. These authors discuss changes in digital assistance services, civic solution development, allowing inclusive decision-making, service delivery, online government service fulfillment, and shared services with public-private partnerships (Razuleu, 2018). Cybersecurity basically defines the use of computer security precautions to provide the highest level of assurance. The term "categorized" means that information should only be visible to those who are allowed to view it. The term "trustworthiness" refers to the rules that allow authorized clients to make changes to data, and those changes will be consistently reflected in all parts of the data. The term "accessibility" refers to the rule that information and computer assets should always be available to authorized customers (Khatoun & Zeadally, 2017; Linkov et al., 2018; Malhotra et al., 2017a; Soni, Anand, Dey et al, 2017; Soni, Dey, Anand et al, 2017). The fundamental problem is that some details are missing. The history of PC security can be said to repeat the same mistakes. Early PC frameworks provided strong security that was nearly inaccessible compared to today's utilities. Information accessibility grew significantly as programming vendors expanded their use, moving to PCs, then distributed registries, and finally online management. However, as a result of this development, difficulties have arisen regarding classification and legality. Several of the driving principles behind creating most of the products focus first on the highlights. The product business has cleaned up over the past few years due to increased safety concerns (Haran, 2016; Ilves, 2016; Jazri & Jat, 2016; Norris et al., 2015; Oxford Analytica, 2016). The core structure of the Internet is built around shared access and trust, followed by security initiatives. Several widely used conventions have little security for their clients, relying instead on trust Figure 2.

3. COVID-19: CYBERSECURITY ISSUES AND CHALLENGES

In high-profile recent cases, hackers attempting to steal $7 million in business documents have been attempted by the hackers. The research includes key conclusions from over 275 of the world's leading specialists in data protection. Many people

Figure 2. Overview challenges and E-Government implementation in Afghanistan (Joshi, 2015)

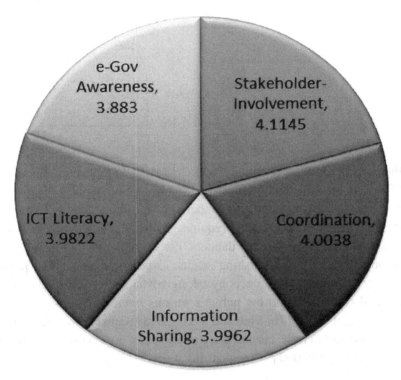

have been compelled to work from home, relying heavily on It's challenging for professionals to mitigate risks remotely because of cloud services and work computing infrastructure (Joshi, 2015; Sithole, 2015; Sony, 2015). When asked what their main concern was, more than 75% said they were concerned that employees would break the rules, exposing company systems and data to new threats. Additionally, 67% are concerned about the vulnerability of systems and networks used by restricted workers, and 65% are concerned about increased attacks by adversaries looking to profit from the problem. COVID-19 will have long-term repercussions for operational security. More than 80% of security experts believe the COVID-19 issue will result in substantial changes in operations methodologies, with only 15% expecting that cyber activities and threat flow will revert to normal once the crisis is over. While the COVID-19 epidemic has put corporate operations in jeopardy, it also raises serious security concerns ahead of the 2020 presidential election in the United States (Angelopoulos et al., 2017; Dubey et al., 2015; Mwangi, 2015; Ramli, 2017). Mobile voting solutions are being considered by local city and state governments in order to meet social distancing requirements, which has security experts concerned.

Figure 3. 48% of working from home, people fall victim to phishing attacks.

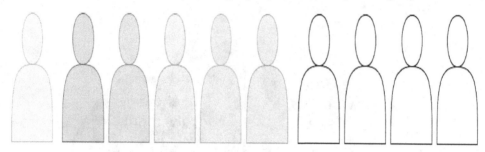

More than two-thirds of survey participants (69%) believe that voting electronically, in any form, is fundamentally dangerous. Using mobile applications for voting, according to 74% of respondents, is an inherently hazardous activity that cannot be safeguarded. The rise of remote work requires greater attention to cybersecurity due to increased vulnerability to cyber dangers. For example, 47% of people working from home were victims of phishing scams. Cybercriminals see the pandemic, this is a way to enhance illegal acts by taking advantage of secluded employees' exposure and capitalising on the public's serious interest in coronavirus-related news (Malhotra et al., 2017b; Meiyanti et al., 2018; Ramzi & Weerakkody, n.d.). Another consideration is the current price of a security breach due to online labour, which can exceed $139,000 per incident Figure 3.

4. COVID-19: CYBERSECURITY AND E-GOVERNMENT

E-government has grown to incorporate both online and offline platforms that provide digital services in addition to giving information via a website. Artificial intelligence and blockchain are among the digital capabilities and services that the e-government infrastructure focuses on. Governments employ the e-government infrastructure to deliver services such as business licensing, birth and debt registration, driver's licence renewal, tax payment services, and public utility payment. Governments have also adopted social media as part of their e-government arrangements to offer timely information to the public and mobilize resources during disasters. E-government delivers substantial benefits to Caribbean countries, including greater access to data and information, speedier and more efficient public service, and streamlining processes. It enables the government to shift away from paper-based transactions and decreases the risk of data and information being lost in the event of a calamity (Alguliyev et al., 2018; Dhonju & Shakya, 2019; Yang et al., 2019). Governments throughout the region have been able to protect their data by using cloud services and investing in cybersecurity technologies. Governments have recently used Up-to-date data is displayed by e-government services about people who have contracted COVID-19, as well as sites to get tested and vaccinated. E-government is a networked system where the government communicates with individuals and offers them enhanced services via electronic apps. E-governance offers the government's once-in-a-lifetime opportunity to improve electronic identity records management and share social and economic outcomes (Abebe, 2019; Alharmoodi & Lakulu, 2020; Gouveia, 2020). According to polls, 80 out of 100 republics have established special provisions to verify e-government e-services used by the most vulnerable members of their population.

5. COVID-19: BUSINESS CYBERSECURITY RISK

Several small and medium-sized organizations are having problems as a result of remote working: they aren't well-prepared for the surge in sophisticated cyber-attacks, and they need to improve significantly to decrease cyber risk. Some companies were averse to permitting remote work before the epidemic, specifically when it came to accessing confidential information. Companies had to expand their capabilities and capacity for working remotely in a relatively short amount of time. Unfortunately, when remote working capabilities were quickly deployed, safety was not always a top consideration. There are ways for businesses to deploy security measures that aren't too intrusive. Host checking is a technique that verifies personal needs on personal devices before granting access to corporate apps. The result of literature review and publicly presented reports that cyber-attacks are increasing and threatening for the business. The object of this survey is to understand cyber-attack in a systemic process (Alqudah & Muradkhanli, 2021; Herawati et al., n.d.; Sharma et al., 2021; Venkatesh et al., 2016; Yang & Wibowo, 2020). Cybersecurity attacks and threats have been categorized based on publicly documented and reported cases and related review articles during the COVID-19 pandemic Figure 4.

6. COVID-19: HEALTHCARE CYBERSECURITY RISK

Healthcare cybersecurity concerns continue to loom over the already overloaded US health service, particularly as the COVID-19 epidemic drags on. Threat actors have staged sophisticated cyber-attacks on vital infrastructure and healthcare industries. Ransomware attacks against hospitals, community clinics, and professional colleagues across the healthcare industry occurred in 2021 as a result of a global epidemic and an incredibly advanced network of cybercriminal groups. Some of

Figure 4. Overview different risks during covid-19

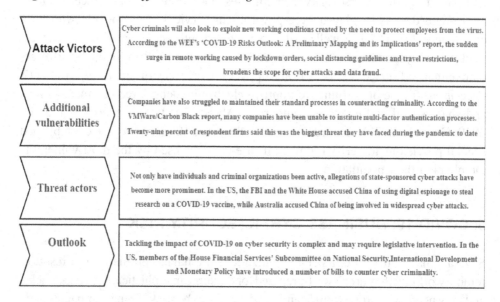

the largest healthcare cybersecurity challenges, according to Mann, are increasingly complex and successful malware cyber-attacks, the uncertainty of COVID-19 on cyber-attacks, and emerging medical device security vulnerabilities (Al-rawahna et al., 2019; AlMendah, 2021; Suleimany, 2021). Mann emphasized the need to make cybersecurity measures a top priority. Healthcare firms must make cyber risk mitigation a top priority in their annual budgets (AlMendah, 2021; Yang et al., 2019). The COVID-19 pandemic has thrown the healthcare industry into disarray around the world, putting it to the test. To add to the sector's already difficult predicament, it has become a direct target or a bystander in cyber-attacks. Hospitals have moved their emphasis and resources to their principal mission, which is to manage this unusual emergency that has put them in a vulnerable position. Hospitals, as well as the entire healthcare industry, must now be prepared (Al-Shboul et al., 2014; Waller & Genius, 2015). Cybercrime evolves in response to the environment it finds itself in. It's not surprising that malware attackers have hopped on the bandwagon in the early stages of a global pandemic like COVID-19.

7. DISCUSSION

Everything has been thrown off by COVID-19. Citizens in every G20 country are significantly reliant on digital technologies to live, work, learn, obtain information, and engage with one another, thanks to stay-at-home directives. Previous patterns of closeness are unlikely to resurface, and virtual contacts will become a more permanent part of everyday life. However, as people's reliance on technology grows, so does the chance for threat actors to commit cybercrime or spread disinformation that harms personal or civic life. This is not the same as cyber warfare or data mining (Al-Soud et al., 2014; Waller & Genius, 2015). The G20 should develop international procedures to assist citizens in avoiding such nefarious activities.

8. COVID-19: CYBERSECURITY ISSUES AND CHALLENGES FOR E-GOVERNMENT

Given the enormous amount of corporate and school disruptions associated with efforts to contain the virus, one of the most surprising outcomes of the COVID-19 global epidemic has been the rapid increase in technological innovation. Companies, health professionals, and educational institutions quickly established virtual operating models when G20 nations proclaimed stay-at-home orders, and consumers flocked online to connect and participate in daily operations (Gorla & Somers, 2014). Aimed to threaten the trust of governments and consumers In Italy, for example, many reports of fake news surfaced, including one claiming that a vaccine could be purchased for 50 Euros (Al-Soud et al., 2014; Rana et al., 2013). Money launderers, cyber terrorists, and other organized crime groups are frequently involved, with the goal of victimization. Phishing is one of the most popular and profitable hacking techniques used by cyber thieves. Phishing emails are said to be responsible for 32% of commercial data breaches and 78% of cyber-espionage operations, according to reports (Waller & Genius, 2015). During the epidemic, cyber thieves exploited the public's fear of the virus by launching phishing attempts using phony World Wide Web addresses. Hackers have been attracted to committing online scams by the rapid growth of video conferencing apps. According to a recent analysis, approximately 6,576 phishing domains for a prominent video conferencing software have been registered since January 2020 Figure 5.

9. COVID-19: INTERNET OF THINGS TECHNOLOGY AND E-GOVERNMENT

We will take a comprehensive look at this chapter on IoT applications in e-government. It outlines the e-government potential of the IoT in numerous application areas, highlighting the difficulties that need to be addressed in each one. A publish-subscribe architecture allows devices to interact. The gadgets used by the end consumer can connect and obtain the final point of use of the information. The

Figure 5. Overview covid-19 cyber-attacks causes

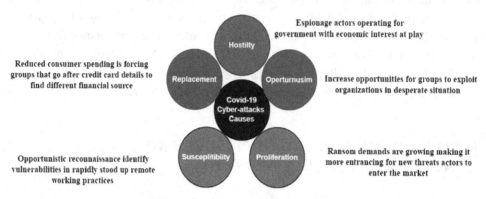

required data will be handled by the endpoint, which will be backed up by the data exchange mechanism. The capabilities of the cybersecurity framework can provide a high-level and strategic focus on the e-government risk management lifecycle related to cybersecurity (Adjei-Bamfo et al., 2019; Al-Mushayt, 2019; Alhawawsha & Panchenko, 2020; Lv et al., 2018). The framework core can be considered essential in identifying significant discrete outcomes for each e-government platform function. The implementation layer of the framework puts the relationship between e-government systems and cybersecurity threats into context (Qi & Wang, 2021). This contextualization occurs within a complete framework that includes comprehensive risk mitigation considerations. These levels are used to describe the level of progress of the organization and its cybersecurity risk reduction management system (Cheng et al., 2017). The authors demonstrate how the IoT can help with economic growth and long-term development. It proposes the connection between e-government and service management, and further proposes that the connection between e-government and supplier government be used to force the government to adopt new reforms and build a new model of high-quality and low-cost services (AlEnezi et al., 2018; Gershon et al., 2018; Nagowah et al., 2018; Sava, 2018). A web-based e-government is presented, which conforms to certain standards and creates a typical hierarchical grid system conceptual structure. In the data age, a cloud computing-based e-government authorization form paradigm has been developed. The framework includes an e-government service model, meets e-government security standards (Chishiro et al., 2017; Elezaj et al., 2018; Henriksen, 2018; Koo, 2019; Pradhan & Shakya, 2018). The separation of the two network systems of the government intranet and the government extranet, the government Internet, is a specially trained office prefab (Chinese Academy of Cyberspace Studies, 2019; Donalds & Osei-Bryson, 2020; Harris & Martin, 2019). Because the Internet and other government affairs are physically separated, some information flow and

Figure 6. Overview of IoT process chart during Covid-19

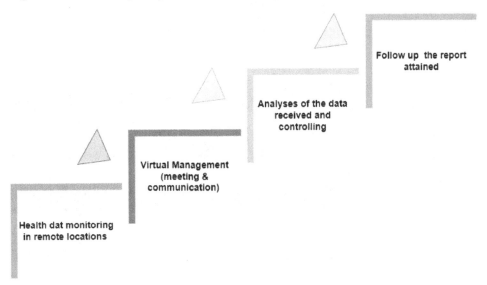

Follow up the report attained

Analyses of the data received and controlling

Virtual Management (meeting & communication)

Health dat monitoring in remote locations

capacity transfers are possible behind firewalls. Such instruments are increasingly abundant in urban environments and are being extensively researched through the Internet of Things Figure 6.

10. COVID-19: BLOCK-CHAIN TECHNOLOGY AND E-GOVERNMENT

The purpose of blockchain-based governance is to create decentralized, efficient, and trustworthy public services. This section looks at how blockchain can be used in various public spaces. Government entities process and maintain a large number of official records of individuals and companies. Block-chain-based applications have the potential to change the way these files are maintained by digitizing, securing, and permanently storing them. Through automation and accountability, blockchain can make government services more efficient and democratically accountable (Hofbauer et al., 2019; Huang & Madnick, 2021; Krishnaraju et al., 2016). The two distinct disciplines of BCT and public administration have been thoroughly explored. In addition to the hurdles and limitations that almost any innovative innovation faces, In the past, there has never been any interference between these two domains (Galvez et al., 2018; Li et al., 2019; Liu, Wang, & Liang, 2020). By combining them, new multidisciplinary solutions can be developed for individuals, companies, and other governments. Likewise, propose and build a new sector, "e-government,"

Figure 7. Overview block-chain challenges applying in e-government

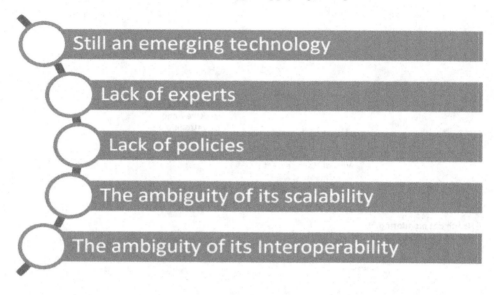

consisting of a series of artefacts developed and built according to basic normative structure and execution principles. Time hijacking is the third well-known cyber-attack in which hackers attempt to modify the timestamps of BCs before they are recorded to the protocol, in order to introduce fake BCs and inauthentic data (Liu & Carter, 2018; Muller & Lind, 2020; Ronchi, 2019; Simonova, 2020). The loss of privacy is another issue that needs to be studied. On the one hand, maintaining all transaction data and information on (Agbo et al., 2019; Twizeyimana & Andersson, 2019; Yazdanmehr et al., 2020; Yoo et al., 2018) each node seems beneficial from a security standpoint, but it also raises questions about the technology's overall usefulness for use cases that require greater anonymity (Bao et al., 2020; De Filippi et al., 2020; Salam & Kumar, 2021). Furthermore, the immutability of the system to all transaction data reveals another flaw, as some business use cases require changes to specific transactions Figure 7.

COVID-19: E-Government and Its Role

Government administrative mechanisms around the world have been transformed through the implementation of e-government technologies that increase efficiency, openness, and accountability. Findings were added based on future research and to support administrators in selecting appropriate models and methods (Almusaylim & Jhanjhi, 2020; Khan, Jhanjhi, Humayun et al, 2020; Lim, Abdullah, Jhanjhi et al, 2019; Liu, Wei, Wang et al, 2020). Manufacturers develop the necessary technical equipment for the next phase of the symbioses. Long-term applications, resources, and infrastructure are considered when developing an e-government plan (Khan, Jhanjhi, Humayun et al, 2020; Korir et al., 2019; Lee et al., 2021; Malhotra et al., 2019; Najmi et al., 2021). Creating the digital/electronic equivalent of a physical service requires a lengthy process to detail roles and responsibilities step-by-step, often hindered by practical limitations. Explore the importance of e-government during a pandemic and provide a framework and standard operating procedures to enable e-government services to operate successfully even during disasters and pandemics involving government personnel and machines. It provides an overview of the various threats and vulnerabilities that can arise in insider activity (Ahmad, 2019; Najmi et al., 2021; Nosiri & Ndoh, 2018; Sangki, 2018). The authors discuss evolving technology trends in e-government in India. Many new trends are explored in his research. Reference was also made to the evolving e-government government strategy. The authors discuss changes in digital assistance services, civic solution development, allowing inclusive decision-making, service delivery, online government service fulfilment, and service sharing with (Huang & Madnick, 2021; Kaur et al., 2018; Le Blond et al., 2017; Liu et al., 2021) public-private partnerships. The 2020 survey shows continued progress in the global e-government development model. Many countries are reducing their EGDI levels. The world is changing as technology spreads. It can help governments simplify (Joshi, 2015; Muzafar & Jhanjhi, 2020; Nosiri & Ndoh, 2018; Sangki, 2018; Shah et al., 2021) speed up, and secure processes. It can be used to automatically and quickly transfer data across multiple departments. Lack of a supportive atmosphere are all challenges (Arabadzhyiev et al., 2021; Herawati et al., n.d.; Malhotra et al., 2017a; Najmi et al., 2021; Walden et al., 2020) The Indonesian government should design comprehensive plans and progress assessments that combine technical, organizational, civic, and environmental elements to aid the development of e-government (De Filippi et al., 2020; Joshi, 2015; Najmi et al., 2021; Waller & Genius, 2015) and how various limitations can potentially affect user dissatisfaction as a measure of e-government performance. In an adverse environment, the study explains more embedded relationships in information systems (IS) success models (Dahwan & Raju, 2021; Najmi et al., 2021; Walden et al., 2020; Watts et al., 2019). IT managers and IT experts PLS Structural Equation Modelling (SEM) was employed due to his high statistical power in handling complex causal models and limited sample size. The findings indicated that service delivery fell short of stakeholder expectations (Le Blond et al., 2017; Liu et al., 2021; Najmi et al., 2021; Sharma, 2021). User dissatisfaction was found to be highly correlated with other parameters. User dissatisfaction was found to be highly correlated with other parameters (Arabadzhyiev et al., 2021; Bhagat et al., 2021; Cowgill & Stevenson, 2020; Dahwan & Raju, 2021; Dorr et al., 2020). With men seeing it as irrelevant and women seeing low system quality as directly related to low service quality. In terms of citizen security, the advent of information and communication technologies has created new difficulties that must be addressed (Linkov et al., 2018; Mehrotra, 2021; Muda et al., 2020; Razuleu, 2018; Sadiq et al., 2021). To remotely detect and manipulate these objects in both the physical and cyber realms. Connected through the Internet, these devices affect every aspect of our lives, including business, industry, education, personal and social aspects, and government (Haran, 2016; Khatoun & Zeadally, 2017; Malhotra et al., 2017a; Soni, Anand, Dey et al, 2017; Soni, Dey, Anand et al, 2017). We connect to a variety of connected smart devices, there are significant threats and risks to privacy and security from a variety of perspectives, including device data theft, authentication, data forgery, and device manipulation (Ilves, 2016; Jazri & Jat, 2016; Joshi, 2015; Norris et al., 2015; Oxford Analytica, 2016). They have the potential to disrupt production and cause financial losses to the company's producers. Some research studies use honeypots to detect botnets as one of various security methods. The authors developed and tested a botnet detection model. Interconnectivity occurs as a result of the exchange of data and information, as well as the aiding of our communication with the things around us (Dubey et al., 2015; Joshi, 2015; Mwangi, 2015; Sony, 2015; Tikkanen et al., 2018). However, major concerns regarding privacy and security remain. Hackers and attackers may benefit from a favourable environment when sharing large amounts of data. They proposed that they concentrate on current security and privacy issues (Dubey et al., 2015; Humayun, Niazi, Jhanjhi et al, 2020; Mwangi, 2015; Sony, 2015; Tikkanen et al., 2018). Cybersecurity information is disseminated via a variety of websites, including security blogs (Dunne, 2019; Lu et al., 2020; Watts et al., 2019; WHO, 2020; World Economic Forum, 2020). The author focuses on the growing e-government technology trends in India. It is understandable that many trends need to grow, such as digital enablement services, support for inclusive decision-making, citizen solution development (Kagame & Ghebreyesus, 2019; Mercer Marsh Benefits, 2019; Muda et al., 2020; O'Neil, n.d.; Watts et al., 2019), institutional efforts, government-to-citizen online service implementation, and public-private partnership services. The authors wanted to learn more about developing an information security self-assessment tool that governments can use to protect e-government systems from cybersecurity risks and attacks (De Filippi et al., 2020; Lee et al., 2018; NHS England, 2014; Walden et al., 2020). The tool employs a web-based architecture that includes specific data security components and methodologies, allowing various data security authorities to examine them. Furthermore, this research (Humayun, Niazi, Jhanjhi et al, 2020; Joshi, 2015; Linkov et al., 2018; U.S. Centers for Medicare & Medicaid Services, 2018; UNDP, 2013) found that, despite significant investment in technical information security measures, governments fail to regularly assess and review their data security efforts. Countries are considering the large-scale introduction of e-government (Department of Health,

Figure 8. Overview of cyber violence during COVID-19 (Alamri et al., 2019)

2017; General Medical Council, 2018; Gershgorn, 2018; NHS, 2019; NHS England, 2014). Building a security wall for data and transactions with complete secrecy in objects is a critical issue that must be addressed if governments are to function properly. According to the authors, this approach requires complete transparency and accountability (Greenspun et al., 2016; Hamid et al., 2020; Lee et al., 2018; Muzafar & Jhanjhi, 2020; Wong et al., 2020). Threats and dangers are significant barriers to using electronic services. Researchers advocate the use of machine learning techniques to analyse several different types of cyber-attacks Figure 8.

Our contribution to this chapter is that, during the COVID-19 pandemic, cybersecurity issues have been raised and investigated. Notable cyber-attacks and vulnerabilities are highlighted and described. Several practical solutions are investigated, as well as potential mitigating approaches, to lessen the threats of cyber-attacks. Cyber criminals and APT groups have taken advantage of the pandemic by attacking vulnerable people and networks. Furthermore, it is unlikely that this stance will alter anytime soon. Healthcare organizations have been one of the most vulnerable targets of cyber-attacks during the epidemic for a variety of reasons. As a result, healthcare businesses must upgrade their cybersecurity defenses to better safeguard their critical information and resources from cyber-attacks. Given the increased potential of a pandemic, cybersecurity needs to be given special attention. The epidemic has taught us that the key to successfully mitigating the harm caused by cyber-attacks is to plan ahead. The capacity to respond fast to unforeseen occurrences can aid in the mitigation of cyber-attack damage. Organizations that already have safe remote working capabilities will be better equipped to deal with the growing number of cyber threats. Organizations that are caught off guard will need to assess their cyber threat exposures as quickly as possible and priorities repair actions based on best practices. Additionally, for companies that provide internet access to private and sensitive data, company-owned devices should be the standard. When granting personal devices access to company data, cyber risks should be assessed and countermeasures did to avoid exposure to cyber threats. Businesses must shift their focus from "if" to "when," and recognize that data breaches and ransomware can have catastrophic financial implications. It's also worth mentioning that hackers aren't solely driven by financial gain. Another issue is "cyberactivism," which aims to harm a company's reputation. Some procedures may be taken to lessen the risk and severity of cyber-attacks, but they involve time and effort. To make remote work practices more resilient to cyber-attacks, companies must improve the development and deployment of security measures. The capabilities of the cybersecurity framework can provide a high-level and strategic focus on the e-government risk management lifecycle related to cybersecurity. The framework core can be considered essential in identifying significant discrete outcomes for each e-government platform function. The implementation layer of the framework puts the relationship between e-government systems and cybersecurity threats into context.

11. CONCLUSION AND FUTURE WORK

Cyber-attacks can steal information by applying different methods and activities of cyber criminals, thereby destroying data, computer programs, and networking on one or more computers. There is an increase in new technology among users, and it provides them with more convenience. On the other hand, cyber-attacks are increasing dramatically today. The world is completely focused on creating social distancing between people. During the WHO-recommended COVID-19 pandemic, billions of people around the world are working from home, with shops and businesses closed. In their investigation of the environment, researchers have uncovered a notable type of cybercrime that has an impact on society and businesses. The pandemic has accelerated the transition of government employees and businesses to an actual workplace ecosystem. Dramatic changes in the workplace have created new and multi-layered challenges in dealing with cybersecurity risks and threats. Cyber-attacks can create problems that are detrimental to the economy, human privacy, and national security. These attacks have different perspectives on the problem and need to be understood first. Furthermore, it needs to continue working on advanced technologies.

REFERENCES

Abebe, B. (2019). *E-government based land administration framework; trends, challenges and prospects* (Doctoral dissertation). https://ir.bdu.edu.et/handle/123456789/10878

Adjei-Bamfo, P., Maloreh-Nyamekye, T., & Ahenkan, A. (2019). The role of e-government in sustainable public procurement in developing countries: A systematic literature review. *Resources, Conservation and Recycling, 142,* 189–203. doi:10.1016/j.resconrec.2018.12.001

Agbo, C. C., Mahmoud, Q. H., & Eklund, J. M. (2019, June). Blockchain technology in healthcare: a systematic review. In *Healthcare* (Vol. 7, No. 2, p. 56). Multidisciplinary Digital Publishing Institute. https://www.mdpi.com/2227-9032/7/2/56

Ahmad, T. (2019). Technology Convergence and Cybersecurity: A Critical Analysis of Cybercrime Trends in India. *27th Convergence India Pragati Maidan,* 29-31. https://papers.ssrn.com/sol3/papers.cfm?abstract_id=3326232

AhmadT. (2020). *Corona virus (covid-19) pandemic and work from home: Challenges of cybercrimes and cybersecurity.* https://papers.ssrn.com/sol3/papers.cfm?abstract_id=3568830 doi:10.2139/ssrn.3568830

Al-Mushayt, O. S. (2019). Automating E-government services with artificial intelligence. *IEEE Access: Practical Innovations, Open Solutions, 7,* 146821–146829. doi:10.1109/ACCESS.2019.2946204

Al-rawahnaA. S. M.ChenS. C.HungC. W. (2019). *The barriers of e-government success: An empirical study from Jordan.* https://papers.ssrn.com/sol3/papers.cfm?abstract_id=3498847 doi:10.2139/ssrn.3498847

Al-Shboul, M., Rababah, O., Ghnemat, R., & Al-Saqqa, S. (2014). Challenges and factors affecting the implementation of e-government in Jordan. *Journal of Software Engineering and Applications, 7*(13), 1111–1127. doi:10.4236/jsea.2014.713098

Al-Soud, A. R., Al-Yaseen, H., & Al-Jaghoub, S. H. (2014). Jordan's e-Government at the crossroads. *Transforming Government: People, Process and Policy.* https://www.emerald.com/insight/content/doi/10.1108/TG-10-2013-0043/full/html

Alamri, M., Jhanjhi, N. Z., & Humayun, M. (2019). Blockchain for Internet of Things (IoT) research issues challenges & future directions: A review. *Int. J. Comput. Sci. Netw. Secur, 19,* 244–258. https://seap.taylors.edu.my/file/rems/publication/109566_6018_1.pdf

AlEnezi, A., AlMeraj, Z., & Manuel, P. (2018, April). Challenges of IoT based smart-government development. In *2018 21st Saudi Computer Society National Computer Conference (NCC)* (pp. 1-6). IEEE. https://ieeexplore.ieee.org/abstract/document/8593168

Alguliyev, R., Aliguliyev, R., & Yusifov, F. (2018). Role of Social Networks in E-government: Risks and Security Threats. *Online Journal of Communication and Media Technologies*, *8*(4), 363–376. https://www.ojcmt.net/article/role-of-social-networks-in-e-government-risks-and-security-threats-3957

Alharmoodi, B. Y. R., & Lakulu, M. M. B. (2020). Transition from e-government to m-government: Challenges and opportunities-case study of UAE. *European Journal of Multidisciplinary Studies*, *5*(1), 61–67. doi:10.26417/453fgx96c

Alhawawsha, M., & Panchenko, T. (2020, January). Open Data Platform Architecture and Its Advantages for an Open E-Government. In *International Conference on Computer Science, Engineering and Education Applications* (pp. 631–639). Springer. https://link.springer.com/chapter/10.1007/978-3-030-55506-1_56

AlMendah, O. M. (2021). A Survey of Blockchain and E-governance applications: Security and Privacy issues. *Turkish Journal of Computer and Mathematics Education*, *12*(10), 3117–3125. https://turcomat.org/index.php/turkbilmat/article/view/4964

Almusaylim, Z. A., & Jhanjhi, N. Z. (2020). Comprehensive review: Privacy protection of user in location-aware services of mobile cloud computing. *Wireless Personal Communications*, *111*(1), 541–564. doi:10.100711277-019-06872-3

Alqudah, M. A., & Muradkhanli, L. (2021). Artificial Intelligence in Electric Government; Ethical Challenges and Governance in Jordan. *Electronic Research Journal of Social Sciences and Humanities, 3*, 65-74. https://papers.ssrn.com/sol3/papers.cfm?abstract_id=3806600

Amir Latif, R. M., Hussain, K., Jhanjhi, N. Z., Nayyar, A., & Rizwan, O. (2020). A remix IDE: Smart contract-based framework for the healthcare sector by using Blockchain technology. *Multimedia Tools and Applications*, 1–24. doi:10.100711042-020-10087-1

Angelopoulos, K., Diamantopoulou, V., Mouratidis, H., Pavlidis, M., Salnitri, M., Giorgini, P., & Ruiz, J. F. (2017, August). A holistic approach for privacy protection in E-government. In *Proceedings of the 12th International Conference on Availability* (pp. 1–10). Reliability and Security. doi:10.1145/3098954.3098960

Arabadzhyiev, D., Popovych, Y., Lytvynchuk, I., Bakbergen, K., & Kyrychenko, Y. (2021). Digital Society: Regulatory and Institutional Support of Electronic Governance in Modern Realities. In *SHS Web of Conferences* (Vol. 100, p. 03008). EDP Sciences. https://www.shsconferences.org/articles/shsconf/abs/2021/11/shsconf_iscsai2021_03008/shsconf_iscsai2021_03008.html

Bao, J., He, D., Luo, M., & Choo, K. K. R. (2020). A survey of blockchain applications in the energy sector. *IEEE Systems Journal*. https://www.revistageintec.net/index.php/revista/article/view/2409

Bhagat, C., Sharma, B., & Kumar Mishra, A. (2021). *Assessment of E Governance for National Development–A Case Study of Province 1 Nepal*. https://papers.ssrn.com/sol3/papers.cfm?abstract_id=3857194

Bhuvana, M., & Vasantha, S. (2021). The Impact of COVID-19 on Rural Citizens for Accessing E-Governance Services: A Conceptual Model Using the Dimensions of Trust and Technology Acceptance Model. *Recent Advances in Technology Acceptance Models and Theories, 335*, 471. https://www.ncbi.nlm.nih.gov/pmc/articles/PMC7979245/

Brohi, S. N., Jhanjhi, N. Z., Brohi, N. N., & Brohi, M. N. (2020). *Key Applications of State-of-the-Art technologies to mitigate and eliminate COVID-19*. file:///C:/Users/imdad/Downloads/Key%20Applications%20of%20State-of-the-Art%20Technologies%20to%20Mitigate%20and%20Eliminate%20COVID-19%20(1).pdf

Burrell, D. N. (2020). Understanding the talent management intricacies of remote cybersecurity teams in covid-19 induced telework organizational ecosystems. *Land Forces Academy Review, 25*(3), 232-244. https://www.armyacademy.ro/reviste/rev3_2020/Burrell.pdf

Carrapico, H., & Farrand, B. (2020). Discursive continuity and change in the time of Covid-19: The case of EU cybersecurity policy. *journal of European Integration, 42*(8), 1111–1126. doi:10.1080/07036337.2020.1853122

Cheng, B., Solmaz, G., Cirillo, F., Kovacs, E., Terasawa, K., & Kitazawa, A. (2017). FogFlow: Easy programming of IoT services over cloud and edges for smart cities. *IEEE Internet of Things Journal, 5*(2), 696–707. doi:10.1109/JIOT.2017.2747214

Chinese Academy of Cyberspace Studies. (2019). The World e-Government Development. *World Internet Development Report 2017*, 159-197. https://link.springer.com/chapter/10.1007/978-3-662-57524-6_6

Chishiro, H., Tsuchiya, Y., Chubachi, Y., Abu Bakar, M. S., & De Silva, L. C. (2017, June). Global PBL for environmental IoT. In *Proceedings of the 2017 International Conference on E-commerce* (pp. 65–71). E-Business and E-Government. https://dl.acm.org/doi/abs/10.1145/3108421.3108437

Cowgill, B., & Stevenson, M. T. (2020, May). Algorithmic social engineering. In *AEA Papers and Proceedings* (Vol. 110, pp. 96-100). https://www.aeaweb.org/articles?id=10.1257/pandp.20201037

Cradduck, L. (2019). E-conveyancing: A consideration of its risks and rewards. *Property Management.* https://www.emerald.com/insight/content/doi/10.1108/PM-04-2019-0021/full/html

Dahwan, A. A., & Raju, V. (2021). The Infleuence of Online Services and Telecommunication Infrastructure on the Implementation of E-government in Military Institutions in Yemen. *Annals of the Romanian Society for Cell Biology,* 1698–1710. https://www.annalsofrscb.ro/index.php/journal/article/view/2689

De Filippi, P., Mannan, M., & Reijers, W. (2020). Blockchain as a confidence machine: The problem of trust & challenges of governance. *Technology in Society, 62,* 101284. doi:10.1016/j.techsoc.2020.101284

Department of Health. (2017). *Report of the second phase of the review of NHS pathology services: chaired by Lord Carter of Coles.* Department of Health. Available from: http://webarc hive.nationalarchives.gov.uk/20130124044941/http:/www.dh.gov.uk/prod_consum_dh/groups/dh_digita lassets/@dh/@en/documents/digitalasset/dh_091984. pdf

Dhonju, G. R., & Shakya, S. (2019). Analyzing Challenges for the Implementation of E-Government in Municipalities within Kathmandu Valley. *Journal of Science and Engineering, 7,* 70–78. doi:10.3126/jsce.v7i0.26795

Ding, D., Han, Q.-L., Xiang, Y., Ge, X., & Zhang, X.-M. (2018). A survey on security control and attack detection for industrial cyber-physical systems. *Neurocomputing, 275,* 1674–1683. doi:10.1016/j.neucom.2017.10.009

Donalds, C., & Osei-Bryson, K. M. (2020). Cybersecurity compliance behavior: Exploring the influences of individual decision style and other antecedents. *International Journal of Information Management, 51,* 102056. doi:10.1016/j.ijinfomgt.2019.102056

Dorr, B., Bhatia, A., Dalton, A., Mather, B., Hebenstreit, B., Santhanam, S., . . . Strzalkowski, T. (2020, April). Detecting asks in social engineering attacks: Impact of linguistic and structural knowledge. In *Proceedings of the AAAI Conference on Artificial Intelligence* (Vol. 34, No. 05, pp. 7675-7682). https://ojs.aaai.org/index.php/AAAI/article/view/6269

Dubey, A., Saquib, Z., & Dwivedi, S. (2015). *Electronic authentication for e-Government services-a survey.* https://digital-library.theiet.org/content/conferences/10.1049/cp.2015.0299

Dunne, D. (2019). *Mosquito-borne diseases could reach extra 'one billion people' as climate warms.* Carbon Brief. Available from: https://www.carbonbrief.org/mosquitobornediseases-could-reach-extra-one-billion-people-asclimate-warms

Elezaj, O., Tole, D., & Baci, N. (2018). Big Data in e-Government Environments: Albania as a Case Study. *Academic Journal of Interdisciplinary Studies, 7*(2), 117. https://www.mcser.org/journal/index.php/ajis/article/view/10285

Ferreira, A., & Cruz-Correia, R. (2021). COVID-19 and cybersecurity: finally, an opportunity to disrupt? *JMIRx Med, 2*(2), e21069. https://xmed.jmir.org/2021/2/e21069/

Galvez, J. F., Mejuto, J., & Simal-Gandara, J. (2018). Future challenges on the use of blockchain for food traceability analysis. *Trends in Analytical Chemistry, 107*, 222–232. doi:10.1016/j.trac.2018.08.011

Gaur, L., Bhatia, U., Jhanjhi, N. Z., Muhammad, G., & Masud, M. (2021). Medical image-based detection of COVID-19 using Deep Convolution Neural Networks. *Multimedia Systems*, 1–10. doi:10.100700530-021-00794-6 PMID:33935377

General Medical Council. (2018). *Regulatory approaches to telemedicine' general medical council.* Available from: www.gmc-uk.org/ about/what-we-do-and-why/dataand-research /research-and-insight-archive/regulatoryapproachesto-telemedicine

Gershgorn, D. (2018). *If AI is going to be the world's doctor, it needs better textbooks.* Quartz. Available from: https://qz.com/1367177/if-ai-is-going-to-betheworlds-doctor-it-needs-bett

Gershon, D., Prince, O., & Opoku, A. M. (2018). Promoting Inclusiveness and Participation in Governance: The Directions of Electronic Government in Ghana. *The International Journal of Social Sciences (Islamabad), 7*(3), 397–406. doi:10.21474/IJAR01/7931

Gorla, N., & Somers, T. M. (2014). The impact of IT outsourcing on information systems success. *Information & Management, 51*(3), 320–335. doi:10.1016/j.im.2013.12.002

Gouveia, L. B. (2020). e-Government and Smart Cities: Contexts and Challenges Taking from Digital Usage and Exploration. *UNU-EGOV\UM DSI PDSI talk.* https://bdigital.ufp.pt/handle/10284/8554

Greenspun, H., Abrams, K., & Kame, A. (2016). *Preparing the doctor of the future Medical school and residency program evolution.* A report by the Deloitte Center for Health Solutions. Available from: https://www.modernhealthcare.com/article/20160728/SPONSORED/307289996/preparing-the-doctor-of-the-future-medical-school-andresidency-program-evolutio

Gupta, R., & Agarwal, S. P. (2017). A Comparative Study of Cyber Threats in Emerging Economies. *Globus: An International Journal of Management & IT, 8*(2), 24-28. https://globusjournal.com/wp-content/uploads/2018/07/826Ruchika.pdf

Hamid, B., Jhanjhi, N. Z., & Humayun, M. (2020). Digital Governance for Developing Countries Opportunities, Issues, and Challenges in Pakistan. In *Employing Recent Technologies for Improved Digital Governance* (pp. 36–58). IGI Global. doi:10.4018/978-1-7998-1851-9.ch003

Haran, M. H. (2016). Framework Based Approach for the Mitigation of Insider Threats in E-governance IT Infrastructure. *International Journal of Scientific Research, 3*(4), 5–10. http://citeseerx.ist.psu.edu/viewdoc/download?doi=10.1.1.5 66.4423&rep=rep1&type=pdf

Harris, M. A., & Martin, R. (2019). Promoting cybersecurity compliance. In *Cybersecurity education for awareness and compliance* (pp. 54–71). IGI Global. doi:10.4018/978-1-5225-7847-5.ch004

He, Y., Aliyu, A., Evans, M., & Luo, C. (2021). Health Care Cybersecurity Challenges and Solutions Under the Climate of COVID-19: Scoping Review. *Journal of Medical Internet Research, 23*(4), e21747. doi:10.2196/21747 PMID:33764885

Henriksen, H. Z. (2018). One step forward and two steps back: e-Government policies in practice. In *Policy Analytics, Modelling, and Informatics* (pp. 79–97). Springer. doi:10.1007/978-3-319-61762-6_4

Herawati, A. R., Warsono, H., Afrizal, T., & Saputra, J. (n.d.). *The Challenges of Industrial Revolution 4.0: An Evidence from Public Administration Ecology in Indonesia.* http://www.ieomsociety.org/singapore2021/papers/846.pdf

Hiscox. (2019). *The hiscox cyber readiness report 2019*. https://www.sciencedirect.com/science/article/pii/S0167404821000729

Hofbauer, D., Ivkic, I., & Tauber, M. (2019). On the Cost of Security Compliance in Information Systems. *10th International Multi-Conference on Complexity, Informatics and Cybernetics 2019 (IMCIC)*. https://www.igi-global.com/chapter/promoting-cybersecurity-compliance/225917

Huang, K., & Madnick, S. (2021, January). Does High Cybersecurity Capability Lead to Openness in Digital Trade? The Mediation Effect of E-Government Maturity. In *Proceedings of the 54th Hawaii International Conference on System Sciences* (p. 4352). https://papers.ssrn.com/sol3/papers.cfm?abstract_id=3542552

Huang, K., Siegel, M., & Madnick, S. (2018). Systematically understanding the cyber attack business: A survey. *ACM Computing Surveys*, *51*(4), 1–36. doi:10.1145/3199674

Humayun, M., Jhanjhi, N. Z., Hamid, B., & Ahmed, G. (2020). Emerging smart logistics and transportation using IoT and blockchain. *IEEE Internet of Things Magazine, 3*(2), 58-62. https://ieeexplore.ieee.org/abstract/document/9125435

Humayun, M., Niazi, M., Jhanjhi, N. Z., Alshayeb, M., & Mahmood, S. (2020). Cyber security threats and vulnerabilities: A systematic mapping study. *Arabian Journal for Science and Engineering*, *45*(4), 3171–3189. doi:10.100713369-019-04319-2

Hussain, S. J., Irfan, M., Jhanjhi, N. Z., Hussain, K., & Humayun, M. (2021). Performance enhancement in wireless body area networks with secure communication. *Wireless Personal Communications*, *116*(1), 1–22. doi:10.100711277-020-07702-7 PMID:33558792

III. (n.d.). https://www.iii.org/fact-statistic/facts-statistics-identity-theft-and-cybercrime

Ilves, T. H. (2016). The consequences of cyber attacks. *Journal of International Affairs*, *70*(1), 175–181.

Jazri, H., & Jat, D. S. (2016, November). A quick cybersecurity wellness evaluation framework for critical organizations. In *2016 International Conference on ICT in Business Industry & Government (ICTBIG)* (pp. 1-5). IEEE. https://ieeexplore.ieee.org/abstract/document/7892725

Joshi, S. (2015). E-Governance in Uttar Pradesh: Challenges and Prospects. *The Indian Journal of Public Administration*, *61*(2), 229–240. doi:10.1177/0019556120150203

Kagame, P., & Ghebreyesus, T. A. (2019). History shows health is the foundation of African prosperity. *Financial Times*. Available from: https://www.ft.com/content/e61cc58c-cfc7-11e9-b018-ca4456540ea6

Kapersky. (n.d.). https://usa.kaspersky.com/resource-center/definitions/what-is-social-engineering

Karpenko, O., Kuczabski, A., & Havryliak, V. (2021). Mechanisms for providing cybersecurity during the COVID-19 pandemic: Perspectives for Ukraine. *Security and Defence Quarterly*. http://yadda.icm.edu.pl/yadda/element/bwmeta1.element.doi-10_35467_sdq_133158

Kaur, K., Garg, S., Aujla, G. S., Kumar, N., Rodrigues, J. J., & Guizani, M. (2018). Edge computing in the industrial internet of things environment: Software-defined-networks-based edge-cloud interplay. *IEEE Communications Magazine, 56*(2), 44–51. doi:10.1109/MCOM.2018.1700622

Khan, A., Jhanjhi, N. Z., Humayun, M., & Ahmad, M. (2020). The Role of IoT in Digital Governance. In *Employing Recent Technologies for Improved Digital Governance* (pp. 128–150). IGI Global. doi:10.4018/978-1-7998-1851-9.ch007

Khan, N. A., Brohi, S. N., & Zaman, N. (2020). *Ten deadly cyber security threats amid COVID-19 pandemic*. https://www.techrxiv.org/articles/preprint/Ten_Deadly_Cyber_Security_Threats_Amid_COVID-19_Pandemic/12278792/1

Khandpur, R. P., Ji, T., Jan, S., Wang, G., Lu, C. T., & Ramakrishnan, N. (2017, November). Crowdsourcing cybersecurity: Cyber attack detection using social media. In *Proceedings of the 2017 ACM on Conference on Information and Knowledge Management* (pp. 1049-1057). https://dl.acm.org/doi/abs/10.1145/3132847.3132866

Khatoun, R., & Zeadally, S. (2017). Cybersecurity and privacy solutions in smart cities. *IEEE Communications Magazine, 55*(3), 51–59. doi:10.1109/MCOM.2017.1600297CM

Koo, E. (2019). *Digital transformation of Government: from E-Government to intelligent E-Government* (Doctoral dissertation). Massachusetts Institute of Technology. https://dspace.mit.edu/handle/1721.1/121792

Korir, G., Thiga, M., & Rono, L. (2019). *Implementing the Tool for Assessing Organisation Information Security Preparedness in E-Governance Implementation*. https://www.easpublisher.com/media/features_articles/EASJECS_210_284-299.pdf

Krishnaraju, V., Mathew, S. K., & Sugumaran, V. (2016). Web personalization for user acceptance of technology: An empirical investigation of E-government services. *Information Systems Frontiers*, *18*(3), 579–595. doi:10.100710796-015-9550-9

Kumar, M. S., Vimal, S., Jhanjhi, N. Z., Dhanabalan, S. S., & Alhumyani, H. A. (2021). Blockchain based peer to peer communication in autonomous drone operation. *Energy Reports*, *7*, 7925–7939. doi:10.1016/j.egyr.2021.08.073

Lallie, H. S., Shepherd, L. A., Nurse, J. R., Erola, A., Epiphaniou, G., Maple, C., & Bellekens, X. (2021). Cyber security in the age of covid-19: A timeline and analysis of cyber-crime and cyber-attacks during the pandemic. *Computers & Security*, *105*, 102248. doi:10.1016/j.cose.2021.102248

Le Blond, S., Gilbert, C., Upadhyay, U., Gomez-Rodriguez, M., & Choffnes, D. R. (2017). A Broad View of the Ecosystem of Socially Engineered Exploit Documents. *NDSS*. https://www.ndss-symposium.org/wp-content/uploads/2017/09/ndss2017_03B-4_LeBlond_paper.pdf

Lee, K. J. P., Raman, W., & Hedrich, R. (2018). *Holding healthcare to ransom: industry perspectives on cyber risks*. Marsh & McLennan Companies. http://www.mmc.com/insights/publications/ 2018/jul/holding-healthcare-to-ransom-industryperspectives-on-cyb

Lee, S., Abdullah, A., Jhanjhi, N., & Kok, S. (2021). Classification of botnet attacks in IoT smart factory using honeypot combined with machine learning. *PeerJ. Computer Science*, *7*, e350. doi:10.7717/peerj-cs.350 PMID:33817000

Li, L., He, W., Xu, L., Ash, I., Anwar, M., & Yuan, X. (2019). Investigating the impact of cybersecurity policy awareness on employees' cybersecurity behavior. *International Journal of Information Management*, *45*, 13–24. doi:10.1016/j.ijinfomgt.2018.10.017

Liang, Y., Qi, G., Wei, K., & Chen, J. (2017). Exploring the determinant and influence mechanism of e-Government cloud adoption in government agencies in China. *Government Information Quarterly*, *34*(3), 481–495. doi:10.1016/j.giq.2017.06.002

Lim, M., Abdullah, A., & Jhanjhi, N. Z. (2019). Performance optimization of criminal network hidden link prediction model with deep reinforcement learning. *Journal of King Saud University-Computer and Information Sciences*. https://onlinelibrary.wiley.com/doi/abs/10.1002/ett.4171

Lim, M., Abdullah, A., Jhanjhi, N. Z., & Supramaniam, M. (2019). Hidden link prediction in criminal networks using the deep reinforcement learning technique. *Computers, 8*(1), 8. https://www.mdpi.com/2073-431X/8/1/8

Linkov, I., Trump, B. D., Poinsatte-Jones, K., & Florin, M. V. (2018). Governance strategies for a sustainable digital world. *Sustainability*, *10*(2), 440. doi:10.3390u10020440

Liu, C., Wang, N., & Liang, H. (2020). Motivating information security policy compliance: The critical role of supervisor-subordinate guanxi and organizational commitment. *International Journal of Information Management*, *54*, 102152. doi:10.1016/j.ijinfomgt.2020.102152

Liu, D., & Carter, L. (2018, May). Impact of citizens' privacy concerns on e-government adoption. In *Proceedings of the 19th Annual International Conference on Digital Government Research* (pp. 1–6). Governance in the Data Age. doi:10.1145/3209281.3209340

Liu, J., Wang, C., Li, C., Li, N., Deng, J., & Pan, J. Z. (2021). DTN: Deep triple network for topic specific fake news detection. *Journal of Web Semantics*, *100646*. doi:10.1016/j.websem.2021.100646

Liu, Z., Wei, W., Wang, L., Ten, C. W., & Rho, Y. (2020). An Actuarial Framework for Power System Reliability Considering Cybersecurity Threats. *IEEE Transactions on Power Systems*. https://dl.acm.org/doi/abs/10.1145/3386723.3387847

Lu, R., Zhao, X., Li, J., Niu, P., Yang, B., Wu, H., Wang, W., Song, H., Huang, B., Zhu, N., Bi, Y., Ma, X., Zhan, F., Wang, L., Hu, T., Zhou, H., Hu, Z., Zhou, W., Zhao, L., ... Tan, W. (2020). Genomic characterisation and epidemiology of 2019 novel coronavirus: Implications for virus origins and receptor binding. *Lancet*, *395*(10224), 565–574. doi:10.1016/S0140-6736(20)30251-8 PMID:32007145

Luh, R., Marschalek, S., Kaiser, M., Janicke, H., & Schrittwieser, S. (2017). Semantics-aware detection of targeted attacks: A survey. *Journal of Computer Virology and Hacking Techniques*, *13*(1), 47–85. doi:10.100711416-016-0273-3

Lv, Z., Li, X., Wang, W., Zhang, B., Hu, J., & Feng, S. (2018). Government affairs service platform for smart city. *Future Generation Computer Systems*, *81*, 443–451. doi:10.1016/j.future.2017.08.047

Malhotra, H., Dave, M., & Lamba, T. (2019, November). Security Analysis of Cyber Attacks Using Machine Learning Algorithms in eGovernance Projects. In *International Conference on Futuristic Trends in Networks and Computing Technologies* (pp. 662-672). Springer.

Malhotra, H., Bhargava, R., & Dave, M. (2017a). Implementation of E-Governance projects: Development, Threats & Targets. *International Journal of Information Communication and Computing Technology, 5*(2), 292-298. https://www.indianjournals.com/ijor.aspx?target=ijor:jims8i&volume=5&issue=2&article=001

Malhotra, H., Bhargava, R., & Dave, M. (2017b, November). Challenges related to information security and its implications for evolving e-government structures: A comparative study between India and African countries. In *2017 International Conference on Inventive Computing and Informatics (ICICI)* (pp. 30-35). IEEE. 10.1109/ICICI.2017.8365370

McKibbin, W., & Fernando, R. (2020). The economic impact of COVID-19. *Economics in the Time of COVID-19, 45*. https://www.incae.edu/sites/default/files/covid-19.pdf#page=52

MehrotraK. (2021). *Data Privacy & Protection*. https://papers.ssrn.com/sol3/papers.cfm?abstract_id=3858581

Meiyanti, R., Utomo, B., Sensuse, D. I., & Wahyuni, R. (2018, August). E-government challenges in developing countries: a literature review. In *2018 6th International Conference on Cyber and IT Service Management (CITSM)* (pp. 1-6). IEEE. 10.1109/CITSM.2018.8674245

Mensah, I. K. (2019). Impact of government capacity and E-government performance on the adoption of E-Government services. *International Journal of Public Administration*. https://www.tandfonline.com/doi/10.1080/01900692.2019.1628059

Mercer Marsh Benefits. (2019). *Health and benefits: health insurance costs – insights & implications. Results of the 2019 medical trends around the world survey*. Available from: https://www.mercermarshbenefits.com/en/intellectualcapital/2019-medical-trends-around-the-world1. html

Muda, J., Tumsa, S., Tuni, A., & Sharma, D. P. (2020). Cloud-Enabled E-Governance Framework for Citizen Centric Services. *Journal of Computer and Communications, 8*(7), 63–78. doi:10.4236/jcc.2020.87006

Muller, S. R., & Lind, M. L. (2020). Factors in Information Assurance Professionals' Intentions to Adhere to Information Security Policies. *International Journal of Systems and Software Security and Protection, 11*(1), 17–32. doi:10.4018/IJSSSP.2020010102

Muzafar, S., & Jhanjhi, N. Z. (2020). Success stories of ICT implementation in Saudi Arabia. In *Employing Recent Technologies for Improved Digital Governance* (pp. 151–163). IGI Global. doi:10.4018/978-1-7998-1851-9.ch008

Mwangi, N. M. (2015). *e-government adoption by Kenya ministries* (Doctoral dissertation). University of Nairobi. http://erepository.uonbi.ac.ke/handle/11295/94091

Nagowah, S. D., Sta, H. B., & Gobin-Rahimbux, B. A. (2018, October). An overview of semantic interoperability ontologies and frameworks for IoT. In *2018 Sixth International Conference on Enterprise Systems (ES)* (pp. 82-89). IEEE. 10.1109/ES.2018.00020

Najmi, K. Y., AlZain, M. A., Masud, M., Jhanjhi, N. Z., Al-Amri, J., & Baz, M. (2021). A survey on security threats and countermeasures in IoT to achieve users confidentiality and reliability. *Materials Today: Proceedings*. https://www.sciencedirect.com/science/article/pii/S221478532102469X

NHS. (2019). *Preparing the healthcare workforce to deliver the digital future: An independent report on behalf of the secretary of state for health and social care.* NHS. Available from: https:// www.forbes.com/sites/adigaskell/2018/11/09/preparing-the-healthcare-workforce-to-deliver-the-digitalfuture/#654cfeef6d34

NHS England. (2014). *National pathology programme. Digital First: Clinical Transformation through Pathology Innovation.* Available from: www.england.nhs.uk/2014/02/nppdi gital-first/

Norris, D., Joshi, A., & Finin, T. (2015, June). *Cybersecurity challenges to American state and local governments. In 15th European Conference on eGovernment.* Academic Conferences and Publishing Int. Ltd. https://ebiquity.umbc.edu/paper/abstract/id/774/Cybersecurity-Challenges-to-American-State-and-Local-Governments

Nosiri, U. D., & Ndoh, J. A. (2018). E-governance. *South East Journal of Political Science, 4*(1). https://journals.aphriapub.com/index.php/SEJPS/article/view/833

NSKT Global. (n.d.). https://nsktglobal.com/what-are-the-biggest-cybersecurity-threats-in-2021-

O'Neil, J. (n.d.). *Rapid diagnostics: Stopping unnecessary use of antibiotics. Review on antimicrobial resistance.* Available from: http://amrreview.org/sites/default/files/Paper-RapidDiagnostics-Stopping-Unnecessa

Okereafor, K., & Adebola, O. (2020). Tackling the cybersecurity impacts of the coronavirus outbreak as a challenge to internet safety. *Int J IT Eng, 8*(2). https://papers.ssrn.com/sol3/papers.cfm?abstract_id=3568830

Oxford Analytica. (2016). Estonia's e-governance model may be unique. *Emerald Expert Briefings*, (oxan-db). https://www.emerald.com/insight/content/doi/10.1108/OXAN-DB214505/full/html

Peng, C., Xu, M., Xu, S., & Hu, T. (2017). Modeling and predicting extreme cyber attack rates via marked point processes. *Journal of Applied Statistics, 44*(14), 2534–2563. doi:10.1080/02664763.2016.1257590

Pradhan, P., & Shakya, S. (2018). Big Data Challenges for e-Government Services in Nepal. *Journal of the Institute of Engineering, 14*(1), 216–222. doi:10.3126/jie.v14i1.20087

Qi, M., & Wang, J. (2021). Using the Internet of Things e-government platform to optimize the administrative management mode. *Wireless Communications and Mobile Computing, 2021*, 1–11. doi:10.1155/2021/2224957

Rajmohan, R., Kumar, T. A., Pavithra, M., Sandhya, S. G., Julie, E. G., Nayahi, J. J. V., & Jhanjhi, N. Z. (2020). Blockchain: Next-generation technology for industry 4.0. *Blockchain Technology*, 177-198. https://www.taylorfrancis.com/chapters/edit/10.1201/9781003004998-11/blockchain-rajmohan-ananth-kumar-pavithra-sandhya

Ramadan, R. A., Aboshosha, B. W., Alshudukhi, J. S., Alzahrani, A. J., El-Sayed, A., & Dessouky, M. M. (2021). Cybersecurity and Countermeasures at the Time of Pandemic. *Journal of Advanced Transportation, 2021*, 1–19. doi:10.1155/2021/6627264

Ramli, R. M. (2017). Challenges and issues in Malaysian e-government. *Electronic Government, an International Journal, 13*(3), 242-273. https://www.inderscienceonline.com/doi/abs/10.1504/EG.2017.086685

Ramzi, E. H., & Weerakkody, V. (n.d.). *E-Government implementation Challenges: A Case study*. https://aisel.aisnet.org/cgi/viewcontent.cgi?article=1318&context=amcis2010

Rana, N. P., Dwivedi, Y. K., & Williams, M. D. (2013). Analysing challenges, barriers and CSF of egov adoption. *Transforming Government: People, Process and Policy*. https://www.emerald.com/insight/content/doi/10.1108/17506161311325350/full/html

Ravi, N., Verma, S., Jhanjhi, N. Z., & Talib, M. N. (2021, August). Securing VANET Using Blockchain Technology. In *Journal of Physics: Conference Series* (Vol. 1979, No. 1, p. 012035). IOP Publishing. https://iopscience.iop.org/article/10.1088/1742-6596/1979/1/012035/meta

Razaque, A., Amsaad, F., Khan, M. J., Hariri, S., Chen, S., Siting, C., & Ji, X. (2019). Survey: Cybersecurity vulnerabilities, attacks and solutions in the medical domain. *IEEE Access: Practical Innovations, Open Solutions*, 7, 168774–168797. doi:10.1109/ACCESS.2019.2950849

Razuleu, L. (2018). *E-Governance and its associated cybersecurity: The challenges and best practices of authentication and authorization among a rapidly growing e-government.* https://scholarworks.calstate.edu/concern/theses/qj72pb20t

Research Gate. (n.d.). https://www.researchgate.net/figure/Number-of-papers-related-to-deepfakes-in-years-from-2015-to-2020-obtained-from_fig3_336058980

Rodela, T. T., Tasnim, S., Mazumder, H., Faizah, F., Sultana, A., & Hossain, M. M. (2020). Economic Impacts of Coronavirus Disease (COVID-19) in Developing Countries. doi:10.31235/osf.io/wygpk

Ronchi, A. M. (2019). e-Government: Background, Today's Implementation and Future Trends. In e-Democracy (pp. 93-196). Springer.

Sadiq, A. A. I., Haning, M. T., Nara, N., & Rusdi, M. (2021). Learning Organization on the Implementation of E-Government in the City of Makassar. *Journal Dimensie Management and Public Sector*, 2(3), 12–21. doi:10.48173/jdmps.v2i3.111

Salam, S., & Kumar, K. P. (2021). Survey on Applications of Blockchain in E-Governance. *Revista Geintec-Gestao Inovacao E Tecnologias, 11*(4), 3807-3822. https://www.revistageintec.net/index.php/revista/article/view/2409

Saleem, J., Adebisi, B., Ande, R., & Hammoudeh, M. (2017, July). A state of the art survey-Impact of cyber attacks on SME's. In *Proceedings of the International Conference on Future Networks and Distributed Systems*. https://dl.acm.org/doi/abs/10.1145/3102304.3109812

Samtani, S., Zhu, H., & Chen, H. (2020). Proactively Identifying Emerging Hacker Threats from the Dark Web: A Diachronic Graph Embedding Framework (D-GEF). *ACM Transactions on Privacy and Security (TOPS), 23*(4), 1-33. https://dl.acm.org/doi/abs/10.1145/3409289

Sangki, J. (2018). Vision of future e-government via new e-government maturity model: Based on Korea's e-government practices. *Telecommunications Policy*, 42(10), 860–871. doi:10.1016/j.telpol.2017.12.002

Sava, A. (2018). IoT Technologies: Realities of the Future. *Social-Economic Debates*, 7(1), 100-105. http://economic-debates.ro/art11-Sava-economic-debates-2018.pdf

Scarfone, K., Hoffman, P., & Souppaya, M. (2009). Guide to enterprise telework and remote access security. *NIST Special Publication, 800*, 46. https://csrc.nist.rip/library/alt-SP800-46r1.pdf

Shah, Rajper, & ZamanJhanjhi. (2021). Using ML and Data-Mining Techniques in Automatic Vulnerability Software Discovery. *International Journal (Toronto, Ont.)*, *10*, 3.

Sharma, S. K., Metri, B., Dwivedi, Y. K., & Rana, N. P. (2021). Challenges common service centers (CSCs) face in delivering e-government services in rural India. *Government Information Quarterly*, *38*(2), 101573. doi:10.1016/j.giq.2021.101573

Sharma, T. (2021). *Evolving Phishing Email Prevention Techniques: A Survey to Pin Down Effective Phishing Study Design Concepts.* https://www.ideals.illinois.edu/handle/2142/109179

Simonova, A. (2020). *An Analysis of Factors Influencing National Institute of Standards and Technology Cybersecurity Framework Adoption in Financial Services: A Correlational Study* (Doctoral dissertation). Capella University. https://www.proquest.com/openview/8482434364a539361dbd14f5dd872752/1?pq-origsite=gscholar&cbl=18750&diss=y

Singh, A. P., Pradhan, N. R., Luhach, A. K., Agnihotri, S., Jhanjhi, N. Z., Verma, S., Kavita, Ghosh, U., & Roy, D. S. (2020). A novel patient-centric architectural framework for blockchain-enabled healthcare applications. *IEEE Transactions on Industrial Informatics*, *17*(8), 5779–5789. doi:10.1109/TII.2020.3037889

Sithole, V. E. (2015). *An e-governance training model for public managers: The case of selected Free State Provincial departments* (Doctoral dissertation). http://repository.nwu.ac.za/handle/10394/16320

Soni, V., Anand, R., Dey, P. K., Dash, A. P., & Banwet, D. K. (2017). Quantifying e-governance efficacy towards Indian–EU strategic dialogue. *Transforming Government: People, Process and Policy.* https://www.emerald.com/insight/content/doi/10.1108/TG-06-2017-0031/full/html

Soni, V., Dey, P. K., Anand, R., Malhotra, C., & Banwet, D. K. (2017). Digitizing grey portions of e-governance. *Transforming Government: People, Process and Policy.* https://www.emerald.com/insight/content/doi/10.1108/TG-11-2016-0076/full/html

Sony, A. L. (2015). Solving e-Governance Challenges in India through the Incremental Adoption to Cloud Service. *Law: J. Higher Sch. Econ.*, 169. https://heinonline.org/HOL/LandingPage?handle=hein.journals/pravo2015&div=15&id=&page=

Stellios, I., Kotzanikolaou, P., Psarakis, M., Alcaraz, C., & Lopez, J. (2018). A survey of iot-enabled cyberattacks: Assessing attack paths to critical infrastructures and services. *IEEE Communications Surveys and Tutorials, 20*(4), 3453–3495. doi:10.1109/COMST.2018.2855563

Suleimany, M. (2021, May). Smart Urban Management and IoT; Paradigm of E-Governance and Technologies in Developing Communities. In *2021 5th International Conference on Internet of Things and Applications (IoT)* (pp. 1-6). IEEE. https://ieeexplore.ieee.org/abstract/document/9469713

Tikkanen, E., Gustafsson, S., & Ingelsson, E. (2018). Associations of fitness, physical activity, strength, and genetic risk with cardiovascular disease: Longitudinal analyses in the UK Biobank study. *Circulation, 137*(24), 2583–2591. doi:10.1161/CIRCULATIONAHA.117.032432 PMID:29632216

Tounsi, W., & Rais, H. (2018). A survey on technical threat intelligence in the age of sophisticated cyber attacks. *Computers & Security, 72*, 212–233. doi:10.1016/j.cose.2017.09.001

Twizeyimana, J. D., & Andersson, A. (2019). The public value of E-Government–A literature review. *Government Information Quarterly, 36*(2), 167–178. doi:10.1016/j.giq.2019.01.001

U.S. Centers for Medicare & Medicaid Services, National Health Expenditure Accounts. (2018). Available from: https://www.cms.gov/ Research-Statistics-Data-and-Systems/StatisticsTrends-and-eports/NationalHealthExpendData/NationalHealthAccountsHistorical.Html

Ullah, A., Pinglu, C., Ullah, S., Abbas, H. S. M., & Khan, S. (n.d.). *The Role of E-Governance in Combating COVID-19 and Promoting Sustainable Development: A Comparative Study of China and Pakistan.* https://link.springer.com/article/10.1007/s41111-020-00167-w

UNDP. (2013). *World economic and social survey 2013 sustainable development challenges.* Available from: https://sustainabledevelopment.un.org/content/documents/2843WESS2013.pdf

Venkatesh, V., Thong, J. Y., Chan, F. K., & Hu, P. J. (2016). Managing citizens' uncertainty in e-government services: The mediating and moderating roles of transparency and trust. *Information Systems Research, 27*(1), 87–111. doi:10.1287/isre.2015.0612

Walden, A., Cortelyou-Ward, K., Gabriel, M. H., & Noblin, A. (2020). To report or not to report health care data breaches. *The American Journal of Managed Care*, *26*(12), e395–e402. doi:10.37765/ajmc.2020.88546 PMID:33315333

Waller, L., & Genius, A. (2015). Barriers to transforming government in Jamaica: Challenges to implementing initiatives to enhance the efficiency, effectiveness and service delivery of government through ICTs (e-Government). *Transforming Government: People, Process and Policy*. https://www.emerald.com/insight/content/doi/10.1108/TG-12-2014-0067/full/html?fullSc=1

Watts, N., Amann, M., Arnell, N., Ayeb-Karlsson, S., Belesova, K., Boykoff, M., Byass, P., Cai, W., Campbell-Lendrum, D., Capstick, S., Chambers, J., Dalin, C., Daly, M., Dasandi, N., Davies, M., Drummond, P., Dubrow, R., Ebi, K. L., Eckelman, M., ... Montgomery, H. (2019). The 2019 report of The Lancet countdown on health and climate change: Ensuring that the health of a child born today is not defined by a changing climate. *Lancet*, *394*(10211), 1836–1878. doi:10.1016/S0140-6736(19)32596-6 PMID:31733928

Weil, T., & Murugesan, S. (2020). IT Risk and Resilience-Cybersecurity Response to COVID-19. *IT Professional*, *22*(3), 4–10. doi:10.1109/MITP.2020.2988330

WHO. (2020). *Report on global surveillance of epidemicprone infectious diseases – introduction*. Switzerland, Geneva: WHO. https://www.ncbi.nlm.nih.gov/pmc/articles/PMC7195982/

Wiggen, J. (2020). *Impact of COVID-19 on cyber crime and state-sponsored cyber activities*. Konrad Adenauer Stiftung. https://www.jstor.org/stable/pdf/resrep25300.pdf?acceptTC=true&coverpage=false

Wijayanto, H., & Prabowo, I. A. (2020). Cybersecurity Vulnerability Behavior Scale in College During the Covid-19 Pandemic. *Jurnal Sisfokom (Sistem Informasi dan Komputer)*, *9*(3),395-399. https://www.aimspress.com/article/id/6087e948ba35de2200eea776

Williams, C. M., Chaturvedi, R., & Chakravarthy, K. (2020). Cybersecurity Risks in a Pandemic. *Journal of Medical Internet Research*, *22*(9), e23692. doi:10.2196/23692 PMID:32897869

Wong, J. C. J., Alla, K. R., Dominic, P. D. D., Rimsan, M., Mahmood, A. K., Umair, M., ... Jhanjhi, N. Z. (2020, October). 6LWL. KDGLMDK% DKDULQ= DOLNKD= XONLflL 6DPVLDK $ KPDG. In *International Conference on Computational Intelligence (ICCI)* (*Vol. 8*, p. 9). Academic Press.

World Economic Forum. (2020). *The global risk report*. Available from: https://www. weforum.org/reports/the-global-risks-report-2020

World Health Organization. (2020). *WHO reports fivefold increase in cyber-attacks, urges vigilance. WHO reports fivefold increase in cyber attacks, urges vigilance*. WHO.

Yang, L., Elisa, N., & Eliot, N. (2019). Privacy and security aspects of E-government in smart cities. In *Smart cities cybersecurity and privacy* (pp. 89–102). Elsevier. doi:10.1016/B978-0-12-815032-0.00007-X

Yang, R., & Wibowo, S. (2020). *Risks and Uncertainties in Citizens' Trust and Adoption of E-Government: A Proposed Framework*. https://aisel.aisnet.org/cgi/viewcontent.cgi?article=1073&context=acis2020

Yazdanmehr, A., Wang, J., & Yang, Z. (2020). Peers matter: The moderating role of social influence on information security policy compliance. *Information Systems Journal*, *30*(5), 791–844. doi:10.1111/isj.12271

Yoo, C. W., Sanders, G. L., & Cerveny, R. P. (2018). Exploring the influence of flow and psychological ownership on security education, training and awareness effectiveness and security compliance. *Decision Support Systems*, *108*, 107–118. doi:10.1016/j.dss.2018.02.009

Zong, S., Ritter, A., Mueller, G., & Wright, E. (2019). *Analyzing the perceived severity of cybersecurity threats reported on social media*. doi:10.18653/v1/N19-1140

Conclusion

INTRODUCTION

Information and communication technologies are advancing, enabling more information to travel across the globe via the internet superhighway. As people become more connected to the virtual world and become more focused, extensive, and smart, solutions need to be applied to cybersecurity measures. When information is processed within an application, it is subject to various attack levels, and it is impractical to handle it alone like previous security solutions Cao (J, Li Q, Xie R 2019). The development of software-defined networking (SDN) has sparked new perspectives on data security, as networking may help create reliable and secure continuity in the face of Internet perils. The structure of SDN, especially the incremental construction and integration of network data and methods, forces us to think about security from a policy perspective (Wang, Y., Jiang 2021). The purpose of this chapter is to provide a comprehensive review of the state-of-the-art in SDN security and its impact on e-government applications.

With smart gadgets and data being connected and updated in real-time, the Internet of Things (IoT) is gaining popularity in everyday life to make critical choices across industries. The Internet of Things is being used to provide digital services to ordinary people in a number of ways. Paying online, buying a home, and sailing are just a few examples. On the other hand, complaints from users about the security and privacy of their personal information are also on the rise (Adjei-Bamfo, P. 2019). The Internet of Things (IoT) is gaining popularity and has the potential to greatly improve E-government. The Internet of Things (IoT) is based on user devices to transmit data and act on that data. At other times, devices work together to achieve a common purpose and communicate over the Internet. In several cases, the IoT can provide strategic and operational advantages to management by building applications that leverage the data generated by these devices. Several Internet (Business Insider, 2019) of Things devices is estimated to reach 65 billion by 2026

Machine learning (ML), the Internet of Things (IoT), and Artificial Intelligence (AI) are among the world's fastest-growing technologies (AI). Cybersecurity is the use of technologies that play a vital role in securing data and lowering the danger of cyber-attacks among users, including computer programs, networks, data, and devices. New security measures must be designed in-depth (Khan, A., Jhanjhi, N. Z 2020). The e-government provides online services for individuals, corporations, and other e-government entities to share services and electronic data. Because digital transformations and hyper-convergence increase the risk of vulnerabilities and failures, a cyber-flexibility strategy is required to keep a firm functioning smoothly. Businesses may reduce risk, reputational harm, financial influence, and status losses by using an effective method. In recent years, cyber security has made great progress in keeping up with the rapid developments in cyberspace (Lee, S., Abdullah 2021). Cyber security may be defined as a tool that any firm can protect its data and goods in cyberspace. Using machine learning approaches such as culture and risk management awareness. The main purpose of this chapter is to focus on relevant research articles, book chapters, and published reports on cybersecurity threats and attacks over the past decade, which focus and underlie e-government applications and emerging technologies for measuring cybersecurity. This research has been used in machine learning techniques to obtain real and scientific results. According to our research, new doors will open for researchers and professionals

As technology advances, hackers are actively gaining access to personal information. They employ various methods and procedures to achieve their goals and easily access information about any individual. When a hacker gains full access to a user's information without the user's permission, it's called a "privacy breach." Security threats and risks arise for many reasons, including technical weaknesses and targeted attacks. Governments provide digital public services to citizens and businesses. Consumers expect e-government to preserve and secure their data and personal information (Dhonju, G. R 2019). Users have expressed concerns about the privacy and security of their personal information. Business and survival rates have improved in recent years as developed countries have increased. Governments need to improve the reliability of their Internet service networks. In general, e-government can save time and resources by facilitating communication between citizens and government agencies. According to various studies, privacy violations in e-government services have increased in recent years (Alharmoodi, B. Y. R 2020). The main purpose of this chapter is to provide strategies for IT professionals and e-government services as they require continuous improvement on privacy and security issues. The findings in this chapter are useful to new researchers and help avoid security breaches and privacy concerns.

As the world becomes more connected, the use of e-government is increasing. However, data and information must be used. As technology evolves, data security systems must be designed to handle new and effective vulnerabilities. There are growing concerns and challenges in securing information infrastructure in today's rapidly changing environment. Due to numerous system flaws, these networks are vulnerable to cyber-attacks (Baharin, A. M. 2021). Therefore, it is critical to accelerating comprehensive security efforts, including application software and infrastructure, to establish a practical governance framework that cannot be easily tampered with. During the evaluation of related papers, it was found that only a small amount of research has been done on e-government and cyber-attacks. Cyber-attacks are affecting e-government and jeopardizing public trust. To improve government services and efficiency. The accelerating IT progress and the improvement of government functions are the two most significant revolutions. Different e-government applications are running, with greater reliance on cyberspace, an area of "business" that few people know about, especially in digital security (Hoffman, I., & Cseh 2021). The main purpose of this chapter is to review research articles over the past fifteen years, and the results have been compared every five years. Our findings offer potential recommendations and solutions.

The Economic Community of West African States (ECOWAS) is a West African economic region. This region has roughly 349 million people, with over 15 nations represented (Asongu, S. A. 2019). Cybersecurity has become a major concern with the rapid advancement of technology in agriculture, healthcare, and personal devices (Orji, U. J. (2018). With dictatorships, corrupt regimes, religious extremists, and other illegal activities on the rise, it is critical that cybersecurity becomes a cornerstone of local governments to safeguard residents' safety.

The COVID-19 virus is a novel virus belonging to the same virus family. This is a national emergency, and forums and organizations worldwide are working together to fight the disease until an accurate vaccine for the virus is developed and normal life resumes. WHO recommends social distancing between people in this situation (El Khatib, M., Nakand 2020). Hundreds of millions of people worldwide work and run businesses from home, including financial activities, buying and selling, and shopping. On the other hand, cyber-attacks are becoming more common. E-government is an information technology application that provides online services (Froehlich, A., Ringas 2020). The COVID-19 pandemic recommended by the World Health Organization, billions of people are working from home (online activities), with shops and businesses closed. The researchers' analysis in this context reveals a surprising amount of cybercrime affecting society and businesses. In this chapter, the focus has been on the deep learning application of e-government in detecting cyber-attacks.

A cyber-attack can damage your business and cause your customers to lose trust in you. Therefore, you may lose customers. The number of sales has decreased. It's no secret that new technologies bring new opportunities for criminal activity. Not only do they pose a danger to the narrow-minded, but they also pose a threat to the positive progress of the world. There are three foundations of information security:

Table 1. Overview of 20 top victim countries year 2020

Name of Victim Country	Complaints Received
'United Kingdom'	217,640
Canada	5,480
India	3,177
Greece	2,518
Australia	2,112
South Africa	1,865
France	1,751
. Germany	1,615
Mexico	1,270
Belgium	1,100
Brazil	982
Philippines	910
Italy	802
Spain	627
Netherlands	512
Nigeria	488
Pakistan	456
China	477
Colombia	420
Hong Kong	410

confidentiality, integrity, and availability (Reda, H. T., Anwar 2021). Needless to say, as new technologies emerge, so do new opportunities for criminal activity. Not only do they pose a danger to the narrow-minded, but they also pose a threat to the positive progress of the world. By exploiting the weaknesses of networked business equipment, an increasing number of cybersecurity breaches are affecting companies' capabilities in the modern technological age, especially in the context of Industry 4.0.

In some cases, a cyberattack on vital industrial equipment could put a company's economic model at risk Najmi, (K. Y., AlZain 2021). The main goal of this chapter is to discover and assess the impact of integrity attacks and threats used in e-government research over the past fifteen years. This research will help assess the security of various organizations' security under e-government table 1 and figure 1.

Currently, implementing blockchain through e-government has raised some complexities. When a region meets the requirements for e-government implementation, new challenges arise. Due to the information technology revolution, governments

Figure 1. Overview the 20 top victim countries

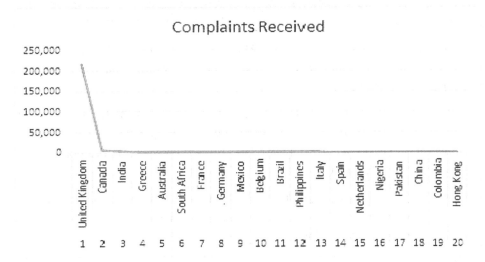

and industries are forced to provide more efficient and secure Internet services. Governments all over the world are trying to provide the public with fast, fast and user-friendly electronic services (Srivastava, A., & Dashora 2022). Blockchain is considered to have significant potential benefits for governments as it is a combination of technologies such as distributed ledgers, privacy, authentication, and consensus mechanisms. However, this advanced technology is still in the development stage, and e-government faces many difficulties and challenges (Sahebi, I. G., Mosayebi 2022). This advanced technology has been evaluated in the context of technical issues such as high-level e-government security and privacy enforcement measures as it adapts.

REFERENCES

Adjei-Bamfo, P., Maloreh-Nyamekye, T., & Ahenkan, A. (2019). The role of e-government in sustainable public procurement in developing countries: A systematic literature review. *Resources, Conservation and Recycling, 142*, 189–203. doi:10.1016/j.resconrec.2018.12.001

Alharmoodi, B. Y. R., & Lakulu, M. M. B. (2020). Transition from e-government to m-government: Challenges and opportunities-case study of UAE. *European Journal of Multidisciplinary Studies, 5*(1), 61–67. doi:10.26417/453fgx96c

Asongu, S. A., Orim, S. M. I., & Nting, R. T. (2019). Inequality, information technology and inclusive education in sub-Saharan Africa. *Technological Forecasting and Social Change, 146*, 380–389. doi:10.1016/j.techfore.2019.06.006

Baharin, A. M., & Zolkipli, M. F. (2021). Review on Current Target of Mobile Attacks. *Borneo International Journal, 4*(2), 17-24. http://majmuah.com/journal/index.php/bij/article/view/84

Cao, J., Li, Q., Xie, R., Sun, K., Gu, G., Xu, M., & Yang, Y. (2019). *The crosspath attack: disrupting the SDN control channel via shared links. In 28th USENIX Security symposium (USENIX Security)* (Vol. 19). https://www.usenix.org/conference/usenixsecurity19/presentation/cao

Dhonju, G. R., & Shakya, S. (2019). Analyzing Challenges for the Implementation of E-Government in Municipalities within Kathmandu Valley. *Journal of Science and Engineering, 7*, 70–78. doi:10.3126/jsce.v7i0.26795

El Khatib, M., Nakand, L., Almarzooqi, S., & Almarzooqi, A. (2020). E-Governance in Project Management: Impact and Risks of Implementation. *American Journal of Industrial and Business Management, 10*(12), 1785–1811. doi:10.4236/ajibm.2020.1012111

Froehlich, A., Ringas, N., & Wilson, J. (2020). E-Governance in Africa and the World. In *Space Supporting Africa* (pp. 53–124). Springer. doi:10.1007/978-3-030-52260-5_2

Hoffman, I., & Cseh, K. B. (2021). E-administration, cybersecurity and municipalities–the challenges of cybersecurity issues for the municipalities in Hungary. *Cybersecurity and Law, 4*(2), 199-211. https://www.cybersecurityandlaw.pl/E-administration-cybersecurity-and-municipalities-the-challenges-of-cybersecurity,133999,0,1.html

Khan, A., Jhanjhi, N. Z., Humayun, M., & Ahmad, M. (2020). The Role of IoT in Digital Governance. In *Employing Recent Technologies for Improved Digital Governance* (pp. 128–150). IGI Global. doi:10.4018/978-1-7998-1851-9.ch007

Lee, S., Abdullah, A., Jhanjhi, N., & Kok, S. (2021). Classification of botnet attacks in IoT smart factory using honeypot combined with machine learning. *PeerJ. Computer Science, 7*, e350. doi:10.7717/peerj-cs.350 PMID:33817000

Najmi, K. Y., AlZain, M. A., Masud, M., Jhanjhi, N. Z., Al-Amri, J., & Baz, M. (2021). A survey on security threats and countermeasures in IoT to achieve users confidentiality and reliability. *Materials Today: Proceedings*. https://www.sciencedirect.com/science/article/pii/S221478532102469X

Orji, U. J. (2018). The African Union Convention on Cybersecurity: A Regional Response Towards Cyber Stability? *Masaryk University Journal of Law and Technology, 12*(2), 91-129.

Qi, M., & Wang, J. (2021). Using the Internet of Things e-government platform to optimize the administrative management mode. *Wireless Communications and Mobile Computing, 2021*, 1–11. doi:10.1155/2021/2224957

Reda, H. T., Anwar, A., Mahmood, A. N., & Tari, Z. (2021). *A Taxonomy of Cyber Defence Strategies Against False Data Attacks in Smart Grid.* https://arxiv.org/abs/2103.16085

Sahebi, I. G., Mosayebi, A., Masoomi, B., & Marandi, F. (2022). Modeling the enablers for blockchain technology adoption in renewable energy supply chain. *Technology in Society, 101871.* doi:10.1016/j.techsoc.2022.101871

Srivastava, A., & Dashora, K. (2022). Application of blockchain technology for agrifood supply chain management: a systematic literature review on benefits and challenges. *Benchmarking: An International Journal.* https://www.emerald.com/insight/content/doi/10.1108/BIJ-08-2021-0495/full/html

Wang, Y., Jiang, D., Huo, L., & Zhao, Y. (2021). A new traffic prediction algorithm to software defined networking. *Mobile Networks and Applications, 26*(2), 716–725. doi:10.100711036-019-01423-3

Compilation of References

Huang, K., & Madnick, S. (2021, January). Does High Cybersecurity Capability Lead to Openness in Digital Trade? The Mediation Effect of E-Government Maturity. In *Proceedings of the 54th Hawaii International Conference on System Sciences* (p. 4352). https://papers.ssrn.com/sol3/papers.cfm?abstract_id=3542552

Jha, R. (n.d.). *Review of Data Mining and Data Warehousing Implementation in E-Governance.* https://ijisrt.com/assets/upload/files/IJISRT20OCT033.pdf

Hammouri, Q. M., Abu-Shanab, E. A., & Nusairat, N. M. (2021). Attitudes Toward Implementing E-Government in Health Insurance Administration. *International Journal of Electronic Government Research, 17*(2), 1–18. doi:10.4018/IJEGR.2021040101

Krishnaraju, V., Mathew, S. K., & Sugumaran, V. (2016). Web personalization for user acceptance of technology: An empirical investigation of E-government services. *Information Systems Frontiers, 18*(3), 579–595.

Galvez, J. F., Mejuto, J., & Simal-Gandara, J. (2018). Future challenges on the use of blockchain for food traceability analysis. *Trends in Analytical Chemistry, 107*, 222–232.

Setiya, R., Pandey, S., Singh, A. K., & Sharma, D. K. (2021). Citizen e-governance using blockchain. In *Blockchain for Smart Cities* (pp. 119–152). Elsevier. doi:10.1016/B978-0-12-824446-3.00010-7

Li, L., He, W., Xu, L., Ash, I., Anwar, M., & Yuan, X. (2019). Investigating the impact of cybersecurity policy awareness on employees' cybersecurity behavior. *International Journal of Information Management, 45*, 13–24. https://www.sciencedirect.com/science/article/abs/pii/S0268401218302093

Gupta, R., Muttoo, S. K., & Pal, S. K. (2020). Regional e-governance development index for developing nations. *Digital Government: Research and Practice, 1*(3), 1-26. https://dl.acm.org/doi/abs/10.1145/3386163

Kim, C., & Kim, K. A. (2021). The institutional change from E-Government toward Smarter City; comparative analysis between royal borough of Greenwich, UK, and Seongdong-gu, South Korea. *Journal of Open Innovation, 7*(1), 42. https://www.mdpi.com/2199-8531/7/1/42

Liu, C., Wang, N., & Liang, H. (2020). Motivating information security policy compliance: The critical role of supervisor-subordinate guanxi and organizational commitment. *International Journal of Information Management, 54*, 102152. https://www.sciencedirect.com/science/article/abs/pii/S0268401219302877

Shivpuri, D. (2021). Cyber Crime: Are the Law Outdated for this Type of Crime. *International Journal of Research in Engineering, Science and Management, 4*(7), 44-49. https://www.journals.resaim.com/ijresm/article/view/958

Shah, Rajper, & ZamanJhanjhi. (2021). Using ML and Data-Mining Techniques in Automatic Vulnerability Software Discovery. *International Journal (Toronto, Ont.), 10*, 3.

Romaniuk, S. N., & Omona, D. A. (2021). Building a Cyber Fortress in Africa: Uganda's cyber security capacities and challenges. In *Routledge Companion to Global Cyber-Security Strategy* (pp. 573–590). Routledge. doi:10.4324/9780429399718-49

Ronchi, A. M. (2019). e-Government: Background, Today's Implementation and Future Trends. In e-Democracy (pp. 93-196). Springer.

Kumar, C., Singh, A. K., & Kumar, P. (2018). A recent survey on image watermarking techniques and its application in e-governance. *Multimedia Tools and Applications, 77*(3), 3597–3622. doi:10.100711042-017-5222-8

Muller, S. R., & Lind, M. L. (2020). Factors in Information Assurance Professionals' Intentions to Adhere to Information Security Policies. *International Journal of Systems and Software Security and Protection, 11*(1), 17–32. https://www.igi-global.com/article/factors-in-information-assurance-professionals-intentions-to-adhere-to-information-security-policies/249763

Alqahtani, M., & Braun, R. (2021). *Examining the Impact of Technical Controls, Accountability and Monitoring towards Cyber Security Compliance in E-government Organizations.* https://web.archive.org/web/20210428072623id_/https://www.researchsquare.com/article/rs-196216/v1.pdf

Shorten, C., Khoshgoftaar, T. M., & Furht, B. (2021). Deep Learning applications for COVID-19. *Journal of Big Data, 8*(1), 1–54. doi:10.118640537-020-00392-9 PMID:33457181

Sahoo, B., Behera, R. N., & Mohanty, S. (2018, July). International Cyber Attackers Eyeing Eastern India: Odisha-A Case Study. In *Science and Information Conference* (pp. 1328–1339). Springer. https://link.springer.com/chapter/10.1007/978-3-030-01177-2_97

Simonova, A. (2020). *An Analysis of Factors Influencing National Institute of Standards and Technology Cybersecurity Framework Adoption in Financial Services: A Correlational Study* (Doctoral dissertation). Capella University. https://www.proquest.com/openview/8482434364a539361dbd14f5dd872752/1?pq-origsite=gscholar&cbl=18750&diss=y

Anand, R., Medhavi, S., Soni, V., Malhotra, C., & Banwet, D. K. (2018). Transforming information security governance in India (A SAP-LAP based case study of security, IT policy and e-governance). *Information & Computer Security.* https://www.emerald.com/insight/content/doi/10.1108/ICS-12-2016-0090/full/html

Twizeyimana, J. D., & Andersson, A. (2019). The public value of E-Government–A literature review. *Government Information Quarterly*, *36*(2), 167–178. https://www.sciencedirect.com/science/article/pii/S0740624X1730196X

Witti, M., & Konstantas, D. (2018, December). A secure and privacy-preserving internet of things framework for smart city. In *Proceedings of the 6th International Conference on Information Technology* (pp. 145–150). IoT and Smart City. doi:10.1145/3301551.3301607

Yazdanmehr, A., Wang, J., & Yang, Z. (2020). Peers matter: The moderating role of social influence on information security policy compliance. *Information Systems Journal*, *30*(5), 791–844. https://onlinelibrary.wiley.com/doi/abs/10.1111/isj.12271

Sharma, L., & Singh, V. (2018, October). India Towards Digital Revolution (Security and Sustainability). In *2018 Second World Conference on Smart Trends in Systems, Security and Sustainability (WorldS4)* (pp. 297-302). IEEE. https://ieeexplore.ieee.org/abstract/document/8611564

Yoo, C. W., Sanders, G. L., & Cerveny, R. P. (2018). Exploring the influence of flow and psychological ownership on security education, training and awareness effectiveness and security compliance. *Decision Support Systems*, *108*, 107–118. https://www.sciencedirect.com/science/article/abs/pii/S0167923618300381

Agbo, C. C., Mahmoud, Q. H., & Eklund, J. M. (2019, June). Blockchain technology in healthcare: a systematic review. In *Healthcare* (Vol. 7, No. 2, p. 56). Multidisciplinary Digital Publishing Institute. https://www.mdpi.com/2227-9032/7/2/56

Wang, H., Ruan, J., Wang, G., Zhou, B., Liu, Y., Fu, X., & Peng, J. (2018). Deep learning-based interval state estimation of AC smart grids against sparse cyber attacks. *IEEE Transactions on Industrial Informatics*, *14*(11), 4766–4778. doi:10.1109/TII.2018.2804669

Komar, M., Sachenko, A., Golovko, V., & Dorosh, V. (2018, May). Compression of network traffic parameters for detecting cyber attacks based on deep learning. In *2018 IEEE 9th International Conference on Dependable Systems, Services and Technologies (DESSERT)* (pp. 43-47). IEEE. https://ieeexplore.ieee.org/abstract/document/8409096

Salam, S., & Kumar, K. P. (2021). Survey on Applications of Blockchain in E-Governance. *Revista Geintec-Gestao Inovacao E Tecnologias*, *11*(4), 3807-3822. https://www.revistageintec.net/index.php/revista/article/view/2409

Bao, J., He, D., Luo, M., & Choo, K. K. R. (2020). A survey of blockchain applications in the energy sector. *IEEE Systems Journal*. https://www.revistageintec.net/index.php/revista/article/view/2409

Taormina, R., & Galelli, S. (2018). Deep-learning approach to the detection and localization of cyber-physical attacks on water distribution systems. *Journal of Water Resources Planning and Management*, *144*(10), 04018065. doi:10.1061/(ASCE)WR.1943-5452.0000983

De Filippi, P., Mannan, M., & Reijers, W. (2020). Blockchain as a confidence machine: The problem of trust & challenges of governance. *Technology in Society*, *62*, 101284. doi:10.1016/j.techsoc.2020

Xin, Y., Kong, L., Liu, Z., Chen, Y., Li, Y., Zhu, H., Gao, M., Hou, H., & Wang, C. (2018). Machine learning and deep learning methods for cybersecurity. *IEEE Access: Practical Innovations, Open Solutions*, *6*, 35365–35381. doi:10.1109/ACCESS.2018.2836950

El Haddouti, S., & El Kettani, M. D. E. C. (2019, April). Analysis of identity management systems using blockchain technology. In *2019 International Conference on Advanced Communication Technologies and Networking (CommNet)* (pp. 1-7). IEEE. https://ieeexplore.ieee.org/abstract/document/8742375/

Sujatha, R., Chatterjee, J. M., Jhanjhi, N. Z., & Brohi, S. N. (2021). Performance of deep learning vs machine learning in plant leaf disease detection. *Microprocessors and Microsystems*, *80*, 103615. doi:10.1016/j.micpro.2020.103615

Fan, K., Wang, S., Ren, Y., Li, H., & Yang, Y. (2018). Medblock: Efficient and secure medical data sharing via blockchain. *Journal of Medical Systems*, *42*(8), 1–11. https://link.springer.com/article/10.1007/s10916-018-0993-7

Tayyab, M., Marjani, M., Jhanjhi, N. Z., & Hashem, I. A. T. (2021, March). A Light-weight Watermarking-Based Framework on Dataset Using Deep Learning Algorithms. In *2021 National Computing Colleges Conference (NCCC)* (pp. 1-6). IEEE. https://ieeexplore.ieee.org/abstract/document/9428845

Avina, G. E., Bogner, K., Carter, J., Friedman, A., Gordon, S. P., Haney, J., . . . Wolf, D. (2017). *Tailoring of cyber security technology adoption practices for operational adoption in complex organizations*. https://citeseerx.ist.psu.edu/viewdoc/download?doi=10.1.1.549.7147&rep=rep1&type=pdf

Sit, M., Demiray, B. Z., Xiang, Z., Ewing, G. J., Sermet, Y., & Demir, I. (2020). A comprehensive review of deep learning applications in hydrology and water resources. *Water Science and Technology*, *82*(12), 2635–2670. doi:10.2166/wst.2020.369 PMID:33341760

Kim, H. M., & Laskowski, M. (2018). Agriculture on the blockchain: Sustainable solutions for food, farmers, and financing. *Supply Chain Revolution*. https://papers.ssrn.com/sol3/papers.cfm?abstract_id=3028164

Han, M., Li, Z., He, J., Wu, D., Xie, Y., & Baba, A. (2018, September). A novel blockchain-based education records verification solution. In *Proceedings of the 19th Annual SIG Conference on Information Technology Education* (pp. 178-183). https://dl.acm.org/doi/abs/10.1145/3241815.3241870

Jhanjhi, N. Z., Brohi, S. N., & Malik, N. A. (2019, December). Proposing a rank and wormhole attack detection framework using machine learning. In *2019 13th International Conference on Mathematics, Actuarial Science, Computer Science and Statistics (MACS)* (pp. 1-9). IEEE. https://ieeexplore.ieee.org/abstract/document/9024821

Khan, M. A., Ashraf, I., Alhaisoni, M., Damaševičius, R., Scherer, R., Rehman, A., & Bukhari, S. A. C. (2020). Multimodal brain tumor classification using deep learning and robust feature selection: A machine learning application for radiologists. *Diagnostics (Basel)*, *10*(8), 565. doi:10.3390/diagnostics10080565 PMID:32781795

Gao, Z., Luo, Z., Zhang, W., Lv, Z., & Xu, Y. (2020). Deep learning application in plant stress imaging: a review. *AgriEngineering, 2*(3), 430-446. https://www.mdpi.com/2624-7402/2/3/29

Mengelkamp, E., Gärttner, J., Rock, K., Kessler, S., Orsini, L., & Weinhardt, C. (2018). Designing microgrid energy markets: A case study: The Brooklyn Microgrid. *Applied Energy, 210*, 870–880. https://dl.acm.org/doi/abs/10.1145/3241815.3241870

Naik, N., & Jenkins, P. (2020, April). Self-Sovereign Identity Specifications: Govern your identity through your digital wallet using blockchain technology. In *2020 8th IEEE International Conference on Mobile Cloud Computing, Services, and Engineering (MobileCloud)* (pp. 90-95). IEEE. https://ieeexplore.ieee.org/abstract/document/9126742

Panwar, H., Gupta, P. K., Siddiqui, M. K., Morales-Menendez, R., & Singh, V. (2020). Application of deep learning for fast detection of COVID-19 in X-Rays using nCOVnet. *Chaos, Solitons, and Fractals, 138*, 109944. doi:10.1016/j.chaos.2020.109944 PMID:32536759

Nawari, N. O., & Ravindran, S. (2019). Blockchain and the built environment: Potentials and limitations. *Journal of Building Engineering, 25*, 100832. https://www.sciencedirect.com/science/article/abs/pii/S2352710218312294

Hong, S. J., Han, Y., Kim, S. Y., Lee, A. Y., & Kim, G. (2019). Application of deep-learning methods to bird detection using unmanned aerial vehicle imagery. *Sensors (Basel)*, *19*(7), 1651. doi:10.339019071651 PMID:30959913

Su, Z., Wang, Y., Xu, Q., Fei, M., Tian, Y. C., & Zhang, N. (2018). A secure charging scheme for electric vehicles with smart communities in energy blockchain. *IEEE Internet of Things Journal, 6*(3), 4601-4613. https://ieeexplore.ieee.org/abstract/document/8457186

Purwins, H., Li, B., Virtanen, T., Schlüter, J., Chang, S. Y., & Sainath, T. (2019). Deep learning for audio signal processing. *IEEE Journal of Selected Topics in Signal Processing*, *13*(2), 206–219. doi:10.1109/JSTSP.2019.2908700

United Nations. (2018). https://publicadministration.un.org/egovkb/en-us/data/compare-countries

Pathirage, C. S. N., Li, J., Li, L., Hao, H., Liu, W., & Wang, R. (2019). Development and application of a deep learning–based sparse autoencoder framework for structural damage identification. *Structural Health Monitoring, 18*(1), 103–122. doi:10.1177/1475921718800363

Zheng, Z., Xie, S., Dai, H. N., Chen, X., & Wang, H. (2018). Blockchain challenges and opportunities: A survey. *International Journal of Web and Grid Services, 14*(4), 352-375. https://www.inderscienceonline.com/doi/abs/10.1504/IJWGS.2018.095647

Singh, A. P., Pradhan, N. R., Luhach, A. K., Agnihotri, S., Jhanjhi, N. Z., Verma, S., ... Roy, D. S. (2020). A novel patient-centric architectural framework for blockchain-enabled healthcare applications. *IEEE Transactions on Industrial Informatics*, *17*(8), 5779–5789. https://ieeexplore. ieee.org/abstract/document/9259231

Tang, B., Pan, Z., Yin, K., & Khateeb, A. (2019). Recent advances of deep learning in bioinformatics and computational biology. *Frontiers in Genetics*, *10*, 214. doi:10.3389/fgene.2019.00214 PMID:30972100

Barrane, F. Z., Karuranga, G. E., & Poulin, D. (2018). Technology adoption and diffusion: A new application of the UTAUT model. *International Journal of Innovation and Technology Management*, *15*(06), 1950004. https://www.worldscientific.com/doi/abs/10.1142/S0219877019500044

Kuutti, S., Bowden, R., Jin, Y., Barber, P., & Fallah, S. (2020). A survey of deep learning applications to autonomous vehicle control. *IEEE Transactions on Intelligent Transportation Systems*, *22*(2), 712–733. doi:10.1109/TITS.2019.2962338

Koirala, A., Walsh, K. B., Wang, Z., & McCarthy, C. (2019). Deep learning–Method overview and review of use for fruit detection and yield estimation. *Computers and Electronics in Agriculture*, *162*, 219–234. doi:10.1016/j.compag.2019.04.017

Kumar, M. S., Vimal, S., Jhanjhi, N. Z., Dhanabalan, S. S., & Alhumyani, H. A. (2021). Blockchain based peer to peer communication in autonomous drone operation. *Energy Reports*. https://www. sciencedirect.com/science/article/pii/S2352484721006752

Ravi, N., Verma, S., Jhanjhi, N. Z., & Talib, M. N. (2021, August). Securing VANET Using Blockchain Technology. In *Journal of Physics: Conference Series* (Vol. 1979, No. 1, p. 012035). IOP Publishing. https://iopscience.iop.org/article/10.1088/1742-6596/1979/1/012035/meta

Singh, K. B., & Arat, M. A. (2019). *Deep learning in the automotive industry: Recent advances and application examples.* https://arxiv.org/abs/1906.08834

Alamri, M., Jhanjhi, N. Z., & Humayun, M. (2019). Blockchain for Internet of Things (IoT) research issues challenges & future directions: A review. *Int. J. Comput. Sci. Netw. Secur*, *19*, 244–258.

Ozdemir, R., & Koc, M. (2019, September). A quality control application on a smart factory prototype using deep learning methods. In *2019 IEEE 14th International Conference on Computer Sciences and Information Technologies (CSIT)* (Vol. 1, pp. 46-49). IEEE. https://ieeexplore.ieee. org/abstract/document/8929734

Choi, B. G., Jeong, E., & Kim, S. W. (2019). Multiple security certification system between blockchain based terminal and internet of things device: Implication for open innovation. *Journal of Open Innovation*, *5*(4), 87.

Kumar, B. S., Sridhar, V., & Sudhindra, K. R. (2019). A Case Study: Risk Rating Methodology for E-Governance Application Security Risks. *i-Manager's Journal on Software Engineering*, *13*(3), 39. www.proquest.com/openview/ee2f52533cd40f06b66288ca835e4501/1?pq-origsite=gscholar&cbl=2030612

Anand, D., & Khemchandani, V. (2019). Unified and integrated authentication and key agreement scheme for e-governance system without verification table. *Sadhana*, *44*(9), 1–14. doi:10.100712046-019-1163-4

Tosh, D. K., Shetty, S., Liang, X., Kamhoua, C., & Njilla, L. (2017, October). Consensus protocols for blockchain-based data provenance: Challenges and opportunities. In *2017 IEEE 8th Annual Ubiquitous Computing, Electronics and Mobile Communication Conference (UEMCON)* (pp. 469-474). IEEE.

Dhaoui, I. (2019). *Electronic governance: An overview of opportunities and challenges.* https://mpra.ub.uni-muenchen.de/92545/

Yang, T., Guo, Q., Tai, X., Sun, H., Zhang, B., Zhao, W., & Lin, C. (2017, November). *Applying blockchain technology to decentralized operation in future energy internet. In 2017 IEEE Conference on Energy Internet and Energy System Integration (EI2).* IEEE. https://ieeexplore.ieee.org/abstract/document/8244418

Loukas, G., Patrikakis, C. Z., & Wilbanks, L. R. (2020). Digital deception: Cyber fraud and online misinformation. *IT Professional*, *22*(2), 19–20. doi:10.1109/MITP.2020.2980090

Tasca, P., & Tessone, C. J. (2017). *Taxonomy of blockchain technologies. Principles of identification and classification.* arXiv preprint arXiv:1708.04872.

El-Gendy, S., & Azer, M. A. (2020, December). Security Framework for Internet of Things (IoT). In *2020 15th International Conference on Computer Engineering and Systems (ICCES)* (pp. 1-6). IEEE. https://ieeexplore.ieee.org/abstract/document/9334589

Xia, Q., Sifah, E. B., Smahi, A., Amofa, S., & Zhang, X. (2017). BBDS: Blockchain-based data sharing for electronic medical records in cloud environments. *Information*, *8*(2), 44. https://www.mdpi.com/2078-2489/8/2/44

Cachin, C., & Vukolić, M. (2017). *Blockchain consensus protocols in the wild.* https://arxiv.org/abs/1707.01873

Calderaro, A., & Craig, A. J. (2020). Transnational governance of cybersecurity: Policy challenges and global inequalities in cyber capacity building. *Third World Quarterly*, *41*(6), 917–938. doi:10.1080/01436597.2020.1729729

McKinney, S. A., Landy, R., & Wilka, R. (2017). Smart contracts, blockchain, and the next frontier of transactional law. *Wash. JL Tech. & Arts*, *13*, 313. https://heinonline.org/HOL/LandingPage?handle=hein.journals/washjolta13&div=18&id=&page=

Mehta, S., Sharma, A., Chawla, P., & Soni, K. (2021, May). The Urgency of Cyber Security in Secure Networks. In *2021 5th International Conference on Intelligent Computing and Control Systems (ICICCS)* (pp. 315-322). IEEE. https://ieeexplore.ieee.org/abstract/document/9432092

Chen, X., Chen, L., & Wu, D. (2018). Factors that influence employees' security policy compliance: An awareness-motivation-capability perspective. *Journal of Computer Information Systems*, *58*(4), 312–324. https://www.tandfonline.com/doi/abs/10.1080/08874417.2016.1258679

Zhang, T., Gao, C., Ma, L., Lyu, M., & Kim, M. (2019, October). An empirical study of common challenges in developing deep learning applications. In *2019 IEEE 30th International Symposium on Software Reliability Engineering (ISSRE)* (pp. 104-115). IEEE. https://ieeexplore.ieee.org/abstract/document/8987482

Millard, J. (2017). European Strategies for e-Governance to 2020 and Beyond. In *Government 3.0–Next Generation Government Technology Infrastructure and Services* (pp. 1–25). Springer. https://link.springer.com/chapter/10.1007/978-3-319-63743-3_1

Nadrah, R., Gambour, Y., Kurdi, R., & Almansouri, R. (2021). E-government service in Saudi Arabia. *PalArch's Journal of Archaeology of Egypt/Egyptology, 18*(16), 21-29. https://archives.palarch.nl/index.php/jae/article/view/8156

Risius, M., & Spohrer, K. (2017). A blockchain research framework. *Business & Information Systems Engineering, 59*(6), 385–409. https://link.springer.com/article/10.1007/s12599-017-0506-0

Sambana, B., Raju, K. N., Satish, D., Raju, S. S., & Raja, P. V. K. (2021). *Impact of Cyber Security in e-Governance and e-Commerce* (No. 5533). EasyChair. file:///C:/Users/USER/Downloads/EasyChair-Preprint-5533%20(1).pdf

Tkatchenko, A. (2020). Machine learning for chemical discovery. *Nature Communications, 11*(1), 1–4. doi:10.103841467-020-17844-8 PMID:32807794

Zambrano, R., Seward, R. K., & Sayo, P. (2017). *Unpacking the disruptive potential of blockchain technology for human development.* https://idl-bnc-idrc.dspacedirect.org/handle/10625/56662

Paintner, P. (2021). *Blockchain technology in the area of e-Governance–Guidelines for implementation* (Doctoral dissertation). https://run.unl.pt/handle/10362/123244

Ahmad, M. S., & Shah, S. M. (2021). Moving Beyond the Crypto-Currency Success of Blockchain: A Systematic Survey. *Scalable Computing: Practice and Experience, 22*(3), 321-346. https://link.springer.com/chapter/10.1007/978-3-030-77637-4_6

Choi, M., Lee, J., & Hwang, K. (2018). Information Systems Security (ISS) of EGovernment for Sustainability: A Dual Path Model of ISS Influenced by Institutional Isomorphism. *Sustainability.* https://www.mdpi.com/2071-1050/10/5/1555

Lee, S. M., Seo, J. B., Yun, J., Cho, Y.-H., Vogel-Claussen, J., Schiebler, M. L., Gefter, W. B., van Beek, E. J. R., Goo, J. M., Lee, K. S., Hatabu, H., Gee, J., & Kim, N. (2019). Deep learning applications in chest radiography and computed tomography. *Journal of Thoracic Imaging, 34*(2), 75–85. doi:10.1097/RTI.0000000000000387 PMID:30802231

Thabit, T. H., & Jasim, Y. A. (2019). The challenges of adopting E-governance in Iraq. *Current Res. J. Soc. Sci. & Human., 2*, 31. https://heinonline.org/HOL/LandingPage?handle=hein.journals/crjssh2&div=6&id=&page=

Donalds, C., & Osei-Bryson, K. M. (2020). Cybersecurity compliance behavior: Exploring the influences of individual decision style and other antecedents. *International Journal of Information Management*, *51*, 102056. https://www.sciencedirect.com/science/article/abs/pii/S0268401218312544

Gupta, R., Pal, S. K., & Muttoo, S. K. (2020). Cyber Security Assessment Education for E-Governance Systems. In *Innovations in Cybersecurity Education* (pp. 181–212). Springer. doi:10.1007/978-3-030-50244-7_10

Harris, M. A., & Martin, R. (2019). Promoting cybersecurity compliance. In *Cybersecurity education for awareness and compliance* (pp. 54–71). IGI Global. https://www.igi-global.com/chapter/promoting-cybersecurity-compliance/225917

Veeramani, K., & Jaganathan, S. (2020). Land registration: Use-case of e-Governance using blockchain technology. *Transactions on Internet and Information Systems (Seoul)*, *14*(9), 3693–3711. https://www.koreascience.or.kr/article/JAKO202030161655507.page

El Khatib, M., Nakand, L., Almarzooqi, S., & Almarzooqi, A. (2020). E-Governance in Project Management: Impact and Risks of Implementation. *American Journal of Industrial and Business Management*, *10*(12), 1785–1811. doi:10.4236/ajibm.2020.1012111

Hofbauer, D., Ivkic, I., & Tauber, M. (2019). On the Cost of Security Compliance in Information Systems. *10th International Multi-Conference on Complexity, Informatics and Cybernetics 2019 (IMCIC)*. https://www.igi-global.com/chapter/promoting-cybersecurity-compliance/225917

Abdulkareem, A. K. (2015). *Challenges of e-government implementation in the Nigerian public service*. https://uilspace.unilorin.edu.ng/handle/20.500.12484/290

Abdullahi, A. (2019). Rural Banditry, Regional Security and Integration in West Africa. *Journal of Social and Political Sciences*, *2*(3). Advance online publication. doi:10.31014/aior.1991.02.03.107

Abebe, B. (2019). *E-government based land administration framework; trends, challenges and prospects* (Doctoral dissertation). https://ir.bdu.edu.et/handle/123456789/10878

Abolhasan, M., Lipman, J., Ni, W., & Hagelstein, B. (2015). Software-defined wireless networking: Centralized, distributed, or hybrid? *IEEE Network*, *29*(4), 32–38. doi:10.1109/MNET.2015.7166188

Adeodato, R., & Pournouri, S. (2020). Secure Implementation of E-Governance: A Case Study About Estonia. In *Cyber Defence in the Age of AI, Smart Societies and Augmented Humanity* (pp. 397–429). Springer. doi:10.1007/978-3-030-35746-7_18

Adjei-Bamfo, P., Maloreh-Nyamekye, T., & Ahenkan, A. (2019). The role of e-government in sustainable public procurement in developing countries: A systematic literature review. *Resources, Conservation and Recycling*, *142*, 189–203. https://www.sciencedirect.com/science/article/abs/pii/S0921344918304579

Afzal, B., Umair, M., Shah, G. A., & Ahmed, E. (2019). Enabling IoT platforms for social IoT applications: Vision, feature mapping, and challenges. *Future Generation Computer Systems*, *92*, 718–731. https://www.sciencedirect.com/science/article/abs/pii/S0167739X17312724

Agbo, C. C., Mahmoud, Q. H., & Eklund, J. M. (2019, June). Blockchain technology in healthcare: a systematic review. In *Healthcare* (Vol. 7, No. 2, p. 56). Multidisciplinary Digital Publishing Institute. https://www.mdpi.com/2227-9032/7/2/56

Agbozo, E., Alhassan, D., & Spassov, K. (2018, November). Personal data and privacy barriers to e-Government adoption, implementation and development in Sub-Saharan Africa. In *International Conference on Electronic Governance and Open Society: Challenges in Eurasia* (pp. 82–91). Springer. https://link.springer.com/chapter/10.1007/978-3-030-13283-5_7

Aglionby, J. (2018, January 29). *African Union accuses China of hacking headquarters.* Retrieved October 27, 2018, from https://www.ft.com/content/c26a9214-04f2-11e8-9650-9c0ad2d7c5b5

Agrafiotis, I., Nurse, J. R., Goldsmith, M., Creese, S., & Upton, D. (2018). A taxonomy of cyber-harms: Defining the impacts of cyber-attacks and understanding how they propagate. *Journal of Cybersecurity, 4*(1), tyy006. doi:10.1093/cybsec/tyy006

Ahmad, R., Asim, M. A., Khan, S. Z., & Singh, B. (2019, March). Green IOT—issues and challenges. In *Proceedings of 2nd International Conference on Advanced Computing and Software Engineering (ICACSE).* https://papers.ssrn.com/sol3/papers.cfm?abstract_id=3350317

Ahmad, T. (2019). Technology Convergence and Cybersecurity: A Critical Analysis of Cybercrime Trends in India. *27th Convergence India Pragati Maidan,* 29-31. https://papers.ssrn.com/sol3/papers.cfm?abstract_id=3326232

Ahmad, S. U., Kashyap, S., Shetty, S. D., & Sood, N. (2022). Cybersecurity During COVID-19. In *Information and Communication Technology for Competitive Strategies (ICTCS 2020)* (pp. 1045–1056). Springer. doi:10.1007/978-981-16-0739-4_96

AhmadT. (2020). *Corona virus (covid-19) pandemic and work from home: Challenges of cybercrimes and cybersecurity.* https://papers.ssrn.com/sol3/papers.cfm?abstract_id=3568830 doi:10.2139/ssrn.3568830

Al Shuhaimi, F., Jose, M., & Singh, A. V. (2016, September). Software defined network as solution to overcome security challenges in IoT. In *2016 5th International Conference on Reliability, Infocom Technologies and Optimization (Trends and Future Directions)(ICRITO)* (pp. 491-496). IEEE. https://ieeexplore.ieee.org/abstract/document/7785005

Albrahim, R., Alsalamah, H., Alsalamah, S., & Aksoy, M. (2018). Access control model for modern virtual e-government services: Saudi Arabian case study. *International Journal of Advanced Computer Science and Applications, 9*(8), 357–364. https://pdfs.semanticscholar.org/ebb0/10ac868b6bb721a9db5d2bc33e24cf48895b.pdf

AlEnezi, A., AlMeraj, Z., & Manuel, P. (2018, April). Challenges of IoT based smart-government development. In *2018 21st Saudi Computer Society National Computer Conference (NCC)* (pp. 1-6). IEEE. https://ieeexplore.ieee.org/abstract/document/8593168

Alexopoulos, C., Lachana, Z., Androutsopoulou, A., Diamantopoulou, V., Charalabidis, Y., & Loutsaris, M. A. (2019, April). How machine learning is changing e-government. In *Proceedings of the 12th International Conference on Theory and Practice of Electronic Governance* (pp. 354-363). https://dl.acm.org/doi/abs/10.1145/3326365.3326412

Alguliyev, R., Aliguliyev, R., & Yusifov, F. (2018a). Role of Social Networks in E-government: Risks and Security Threats. *Online Journal of Communication and Media Technologies*, 8(4), 363–376. https://www.ojcmt.net/article/role-of-social-networks-in-e-government-risks-and-security-threats-3957

Alguliyev, R., Aliguliyev, R., & Yusifov, F. (2018b, October). MCDM Model for Evaluation of Social Network Security Threats. In *the book*. In R. Bouzas-Lorenzo & A. Cernadas Ramos (Eds.), *ECDG 2018 18th European Conference on Digital Government* (pp. 1–7). University Santiago de Compostela. https://www.proquest.com/openview/bc2d4527ea3a433a65db63414c023e96/1?pq-origsite=gscholar&cbl=1796415

Alharmoodi, B. Y. R., & Lakulu, M. M. B. (2020). Transition from e-government to m-government: Challenges and opportunities-case study of UAE. *European Journal of Multidisciplinary Studies*, 5(1), 61–67. https://journals.euser.org/files/articles/ejms_v5_i1_20/Alharmoodi.pdf

Alhawawsha, M., & Panchenko, T. (2020, January). Open Data Platform Architecture and Its Advantages for an Open E-Government. In *International Conference on Computer Science, Engineering and Education Applications* (pp. 631–639). Springer. https://link.springer.com/chapter/10.1007/978-3-030-55506-1_56

Aliwa, E., Rana, O., Perera, C., & Burnap, P. (2021). Cyberattacks and countermeasures for in-vehicle networks. *ACM Computing Surveys*, 54(1), 1–37. doi:10.1145/3431233

Alketbi, H. (2018). *An evaluation of e-government effectiveness in Dubai smart government departments* (Doctoral dissertation). Southampton Solent University. https://ssudl.solent.ac.uk/id/eprint/3809/

AlMendah, O. M. (2021). A Survey of Blockchain and E-governance applications: Security and Privacy issues. *Turkish Journal of Computer and Mathematics Education*, 12(10), 3117–3125. https://turcomat.org/index.php/turkbilmat/article/view/4964

Almusaylim, Z. A., & Jhanjhi, N. Z. (2020). Comprehensive review: Privacy protection of user in location-aware services of mobile cloud computing. *Wireless Personal Communications*, 111(1), 541–564. doi:10.100711277-019-06872-3

Almusaylim, Z., Jhanjhi, N. Z., & Alhumam, A. (2020). Detection and Mitigation of RPL Rank and Version Number Attacks in the Internet of Things: SRPL-RP. *Sensors (Basel)*, 20(21), 5997. doi:10.339020215997 PMID:33105891

Al-Mushayt, O. S. (2019). Automating E-government services with artificial intelligence. *IEEE Access: Practical Innovations, Open Solutions*, 7, 146821–146829. https://ieeexplore.ieee.org/abstract/document/8862835

Al-Najjar, A., Layeghy, S., & Portmann, M. (2016). Pushing SDN to the end-host, network load balancing using OpenFlow. *Proc. PCCW'16,* 1–6. https://ieeexplore.ieee.org/abstract/document/7457129

Al-Nidawi, W. J. A., Al-Wassiti, S. K. J., Maan, M. A., & Othman, M. (2018). A review in E-government service quality measurement. *Indonesian Journal of Electrical Engineering and Computer Science, 10*(3), 1257–1265. https://www.mustaqbal-college.edu.iq/lecture/2018%20dr%20wael%20Paper.pdf

Alqudah, M. A., & Muradkhanli, L. (2021). Artificial Intelligence in Electric Government; Ethical Challenges and Governance in Jordan. *Electronic Research Journal of Social Sciences and Humanities, 3,* 65-74. https://papers.ssrn.com/sol3/papers.cfm?abstract_id=3806600

Al-Rawahna, A. S. M., Chen, S. C., & Hung, C. W. (2019). The barriers of e-government success: An empirical study from Jordan. *Available at SSRN 3498847.* https://papers.ssrn.com/sol3/papers.cfm?abstract_id=3498847

Al-rawahnaA. S. M.ChenS. C.HungC. W. (2019). *The barriers of e-government success: An empirical study from Jordan.* https://papers.ssrn.com/sol3/papers.cfm?abstract_id=3498847 doi:10.2139/ssrn.3498847

Al-Shboul, M., Rababah, O., Ghnemat, R., & Al-Saqqa, S. (2014). Challenges and factors affecting the implementation of e-government in Jordan. *Journal of Software Engineering and Applications, 7*(13), 1111. https://www.scirp.org/html/5-9302011_52812.htm?pagespeed=noscript

Alshehri, M., & Drew, S. (2010). Implementation of e-government: advantages and challenges. *International Association for Scientific Knowledge (IASK).* https://research-repository.griffith.edu.au/bitstream/handle/10072/40620/72631_1.pdf

Al-Soud, A. R., Al-Yaseen, H., & Al-Jaghoub, S. H. (2014). Jordan's e-Government at the crossroads. *Transforming Government: People, Process and Policy.* https://www.emerald.com/insight/content/doi/10.1108/TG-10-2013-0043/full/html

Amir Latif, R. M., Hussain, K., Jhanji, N. Z., Nayyar, A., & Rizwan, O. (2020). A remix IDE: Smart contract-based framework for the healthcare sector by using Blockchain technology. *Multimedia Tools and Applications,* 1–24. doi:10.100711042-020-10087-1

Angelopoulos, K., Diamantopoulou, V., Mouratidis, H., Pavlidis, M., Salnitri, M., Giorgini, P., & Ruiz, J. F. (2017, August). A holistic approach for privacy protection in E-government. In *Proceedings of the 12th International Conference on Availability* (pp. 1–10). Reliability and Security. https://dl.acm.org/doi/abs/10.1145/3098954.3098960

Anwar, A., Cheng, Y., Huang, H., Han, J., Sim, H., Lee, D., . . . Butt, A. R. (2018, November). BESPOKV: Application tailored scale-out key-value stores. In *SC18: International Conference for High Performance Computing, Networking, Storage and Analysis* (pp. 14-29). IEEE. https://ieeexplore.ieee.org/abstract/document/8665756

Arabadzhyiev, D., Popovych, Y., Lytvynchuk, I., Bakbergen, K., & Kyrychenko, Y. (2021). Digital Society: Regulatory and Institutional Support of Electronic Governance in Modern Realities. In *SHS Web of Conferences* (Vol. 100, p. 03008). EDP Sciences. https://www.shsconferences. org/articles/shsconf/abs/2021/11/shsconf_iscsai2021_03008/shsconf_iscsai2021_03008.html

Arampatzis, A., & O'Hagan, L. (2022). Cybersecurity and Privacy in the Age of the Pandemic. In *Handbook of Research on Cyberchondria, Health Literacy, and the Role of Media in Society's Perception of Medical Information* (pp. 35-53). IGI Global. https://www.igi-global.com/chapter/ cybersecurity-and-privacy-in-the-age-of-the-pandemic/293432

Ari, A. A. A., Ngangmo, O. K., Titouna, C., Thiare, O., Mohamadou, A., & Gueroui, A. M. (2020). Enabling privacy and security in Cloud of Things: Architecture, applications, security & privacy challenges. *Applied Computing and Informatics.* https://www.emerald.com/insight/ content/doi/10.1016/j.aci.2019.11.005/full/pdf

Arief, A., Wahab, I. H. A., & Muhammad, M. (2021, May). Barriers and Challenges of e-Government Services: A Systematic Literature Review and Meta-Analyses. In *IOP Conference Series: Materials Science and Engineering* (Vol. 1125, No. 1, p. 012027). IOP Publishing. https:// iopscience.iop.org/article/10.1088/1757-899X/1125/1/012027/meta

Asongu, S. A., Orim, S. M. I., & Nting, R. T. (2019). Inequality, information technology and inclusive education in sub-Saharan Africa. *Technological Forecasting and Social Change, 146,* 380–389. doi:10.1016/j.techfore.2019.06.006

Assiri, H., Nanda, P., & Mohanty, M. (2020). *Secure e-Governance Using Blockchain.* https:// ieeexplore.ieee.org/abstract/document/9428825

Baharin, A. M., & Zolkipli, M. F. (2021). Review on Current Target of Mobile Attacks. *Borneo International Journal, 4*(2), 17-24. http://majmuah.com/journal/index.php/bij/article/view/84

Balaji, R. D., Jaboob, S., & Malathi, R. (2021). A Block Chain and IoT Based Hybrid Students Record System for E-Governance. *Current Journal of Applied Science and Technology,* 59-71. https://journalbank.org/index.php/CJAST/article/view/2453

Bannour, F., Souihi, S., & Mellouk, A. (2017). Distributed SDN control: Survey, taxonomy, and challenges. *IEEE Communications Surveys and Tutorials, 20*(1), 333–354. doi:10.1109/ COMST.2017.2782482

Bao, J., He, D., Luo, M., & Choo, K. K. R. (2020). A survey of blockchain applications in the energy sector. *IEEE Systems Journal.* https://www.revistageintec.net/index.php/revista/article/ view/2409

Basyal, D. K., Poudyal, N., & Seo, J. W. (2018). Does E-government reduce corruption? Evidence from a heterogeneous panel data model. *Transforming Government: People, Process and Policy.* https://www.emerald.com/insight/content/doi/10.1108/TG-12-2017-0073/full/html

Baxter, D. J. (2017). E-governance and e-participation via online citizen budgets and electronic lobbying: Promises and challenges. *World Affairs, 180*(4), 4-24. https://scholar.google.com/scholar?q=IoT+and+e-governance+challenges&hl=en&as_sdt=0%2C5&as_ylo=2017&as_yhi=2017

BBC. (2015, January 21). *Ghana government websites targeted by hackers.* Retrieved October 27, 2018, from https://www.bbc.com/news/world-africa-30914000

Bhagat, C., Sharma, B., & Kumar Mishra, A. (2021). *Assessment of E Governance for National Development–A Case Study of Province 1 Nepal.* https://papers.ssrn.com/sol3/papers.cfm?abstract_id=3857194

Bhattacharya, K., & Suri, T. (2017). The curious case of e-governance. *IEEE Internet Computing, 21*(1), 62–67. https://ieeexplore.ieee.org/abstract/document/7839849

Bhuvana, M., & Vasantha, S. (2021). The Impact of COVID-19 on Rural Citizens for Accessing E-Governance Services: A Conceptual Model Using the Dimensions of Trust and Technology Acceptance Model. *Recent Advances in Technology Acceptance Models and Theories, 335,* 471. https://www.ncbi.nlm.nih.gov/pmc/articles/PMC7979245/

Bindu, N., Sankar, C. P., & Kumar, K. S. (2019). From conventional governance to e-democracy: Tracing the evolution of e-governance research trends using network analysis tools. *Government Information Quarterly, 36*(3), 385–399. doi:10.1016/j.giq.2019.02.005

Birkel, H. S., & Hartmann, E. (2019). Impact of IoT challenges and risks for SCM. *Supply Chain Management: An International Journal.* https://www.emerald.com/insight/content/doi/10.1108/SCM-03-2018-0142/full/html

Botelho, F., Bessani, A., Ramos, F. M., & Ferreira, P. (2014, September). *On the design of practical fault-tolerant SDN controllers. In 2014 third European workshop on software defined networks.* IEEE. https://ieeexplore.ieee.org/abstract/document/7780356

Brohi, S. N., Jhanjhi, N. Z., Brohi, N. N., & Brohi, M. N. (2020). *Key Applications of State-of-the-Art technologies to mitigate and eliminate COVID-19.* file:///C:/Users/imdad/Downloads/Key%20Applications%20of%20State-of-the-Art%20Technologies%20to%20Mitigate%20and%20Eliminate%20COVID-19%20(1).pdf

Burrell, D. N. (2020). Understanding the talent management intricacies of remote cybersecurity teams in covid-19 induced telework organizational ecosystems. *Land Forces Academy Review, 25*(3), 232-244. https://www.armyacademy.ro/reviste/rev3_2020/Burrell.pdf

Cabaj, K., Gregorczyk, M., & Mazurczy, W. (2018). Softwaredefined networking-based crypto ransomware detection using http traffic characteristics. *Computers & Electrical Engineering, 66,* 353–368. doi:10.1016/j.compeleceng.2017.10.012

Cao, J., Li, Q., Xie, R., Sun, K., Gu, G., Xu, M., & Yang, Y. (2019). *The crosspath attack: disrupting the SDN control channel via shared links. In 28th USENIX Security symposium (USENIX Security* (Vol. 19). https://www.usenix.org/conference/usenixsecurity19/presentation/cao

Cao, J., Li, Q., Xie, R., Sun, K., Gu, G., Xu, M., & Yang, Y. (2019). *The crosspath attack: disrupting the SDN control channel via shared links. In 28th USENIX Security symposium (USENIX Security)* (Vol. 19). https://www.usenix.org/conference/usenixsecurity19/presentation/cao

Carlton, M., Levy, Y., & Ramim, M. (2019). Mitigating cyber attacks through the measurement of non-IT professionals' cybersecurity skills. *Information & Computer Security.* https://www.emerald.com/insight/content/doi/10.1108/ICS-11-2016-0088/full/html

Carrapico, H., & Farrand, B. (2020). Discursive continuity and change in the time of Covid-19: The case of EU cybersecurity policy. *journal of European Integration, 42*(8), 1111–1126. doi: 10.1080/07036337.2020.1853122

Carstens, D. S., Kies, S., & Stockman, R. (2015). E-government transparency and citizen engagement increasing accountability. In *Digital Solutions for Contemporary Democracy and Government* (pp. 189–214). IGI Global. doi:10.4018/978-1-4666-8430-0.ch011

Chakraborty, C., & Abougreen, A. N. (2021). Intelligent internet of things and advanced machine learning techniques for COVID-19. *EAI Endorsed Transactions on Pervasive Health and Technology, 7*(26), e1. http://eprints.eudl.eu/id/eprint/2578/1/eai.28-1-2021.168505.pdf

Chaturvedi, M. M., Gupta, M. P., & Bhattacharya, J. (2008). Cyber Security Infrastructure in India: A Study. In *Emerging Technologies in E-Government.* CSI Publication. http://citeseerx.ist.psu.edu/viewdoc/download?doi=10.1.1.542.8083&rep=rep1&type=pdf

Cheng, B., Solmaz, G., Cirillo, F., Kovacs, E., Terasawa, K., & Kitazawa, A. (2017). FogFlow: Easy programming of IoT services over cloud and edges for smart cities. *IEEE Internet of Things Journal, 5*(2), 696-707. https://ieeexplore.ieee.org/abstract/document/8022859/

Cheng, B., Solmaz, G., Cirillo, F., Kovacs, E., Terasawa, K., & Kitazawa, A. (2017). FogFlow: Easy programming of IoT services over cloud and edges for smart cities. *IEEE Internet of Things Journal, 5*(2), 696–707. doi:10.1109/JIOT.2017.2747214

Cheng, J., Chen, W., Tao, F., & Lin, C. L. (2018). Industrial IoT in 5G environment towards smart manufacturing. *Journal of Industrial Information Integration, 10*, 10–19. doi:10.1016/j.jii.2018.04.001

Cheng, L., Li, Z., Zhang, Y., Zhang, Y., & Lee, I. (2017). Protecting interoperable clinical environment with authentication. *SIGBED Rev, 14*(2), 34–43. doi:10.1145/3076125.3076129

Chen-xu, N., & Jie-sheng, W. (2015, July). Auto regressive moving average (ARMA) prediction method of bank cash flow time series. In *2015 34th Chinese Control Conference (CCC)* (pp. 4928-4933). IEEE. https://ieeexplore.ieee.org/abstract/document/7260405

Chhajed, Deshmukh, & Kulkarni. (2011). Review on Binary image Stegnography and Watermarking. *International Journal in Computer Science and Engineering, 3*(11), 3545-3651.

Chhajed, Inamdar, & Attar. (2008). Steganography in Black and White Picture Images. In *Congress on Image and Signal Processing, CISP 2008.* IEEE Computer Society. Doi:10.1109/CISP.2008.626

Chhajed, G. J., & Shinde, S. A. (2010). Efficient Embedding in B&W picture Images. *2nd IEEE International conference ICIME 2010*, 525-528. 10.1109/ICIME.2010.5478204

Chiew & Pieprzyk. (2010). Binary Image Steganographic Techniques Classification Based on Multi-class Steganalysis. LNCS, 6047, 341–358.

Chin, T., Xiong, K., & Rahouti, M. (2018). Kernel-Space Intrusion Detection Using Software-Deðned Networking. *EAI Endorsed Transactions on Security and Safety, 5*(15), e2. http://eprints.eudl.eu/id/eprint/2088/

Chinese Academy of Cyberspace Studies. (2019). The World e-Government Development. *World Internet Development Report 2017*, 159-197. https://link.springer.com/chapter/10.1007/978-3-662-57524-6_6

Chin, T., Rahouti, M., & Xiong, K. (2018). Applying software-defined networking to minimize the end-to-end delay of network services. *Applied Computing Review, 18*(1), 30–40. doi:10.1145/3212069.3212072

Chishiro, H., Tsuchiya, Y., Chubachi, Y., Abu Bakar, M. S., & De Silva, L. C. (2017, June). Global PBL for environmental IoT. In *Proceedings of the 2017 International Conference on E-commerce* (pp. 65–71). E-Business and E-Government. https://dl.acm.org/doi/abs/10.1145/3108421.3108437

CIRNU. (2016). *How EU and Japan Deal with the Challenges of Cybersecurity in the eGovernment Domain in the Emerging Age of IoT?* https://www.kgri.keio.ac.jp/en/docs/GWP_33.pdf

College, C. C. C., Rajasingh, J. P., & Ramapuram, C. (2020). A Systematic Conceptual Review-Blockchain As A Next Generation E-Government Information Infrastructure. *European Journal of Molecular & Clinical Medicine, 7*(06). https://www.ejmcm.com/article_3906_fb90616fc37a6dd3497cdf923eff0558.pdf

Correia, S., Boukerche, A., & Meneguette, R. I. (2017). An architecture for hierarchical software-defined vehicular networks. *IEEE Communications Magazine, 55*(7), 80–86. doi:10.1109/MCOM.2017.1601105

Cowgill, B., & Stevenson, M. T. (2020, May). Algorithmic social engineering. In *AEA Papers and Proceedings* (Vol. 110, pp. 96-100). https://www.aeaweb.org/articles?id=10.1257/pandp.20201037

Cradduck, L. (2019). E-conveyancing: a consideration of its risks and rewards. *Property Management.* https://www.emerald.com/insight/content/doi/10.1108/PM-04-2019-0021/full/html

Cradduck, L. (2019). E-conveyancing: A consideration of its risks and rewards. *Property Management.* https://www.emerald.com/insight/content/doi/10.1108/PM-04-2019-0021/full/html

Cybersecurity Technologies: An Overview of Trends & Activities in Switzerland and Abroad. (2022). https://papers.ssrn.com/sol3/papers.cfm?abstract_id=4013762

da Silva, L. E., & Coury, D. V. (2020). Network traffic prediction for detecting DDoS attacks in IEC 61850 communication networks. *Computers & Electrical Engineering, 87*, 106793. doi:10.1016/j.compeleceng.2020.106793

DagbaG. (2020). *Exploring Citizens' Perceptions of Social Media Use in E-governance in Punjab.* https://papers.ssrn.com/sol3/papers.cfm?abstract_id=3763121 doi:10.2139/ssrn.3763121

Dahwan, A. A., & Raju, V. (2021). The Infleuence of Online Services and Telecommunication Infrastructure on the Implementation of E-government in Military Institutions in Yemen. *Annals of the Romanian Society for Cell Biology*, 1698–1710. https://www.annalsofrscb.ro/index.php/journal/article/view/2689

De, S. J., & Shukla, R. (2020). Privacy policies of e-governance initiatives: Evidence from India. *Journal of Public Affairs, 20*(4), e2160. https://onlinelibrary.wiley.com/doi/abs/10.1002/pa.2160

Department of Health. (2017). *Report of the second phase of the review of NHS pathology services: chaired by Lord Carter of Coles.* Department of Health. Available from: http://webarc hive.nationalarchives.gov.uk/20130124044941/http:/www.dh.gov.uk/prod_consum_dh/groups/dh_digita lassets/@dh/@en/documents/digitalasset/dh_091984. pdf

Dhonju, G. R., & Shakya, S. (2019). Analyzing Challenges for the Implementation of E-Government in Municipalities within Kathmandu Valley. *Journal of Science and Engineering, 7*, 70–78. https://www.nepjol.info/index.php/jsce/article/view/26795

Díaz-López, D., Dólera-Tormo, G., Gómez-Mármol, F., & Martínez-Pérez, G. (2016). Dynamic counter-measures for risk-based access control systems: An evolutive approach. *Future Generation Computer Systems, 55*, 321–335. doi:10.1016/j.future.2014.10.012

Dimolianis, M., Pavlidis, A., & Maglaris, V. (2020, February). A multi-feature DDoS detection schema on P4 network hardware. In *2020 23rd Conference on Innovation in Clouds, Internet and Networks and Workshops (ICIN)* (pp. 1-6). IEEE. https://ieeexplore.ieee.org/abstract/document/9125016

Ding, D., Han, Q.-L., Xiang, Y., Ge, X., & Zhang, X.-M. (2018). A survey on security control and attack detection for industrial cyber-physical systems. *Neurocomputing, 275*, 1674–1683. doi:10.1016/j.neucom.2017.10.009

Ding, W., & Wang, Y. (2018). Data Hiding in Binary Image with High Payload. *Arabian Journal for Science and Engineering, 2018*(43), 7737–7745. doi:10.100713369-018-3130-5

Distel, B. (2018). Bringing Light into the Shadows: A Qualitative Interview Study on Citizens' Non-Adoption of e-Government. *Electronic. Journal of E-Government, 16*(2), 98–105. https://academic-publishing.org/index.php/ejeg/article/view/654

Dong, B. (2017). Software Defined Networking Based On-Demand Routing Protocol in Vehicle Ad-Hoc Networks. *ZTE Commun., 15*(2), 11-18. https://ieeexplore.ieee.org/abstract/document/7950235

Dorr, B., Bhatia, A., Dalton, A., Mather, B., Hebenstreit, B., Santhanam, S., . . . Strzalkowski, T. (2020, April). Detecting asks in social engineering attacks: Impact of linguistic and structural knowledge. In *Proceedings of the AAAI Conference on Artificial Intelligence* (Vol. 34, No. 05, pp. 7675-7682). https://ojs.aaai.org/index.php/AAAI/article/view/6269

Dorr, B., Bhatia, A., Dalton, A., Mather, B., Hebenstreit, B., Santhanam, S., . . . Strzalkowski, T. (2020, April). Detecting asks in social engineering attacks: Impact of linguistic and structural knowledge. In *Proceedings of the AAAI Conference on Artificial Intelligence* (Vol. 34, No. 5, pp. 7675-7682). https://ojs.aaai.org/index.php/AAAI/article/view/6269

Dreamstime. (n.d.). *Online Services Illustrations & Vectors*. Retrieved from https://www.dreamstime.com/illustration/online-services.html

Dubey, A., Saquib, Z., & Dwivedi, S. (2015). *Electronic authentication for e-Government services-a survey*. https://digital-library.theiet.org/content/conferences/10.1049/cp.2015.0299

Dunhill, J. (2020). *Critical patient dies after cyber attack disables hospital computers*. https://www.iflscience.com/technology/critical-patient-dies-after-cyber-attack-disables-hospital-computers

Dunne, D. (2019). *Mosquito-borne diseases could reach extra 'one billion people' as climate warms*. Carbon Brief. Available from: https://www.carbonbrief.org/mosquitobornediseases-could-reach-extra-one-billion-people-asclimate-warms

Durst, M. (2019). Internet of things-enabled smart governance and the sustainable development of innovative data-driven urban ecosystems. *Geopolitics, History, and International Relations, 11*(2), 20-26. https://www.ceeol.com/search/article-detail?id=804059

ECOWAS. (n.d.). *Economic Community of West African States (ECOWAS)*. Retrieved October 27, 2018, from https://www.ecowas.int/member-states/

Edelson, E. (2003). The 419 scam: Information warfare on the spam front and a proposal for local filtering. *Computers & Security, 22*(5), 392–401. doi:10.1016/S0167-4048(03)00505-4

Elbahnasawy, N. G. (2021). Can e-government limit the scope of the informal economy? *World Development, 139*, 105341. doi:10.1016/j.worlddev.2020.105341

Elezaj, O., Tole, D., & Baci, N. (2018). Big Data in e-Government Environments: Albania as a Case Study. *Academic Journal of Interdisciplinary Studies, 7*(2), 117. https://www.mcser.org/journal/index.php/ajis/article/view/10285

El-Hassany, A., Miserez, J., Bielik, P., Vanbever, L., & Vechev, M. (2016). SDNRacer: Concurrency Analysis for Software-defined Networks. In *37th ACM SIGPLAN Conference on Programming Language Design and Implementation (PLDI 16)*. ACM. https://dl.acm.org/doi/abs/10.1145/2908080.2908124

Elijah, O., Rahman, T. A., Orikumhi, I., Leow, C. Y., & Hindia, M. N. (2018). An overview of Internet of Things (IoT) and data analytics in agriculture: Benefits and challenges. *IEEE Internet of Things Journal, 5*(5), 3758-3773. https://ieeexplore.ieee.org/abstract/document/8372905

Engineering, C. (n.d.). *The Beginner's Guide to Cybersecurity*. Retrieved from https://bootcamp.cvn.columbia.edu/blog/the-beginners-guide-to-cybersecurity/

Fang, X., Xu, M., Xu, S., & Zhao, P. (2019). A deep learning framework for predicting cyber attacks rates. *EURASIP Journal on Information Security, 2019*(1), 1-11. https://link.springer.com/article/10.1186/s13635-019-0090-6

Feng, B., & Weng, J. (2017). *Stegnalysis of content adaptive binary image data hiding.* Elsevier ScienceDirect., doi:10.1016/j.jvcir.2017.01.008

Fernandez Maimo, L., Huertas Celdran, A., Perales Gomez, A.L., Garcıa Clemente, F.J., Weimer, J., & Lee, I. (2019). Intelligent and dynamic ransomware spread detection and mitigation in integrated clinical environments. *Sensors, 19*(5). doi:10.3390/s19051114

Ferrag, M. A., Shu, L., Yang, X., Derhab, A., & Maglaras, L. (2020). Security and privacy for green IoT-based agriculture: Review, blockchain solutions, and challenges. *IEEE Access: Practical Innovations, Open Solutions, 8*, 32031–32053. https://ieeexplore.ieee.org/abstract/document/8993722

Ferreira, A., & Cruz-Correia, R. (2021). COVID-19 and cybersecurity: finally, an opportunity to disrupt? *JMIRx Med, 2*(2), e21069. https://xmed.jmir.org/2021/2/e21069/

Froehlich, A., Ringas, N., & Wilson, J. (2020). E-Governance in Africa and the World. In *Space Supporting Africa* (pp. 53–124). Springer. doi:10.1007/978-3-030-52260-5_2

Fu, Y. (2020, April). Evaluation Method of Big Data Reliability in Electronic Government. In *2020 International Conference on E-Commerce and Internet Technology (ECIT)* (pp. 142-144). IEEE. https://ieeexplore.ieee.org/abstract/document/9134119

Gajendra, S., Xi, B., & Wang, Q. (2012). E-government: Public participation and ethical issues. *Journal of e-Governance, 35*(4), 195-204. https://content.iospress.com/articles/journal-of-e-governance/gov00320

Garg, B. (2016). *Enhanced accuracy of fuzzy time series model using ordered weighted aggregation. Elsevier Applied Soft Computing, 48.*

Garg, B., Aggarwal, S., & Sokhal, J. (2018). Crop yield forecasting using fuzzy logic and regression model. *Computers & Electrical Engineering, 67*, 383–403. doi:10.1016/j.compeleceng.2017.11.015

Gaur, L., Bhatia, U., Jhanjhi, N. Z., Muhammad, G., & Masud, M. (2021). Medical image-based detection of COVID-19 using Deep Convolution Neural Networks. *Multimedia Systems*, 1–10. doi:10.100700530-021-00794-6 PMID:33935377

General Medical Council. (2018). *Regulatory approaches to telemedicine' general medical council.* Available from: www.gmc-uk.org/ about/what-we-do-and-why/dataand-research /research-and-insight-archive/regulatoryapproachesto-telemedicine

Gershgorn, D. (2018). *If AI is going to be the world's doctor, it needs better textbooks.* Quartz. Available from: https://qz.com/1367177/if-ai-is-going-to-betheworlds-doctor-it-needs-bett

Gershon, D., Prince, O., & Opoku, A. M. (2018). Promoting Inclusiveness and Participation in Governance: The Directions of Electronic Government in Ghana. *The International Journal of Social Sciences (Islamabad)*, *7*(3), 397–406. https://www.indianjournals.com/ijor.aspx?target=ijor:ijsw&volume=7&issue=3&article=007

GhiorghitaE.GherasimZ.AndronieM. (2010). E-Government Implications on Project Management in the Metallurgical Fields. *Available at* SSRN 1741882. doi:10.2139/ssrn.1741882

Giles, M. (2019). Five emerging cyber-threats to worry about in 2019. *MIT Technology Review.* Retrived from https://www.technologyreview.com/2019/01/04/66232/five-emerging-cyber-threats-2019/

Gill, S. H., Razzaq, M. A., Ahmad, M., Almansour, F. M., Haq, I. U., Jhanjhi, N. Z., ... Masud, M. (2022). Security and Privacy Aspects of Cloud Computing: A Smart Campus Case Study. *Intelligent Automation & Soft Computing*, *31*(1), 117–128. doi:10.32604/iasc.2022.016597

Giraldo, J., Cardenas, A. A., & Kantarcioglu, M. (2017, May). Security vs. privacy: How integrity attacks can be masked by the noise of differential privacy. In *2017 American Control Conference (ACC)* (pp. 1679-1684). IEEE. https://ieeexplore.ieee.org/abstract/document/7963194

Glyptis, L., Christofi, M., Vrontis, D., Del Giudice, M., Dimitriou, S., & Michael, P. (2020). E-Government implementation challenges in small countries: The project manager's perspective. *Technological Forecasting and Social Change*, *152*, 119880. doi:10.1016/j.techfore.2019.119880

Gorla, N., & Somers, T. M. (2014). The impact of IT outsourcing on information systems success. *Information & Management*, *51*(3), 320–335. https://www.sciencedirect.com/science/article/abs/pii/S0378720614000020

Gouveia, L. B. (2020). e-Government and Smart Cities: Contexts and Challenges Taking from Digital Usage and Exploration. *UNU-EGOV UM DSI PDSI talk*. https://bdigital.ufp.pt/handle/10284/8554

Gouveia, L. B. (2020). e-Government and Smart Cities: Contexts and Challenges Taking from Digital Usage and Exploration. *UNU-EGOV|UM DSI PDSI talk*. https://bdigital.ufp.pt/handle/10284/8554

Greenspun, H., Abrams, K., & Kame, A. (2016). *Preparing the doctor of the future Medical school and residency program evolution*. A report by the Deloitte Center for Health Solutions. Available from: https://www.modernhealthcare.com/article/20160728/SPONSORED/307289996/preparing-the-doctor-of-the-future-medical-school-andresidency-program-evolutio

Grinin, L., Grinin, A., & Korotayev, A. (2022). COVID-19 pandemic as a trigger for the acceleration of the cybernetic revolution, transition from e-government to e-state, and change in social relations. *Technological Forecasting and Social Change*, *175*, 121348. https://www.sciencedirect.com/science/article/pii/S0040162521007794

Gupta, R., & Agarwal, S. P. (2017). A Comparative Study of Cyber Threats in Emerging Economies. *Globus: An International Journal of Management & IT, 8*(2), 24-28. https://globusjournal.com/wp-content/uploads/2018/07/826Ruchika.pdf

Gupta, R., Muttoo, S. K., & Pal, S. K. (2017, March). Proposed framework for information systems security for e-governance in developing nations. In *Proceedings of the 10th International Conference on Theory and Practice of Electronic Governance* (pp. 546-547). https://dl.acm.org/doi/abs/10.1145/3047273.3047285

Gupta, B. B., & Quamara, M. (2020). An overview of Internet of Things (IoT): Architectural aspects, challenges, and protocols. *Concurrency and Computation, 32*(21), e4946. https://onlinelibrary.wiley.com/doi/abs/10.1002/cpe.4946

Hackmageddon. (2021). https://www.hackmageddon.com/2021/04/13/q1-2021-cyber-attack-statistics/

Halder, D., & Jaishankar, K. (2021). Cyber governance and data protection in India: A critical legal analysis. In *Routledge Companion to Global Cyber-Security Strategy* (pp. 337–348). Routledge. doi:10.4324/9780429399718-28

Hamid, B., Jhanjhi, N. Z., & Humayun, M. (2020). Digital Governance for Developing Countries Opportunities, Issues, and Challenges in Pakistan. In *Employing Recent Technologies for Improved Digital Governance* (pp. 36–58). IGI Global. doi:10.4018/978-1-7998-1851-9.ch003

Haran, M. H. (2016). Framework Based Approach for the Mitigation of Insider Threats in E-governance IT Infrastructure. *International Journal of Scientific Research, 3*(4), 5–10. http://citeseerx.ist.psu.edu/viewdoc/download?doi=10.1.1.566.4423&rep=rep1&type=pdf

Harris, S., & Meyers, M. (2002). *CISSP*. McGraw-Hill/Osborne.

He, Z., Zhang, D., Zhu, S., Cao, J., & Liu, X. (2016, September). Sdn enabled high performance multicast in vehicular networks. In *2016 IEEE 84th Vehicular Technology Conference (VTC-Fall)* (pp. 1-5). IEEE. 10.1109/VTCFall.2016.7881215

Henriksen, H. Z. (2018). One step forward and two steps back: e-Government policies in practice. In *Policy Analytics, Modelling, and Informatics* (pp. 79–97). Springer. https://link.springer.com/chapter/10.1007/978-3-319-61762-6_4

Herawati, A. R., Warsono, H., Afrizal, T., & Saputra, J. (n.d.). *The Challenges of Industrial Revolution 4.0: An Evidence from Public Administration Ecology in Indonesia.* http://www.ieomsociety.org/singapore2021/papers/846.pdf

He, Y., Aliyu, A., Evans, M., & Luo, C. (2021). Health Care Cybersecurity Challenges and Solutions Under the Climate of COVID-19: Scoping Review. *Journal of Medical Internet Research, 23*(4), e21747. doi:10.2196/21747 PMID:33764885

He, Z., Zhang, D., & Liang, J. (2016). Cost-efficient sensory data transmission in heterogeneous software-defined vehicular networks. *IEEE Sensors Journal, 16*(20), 7342–7354. doi:10.1109/JSEN.2016.2562699

HIPAA Journal. (2021). *Healthcare Data Breach Report.* https://www.hipaajournal.com/may-2021-healthcare-data-breach-report/

Hiscox. (2019). *The hiscox cyber readiness report 2019.* https://www.sciencedirect.com/science/article/pii/S0167404821000729

Hofbauer, D., Ivkic, I., & Tauber, M. (2019). On the Cost of Security Compliance in Information Systems. *10th International Multi-Conference on Complexity, Informatics and Cybernetics 2019 (IMCIC).* https://www.igi-global.com/chapter/promoting-cybersecurity-compliance/225917

Hoffman, I., & Cseh, K. B. (2021). E-administration, cybersecurity and municipalities–the challenges of cybersecurity issues for the municipalities in Hungary. *Cybersecurity and Law, 4*(2), 199-211. https://www.cybersecurityandlaw.pl/E-administration-cybersecurity-and-municipalities-the-challenges-of-cybersecurity,133999,0,1.html

Holt, T. J., Stonhouse, M., Freilich, J., & Chermak, S. M. (2021). Examining ideologically motivated cyberattacks performed by far-left groups. *Terrorism and Political Violence, 33*(3), 527–548. doi:10.1080/09546553.2018.1551213

Honey Mol, M., & Reji, P. I. (2016). A secure binary data hiding and comparison technique. *International Journal of Scientific & Engineering Research, 7*(7).

Hoque, T., Wang, X., Basak, A., Karam, R., & Bhunia, S. (2018, April). Hardware trojan attacks in embedded memory. In *2018 IEEE 36th VLSI Test Symposium (VTS)* (pp. 1-6). IEEE. https://ieeexplore.ieee.org/abstract/document/8368630

Huang, K., & Madnick, S. (2021, January). Does High Cybersecurity Capability Lead to Openness in Digital Trade? The Mediation Effect of E-Government Maturity. In *Proceedings of the 54th Hawaii International Conference on System Sciences* (p. 4352). https://papers.ssrn.com/sol3/papers.cfm?abstract_id=3542552

Huang, K., Siegel, M., & Madnick, S. (2018). Systematically understanding the cyber attack business: A survey. *ACM Computing Surveys, 51*(4), 1–36. doi:10.1145/3199674

Huang, X., Yu, R., Kang, J., He, Y., & Zhang, Y. (2017). Exploring mobile edge computing for 5G-enabled software defined vehicular networks. *IEEE Wireless Communications, 24*(6), 55–63. doi:10.1109/MWC.2017.1600387

Huertas Celdran, A., Garcıa Clemente, F.J., Weimer, J., & Lee, I. (2018). Ice++: Im-proving security, QoS, and high availability of medical cyber-physical systems through mobile edge computing. *IEEE 20th international conference one-health networking, applications and services (Healthcom),* 1–8. 10.1109/HealthCom.2018.8531185

Humayun, M., Jhanjhi, N. Z., Alsayat, A., & Ponnusamy, V. (2021). Internet of things and ransomware: Evolution, mitigation and prevention. *Egyptian Informatics Journal, 22*(1), 105-117. https://www.sciencedirect.com/science/article/pii/S1110866520301304

Humayun, M., Jhanjhi, N. Z., Hamid, B., & Ahmed, G. (2020). Emerging smart logistics and transportation using IoT and blockchain. *IEEE Internet of Things Magazine, 3*(2), 58-62. https://ieeexplore.ieee.org/abstract/document/9125435

Humayun, M. (2021). Industry 4.0 and Cyber Security Issues and Challenges. *Turkish Journal of Computer and Mathematics Education, 12*(10), 2957–2971. https://turcomat.org/index.php/turkbilmat/article/view/4946

Humayun, M., Jhanjhi, N., Alruwaili, M., Amalathas, S. S., Balasubramanian, V., & Selvaraj, B. (2020). Privacy protection and energy optimization for 5G-aided industrial Internet of Things. *IEEE Access: Practical Innovations, Open Solutions, 8*, 183665–183677. doi:10.1109/ACCESS.2020.3028764

Humayun, M., Niazi, M., Jhanjhi, N. Z., Alshayeb, M., & Mahmood, S. (2020). Cyber security threats and vulnerabilities: A systematic mapping study. *Arabian Journal for Science and Engineering, 45*(4), 3171–3189. doi:10.100713369-019-04319-2

Hussain, S. J., Ahmed, U., Liaquat, H., Mir, S., Jhanjhi, N. Z., & Humayun, M. (2019, April). IMIAD: intelligent malware identification for android platform. In *2019 International Conference on Computer and Information Sciences (ICCIS)* (pp. 1-6). IEEE. https://ieeexplore.ieee.org/abstract/document/8716471

Hussain, S. J., Irfan, M., Jhanjhi, N. Z., Hussain, K., & Humayun, M. (2021). Performance enhancement in wireless body area networks with secure communication. *Wireless Personal Communications, 116*(1), 1–22. doi:10.100711277-020-07702-7 PMID:33558792

III. (n.d.). https://www.iii.org/fact-statistic/facts-statistics-identity-theft-and-cybercrime

Ilves, T. H. (2016). The consequences of cyber attacks. *Journal of International Affairs, 70*(1), 175–181.

Isacenkova, J., Thonnard, O., Costin, A., Francillon, A., & Balzarotti, D. (2014). Inside the scam jungle: A closer look at 419 scam email operations. *EURASIP Journal on Information Security, 2014*(1), 4. doi:10.1186/1687-417X-2014-4

Islam, M. J., Mahin, M., Roy, S., Debnath, B. C., & Khatun, A. (2019, February). Distblacknet: A distributed secure black sdn-iot architecture with nfv implementation for smart cities. In *2019 International Conference on Electrical, Computer and Communication Engineering (ECCE)* (pp. 1-6). IEEE. https://ieeexplore.ieee.org/abstract/document/8679167

Jacquenet, C., & Boucadair, M. (2016). A software-defined approach to IoT networking. *ZTE Commun., 1*, 1–12.

Jashari, R., & Avdyli, M. (2020). *Security of information systems-legal and ethical rules, chalenges of appying in Kosova.* https://knowledgecenter.ubt-uni.net/conference/2020/all_events/61/

Javaid, M., Haleem, A., Vaishya, R., Bahl, S., Suman, R., & Vaish, A. (2020). Industry 4.0 technologies and their applications in fighting COVID-19 pandemic. *Diabetes & Metabolic Syndrome, 14*(4), 419–422. doi:10.1016/j.dsx.2020.04.032 PMID:32344370

Javed, M. A., Khan, M. Z., Zafar, U., Siddiqui, M. F., Badar, R., Lee, B. M., & Ahmad, F. (2020). ODPV: An efficient protocol to mitigate data integrity attacks in intelligent transport systems. *IEEE Access: Practical Innovations, Open Solutions, 8*, 114733–114740. doi:10.1109/ACCESS.2020.3004444

Jazri, H., & Jat, D. S. (2016, November). A quick cybersecurity wellness evaluation framework for critical organizations. In *2016 International Conference on ICT in Business Industry & Government (ICTBIG)* (pp. 1-5). IEEE. https://ieeexplore.ieee.org/abstract/document/7892725

Joshi, P. R., & Islam, S. (2018). E-government maturity model for sustainable e-government services from the perspective of developing countries. *Sustainability, 10*(6), 1882. https://www.mdpi.com/2071-1050/10/6/1882

Joshi, S. (2015). E-Governance in Uttar Pradesh: Challenges and Prospects. *The Indian Journal of Public Administration, 61*(2), 229–240. doi:10.1177/0019556120150203

Kabanov, Y., Chugunov, A. V., & Nizomutdinov, B. (2019, September). E-Government Research Domain: Comparing the International and Russian Research Agenda. In *International Conference on Electronic Government* (pp. 18–30). Springer. doi:10.1007/978-3-030-27325-5_2

Kagame, P., & Ghebreyesus, T. A. (2019). History shows health is the foundation of African prosperity. *Financial Times.* Available from: https://www.ft.com/content/e61cc58c-cfc7-11e9-b018-ca4456540ea6

Kalakuntla, R., Vanamala, A. B., & Kolipyaka, R. R. (2019). Cyber security. *HOLISTICA– Journal of Business and Public Administration, 10*(2), 115-128. https://sciendo.com/pdf/10.2478/hjbpa-2019-0020

Kamiya, S., Kang, J. K., Kim, J., Milidonis, A., & Stulz, R. M. (2021). Risk management, firm reputation, and the impact of successful cyberattacks on target firms. *Journal of Financial Economics, 139*(3), 719–749. doi:10.1016/j.jfineco.2019.05.019

Kapersky. (n.d.). https://usa.kaspersky.com/resource-center/definitions/what-is-social-engineering

Karakus, M., & Durresi, A. (2017a). A survey: Control plane scalability issues and approaches in software-defined networking (SDN). *Computer Networks, 112*, 279–293. doi:10.1016/j.comnet.2016.11.017

Karakus, M., & Durresi, A. (2017b). Quality of service (QoS) in software defined networking (SDN): A survey. *Journal of Network and Computer Applications, 80*, 200–218. doi:10.1016/j.jnca.2016.12.019

Karki, S., Nguyen, B., & Zhang, X. (2018). QoS Support for Scientific Workflows Using Software-Defined Storage Resource Enclaves. In *2018 IEEE International Parallel and Distributed Processing Symposium (IPDPS 18).* IEEE. https://ieeexplore.ieee.org/abstract/document/8425164

Karpenko, O., Kuczabski, A., & Havryliak, V. (2021). Mechanisms for providing cybersecurity during the COVID-19 pandemic: Perspectives for Ukraine. *Security and Defence Quarterly.* http://yadda.icm.edu.pl/yadda/element/bwmeta1.element.doi-10_35467_sdq_133158

Kaspersky. (n.d.). *What is Social Engineering?* Retrieved from https://usa.kaspersky.com/resource-center/definitions/what-is-social-engineering

Kassen, M. (2022). Blockchain and e-government innovation: Automation of public information processes. *Information Systems, 103*, 101862. doi:10.1016/j.is.2021.101862

Kaur, K., Garg, S., Aujla, G. S., Kumar, N., Rodrigues, J. J., & Guizani, M. (2018). Edge computing in the industrial internet of things environment: Software-defined-networks-based edge-cloud interplay. *IEEE Communications Magazine, 56*(2), 44–51. doi:10.1109/MCOM.2018.1700622

Khan, N. A., Brohi, S. N., & Zaman, N. (2020). *Ten deadly cyber security threats amid COVID-19 pandemic*. https://www.techrxiv.org/articles/preprint/Ten_Deadly_Cyber_Security_Threats_Amid_COVID-19_Pandemic/12278792/1

Khan, S. N., Shael, M., & Majdalawieh, M. (2019, July). Blockchain technology as a support infrastructure in E-Government evolution at Dubai economic department. In *Proceedings of the 2019 International Electronics Communication Conference* (pp. 124-130). https://dl.acm.org/doi/abs/10.1145/3343147.3343164

Khan, A., Jhanjhi, N. Z., Humayun, M., & Ahmad, M. (2020). The Role of IoT in Digital Governance. In *Employing Recent Technologies for Improved Digital Governance* (pp. 128–150). IGI Global. doi:10.4018/978-1-7998-1851-9.ch007

Khandpur, R. P., Ji, T., Jan, S., Wang, G., Lu, C. T., & Ramakrishnan, N. (2017, November). Crowdsourcing cybersecurity: Cyber attack detection using social media. In *Proceedings of the 2017 ACM on Conference on Information and Knowledge Management* (pp. 1049-1057). https://dl.acm.org/doi/abs/10.1145/3132847.3132866

Khan, M. A., & Salah, K. (2018). IoT security: Review, blockchain solutions, and open challenges. *Future Generation Computer Systems, 82*, 395–411. https://www.sciencedirect.com/science/article/abs/pii/S0167739X17315765

Khan, N. A., Brohi, S. N., & Jhanjhi, N. Z. (2020). UAV's applications, architecture, security issues and attack scenarios: a survey. In *Intelligent Computing and Innovation on Data Science* (pp. 753–760). Springer. doi:10.1007/978-981-15-3284-9_81

Khatoun, R., & Zeadally, S. (2017). Cybersecurity and privacy solutions in smart cities. *IEEE Communications Magazine, 55*(3), 51–59. doi:10.1109/MCOM.2017.1600297CM

Kiilu, P., Shingala, H., & Bondavalli, A. (n.d.). *Framework Based Approach for the Mitigation of Insider Threats in E-governance IT Infrastructure*. file:///C:/Users/imdad/Downloads/Framework_Based_Approach_for_the_Mitigat%20(1).pdf

Kim, H. Y., & de Queiroz, R. L. (2004). Alteration-locating authentication watermarking for binary images. *Proc. Int. Workshop Digital Watermarking*, 125–136.

Koo, E. (2019). *Digital transformation of Government: from E-Government to intelligent E-Government* (Doctoral dissertation). Massachusetts Institute of Technology. https://dspace.mit.edu/handle/1721.1/121792

Korir, G., Thiga, M., & Rono, L. (2019). *Implementing the Tool for Assessing Organisation Information Security Preparedness in E-Governance Implementation.* https://www.easpublisher. com/media/features_articles/EASJECS_210_284-299.pdf

Kotenko, I., Saenko, I., & Lauta, O. (2019). Modeling the impact of cyber attacks. In *Cyber Resilience of Systems and Networks* (pp. 135–169). Springer. doi:10.1007/978-3-319-77492-3_7

Krundyshev, V., & Kalinin, M. (2019, September). Hybrid neural network framework for detection of cyber attacks at smart infrastructures. In *Proceedings of the 12th International Conference on Security of Information and Networks* (pp. 1-7). https://dl.acm.org/doi/ abs/10.1145/3357613.3357623

Kumar, P., Kunwar, R. S., & Sachan, A. (2016). A survey report on: Security & challenges in internet of things. In *Proc National Conference on ICT & IoT* (pp. 35-39). https://shop.iotone. ir/public/upload/article/5b8e38ead1f31.pdf

Kumar, B. S., Sridhar, V., & Sudhindra, K. R. (2022). Generic Security Risk Profile of e-Governance Applications—a Case Study. In *Emerging Research in Computing, Information, Communication and Applications* (pp. 731–741). Springer. doi:10.1007/978-981-16-1342-5_57

Kumar, M. S., Raut, R. D., Narwane, V. S., & Narkhede, B. E. (2020). Applications of industry 4.0 to overcome the COVID-19 operational challenges. *Diabetes & Metabolic Syndrome, 14*(5), 1283–1289. doi:10.1016/j.dsx.2020.07.010 PMID:32755822

Kumar, M. S., Vimal, S., Jhanjhi, N. Z., Dhanabalan, S. S., & Alhumyani, H. A. (2021). Blockchain based peer to peer communication in autonomous drone operation. *Energy Reports, 7,* 7925–7939. doi:10.1016/j.egyr.2021.08.073

Lallie, H. S., Shepherd, L. A., Nurse, J. R., Erola, A., Epiphaniou, G., Maple, C., & Bellekens, X. (2021). Cyber security in the age of covid-19: A timeline and analysis of cyber-crime and cyber-attacks during the pandemic. *Computers & Security, 105,* 102248. doi:10.1016/j.cose.2021.102248

Le Blond, S., Gilbert, C., Upadhyay, U., Gomez-Rodriguez, M., & Choffnes, D. R. (2017). A Broad View of the Ecosystem of Socially Engineered Exploit Documents. *NDSS.* https://www. ndss-symposium.org/wp-content/uploads/2017/09/ndss2017_03B-4_LeBlond_paper.pdf

Le, N. T., & Hoang, D. B. (2016, December). Can maturity models support cyber security? In *2016 IEEE 35th international performance computing and communications conference (IPCCC)* (pp. 1-7). IEEE. https://ieeexplore.ieee.org/abstract/document/7820663

Lee, K. J. P., Raman, W., & Hedrich, R. (2018). *Holding healthcare to ransom: industry perspectives on cyber risks.* Marsh & McLennan Companies. http://www.mmc.com/insights/publications/ 2018/jul/holding-healthcare-to-ransom-industryperspectives-on-cyb

Lee, S., Kim, J., Shin, S., Porras, P., & Yegneswaran, V. (2017, June). Athena: A framework for scalable anomaly detection in software-defined networks. In *2017 47th Annual IEEE/IFIP International Conference on Dependable Systems and Networks (DSN)* (pp. 249-260). IEEE. https://ieeexplore.ieee.org/abstract/document/8023127

Lee-Geiller, S., & Lee, T. D. (2019). Using government websites to enhance democratic E-governance: A conceptual model for evaluation. *Government Information Quarterly, 36*(2), 208–225. doi:10.1016/j.giq.2019.01.003

Lee, S., Abdullah, A., Jhanjhi, N., & Kok, S. (2021). Classification of botnet attacks in IoT smart factory using honeypot combined with machine learning. *PeerJ. Computer Science, 7,* e350. doi:10.7717/peerj-cs.350 PMID:33817000

Lee, S., Kim, J., Woo, S., Yoon, C., Scott-Hayward, S., Yegneswaran, V., Porras, P., & Shin, S. (2020). A comprehensive security assessment framework for software-defined networks. *Computers & Security, 91,* 101720. doi:10.1016/j.cose.2020.101720

Lee, Y., Kim, H., & Park, Y. (2009). A new data hiding scheme for binary image authentication with small image distortion. *Information Sciences, 179*(22), 3866–3884. doi:10.1016/j.ins.2009.07.014

Li, Y., Liu, H., & Yang, W. (2017) Predicting inter-data-center network traffic using elephant flow and sublink information. *IEEE Trans Netw Serv Manag, 13*(4), 782–792. https://ieeexplore.ieee.org/abstract/document/8079318/

Liang, Y., Qi, G., Wei, K., & Chen, J. (2017). Exploring the determinant and influence mechanism of e-Government cloud adoption in government agencies in China. *Government Information Quarterly, 34*(3), 481–495. doi:10.1016/j.giq.2017.06.002

Lim, M., Abdullah, A., & Jhanjhi, N. Z. (2019). Performance optimization of criminal network hidden link prediction model with deep reinforcement learning. *Journal of King Saud University-Computer and Information Sciences.* https://onlinelibrary.wiley.com/doi/abs/10.1002/ett.4171

Lim, M., Abdullah, A., & Jhanjhi, N. Z. (2019). Performance optimization of criminal network hidden link prediction model with deep reinforcement learning. *Journal of King Saud University-Computer and Information Sciences.* https://www.sciencedirect.com/science/article/pii/S1319157819308584

Lim, M., Abdullah, A., Jhanjhi, N. Z., & Supramaniam, M. (2019). Hidden link prediction in criminal networks using the deep reinforcement learning technique. *Computers, 8*(1), 8. https://www.mdpi.com/2073-431X/8/1/8

Lim, M., Abdullah, A., Jhanjhi, N. Z., Khan, M. K., & Supramaniam, M. (2019). Link prediction in time-evolving criminal network with deep reinforcement learning technique. *IEEE Access: Practical Innovations, Open Solutions, 7,* 184797–184807. doi:10.1109/ACCESS.2019.2958873

Lin, J., Yu, W., Zhang, N., Yang, X., & Ge, L. (2017, January). On data integrity attacks against route guidance in transportation-based cyber-physical systems. In *2017 14th IEEE Annual Consumer Communications & Networking Conference (CCNC)* (pp. 313-318). IEEE. https://ieeexplore.ieee.org/abstract/document/7983125

Li, N., Jiang, H., Feng, D., & Shi, Z. (2017). Customizable SLO and its near-precise enforcement for storage bandwidth. *ACM Transactions on Storage, 13*(1), 1–25. doi:10.1145/2998454

Linkov, I., Trump, B. D., Poinsatte-Jones, K., & Florin, M. V. (2018). Governance strategies for a sustainable digital world. *Sustainability*, *10*(2), 440. doi:10.3390u10020440

Liu, Z., Wei, W., Wang, L., Ten, C. W., & Rho, Y. (2020). An Actuarial Framework for Power System Reliability Considering Cybersecurity Threats. *IEEE Transactions on Power Systems*. https://dl.acm.org/doi/abs/10.1145/3386723.3387847

Liu, D., & Carter, L. (2018, May). Impact of citizens' privacy concerns on e-government adoption. In *Proceedings of the 19th Annual International Conference on Digital Government Research* (pp. 1–6). Governance in the Data Age. https://dl.acm.org/doi/abs/10.1145/3209281.3209340

Liu, J., Wang, C., Li, C., Li, N., Deng, J., & Pan, J. Z. (2021). DTN: Deep triple network for topic specific fake news detection. *Journal of Web Semantics*, *100646*. doi:10.1016/j. websem.2021.100646

Lu, H., Shi, X., Shi, Y. Q., Kot, A. C., & Chen, L. (2002). Watermark embedding in DC components of DCT for binary images. *Proc., IEEE Workshop on Multimedia Signal Processing*, 300–303.

Luh, R., Marschalek, S., Kaiser, M., Janicke, H., & Schrittwieser, S. (2017). Semantics-aware detection of targeted attacks: A survey. *Journal of Computer Virology and Hacking Techniques*, *13*(1), 47–85. doi:10.100711416-016-0273-3

Luo, P., Zou, D., Du, Y., Jin, H., Liu, C., & Shen, J. (2020). Static detection of real-world buffer overflow induced by loop. *Computers & Security*, *89*, 101,616. doi:10.1016/j.cose.2019.101616

Lu, R., Zhao, X., Li, J., Niu, P., Yang, B., Wu, H., Wang, W., Song, H., Huang, B., Zhu, N., Bi, Y., Ma, X., Zhan, F., Wang, L., Hu, T., Zhou, H., Hu, Z., Zhou, W., Zhao, L., ... Tan, W. (2020). Genomic characterisation and epidemiology of 2019 novel coronavirus: Implications for virus origins and receptor binding. *Lancet*, *395*(10224), 565–574. doi:10.1016/S0140-6736(20)30251-8 PMID:32007145

Lv, Z., & Kumar, N. (2020). Software defined solutions for sensors in 6G/IoE. *Computer Communications*, *153*, 42–47. doi:10.1016/j.comcom.2020.01.060

Lv, Z., Li, X., Wang, W., Zhang, B., Hu, J., & Feng, S. (2018). Government affairs service platform for smart city. *Future Generation Computer Systems*, *81*, 443–451. https://www.sciencedirect.com/science/article/abs/pii/S0167739X17311391

Mace, J., Roelke, R., & Fonseca, R. (2018). Pivot tracing: Dynamic causal monitoring for distributed systems. *ACM Transactions on Computer Systems*, *35*(4), 1–28. doi:10.1145/3208104

Máchová, R. (2017). Measuring the effects of open data on the level of corruption. In *Proceedings of the 21st International Conference Current Trends in Public Sector Research*. Masarykova univerzita. https://dk.upce.cz/handle/10195/66979

Maharaj, M. S., & Munyoka, W. (2019). Privacy, security, trust, risk and optimism bias in e-government use: The case of two Southern African Development Community countries. *South African Journal of Information Management*, *21*(1), 1–9. https://journals.co.za/doi/abs/10.4102/sajim.v21i1.983

Mahmood, Z. (Ed.). (2016). *Connectivity frameworks for smart devices: the internet of things from a distributed computing perspective.* Springer. https://link.springer.com/book/10.1007%2F978-3-319-33124-9

Makhshari, A., & Mesbah, A. (2021, May). IoT bugs and development challenges. In *2021 IEEE/ACM 43rd International Conference on Software Engineering (ICSE)* (pp. 460-472). IEEE. https://ieeexplore.ieee.org/abstract/document/9402092

Ma, L., & Zheng, Y. (2019). National e-government performance and citizen satisfaction: A multilevel analysis across European countries. *International Review of Administrative Sciences, 85*(3), 506–526. https://journals.sagepub.com/doi/abs/10.1177/0020852317703691

Malhotra, H., Bhargava, R., & Dave, M. (2017). Implementation of E-Governance projects: Development, Threats & Targets. *International Journal of Information Communication and Computing Technology, 5*(2), 292-298. https://www.indianjournals.com/ijor.aspx?target=ijor:jims8i&volume=5&issue=2&article=001

Malhotra, H., Bhargava, R., & Dave, M. (2017). Implementation of E-Governance projects: Development, Threats & Targets. *JIMS8I-International Journal of Information Communication and Computing Technology, 5*(2), 292-298. https://www.indianjournals.com/ijor.aspx?target=ijor:jims8i&volume=5&issue=2&article=001

Malhotra, H., Bhargava, R., & Dave, M. (2017a). Implementation of E-Governance projects: Development, Threats & Targets. *International Journal of Information Communication and Computing Technology, 5*(2), 292-298. https://www.indianjournals.com/ijor.aspx?target=ijor:jims8i&volume=5&issue=2&article=001

Malhotra, H., Bhargava, R., & Dave, M. (2017, November). Challenges related to information security and its implications for evolving e-government structures: A comparative study between India and African countries. In *2017 International Conference on Inventive Computing and Informatics (ICICI)* (pp. 30-35). IEEE.

Malhotra, H., Dave, M., & Lamba, T. (2019, November). Security Analysis of Cyber Attacks Using Machine Learning Algorithms in eGovernance Projects. In *International Conference on Futuristic Trends in Networks and Computing Technologies* (pp. 662-672). Springer.

Malodia, S., Dhir, A., Mishra, M., & Bhatti, Z. A. (2021). Future of e-Government: An integrated conceptual framework. *Technological Forecasting and Social Change, 173*, 121102. https://www.sciencedirect.com/science/article/pii/S0040162521005357

Manikandan, V. M., & Masilamani, V. (2018). Reversible data hiding scheme during encryption using machine learning. *Procedia Computer Science, 133*, 348–356. doi:10.1016/j.procs.2018.07.043

Manoharan, A. P., Ingrams, A., Kang, D., & Zhao, H. (2021). Globalization and worldwide best practices in E-Government. *International Journal of Public Administration, 44*(6), 465–476. doi:10.1080/01900692.2020.1729182

Mármol, F. G., Pérez, M. G., & Pérez, G. M. (2016, July). I don't trust ICT: Research challenges in cyber security. In *IFIP International Conference on Trust Management* (pp. 129-136). Springer. 10.1007/978-3-319-41354-99

Martins, I. (2018). The role of e-government in nigeria: Legal issues and barriers against complete implementation. In *The Stances of e-GovernmentPolicies* (pp. 23-30). Chapman and Hall/CRC. https://www.taylorfrancis.com/chapters/edit/10.1201/9780203731451-3/role-government-nigeria-legal-issues-barriers-complete-implementation-ishaya-martins

Maseko, F. (2018, September 17). *Nigeria: Cyber security advocacy group calls president to sign electronic transaction bill*. Retrieved October 27, 2018, from http://www.itnewsafrica.com/2018/09/nigeria-cyber-security-advocacy-group-calls-president-to-sign-electronic-transaction-bill/

Matteson. (2021). *Cybersecurity: There's no such thing as a false positive*. TechRepublic. https://www.techrepublic.com/article/cybersecurity-theres-no-such-thing-as-a-false-positive/

McDonnell, T. (2019, November 24). *The Powerlessness Of Nigeria's Tech Startups*. Retrieved October 12, 2020, from https://www.npr.org/sections/goatsandsoda/2019/11/24/781132932/the-powerlessness-of-nigerias-tech-startups

McKibbin, W., & Fernando, R. (2020). The economic impact of COVID-19. *Economics in the Time of COVID-19, 45*. https://www.incae.edu/sites/default/files/covid-19.pdf#page=52

MehrotraK. (2021). Data Privacy & Protection. *Available at* SSRN 3858581. https://papers.ssrn.com/sol3/papers.cfm?abstract_id=3858581

MehrotraK. (2021). *Data Privacy & Protection*. https://papers.ssrn.com/sol3/papers.cfm?abstract_id=3858581

Mei, Q., Wong, E. K., & Memon, N. (2001). Data hiding in binary text document. *Proceedings of the Society for Photo-Instrumentation Engineers, 4314*, 369–375. doi:10.1117/12.435420

Meiyanti, R., Utomo, B., Sensuse, D. I., & Wahyuni, R. (2018, August). E-government challenges in developing countries: a literature review. In *2018 6th International Conference on Cyber and IT Service Management (CITSM)* (pp. 1-6). IEEE.

Meiyanti, R., Utomo, B., Sensuse, D. I., & Wahyuni, R. (2018, August). E-government challenges in developing countries: a literature review. In *2018 6th International Conference on Cyber and IT Service Management (CITSM)* (pp. 1-6). IEEE. 10.1109/CITSM.2018.8674245

Mello, J. (2021). *DNS Flaws Expose Millions of IoT Devices to Hacker Threats*. Tech News World. Retrieved from https://www.technewsworld.com/story/87096.html

Meng, Y., & Kwok, L. F. (2013). Enhancing false alarm reduction using voted ensemble selection in intrusion detection. *International Journal of Computational Intelligence Systems, 6*(4), 626–638. doi:10.1080/18756891.2013.802114

Meng, Y., & Li, W. (2012, December). Intelligent alarm filter using knowledge-based alert verification in network intrusion detection. In *International Symposium on Methodologies for Intelligent Systems* (pp. 115–124). Springer. doi:10.1007/978-3-642-34624-8_14

Mensah, I. K. (2019). Impact of government capacity and E-government performance on the adoption of E-Government services. *International Journal of Public Administration*. https://www.tandfonline.com/doi/10.1080/01900692.2019.1628059

Mercer Marsh Benefits. (2019). *Health and benefits: health insurance costs – insights & implications. Results of the 2019 medical trends around the world survey.* Available from: https://www.mercermarshbenefits.com/en/intellectualcapital/2019-medical-trends-around-the-world1.html

Mitrokotsa, A., & Douligeris, C. (2007). E-Government and Denial of Service Attacks. In *Secure E-Government Web Services* (pp. 124–142). IGI Global. doi:10.4018/978-1-59904-138-4.ch008

Muda, J., Tumsa, S., Tuni, A., & Sharma, D. P. (2020). Cloud-Enabled E-Governance Framework for Citizen Centric Services. *Journal of Computer and Communications, 8*(7), 63–78. doi:10.4236/jcc.2020.87006

Mukherjee, B. K., Pappu, S. I., Islam, M. J., & Acharjee, U. K. (2020, February). An SDN based distributed IoT network with NFV implementation for smart cities. In *International Conference on Cyber Security and Computer Science* (pp. 539–552). Springer. doi:10.1007/978-3-030-52856-0_43

Muzafar, S., & Jhanjhi, N. Z. (2020). Success Stories of ICT Implementation in Saudi Arabia. In *Employing Recent Technologies for Improved Digital Governance* (pp. 151–163). IGI Global. doi:10.4018/978-1-7998-1851-9.ch008

Muzammal, S. M., Murugesan, R. K., & Jhanjhi, N. Z. (2020). A comprehensive review on secure routing in internet of things: Mitigation methods and trust-based approaches. *IEEE Internet of Things Journal*. https://ieeexplore.ieee.org/abstract/document/9223748

Mwangi, N. M. (2015). *e-government adoption by Kenya ministries* (Doctoral dissertation). University of Nairobi. http://erepository.uonbi.ac.ke/handle/11295/94091

Nagowah, S. D., Sta, H. B., & Gobin-Rahimbux, B. A. (2018, October). An overview of semantic interoperability ontologies and frameworks for IoT. In *2018 Sixth International Conference on Enterprise Systems (ES)* (pp. 82-89). IEEE.

Najmi, K. Y., AlZain, M. A., Masud, M., Jhanjhi, N. Z., Al-Amri, J., & Baz, M. (2021). A survey on security threats and countermeasures in IoT to achieve users confidentiality and reliability. *Materials Today: Proceedings*. https://www.sciencedirect.com/science/article/pii/S221478532102469X

Nautiyal, L., Malik, P., & Agarwal, A. (2018). Cybersecurity system: an essential pillar of smart cities. In *Smart Cities* (pp. 25–50). Springer. doi:10.1007/978-3-319-76669-0_2

Ndiaye, M., Oyewobi, S. S., Abu-Mahfouz, A. M., Hancke, G. P., Kurien, A. M., & Djouani, K. (2020). IoT in the wake of COVID-19: A survey on contributions, challenges and evolution. *IEEE Access: Practical Innovations, Open Solutions*, 8, 186821–186839. doi:10.1109/ACCESS.2020.3030090 PMID:34786294

Neměšanu, F., & Păžnzaru, F. (2017). Smart city management based on IoT. *Smart Cities and Regional Development (SCRD) Journal, 1*(1), 91-97. https://www.ceeol.com/search/article-detail?id=624232

Nespoli, P., Papamartzivanos, D., Mármol, F. G., & Kambourakis, G. (2017). Optimal countermeasures selection against cyber attacks: A comprehensive survey on reaction frameworks. *IEEE Communications Surveys and Tutorials*, 20(2), 1361–1396. doi:10.1109/COMST.2017.2781126

Networking, S.-D. (n.d.). *The New Norm for Networks*. Available online: https://www.opennetworking.org/images/stories/downloads/sdn-resources/white-papers/wp-sdn-newnorm.pdf

Nguyen, H., Acharya, B., Ivanov, R., Haeberlen, A., Phan, L. T. X., Sokolsky, O., Walker, J., Weimer, J., Hanson, W., & Lee, I. (2016). Cloud-based secure logger for medical devices. *Proceedings of the IEEE first international conference on connected health: applications, systems and engineering technologies (CHASE)*, 89–94. 10.1109/CHASE.2016.48

Nguyen. (2015). *High capacity data hiding for binary image based on block classification*. Springer. doi:10.100711042-015-2768-1

NHS England. (2014). *National pathology programme. Digital First: Clinical Transformation through Pathology Innovation*. Available from: www.england.nhs.uk/2014/02/nppdi gital-first/

NHS. (2019). *Preparing the healthcare workforce to deliver the digital future: An independent report on behalf of the secretary of state for health and social care*. NHS. Available from: https://www.forbes.com/sites/adigaskell/2018/11/09/prepar ing-the-healthcare-workforce-to-deliver-the-digitalfuture/#654cfeef6d34

Ni, H., Rahouti, M., Chakrabortty, A., Xiong, K., & Xin, Y. (2018, August). A distributed cloud-based wide-area controller with sdn-enabled delay optimization. In *2018 IEEE Power & Energy Society General Meeting (PESGM)* (pp. 1-5). IEEE. https://ieeexplore.ieee.org/abstract/document/8586040

Nižetić, S., Šolić, P., González-de, D. L. D. I., & Patrono, L. (2020). Internet of Things (IoT): Opportunities, issues and challenges towards a smart and sustainable future. *Journal of Cleaner Production, 274*, 122877. https://www.sciencedirect.com/science/article/pii/S095965262032922X

Norris, D., Joshi, A., & Finin, T. (2015, June). *Cybersecurity challenges to American state and local governments. In 15th European Conference on eGovernment*. Academic Conferences and Publishing Int. Ltd. https://ebiquity.umbc.edu/paper/abstract/id/774/Cybersecurity-Challenges-to-American-State-and-Local-Governments

Nosiri, U. D., & Ndoh, J. A. (2018). E-governance. *South East Journal of Political Science, 4*(1). https://journals.aphriapub.com/index.php/SEJPS/article/view/833

Nosiri, U. D., & Ndoh, J. A. (2018). E-Governance. *South East Journal of Political Science, 4*(1). https://journals.aphriapub.com/index.php/SEJPS/article/view/833

NSKT Global. (2020). What are the biggest cybersecurity threats in 2021? *NSKT*. Retrieved from https://nsktglobal.com/what-are-the-biggest-cybersecurity-threats-in-2021-

NSKT Global. (n.d.). https://nsktglobal.com/what-are-the-biggest-cybersecurity-threats-in-2021-

Nzimakwe, T. I. (2018). Government's Dynamic Approach to Addressing Challenges of Cybersecurity in South Africa. In *Handbook of Research on Information and Cyber Security in the Fourth Industrial Revolution* (pp. 364–381). IGI Global. doi:10.4018/978-1-5225-4763-1.ch013

O'Neil, J. (n.d.). *Rapid diagnostics: Stopping unnecessary use of antibiotics. Review on antimicrobial resistance.* Available from: http://amrreview.org/sites/default/files/Paper-RapidDiagnostics-Stopping-Unnecessa

Ogunniyi, O. J., & Akpu, J. O. (2019). The Challenge of Drug Trafficking to Democratic Governance and Human Security in West Africa. *Africa Development. Afrique et Developpement, 44*(4), 29–50. https://www.jstor.org/stable/26873443

Oke, O. (2009). *Evaluating the Security of E-government in West Africa.* http://cs.lewisu.edu/mathcs/msis/projects/msis595_SolaOke.pdf

Okereafor, K., & Adebola, O. (2020). Tackling the cybersecurity impacts of the coronavirus outbreak as a challenge to internet safety. *Int J IT Eng, 8*(2). https://papers.ssrn.com/sol3/papers.cfm?abstract_id=3568830

Orji, U. J. (2018). The African Union Convention on Cybersecurity: A Regional Response Towards Cyber Stability? *Masaryk University Journal of Law and Technology, 12*(2), 91-129.

Ouyang, J., Lin, S., Jiang, S., Hou, Z., Wang, Y., & Wang, Y. (2014, February). SDF: Software-defined flash for web-scale internet storage systems. In *Proceedings of the 19th international conference on Architectural support for programming languages and operating systems* (pp. 471-484). https://dl.acm.org/doi/abs/10.1145/2541940.2541959

Oxford Analytica. (2016). Estonia's e-governance model may be unique. *Emerald Expert Briefings*, (oxan-db). https://www.emerald.com/insight/content/doi/10.1108/OXAN-DB214505/full/html

Oxford Analytica. (2016). Estonia's e-governance model may be unique. *Emerald Expert Briefings*. https://www.emerald.com/insight/content/doi/10.1108/OXAN-DB214505/full/html

Pal, S. K. (2019). Changing technological trends for E-governance. In *E-governance in India* (pp. 79-105). Palgrave Macmillan. https://link.springer.com/chapter/10.1007/978-981-13-8852-1_5

Pal, S. K. (2019). Changing technological trends for E-governance. In *E-governance in India* (pp. 79-105). Palgrave Macmillan. https://link.springer.com/chapter/10.1007/978-981-15-4451-4_52

Palanisamy, R., & Mukerji, B. (2014). Security and Privacy issues in e-Government. In *Cyber Behavior: Concepts, Methodologies, Tools, and Applications* (pp. 880-892). IGI Global. https://www.igi-global.com/chapter/security-and-privacy-issues-in-e-government/107765

Palvia, S., Aeron, P., Gupta, P., Mahapatra, D., Parida, R., Rosner, R., & Sindhi, S. (2018). *Online education: Worldwide status, challenges, trends, and implications.* https://www.tandfonline.com/doi/full/10.1080/1097198X.2018.1542262

Pandey, D. L., & Risal, N. (2019). Impact of social governance on e-governance in Nepal. *ITIHAS The Journal of Indian Management, 9*(4), 40-48. https://www.indianjournals.com/ijor.aspx?target=ijor:ijim&volume=9&issue=4&article=006

Papadopoulou, P., Kolomvatsos, K., & Hadjiefthymiades, S. (2020). Internet of things in E-government: Applications and challenges. *International Journal of Artificial Intelligence and Machine Learning, 10*(2), 99–118. https://www.igi-global.com/article/internet-of-things-in-e-government/257274

Pathak, A., AmazUddin, M., Abedin, M. J., Andersson, K., Mustafa, R., & Hossain, M. S. (2019). IoT based smart system to support agricultural parameters: A case study. *Procedia Computer Science, 155*, 648-653. https://www.sciencedirect.com/science/article/pii/S1877050919310087

Pena, J. G. V., & Yu, W. E. (2014, April). *Development of a distributed firewall using software defined networking technology. In 2014 4th IEEE International Conference on Information Science and Technology.* IEEE. https://ieeexplore.ieee.org/abstract/document/6920514

Peng, C., Sun, H., Yang, M., & Wang, Y. L. (2019). A survey on security communication and control for smart grids under malicious cyber attacks. *IEEE Transactions on Systems, Man, and Cybernetics. Systems, 49*(8), 1554–1569. doi:10.1109/TSMC.2018.2884952

Peng, C., Xu, M., Xu, S., & Hu, T. (2017). Modeling and predicting extreme cyber attack rates via marked point processes. *Journal of Applied Statistics, 44*(14), 2534–2563. doi:10.1080/02664763.2016.1257590

Prabadevi, B., Jeyanthi, N., & Abraham, A. (2020). An analysis of security solutions for ARP poisoning attacks and its effects on medical computing. *International Journal of System Assurance Engineering and Management, 11*(1), 1–14. 1. doi:10.100713198-019-00919-1

Pradhan, P., & Shakya, S. (2018). Big Data Challenges for e-Government Services in Nepal. *Journal of the Institute of Engineering, 14*(1), 216–222. https://www.nepjol.info/index.php/JIE/article/view/20087

Qian, Y., Li, X., Ihara, S., Zeng, L., Kaiser, J., Süß, T., & Brinkmann, A. (2017, November). A configurable rule based classful token bucket filter network request scheduler for the lustre file system. In *Proceedings of the International Conference for High Performance Computing* (pp. 1–12). Networking, Storage and Analysis. doi:10.1145/3126908.3126932

Qi, M., & Wang, J. (2021). Using the Internet of Things e-government platform to optimize the administrative management mode. *Wireless Communications and Mobile Computing*. https://www.hindawi.com/journals/wcmc/2021/2224957/

Qi, R., Feng, C., Liu, Z., & Mrad, N. (2017). Blockchain-powered internet of things, e-governance and e-democracy. In *E-Democracy for Smart Cities* (pp. 509–520). Springer. https://link.springer.com/chapter/10.1007/978-981-10-4035-1_17

Rahman, A., Islam, M. J., Sunny, F. A., & Nasir, M. K. (2019, December). DistBlockSDN: A distributed secure blockchain based SDN-IoT architecture with NFV implementation for smart cities. In *2019 2nd International Conference on Innovation in Engineering and Technology (ICIET)* (pp. 1-6). IEEE. https://ieeexplore.ieee.org/abstract/document/9290627

Rahouti, M., Xiong, K., Ghani, N., & Shaikh, F. (2021). SYNGuard: Dynamic threshold-based SYN flood attack detection and mitigation in software-defined networks. *IET Networks*, *10*(2), 76–87. doi:10.1049/ntw2.12009

Rajmohan, R., Kumar, T. A., Pavithra, M., Sandhya, S. G., Julie, E. G., Nayahi, J. J. V., & Jhanjhi, N. Z. (2020). Blockchain: Next-generation technology for industry 4.0. *Blockchain Technology*, 177-198. https://www.taylorfrancis.com/chapters/edit/10.1201/9781003004998-11/blockchain-rajmohan-ananth-kumar-pavithra-sandhya

Ramadan, R. A., Aboshosha, B. W., Alshudukhi, J. S., Alzahrani, A. J., El-Sayed, A., & Dessouky, M. M. (2021). Cybersecurity and Countermeasures at the Time of Pandemic. *Journal of Advanced Transportation*, *2021*, 1–19. doi:10.1155/2021/6627264

Ramli, R. M. (2017). Challenges and issues in Malaysian e-government. *Electronic Government, an International Journal*, *13*(3), 242-273. https://www.inderscienceonline.com/doi/abs/10.1504/EG.2017.086685

Ramzi, E. H., & Weerakkody, V. (n.d.). *E-Government implementation Challenges: A Case study*. https://aisel.aisnet.org/cgi/viewcontent.cgi?article=1318&context=amcis2010

Rana, N. P., Dwivedi, Y. K., & Williams, M. D. (2013). Analysing challenges, barriers and CSF of egov adoption. *Transforming Government: People, Process and Policy*. https://www.emerald.com/insight/content/doi/10.1108/17506161311325350/full/html

Rao, P. M., & Deebak, B. D. (2022). Security and privacy issues in smart cities/industries: Technologies, applications, and challenges. *Journal of Ambient Intelligence and Humanized Computing*, 1–37. doi:10.100712652-022-03707-1

Ravi, N., Verma, S., Jhanjhi, N. Z., & Talib, M. N. (2021, August). Securing VANET Using Blockchain Technology. In *Journal of Physics: Conference Series* (Vol. 1979, No. 1, p. 012035). IOP Publishing. https://iopscience.iop.org/article/10.1088/1742-6596/1979/1/012035/meta

Razaque, A., Amsaad, F., Khan, M. J., Hariri, S., Chen, S., Siting, C., & Ji, X. (2019). Survey: Cybersecurity vulnerabilities, attacks and solutions in the medical domain. *IEEE Access: Practical Innovations, Open Solutions*, 7, 168774–168797. doi:10.1109/ACCESS.2019.2950849

Razuleu, L. (2018). *E-Governance and its associated cybersecurity: The challenges and best practices of authentication and authorization among a rapidly growing e-government.* https://scholarworks.calstate.edu/concern/theses/qj72pb20t

Razuleu, L. A. (2018). *E-Governance and Its Associated Cybersecurity: The Challenges and Best Practices of Authentication and Authorization Among a Rapidly Growing E-government* (Doctoral dissertation). California State University, Northridge. https://scholarworks.calstate.edu/downloads/mc87pt75n

Reda, H. T., Anwar, A., Mahmood, A. N., & Tari, Z. (2021). *A Taxonomy of Cyber Defence Strategies Against False Data Attacks in Smart Grid.* https://arxiv.org/abs/2103.16085

Rehman, S., Khaliq, M., Imtiaz, S. I., Rasool, A., Shafiq, M., Javed, A. R., ... Bashir, A. K. (2021). DIDDOS: An approach for detection and identification of Distributed Denial of Service (DDoS) cyberattacks using Gated Recurrent Units (GRU). *Future Generation Computer Systems, 118*, 453-466. https://www.sciencedirect.com/science/article/abs/pii/S0167739X21000327

Research Gate. (n.d.). https://www.researchgate.net/figure/Number-of-papers-related-to-deepfakes-in-years-from-2015-to-2020-obtained-from_fig3_336058980

Rodela, T. T., Tasnim, S., Mazumder, H., Faizah, F., Sultana, A., & Hossain, M. M. (2020). Economic Impacts of Coronavirus Disease (COVID-19) in Developing Countries. doi:10.31235/osf.io/wygpk

Romansky, R., & Noninska, I. (2020). Business virtual system in the context of e-governance: Investigation of secure access to information resources. *Journal of Public Affairs, 20*(3), e2072. doi:10.1002/pa.2072

Ronchi, A. M. (2019). e-Government: Background, Today's Implementation and Future Trends. In e-Democracy (pp. 93-196). Springer.

Roopak, M., Tian, G. Y., & Chambers, J. (2020, January). *An intrusion detection system against ddos attacks in iot networks. In 2020 10th Annual Computing and Communication Workshop and Conference (CCWC) (pp. 0562-0567).* IEEE. https://ieeexplore.ieee.org/abstract/document/9031206/

Rose, S. W., Nightingale, S. J., Garfinkel, S. L., & Chandramouli, R. (2016). *Trustworthy Email.* doi:10.6028/NIST.SP.800-177

Ross, R. S. (2013). *Security and Privacy Controls for Federal Information Systems and Organizations (includes updates as of 5/7/13).* No. Special Publication (NIST SP)-800-53 Rev 4.

Russo, A. M., Rankothge, W., Ma, J., Le, F., & Lobo, J. (n.d.). *Towards making network function virtualization a cloud computing service.* https://ieeexplore.ieee.org/abstract/document/7140280

Ryu. (2018, May). Https://osrg.github.io/ryu/

Sabani, A., Deng, H., & Thai, V. (2019, January). Evaluating the development of E-government in Indonesia. In *Proceedings of the 2nd International Conference on Software Engineering and Information Management* (pp. 254-258). https://dl.acm.org/doi/abs/10.1145/3305160.3305191

Sadeeq, M. M., Abdulkareem, N. M., Zeebaree, S. R., Ahmed, D. M., Sami, A. S., & Zebari, R. R. (2021). IoT and Cloud computing issues, challenges and opportunities: A review. *Qubahan Academic Journal, 1*(2), 1-7. https://journal.qubahan.com/index.php/qaj/article/view/36

Sadiq, A. A. I., Haning, M. T., Nara, N., & Rusdi, M. (2021). Learning Organization on the Implementation of E-Government in the City of Makassar. *Journal Dimensie Management and Public Sector, 2*(3), 12–21. doi:10.48173/jdmps.v2i3.111

Saeed, S., Jhanjhi, N. Z., Naqvi, M., & Humayun, M. (2019). Analysis of Software Development Methodologies. *International Journal of Computing and Digital Systems, 8*(5), 446–460. http://journal.uob.edu.bh/handle/123456789/3583

Sagarik, D., Chansukree, P., Cho, W., & Berman, E. (2018). E-government 4.0 in Thailand: The role of central agencies. *Information Polity, 23*(3), 343-353. https://content.iospress.com/articles/information-polity/ip180006

Sahay, R., Meng, W., & Jensen, C. D. (2019). The application of Software Defined Networking on securing computer networks: A survey. *Journal of Network and Computer Applications, 131*, 89–108. doi:10.1016/j.jnca.2019.01.019

Sahebi, I. G., Mosayebi, A., Masoomi, B., & Marandi, F. (2022). Modeling the enablers for blockchain technology adoption in renewable energy supply chain. *Technology in Society, 101871*. doi:10.1016/j.techsoc.2022.101871

Salam, S., & Kumar, K. P. (2021). Survey on Applications of Blockchain in E-Governance. *Revista Geintec-Gestao Inovacao E Tecnologias, 11*(4), 3807-3822. https://www.revistageintec.net/index.php/revista/article/view/2409

Saleem, J., Adebisi, B., Ande, R., & Hammoudeh, M. (2017, July). A state of the art survey-Impact of cyber attacks on SME's. In *Proceedings of the International Conference on Future Networks and Distributed Systems*. https://dl.acm.org/doi/abs/10.1145/3102304.3109812

Saleem, J., Adebisi, B., Ande, R., & Hammoudeh, M. (2017, July). A state of the art survey-Impact of cyber attacks on SME's. *Proceedings of the International Conference on Future Networks and Distributed Systems*. https://dl.acm.org/doi/abs/10.1145/3102304.3109812

Saleem, J., Hammoudeh, M., Raza, U., Adebisi, B., & Ande, R. (2018, June). IoT standardisation: Challenges, perspectives and solution. In *Proceedings of the 2nd international conference on future networks and distributed systems* (pp. 1-9). https://dl.acm.org/doi/abs/10.1145/3231053.3231103

Saleh, M., Jhanjhi, N. Z., Abdullah, A., & Saher, R. (n.d.). *Design Challenges of Securing IoT Devices: A survey*. http://www.ripublication.com/irph/ijert20/ijertv13n12_149.pdf

Sambana, B., Raju, K. N., Satish, D., Raju, S. S., & Raja, P. V. K. (2021). *Impact of Cyber Security in e-Governance and e-Commerce* (No. 5533). EasyChair. file:///C:/Users/imdad/Downloads/EasyChair-Preprint-5533%20(1).pdf

Sambana, B., Raju, K. N., Satish, D., Raju, S. S., & Raja, P. V. K. (2021). *Impact of Cyber Security in e-Governance and e-Commerce* (No. 5533). EasyChair. file:///C:/Users/imdad/Downloads/EasyChair-Preprint-5533.pdf

Sambana, B., Raju, K. N., Satish, D., Raju, S. S., & Raja, P. V. K. (2021). *Impact of Cyber Security in e-Governance and e-Commerce* (No. 5533). EasyChair. file:///C:/Users/USER/Downloads/EasyChair-Preprint-5533%20(4).pdf

Samsor, A. M. (2020). Challenges and Prospects of e-Government implementation in Afghanistan. *International Trade, Politics and Development.* https://www.proquest.com/openview/8aabcd1bad4fe2b6ff590619c704defd/1?pq-origsite=gscholar&cbl=4931636

Samtani, S., Zhu, H., & Chen, H. (2020). Proactively Identifying Emerging Hacker Threats from the Dark Web: A Diachronic Graph Embedding Framework (D-GEF). *ACM Transactions on Privacy and Security (TOPS), 23*(4), 1-33. https://dl.acm.org/doi/abs/10.1145/3409289

Samtani, S., Zhu, H., & Chen, H. (2020). Proactively Identifying Emerging Hacker Threats from the Dark Web: A Diachronic Graph Embedding Framework (D-GEF). *ACM Transactions on Privacy and Security, 23*(4), 1-33. https://dl.acm.org/doi/abs/10.1145/3409289

Sangki, J. (2018). Vision of future e-government via new e-government maturity model: Based on Korea's e-government practices. *Telecommunications Policy, 42*(10), 860–871. doi:10.1016/j.telpol.2017.12.002

Saqib, M., & Al-Muqrashi, N. (2017). Role and Importance of IoT in the smart city and E-Governance. *Journal of Student Research.* https://jsr.org/index.php/path/article/view/544

Sava, A. (2018). IoT Technologies: Realities of the Future. *Social-Economic Debates, 7*(1), 100-105. http://economic-debates.ro/art11-Sava-economic-debates-2018.pdf

Savaş, S., & Karataş, S. (2022). Cyber governance studies in ensuring cybersecurity: an overview of cybersecurity governance. *International Cybersecurity Law Review,* 1-28. https://link.springer.com/article/10.1365/s43439-021-00045-4

Saxena, S. (2017). Factors influencing perceptions on corruption in public service delivery via e-government platform. *Foresight.* https://www.emerald.com/insight/content/doi/10.1108/FS-05-2017-0013/full/html

Scarfone, K. A., Souppaya, M. P., Cody, A., & Orebaugh, A. D. (2008). *Technical guide to information security testing and assessment.* doi:10.6028/NIST.SP.800-115

Scarfone, K., Hoffman, P., & Souppaya, M. (2009). Guide to enterprise telework and remote access security. *NIST Special Publication, 800,* 46. https://csrc.nist.rip/library/alt-SP800-46r1.pdf

Schiff, L., Schmid, S., & Kuznetsov, P. (2016). In-Band Synchronization for Distributed SDN Control Planes. *Computer Communication Review, 46*(1), 37–43. doi:10.1145/2875951.2875957

Shafiq, D. A., Jhanjhi, N. Z., & Abdullah, A. (2021, March). Machine Learning Approaches for Load Balancing in Cloud Computing Services. In *2021 National Computing Colleges Conference (NCCC)* (pp. 1-8). IEEE.

Sharef, B. T., Alsaqour, R. A., & Ismail, M. (2014). Vehicular communication ad hoc routing protocols: A survey. *Journal of Network and Computer Applications, 40*, 363–396. doi:10.1016/j.jnca.2013.09.008

Sharma, P., Zawar, S., & Patil, S. B. (2016). Ransomware Analysis: Internet of Things (Iot) Security Issues, Challenges and Open Problems In the Context of Worldwide Scenario of Security of Systems and Malware Attacks. In *International conference on recent Innovation in Engineering and Management* (Vol. 2, No. 3, pp. 177-184). http://www.ijirse.com/wp-content/upload/2016/02/1089B.pdf

Sharma, S. (2018). *Good Governance and its Challenges in India.* https://www.indianjournals.com/ijor.aspx?target=ijor:ijmss&volume=6&issue=11&article=009

Sharma, T. (2021). *Evolving Phishing Email Prevention Techniques: A Survey to Pin Down Effective Phishing Study Design Concepts.* https://www.ideals.illinois.edu/handle/2142/109179

Sharma, P. K., Singh, S., Jeong, Y. S., & Park, J. H. (2017). Distblocknet: A distributed blockchains-based secure sdn architecture for iot networks. *IEEE Communications Magazine, 55*(9), 78–85. doi:10.1109/MCOM.2017.1700041

Sharma, S. K., Metri, B., Dwivedi, Y. K., & Rana, N. P. (2021). Challenges common service centers (CSCs) face in delivering e-government services in rural India. *Government Information Quarterly, 38*(2), 101573.

Sibi Chakkaravarthy, S., Sangeetha, D., Venkata Rathnam, M., Srinithi, K., & Vaidehi, V. (2018). Futuristic cyber-attacks. *International Journal of Knowledge-based and Intelligent Engineering Systems, 22*(3), 195–204. doi:10.3233/KES-180384

Simonova, A. (2020). *An Analysis of Factors Influencing National Institute of Standards and Technology Cybersecurity Framework Adoption in Financial Services: A Correlational Study* (Doctoral dissertation). Capella University. https://www.proquest.com/openview/8482434364a539361dbd14f5dd872752/1?pq-origsite=gscholar&cbl=18750&diss=y

Sithole, V. E. (2015). *An e-governance training model for public managers: The case of selected Free State Provincial departments* (Doctoral dissertation). http://repository.nwu.ac.za/handle/10394/16320

Smyth, D., Cionca, V., McSweeney, S., & O'Shea, D. (2016). *Exploiting pitfalls in software-defined networking implementation. In 2016 International conference on cyber security and protection of digital services (Cyber Security).* IEEE. doi:10.1109/CyberSecPODS.2016.7502354

Soni, V., Anand, R., Dey, P. K., Dash, A. P., & Banwet, D. K. (2017). Quantifying e-governance efficacy towards Indian–EU strategic dialogue. *Transforming Government: People, Process and Policy.* https://www.emerald.com/insight/content/doi/10.1108/TG-06-2017-0031/full/html

Soni, V., Dey, P. K., Anand, R., Malhotra, C., & Banwet, D. K. (2017). Digitizing grey portions of e-governance. *Transforming Government: People, Process and Policy.* https://www.emerald.com/insight/content/doi/10.1108/TG-11-2016-0076/full/html

Sony, A. L. (2015). Solving e-Governance Challenges in India through the Incremental Adoption to Cloud Service. *Law: J. Higher Sch. Econ.,* 169. https://heinonline.org/HOL/LandingPage?handle=hein.journals/pravo2015&div=15&id=&page=

Srivastava, A., & Dashora, K. (2022). Application of blockchain technology for agrifood supply chain management: a systematic literature review on benefits and challenges. *Benchmarking: An International Journal.* https://www.emerald.com/insight/content/doi/10.1108/BIJ-08-2021-0495/full/html

Stankovic, J. A. (2016). Research directions for cyber physical systems in wireless and mobile healthcare. *ACM Transactions on Cyber-Physical Systems, 1*(1), 1-12. https://dl.acm.org/doi/pdf/10.1145/2899006

Steichen, M., Hommes, S., & State, R. (2017, September). ChainGuard—A firewall for blockchain applications using SDN with OpenFlow. In *2017 Principles, Systems and Applications of IP Telecommunications (IPTComm)* (pp. 1-8). IEEE. https://ieeexplore.ieee.org/abstract/document/8169748

Stellios, I., Kotzanikolaou, P., Psarakis, M., Alcaraz, C., & Lopez, J. (2018). A survey of iot-enabled cyberattacks: Assessing attack paths to critical infrastructures and services. *IEEE Communications Surveys and Tutorials, 20*(4), 3453–3495. doi:10.1109/COMST.2018.2855563

Suleimany, M. (2021, May). Smart Urban Management and IoT; Paradigm of E-Governance and Technologies in Developing Communities. In *2021 5th International Conference on Internet of Things and Applications (IoT)* (pp. 1-6). IEEE. https://ieeexplore.ieee.org/abstract/document/9469713

Susha, I., & Grönlund, Å. (2014). Context clues for the stall of the Citizens' Initiative: Lessons for opening up e-participation development practice. *Government Information Quarterly, 31*(3), 454–465. https://www.sciencedirect.com/science/article/abs/pii/S0740624X14000860

Swanson, M., Bowen, P., Phillips, A. W., Gallup, D., & Lynes, D. (2010). *Contingency planning guide for federal information systems.* doi:10.6028/NIST.SP.800-34r1

Tan, Y., Cheng, J., Zhu, H., Hu, Z., Li, B., & Liu, S. (2017, July). Real-time life prediction of equipment based on optimized ARMA model. In *2017 Prognostics and System Health Management Conference (PHM-Harbin)* (pp. 1-6). IEEE. https://ieeexplore.ieee.org/abstract/document/8079318

Tawalbeh, L. A., Muheidat, F., Tawalbeh, M., & Quwaider, M. (2020). IoT Privacy and security: Challenges and solutions. *Applied Sciences (Basel, Switzerland), 10*(12), 4102. https://www.mdpi.com/2076-3417/10/12/4102

Teiu, C. (2011). The Impact Of The Financial Crisis On European E-Government Development. *CES Working Papers, 3*(3), 429-439. https://www.ceeol.com/search/article-detail?id=137053

Thakkar, A., & Lohiya, R. (2021). A review on machine learning and deep learning perspectives of IDS for IoT: Recent updates, security issues, and challenges. *Archives of Computational Methods in Engineering, 28*(4), 3211–3243. https://link.springer.com/article/10.1007/s11831-020-09496-0

Tikkanen, E., Gustafsson, S., & Ingelsson, E. (2018). Associations of fitness, physical activity, strength, and genetic risk with cardiovascular disease: Longitudinal analyses in the UK Biobank study. *Circulation, 137*(24), 2583–2591. https://www.ahajournals.org/doi/full/10.1161/CIRCULATIONAHA.117.032432

Tilouine, J., & Kadiri, G. (2018, January 27). *A Addis-Abeba, le siège de l'Union africaine espionné par Pékin*. Retrieved October 27, 2018, from https://www.lemonde.fr/afrique/article/2018/01/26/a-addis-abeba-le-siege-de-l-union-africaine-espionne-par-les-chinois_5247521_3212.html

Tingjun, Z. (2015). The Analysis of Behavior and Effectiveness of Public Participating in E-government Platform of City Public Service—A Case Study of the Mayor's Hotline in Fuzhou. *Journal of Public Management*, 2. https://en.cnki.com.cn/Article_en/CJFDTotal-GGGL201502003.htm

Tounsi, W., & Rais, H. (2018). A survey on technical threat intelligence in the age of sophisticated cyber attacks. *Computers & Security, 72*, 212–233. doi:10.1016/j.cose.2017.09.001

Trippel, T., Weisse, O., Xu, W., Honeyman, P., & Fu, K. (2017, April). WALNUT: Waging doubt on the integrity of MEMS accelerometers with acoustic injection attacks. In *2017 IEEE European symposium on security and privacy (EuroS&P)* (pp. 3-18). IEEE. https://ieeexplore.ieee.org/abstract/document/7961948

Tseng, Y. C., & Pan, H.-K. (2002). Data hiding in 2-color images. *IEEE Transactions on Computers, 51*(7), 873–878. doi:10.1109/TC.2002.1017706

Tsesmelis, M., Percia David, D., Maillart, T., Dolamic, L., Tresoldi, G., Lacube, W., . . . Mermoud, A. (2022). *Cybersecurity Technologies: An Overview of Trends & Activities in Switzerland and Abroad*. https://papers.ssrn.com/sol3/papers.cfm?abstract_id=4013762

U.S. Centers for Medicare & Medicaid Services, National Health Expenditure Accounts. (2018). Available from: https://www.cms.gov/ Research-Statistics-Data-and-Systems/StatisticsTrends-and-eports/NationalHealthExpendData/NationalHealthAccountsHistorical.Html

Udhayavene, S., & Aathira, T. (2015). New data hiding technique in encrypted image:DKL algorithm. *Procedia Computer Science, 54*, 790–798. doi:10.1016/j.procs.2015.06.093

Ullah, A., Pinglu, C., Ullah, S., Abbas, H. S. M., & Khan, S. (2021). The role of E-governance in combating COVID-19 and promoting sustainable development: a comparative study of China and Pakistan. *Chinese Political Science Review, 6*(1), 86-118. https://link.springer.com/article/10.1007/s41111-020-00167-w

Ullah, A., Pinglu, C., Ullah, S., Abbas, H. S. M., & Khan, S. (n.d.). *The Role of E-Governance in Combating COVID-19 and Promoting Sustainable Development: A Comparative Study of China and Pakistan.* https://link.springer.com/article/10.1007/s41111-020-00167-w

Ullah, A., Azeem, M., Ashraf, H., Alaboudi, A. A., Humayun, M., & Jhanjhi, N. Z. (2021). Secure healthcare data aggregation and transmission in IoT—A survey. *IEEE Access: Practical Innovations, Open Solutions, 9*, 16849–16865. doi:10.1109/ACCESS.2021.3052850

Ullah, A., Pinglu, C., Ullah, S., Abbas, H. S. M., & Khan, S. (2021). The role of e-governance in combating COVID-19 and promoting sustainable development: A comparative study of China and Pakistan. *Chinese Political Science Review, 6*(1), 86–118. doi:10.100741111-020-00167-w

UNDP. (2013). *World economic and social survey 2013 sustainable development challenges.* Available from: https://sustainabledevelopment.un.org/content/documents/2843WESS2013.pdf

Uyar, A., Nimer, K., Kuzey, C., Shahbaz, M., & Schneider, F. (2021). Can e-government initiatives alleviate tax evasion? The moderation effect of ICT. *Technological Forecasting and Social Change, 166*, 120597. doi:10.1016/j.techfore.2021.120597

Vaddiraju, A. K., & Manasi, S. (2019). E-governance: Learning from Karnataka. *The Indian Journal of Public Administration, 65*(2), 416–429. doi:10.1177/0019556119844582

Vardell, E., Wang, T., & Thomas, P. A. (2021). "I found what I needed, which was a supportive community": An ethnographic study of shared information practices in an online cosplay community. *Journal of Documentation.* https://www.emerald.com/insight/content/doi/10.1108/JD-02-2021-0034/full/html

Véliz, C. (2021). Privacy and digital ethics after the pandemic. *Nature Electronics, 4*(1), 10-11. https://www.nature.com/articles/s41928-020-00536-y

Venkatesh, V., Thong, J. Y., Chan, F. K., & Hu, P. J. (2016). Managing citizens' uncertainty in e-government services: The mediating and moderating roles of transparency and trust. *Information Systems Research, 27*(1), 87–111. https://pubsonline.informs.org/doi/abs/10.1287/isre.2015.0612

Walden, A., Cortelyou-Ward, K., Gabriel, M. H., & Noblin, A. (2020). To report or not to report health care data breaches. *The American Journal of Managed Care, 26*(12), e395–e402. doi:10.37765/ajmc.2020.88546 PMID:33315333

Waller, L., & Genius, A. (2015). Barriers to transforming government in Jamaica: Challenges to implementing initiatives to enhance the efficiency, effectiveness and service delivery of government through ICTs (e-Government). *Transforming Government: People, Process and Policy.* https://www.emerald.com/insight/content/doi/10.1108/TG-12-2014-0067/full/html?fullSc=1

Wang, N., Wang, P., Alipour-Fanid, A., Jiao, L., & Zeng, K. (2019). Physical-layer security of 5G wireless networks for IoT: Challenges and opportunities. *IEEE Internet of Things Journal*, 6(5), 8169-8181. https://ieeexplore.ieee.org/abstract/document/8758230

Wang, Y., Jiang, D., Huo, L., & Zhao, Y. (2021). A new traffic prediction algorithm to software defined networking. *Mobile Networks and Applications*, 26(2), 716–725. doi:10.100711036-019-01423-3

Watts, N., Amann, M., Arnell, N., Ayeb-Karlsson, S., Belesova, K., Boykoff, M., Byass, P., Cai, W., Campbell-Lendrum, D., Capstick, S., Chambers, J., Dalin, C., Daly, M., Dasandi, N., Davies, M., Drummond, P., Dubrow, R., Ebi, K. L., Eckelman, M., ... Montgomery, H. (2019). The 2019 report of The Lancet countdown on health and climate change: Ensuring that the health of a child born today is not defined by a changing climate. *Lancet*, 394(10211), 1836–1878. doi:10.1016/S0140-6736(19)32596-6 PMID:31733928

Weil, T., & Murugesan, S. (2020). IT Risk and Resilience-Cybersecurity Response to COVID-19. *IT Professional*, 22(3), 4–10. doi:10.1109/MITP.2020.2988330

Wen, H., Cao, Z., Zhang, Y., Cao, X., Fan, Z., Voigt, D., & Du, D. (2018, September). Joins: Meeting latency slo with integrated control for networked storage. In *2018 IEEE 26th International Symposium on Modeling, Analysis, and Simulation of Computer and Telecommunication Systems (MASCOTS)* (pp. 194-200). IEEE.

WHO. (2020). *Report on global surveillance of epidemicprone infectious diseases – introduction*. Switzerland, Geneva: WHO. https://www.ncbi.nlm.nih.gov/pmc/articles/PMC7195982/

Wiggen, J. (2020). *Impact of COVID-19 on cyber crime and state-sponsored cyber activities*. Konrad Adenauer Stiftung. https://www.jstor.org/stable/pdf/resrep25300.pdf?acceptTC=true&coverpage=false

Wijayanto, H., & Prabowo, I. A. (2020). Cybersecurity Vulnerability Behavior Scale in College During the Covid-19 Pandemic. *Jurnal Sisfokom (Sistem Informasi dan Komputer)*, 9(3), 395-399. https://www.aimspress.com/article/id/6087e948ba35de2200eea776

Wijayanto, H., & Prabowo, I. A. (2020). Cybersecurity Vulnerability Behavior Scale in College During the Covid-19 Pandemic. *Jurnal Sisfokom (Sistem Informasi dan Komputer)*, 9(3),395-399. https://www.aimspress.com/article/id/6087e948ba35de2200eea776

Williams, C. M., Chaturvedi, R., & Chakravarthy, K. (2020). Cybersecurity Risks in a Pandemic. *Journal of Medical Internet Research*, 22(9), e23692. doi:10.2196/23692 PMID:32897869

Wilson, M., Zafra, D. E. D., Pitcher, S. I., Tressler, J. D., & Ippolito, J. B. (1998). *Information technology security training requirements*. doi:10.6028/NIST.SP.800-16

Wong, J. C. J., Alla, K. R., Dominic, P. D. D., Rimsan, M., Mahmood, A. K., Umair, M., . . . Jhanjhi, N. Z. (2020, October). 6LWL. KDGLMDK% DKDULQ= DOLNKD= XONLflL 6DPVLDK $ KPDG. In *International Conference on Computational Intelligence (ICCI)* (*Vol. 8*, p. 9). Academic Press.

World Economic Forum. (2020). *The global risk report.* Available from: https://www. weforum. org/reports/the-global-risks-report-2020

World Health Organization. (2020). *WHO reports fivefold increase in cyber-attacks, urges vigilance. WHO reports fivefold increase in cyber attacks, urges vigilance.* WHO.

Wu. (2016). *Separable Reversible data hiding for encrypted palette images with color partitioning and flipping verification.* IEEE. doi:10.1109/TCSVT.2016.2556585

Wu. (2017). *Development of data hiding schema based on combination theory for lowering the visual noise in binary image.* Elsevier ScienceDirect. doi:10.1016/j.displa.2017.07.009

Wu, M., & Liu, B. (2004). Data hiding in binary images for authentication and annotation. *IEEE Transactions on Multimedia, 6*(4), 528–538. doi:10.1109/TMM.2004.830814

Xiao, F., Zhang, J., Huang, J., Gu, G., Wu, D., & Liu, P. (2020). *Unexpected data dependency creation and chaining: a new attack to SDN. 2020 IEEE Symposium on Security and Privacy.*

Xuan, G., & Yun, Q. (2008). Reversible Binary Image Data Hiding By Run-Length Histogram Modification. *International Conference on Pattern Recognition,* 1651-1653.

Yadav, E. P., Mittal, E. A., & Yadav, H. (2018, February). IoT: Challenges and issues in indian perspective. In *2018 3rd International Conference on Internet of Things: Smart Innovation and Usages (IoT-SIU)* (pp. 1-5). IEEE. https://ieeexplore.ieee.org/abstract/document/8519869

Yang, R., & Wibowo, S. (2020). *Risks and Uncertainties in Citizens' Trust and Adoption of E-Government: A Proposed Framework.* https://aisel.aisnet.org/cgi/viewcontent.cgi?article=1073&context=acis2020

Yang, H., & Kot, A. C. (2006). Binary Image Authentication With Tampering Localization by Embedding Cryptographic Signature and Block Identifier. *IEEE Signal Processing Letters, 13*(12), 741–744. doi:10.1109/LSP.2006.879829

Yang, H., & Kot, A. C. (2007). Pattern-based date hiding for binary images authentication by connectivity-preserving. *IEEE Transactions on Multimedia, 9*(3), 475–486. doi:10.1109/TMM.2006.887990

Yang, H., Kot, A. C., & Rahardja, S. (2008). Orthogonal data embedding for binary images in Morphological Transform domain-A high capacity approach. *IEEE Transactions on Multimedia, 10*(3), 339–351. doi:10.1109/TMM.2008.917404

Yang, L., Elisa, N., & Eliot, N. (2019). Privacy and security aspects of E-government in smart cities. In *Smart cities cybersecurity and privacy* (pp. 89–102). Elsevier. https://www.sciencedirect. com/science/article/pii/B978012815032000007X

Yang, Q., An, D., Min, R., Yu, W., Yang, X., & Zhao, W. (2017). On optimal PMU placement-based defense against data integrity attacks in smart grid. *IEEE Transactions on Information Forensics and Security, 12*(7), 1735–1750. doi:10.1109/TIFS.2017.2686367

Yarovoy, T. S., Kozyrieva, O. V., Bielska, T. V., Zhuk, I. I., & Mokhova, I. L. (2020). The E-government development in ensuring the country financial and information security. *Financial and credit activity: Problems of theory and practice, 2*(33), 268-275. http://fkd1.ubs.edu.ua/article/view/206853

Yassein, M. B., Aljawarneh, S., Al-Rousan, M., Mardini, W., & Al-Rashdan, W. (2017, November). Combined software-defined network (SDN) and Internet of Things (IoT). In *2017 international conference on electrical and computing technologies and applications (ICECTA)* (pp. 1-6). IEEE. https://ieeexplore.ieee.org/abstract/document/8252003

Yau. (2021) *What is Data Integrity?* Precisely. https://www.precisely.com/blog/data-integrity/what-is-data-integrity

Zaoui, I., Elmaghraoui, H., Chiadmi, D., & Benhlima, L. (2014). Towards a personalized e-government platform. *International Journal of Computer Science: Theory and Application, 2*(2), 35–40. https://citeseerx.ist.psu.edu/viewdoc/download?doi=10.1.1.1018.918&rep=rep1&type=pdf

Zhu, T., Kozuch, M. A., & Harchol-Balter, M. (2017). WorkloadCompactor: Reducing Datacenter Cost While Providing Tail Latency SLO Guarantees. In *8th ACM Symposium on Cloud Computing (SoCC 17)*. ACM. https://dl.acm.org/doi/abs/10.1145/3127479.3132245

Zong, S., Ritter, A., Mueller, G., & Wright, E. (2019). *Analyzing the perceived severity of cybersecurity threats reported on social media*. doi:10.18653/v1/N19-1140

Zoppelt, M., & Kolagari, R. T. (2019, October). What today's serious cyber attacks on cars tell us: consequences for automotive security and dependability. In *International Symposium on Model-Based Safety and Assessment* (pp. 270–285). Springer. doi:10.1007/978-3-030-32872-6_18

About the Contributors

Noor Zaman received the Ph.D. degree in IT from UTP, Malaysia. He has great international exposure in academia, research, administration, and academic quality accreditation. He was with ILMA University, KFU for a decade, and currently with Taylor's University, Malaysia. He has 19 years of teaching & administrative experience. He has an intensive background of academic quality accreditation in higher education besides scientific research activities, he had worked a decade for academic accreditation and earned ABET accreditation twice for three programs at CCSIT, King Faisal University, Saudi Arabia. Dr. Noor Zaman has awarded as top reviewer 1% globally by WoS/ISI (Publons) recently. He has edited/authored more than 11 research books with international reputed publishers, earned several research grants, and a great number of indexed research articles on his credit. He has supervised several postgraduate students including masters and Ph.D. Dr. Jhanjhi is an Associate Editor of IEEE ACCESS, Guest editor of several reputed journals, member of the editorial board of several research journals, and active TPC member of reputed conferences around the globe.

* * *

Gyankamal Chhajed obtained her B.E. Degree in Computer Science and Engineering in 1991-95 from S.G.G.S.I.E. & T., Nanded and Postgraduate Degree (M.Tech.) in Computer Engineering from College of Engineering, Pune (COEP) in 2005-2007 both with Distinction. She is GATE qualified (96.76 percentile) and pursuing Ph.D. in Computer Engineering. She is approved Undergraduate and recognized Postgraduate teacher of Pune University and has about 24 yrs. of experience. Gyankamal is Principal and Co-investigator for research project . She guided 23 postgraduate dissertation work .She authored a book and has total 54 Publications in all at the National, International Conferences and Journals. She judged paper presentation event at National Conference, delivered expert talk and reviewed paper for IEEE International Conference. She has membership of IEEE, LMCSI, IET, LMISTE, and International Association LMIACSIT.

Maurice Dawson is an Assistant Professor of Information Technology and Management within the College of Computing at Illinois Institute of Technology. Additionally, he serves as Director and Distinguished Member of the IIT Center for Cyber Security and Forensics Education (C2SAFE) and responsible for working with the faculty who are members of this center. Before joining academia, he was an engineering manager for unmanned air systems and senior program manager for rotary-wing aircraft. He has a Doctor of Computer Science from Colorado Technical University and a Doctor of Philosophy in Cyber Security from the Intelligent Systems Research Centre at London Metropolitan University. Additionally, he is the co-editor of Developing Next-Generation Countermeasures for Homeland Security Threat Prevention, and New Threats and Countermeasures in Digital Crime and Cyber Terrorism, published by IGI Global in 2017, and 2015 respectively. He has received for Fulbright Scholar Grants.

Bindu Garg is working as Professor and HOD, Computer Science Engineering department of Bharati Vidyapeeth's Deemed University College of Engineering, Pune. She is also heading innovation cell- "Institution Innovation Council (IICA)" formed at BVDUCOE Institution Innovation Council(IIC) at BDUCOE, Pune. Previously,She was serving Bharati Vidyapeeth's College of Engineering at New Delhi as Dean R&D and HOD of Computer Science department. she is always served the institute and University with best of my knowledge & capabilities. She has published more than 100 research papers (100 – includes reputed journals of SCI and Scopus indexed) in credit. Her area of research and specialization are Time Series Analysis, Soft Computing, Neural networks, Fuzzy logic, Genetic Algorithm, Forecasting Applications, Analysis and Designing of Algorithm, Data Structure, Object Oriented Programming, Numerical Analysis, Cloud Computing and Big data.

Loveleen Gaur is the Professor and Program Director (Artificial Intelligence & Business Intelligence and Data Analytics of the Amity International Business School, Amity University, Noida, India. She is a senior IEEE member and Series Editor with CRC and Wiley. Prof. Gaur has significantly contributed to enhancing scientific understanding by participating in over three hundred scientific conferences, symposia, and seminars, by chairing technical sessions and delivering plenary and invited talks. She has specialized in the fields of Artificial Intelligence, Machine Learning, Pattern Recognition, Internet of Things, Data Analytics and Business Intelligence. She has chaired various positions in International Conferences of repute and is a reviewer with top rated journals of IEEE, SCI and ABDC Journals. She has been honoured with prestigious National and International awards. She is also actively involved in various reputed projects of Government of India and abroad.

Mamoona Humayun has completed her PhD. in Computer Sciences from Harbin Institute of Technology, China. She has 15 years of teaching and administrative experience internationally. She has extensive background of teaching, research supervision and administrative work. She has experience in teaching advanced era technological courses including, Mobile application development (Android), Cyber security and .Net Framework programming besides other undergraduate and postgraduate courses, graduation projects and thesis supervisions. Dr. Mamoona Humayun is the guest Editor and reviewer for several reputable journals and conferences around the globe. She has authored several research papers, supervised a great number of postgraduate students, and external thesis examiner to her credit. She has strong analytical, problem solving, interpersonal and communication skills. Her areas of interest include Cyber Security, Wireless Sensor Network (WSN), Internet of Things (IoT), Requirement Engineering, Global Software Development and Knowledge Management.

Khalid Hussain is working as Professor Cyber Security in Superior University Lahore and Campus Director in National Superior Institute of Science and Technology (NSIST) Islamabad, previously he had served as Dean Faculty of Computer Science and also Campus Director in Barani Institute of Sciences ARID Agriculture University, for the last one and half years. He also served at The University of Lahore as Dean Faculty of Computer Science and Information Technology for a period of three years. Dr. Khalid has vast university/industry experience. During his tenure in the industry, he served in defense-related projects, and in recognition of his services, he has been awarded commendation certificates by multiple government agencies. He joined academia in 2008 as a full-time faculty member. In addition to his teaching role, he has been involved in numerous research projects, ICT pieces of training, seminars, and workshops especially in the domain of Cyber Security. He helps set up a pioneer setup for information/ network security certification in Pakistan. He also introduced EC Council certification under the first academia-industry partnership. That project started from a one-room office and has grown into a fully functional campus of RIPHAH University. He did his Ph.D. from Malaysia, under a fully funded UTM / HEC scholarship. Up till now, he published 64 papers. In which 28 are ISI Indexed Impact Factor, 13 are in HEC approved journal and 23 are in IEEE and ACM conferences. Except for this, he also has seven book chapters and three books for his credit. His Cumulative Impact Factor is 83.032. He has successfully completed six applied research projects in the domain of Information Security funded by NESCOM and other funding agencies. Up till now 21 MS and 03 Ph.D. students completed their research thesis under his supervision. Currently, he is supervising 13 MS and five Ph.D. students. In reward of his contribution towards Information Security SATHA awarded him, Gold Medal, in 2015.

Muhammad Amir Khan is an Assistant Professor in Computer Science department at COMSATS University Islamabad, Abbottabad Campus, Pakistan. He obtained his PhD in Information Technology from the Universiti Teknologi PETRONAS, Malaysia. He received his MS in Computer Engineering from the COMSATS University Islamabad, Abbottabad Campus. His research interest includes Communication Protocols for Internet of Things (IOT), Wireless Sensor Networks, Wireless ad hoc Network, Software Defined Networking (SDN) and Network Security. He has published more than 23 research papers in ISI / Impact Factor journals and international conferences.

Navid Ali Khan holds a PhD in Computer Science and currently working as a Senior Lecturer at Taylor's University, Malaysia.

Mir Sajjad Hussain Talpur received Master's degree in Information Technology from Shah Abdul Latif University (SALU) in 2003, PGD (Science and Technology Policy Development) from Mehran University of Engineering and Technology (MUET) in 2008, and Ph.D. degree in Computer Science from Central South University (CSU) China in 2015. He is presently the Associate Professor/Researcher/ Senior Software Engineer, and Doctoral Supervisor of Information Technology Centre at SAU, Sindh, Pakistan. His research interests include Internet of Things, smart agriculture, smart transportation, smart healthcare, smart city, smart robotics, RFID, green computing, mobile edge computing, transparent computing, human computer interaction (HCI), brain computer interaction (BCI), and software engineering. He has published more than 35 research papers in the international journals of the above areas. Dr. Talpur joined ITC-SAU from 31st Jan 2004.

Damon Walker completed a Master of Business Administration (MBA) at the University of Missouri - Saint Louis (UMSL) which is an AACSB, and NSA & DHS Center for Academic Excellence (CAE) in Cyber Defense Education (CDE). This is a rigorous program which is the metropolitan's only NSA & DHS accredited program and state's only university that has an NSA focus area. International Information Technology (IT) experience in Guinea, Senegal, and Benin, West Africa through the United States Agency for International Development (USAID), Catholic Relief Services, and Winrock International with the Ministry of Agriculture of Information Communications Technology (ICT) Training. Recipient of the President's Volunteer Service Award (PVSA) and on the UMSL's Dean List multiple times.

Index

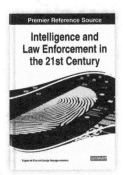
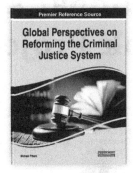

Ensure Quality Research is Introduced to the Academic Community

Become an Evaluator for IGI Global Authored Book Projects

Premier Reference Source

Stabilizing Currency and Preserving Economic Sovereignty Using the Grondona System

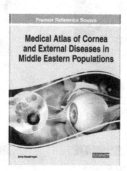

Premier Reference Source

Medical Atlas of Cornea and External Diseases in Middle Eastern Populations

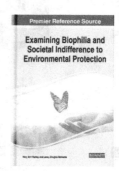

Premier Reference Source

Examining Biophilia and Societal Indifference to Environmental Protection

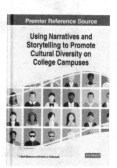

Premier Reference Source

Using Narratives and Storytelling to Promote Cultural Diversity on College Campuses

The overall success of an authored book project is dependent on quality and timely manuscript evaluations.

Applications and Inquiries may be sent to:
development@igi-global.com

Applicants must have a doctorate (or equivalent degree) as well as publishing, research, and reviewing experience. Authored Book Evaluators are appointed for one-year terms and are expected to complete at least three evaluations per term. Upon successful completion of this term, evaluators can be considered for an additional term.

If you have a colleague that may be interested in this opportunity, we encourage you to share this information with them.

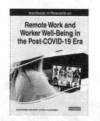

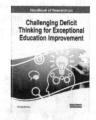

Printed in the United States
by Baker & Taylor Publisher Services